The
GREAT WESTERN
at
SWINDON WORKS

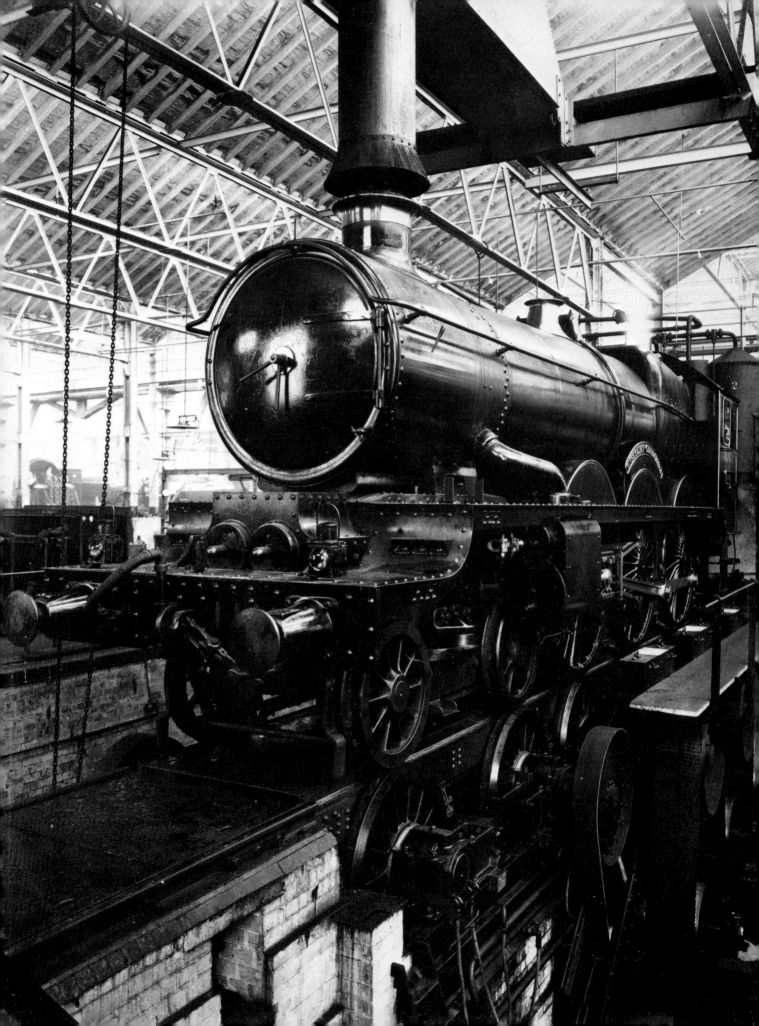

The
GREAT WESTERN
at
SWINDON WORKS

Alan S. Peck C. Eng., F. I. Mech E.

Foreword by
Sir Peter Parker M.V.O.

Oxford Publishing Co.

Copyright © 1983 Oxford Publishing Company

ISBN 0-86093-177-3

Frontispiece: GWR 'Castle' class 4-6-0, No. 111 *Viscount Churchill* on the test bed at Swindon Works.

British Rail

Typeset by Aquarius Typesetting Services, New Milton

Photo-reproduction and offset printing plates by
Oxford Litho Plates Ltd, Oxford.

Printed in Great Britain by:
B. H. Blackwell Limited
in the City of Oxford.

Published by:
Oxford Publishing Company,
Link House,
West Street,
POOLE,
Dorset.

Foreword by *Sir Peter Parker* M.V.O.

Here is the story of the genesis and growth of a railway town, a railway community and a railway factory under the direction of Victorian and Edwardian autocrats with an immensely strong and paternalistic sense of duty to those whom they employed and to their families: Lords of an enormous manor but, at the same time, distinguished engineers, honourable men.

Much has been written about the Great Western Railway, almost, one might say, too much. A legend has long been created, a legend which ignores much that was unpleasant or uncomplimentary but here we have legend incarnate, the true story of Swindon, town, factory and people, told by a man who, with his family, served the Great Western Railway and who, after retirement, deemed the production of this book to be his life's work. He has succeeded nobly.

One has only to read a few pages to become absorbed with what becomes, not only an exhaustive study of technical matters, of railway management and of factory life, but a fascinating exposition of social history over 140 years. Alan Peck takes us behind the scenes with the authenticity and authority of a railway engineer, supported by access to papers. He writes in depth, with conviction and, at times, with quiet and subtle humour. One is gripped by historical significance.

The drawings are fascinating. Study the building constructed in the very early days which housed not only the Accountant but, by no means far away, the enginemen, with their bathroom. Only the GWR would have the courage to put these widely differing breeds in such close proximity — perhaps we have something to learn from this today.

The giants of the past emerge, not just as names but as human beings with strengths and failings, fascinating and alive. Gooch, the creator of Swindon and he who chose the site with such simple practicality, is literally world famous but justice is done to such as Joseph Armstrong who followed Gooch, as a man who gave his life to the railway and who is remembered less as an engineer than as the great and good father figure of an enormous railway family.

Today, it is difficult to comprehend the power of the great Swindon organization at its zenith. Until 1921, when Churchward retired, the Chief Mechanical Engineer had reported direct to the Board, bypassing the General Manager. Churchward had the power, the ability to create and use the right team, to innovate and to fashion an efficient locomotive fleet, years ahead of its time; his strength of personality persuaded his Board of the rightness of all things Swindon.

He must have been present at the Annual Children's fete to preside over the affairs of the 38,000 people that drank 680 gallons of tea and ate 4 tons of cake. Swindon is rightly famous for its locomotive, carriage and wagon construction but nothing delights my imagination more than the preparation of this gargantuan feast and the employment of a Great Western Railway Cake Cutting machine. Could that factory really produce a machine that would have delighted Mr Heath Robinson himself? Nothing was impossible in the great days.

Finally, one reads of the decline, the virtual extinction and then, at the eleventh hour, of the resurgence of the spirit of this historic works. It is said of Swindon that if you scratch the surface of its life, it is railway blood that runs — this book demonstrates why. Alan Peck epitomises the spirit of Swindon — indeed of the railway community — proud of its tradition but totally aware of the part that it can play in the years ahead.

Sir Peter Parker MVO
April 1983

Acknowledgements

My first acknowledgement must be to the innumerable friends and working colleagues of the GWR and its successors who have satisfied my curiosity over a lifetime's service and given me so much of the background for this history. My debt to them is beyond expression. There are, however, some who must be named. Past Works Managers, Harold Johnson, Herbert Mear and Harry Roberts, and the present Manager, Harold Taylor, all gave a great deal of help and encouragement. Also a special word to my one-time chief, the late Bill Pellow, who sadly died during the final preparation of this volume. The archivist of the former BR archives at Porchester Place, London, and latterly the staff of the Public Records Office at Kew were of great help, as also locally was the Wiltshire County Council librarian. In particular the reference librarian at Swindon Central Library, Roger Trayhurn, always proffered knowledgeable and enthusiastic assistance. John Woodward, curator of Swindon Museums and his assistant, Ernest Wood, helped in many ways, and assistance was always forthcoming from the members and staff of Thamesdown Borough Council. Dr. John Coiley, Keeper of the National Railway Museum at York was always ready to place the resources of that institution at my disposal and this was always supported fully by his librarians Philip Atkinson and Mike Rutherford.

Amongst my working colleagues, my special thanks go to Selborne Smith who is even more enthusiastic about railway industrial archaeology than I. Joe Silto, John Walter, Ken Brown and Peter Wicks were of help in providing either social information or in producing old drawings for reference. Roy Nash and Denis Bird must also receive special thanks for granting me permission to use illustrations from their extensive libraries of photographs.

To Sir Peter Parker who so readily found time to provide the Foreword to this book, I offer my most sincere thanks. To the directors and staff of the Oxford Railway Publishing Co. Ltd., in particular Colin Judge, Rex Kennedy and Jim Russell; my thanks for their help and forebearance to a first-time author, are suitably great. A most unenviable task was undertaken by my friend Bob Perkins who read my faltering manuscript as it was written, chapter by chapter and gave invaluable advice and many welcome criticisms. I am glad to say we are still friends.

Finally, without the devoted help, advice, encouragement and sheer hard work by my wife, Peggy, this book would never have seen the light of day. It was she who provided a comfortable background thus enabling me to concentrate on the writing, then painstakingly translating my scribble into respectable typescript, often several times over. To her I dedicate this history with my love and gratitude.

Alan Peck
Swindon
1982

Contents

Bibliography

The following is a list of volumes, from the author's bookshelf, which have been consulted during the preparation of this book and which may provide further information on their particular subjects.

Title	Author	Publisher	Date
Our Iron Roads	F. S. Williams	Bemrose & Son	1883
Swindon Reminiscences	W. Morris	Tabard Press	1885
A History of the GWR	G. A. Sekon	Digby Long	1895
Life in a Railway Factory	A. Williams	Duckworth	1915
War Record of the GWR	E. A. Pratt	Selwyn & Blount	1922
A History of the GWR — Vol. 1 & 2	E. T. MacDermott	GWR	1927
A Swindon Retrospect 1855-1930	F. Large	Borough Press	1932
GW Progress 1835-1935	—	The Times	1935
Nine Fifteen from Victoria	V. Bayley	Robert Hale	1937
British Railways in Peace & War	—	BR Press Office	1944
It can now be revealed	—	BR Press Office	1945
St. Mark's Church Swindon 1845-1945	Priests & People	Swindon Press	1945
A Century of Medical Service	B. Darwin	GWR Medical Fund Society	1947
British Machine Tool Engineering (Vol. XXXII No. 160)			
Studies in the History of Swindon	L. V. Grinsell & others	Swindon Borough Council	1950
Locomotives of the GWR Parts 1—12	Various	RCTS	1951-74
British Canals	C. Hadfield	Readers Union	1952
The Armstrongs of the Great Western	H. Holcroft	Railway World	1953
An Outline of GW Locomotive Practice 1837-1947	H. Holcroft	Ian Allan	1957
The Reshaping of British Railways	BRB	HMSO	1963
Great Western Coaches 1890-1954	M. Harris	David & Charles	1966
A History of the GWR — Vol. 3	O. S. Nock	Ian Allan	1967
The Age of the Railway	H. Perkin	David & Charles	1970
Sir Daniel Gooch, Memoirs & Diary	Ed. R. B. Wilson	David & Charles	1972
The Swindon Tramways	L. J. Dalby	Oakwood Press	1973
Swindon Steam 1921-1951	K. J. Cook	Ian Allan	1974
G. J. Churchward, A Locomotive Biography	Col. H. C. B. Rogers	Geo. Allen & Unwin	1975
Rail 150	Ed. Jack Simmons	Eyre Methuen	1975
The Victoria County History of Wiltshire	—	Oxford University Press	
The Great Western Railway Magazine			
Astil's Directory (various years)			
Swindon & North Wilts Directory (various years)			
Proceedings of the GWR Swindon Engineering Society			

Introduction

This book is an attempt to set out the history of an engineering works over the 140 years of its existence. Its establishment in the fields of North Wiltshire stimulated the birth of a completely new town. Although it took its name from the Domesday village of Swindon on the nearby hill, it was only loosely connected with that community during its early development. The story of the new undertaking is an excellent example of the effects of the later part of the Industrial Revolution in England, and it must be assumed that those people who nurtured it were well aware of the problems and pitfalls of earlier and similar developments during the previous fifty years, where industrial development of former agricultural areas had taken place. The story which follows, therefore, cannot just be a catalogue recounting the building, equipping, and later extensions of a factory. The people who controlled it and worked there are an inextricable part of the story, as is the town which they themselves developed. These three, factory, people, and town, cannot and should not be separated. In the nature of things, as both factory and town grew to maturity, the close bonds of earlier years would loosen, but even the incorporation of the Borough of Swindon in 1900, after 60 years of growth, could not sever the close ties between the two organizations. In fact it was to be another 50 years before the town's complete dependence on the presence of the railway factory was to be gradually eased but only after the demise of the Great Western Railway when it disappeared in the Nationalization upheaval of 1948.

Swindon Works was one of the largest single assets of the GWR and its fortunes and misfortunes through the years were closely connected with both the short-term and overall policy of the Board of Directors of the Company at any period. It has been necessary, therefore, to acquaint the reader from time to time with many of the historic decisions which were to affect life there. Of particular importance, and one which was rarely overlooked by the Board, was the personality of the senior officers whom they selected, and in most cases previously prepared, for high office at Swindon. There was an obvious awareness that not only should this person be the best professional engineer available, and an expert and capable leader of men at work, but also suitable from a civic and social standpoint. That the Board was successful in this for nearly 100 years is plain. Of this succession of great men, two, Daniel Gooch and Joseph Armstrong, tower above the others in their efforts for the community, and in the author's opinion their great achievements have never gained locally the recognition they deserve. It may sound a brutal thing to say, but, Isambard Kingdom Brunel, great engineer and progenitor of the GWR that he was, had very

little to do directly with the building of the factory and town. This was mainly the brainchild of Gooch. It was left to his successor Armstrong, in thirteen years of feverish activity which eventually wore him out, to complete the work. In that short period this great man not only doubled the size of the works, turning it into an efficient manufacturing organization, but also inaugurated those things necessary to complete the transformation of a collection of dwellings into a well organized and thriving township. The work of his successors, William Dean and George Jackson Churchward, was to keep the initiative and momentum going to the ultimate benefit not only of the GWR, but more importantly, of Swindon as a whole.

This volume could have become a collection of tales and reminiscences, which in themselves might prove interesting and amusing. However, I have included such items only where it proves relevant to the matter under discussion, (and indeed a complete volume could be written on such material alone). Similarly the book could have been a long dissertation on the locomotives, carriages and wagons which have been built and maintained over the years at Swindon. Such an approach would confuse my object, and in any case, this information is already available from a host of railway writers much better informed and equipped to present such facts. Again only where the information is relevant to the development of Swindon as an engineering centre have such details been included.

This book is therefore an amalgam of industrial archaeology, social history, and a study in the development of railway rolling stock engineering. It is presented in the unified way that the subject of the town and Railway Works at Swindon demand and which, it is believed, has not been attempted in this way hitherto. Whilst doubtless it will be of local interest, it is hoped that the book will be acceptable in wider circles as a commentary on urban development based on industry which, because of the almost diametrically opposite approach as evidenced in the 20th century new town corporation concept, is not likely to be repeated. One thing is certain, in researching for the book, the author has been reminded time and again of the dictum that 'it has all happened before'.

A few words of explanation regarding terminology are required. The GWR always referred to the Broad Gauge (7 ft. 0¼ in.), and the Narrow Gauge (4 ft. 8½ in.) until the Broad Gauge was finally converted in 1892. Only then did the 4 ft. 8½ in. gauge become known as the Standard Gauge. This is but one example of the many things which helped to make the GWR different from other undertakings. The author, as a member of a family with long connections with the Great Western Railway, has retained these particular terms and phrases in the text of this book. Finally, the use of the words 'the Borough' should be explained. This refers from 1900 until 1974 to the Borough of Swindon. In 1974 the reorganization of Local Government throughout the country resulted in the formation locally of the Borough of Thamesdown, comprising a large part of the north-east corner of Wiltshire. However, these political changes made no difference to the naming of the actual town of Swindon, and this is still the name to be found on maps and used by the Post Office, and indeed everyone, except the local authority. So as not to confuse the reader, therefore, the name Swindon is used throughout the book. Swindon's fame as a railway engineering centre is acknowledged world-wide, and that is a good enough reason for its retention and continued use.

Chapter One

Before 1841~From Stone Age to Steam Age

Until the early 19th century, history passed Swindon by. Even in the Neolithic Age, when the area of the Berkshire and Wiltshire Downs was one of the higher populated areas of Britain centred upon Avebury, the small hill on which the village of Swindon developed was just an outcrop to the north, although its numerous springs of fresh water may have attracted a few temporary settlements. The Romans served it similarly. Their military road from Corinium (Cirencester) to Venta Bulgarum (Winchester), branched at its first staging camp some two miles east of Swindon Hill, whence another road, the Ermine Way, led in an easterly direction to Calleva (Silchester). This staging camp could be called the first Swindon Junction! The camp area is thought by some authorities to have been named Durocornovium, and this is supported by the name of the stream running through the area, known as Dorcan brook, which appears in Anglo-Saxon land charters with the same name, but with the inevitable spelling variations. Some small signs of a Roman habitation were found at Okus, the westerly part of Swindon Hill, in the early 19th century.

As Saxon Britain developed, however, a small village did slowly grow, attracted, no doubt, by the strangely spaced springs, now mainly dried up, that appeared all round the crest of this geologically complex hill, where many types of clays, sands and Portland and Purbeck stone are to be found. The main attraction was, no doubt, the opportunity of harnessing some of this spring water, by means of keep ponds, to operate water-mills. One such mill continued to be used on the south side of the hill until about the middle of the 19th century. These activities were certainly in being by the reign of King Edward the Confessor, as there are six entries for the village of Swindon in the Domesday Book, and many entries refer to holdings prior to the Norman Conquest. Even so, the land in the area was not important enough to form one large holding, but at least five landlords, and possibly more, were involved. The only person of note amongst these was Bishop Odo of Bayeux, the Conqueror's half-brother, who played a prominent part in the invading expedition, and that worthy at least is depicted on the Bayeux Tapestry. Development thereafter was exceedingly slow, and other villages within a radius of ten miles or so, such as Marlborough, Highworth, Cricklade and Wootton Bassett, seemed to develop more satisfactorily. Certain families throughout this long period have persisted, and names such as Avenell, Ruddle, Lawrence and Haggard — to quote but a few — appear again and again in old records. The name of Avenell occurs as early as 1316, and at the time of writing there is at least one of the same name on the Swindon Works payroll.

The Lordship of the Manor of Swindon passed into the hands of the Goddard family in 1563, and the family remained in residence at successive manor houses at 'The Lawn' until a few years ago. It is possible that an early market was set up at Swindon, probably about 1257. Thomas Goddard was granted a Monday Market by Charles I in 1626 together with two fairs a year. The Market is still in being, and the fairs observed, although the latter only by road showmen. This market prospered, since agriculture was the main occupation in the area, and Swindon was a little too far east to become very much involved in the broadcloth manufacturing areas of West Wiltshire, and too far south to come within the Cotswold wool and cloth region, in an era of poor communications. The Goddard family commenced quarrying activities in the area some time after 1640. The stone was said, by the historian John Aubrey, to be very good for paving halls and staircases, but much may also have been used as road stone and as common building material. But since Swindon was on no particular road to anywhere, (unlike Marlborough on the Great West Road to Bath and Bristol from London) the difficulties of distribution of such a heavy commodity as stone must have been a considerable deterrent to the expansion of this industry. Nevertheless, after agriculture, it was the main employment activity of the village.

It was only with the inauguration of the Wilts & Berks Canal, built under the Act of 1795, from Semington on the Kennet & Avon Canal to the River Thames at Abingdon, that an improvement in communications to Swindon took place with a corresponding uplift to the local economy. This was a narrow canal built mainly for coal carrying and serving the agricultural communities. It navigated around the north side of Swindon Hill. Business increased even more when the North Wilts Canal, from Latton on the Thames & Severn Canal to a junction at Swindon with the Wilts & Berks, was promoted in 1813. This gave a second 'Swindon Junction' about 1700 years after the Romans. Thus, within about 20 years, commercial transit by narrow boat could be made to London via the Thames at Abingdon; to the Midlands, via Abingdon and Oxford; to Trowbridge, Bath and Bristol, via the Kennet & Avon; and northwards through the Sapperton Canal Tunnel to Stroud, Gloucester, and the Severn Basin. Although Swindon was comparatively isolated from the main road system of the

Plate 1: The Seal of the Wilts and Berks Canal Co.
Wiltshire Museums & Libraries

country, there was a reasonable stage-coach service for passenger traffic. At its height there was a service three days a week from Swindon to London, with a complementary return service, the single journey taking about ten hours. A coach service between Oxford and Bath also made a daily call at Swindon in each direction, and a similar arrangement was made in the Cheltenham to Southampton service. In addition the 'carriers' undertook local services within the area.

This was how matters stood in the earlier years of the 19th century. Railways were already being projected, particularly in those areas of the country which were dependent on the heavy industries of mining and iron making. The population of Swindon had risen with the opening up of communications by the canals, as shown by the census returns:

Year	Population
1801	1,198
1811	1,341
1821	1,580
1831	1,742

Before the Stockton & Darlington railway was opened, some Bristol merchants, in 1824, were promoting the idea of a railway operated by locomotives between their city, still the second largest port in the country, and London. The first known proposal was to be the London & Bristol Rail-Road Company. It was certainly a very adventurous proposal, since no railway of such a length had by then been considered, when a steam locomotive's capability was very questionable. This first proposal, if it had continued, would certainly have passed close to Swindon, as the

Vale of the White Horse was part of the selected route. Even though it was said that all the shares for a £1½ million stock issue had been taken up, and steps had been taken to apply to Parliament for the necessary Act, little further action appears to have taken place.

Doubtless, the success of the Liverpool & Manchester Railway opened in 1830 rekindled discussion of this important route. So again, in 1832, a new proposal for a 'Bristol & London Railway' took shape. This project, in its original form, failed to get the necessary support, but a further meeting was convened at the Bristol Council House on 21st January 1833. This meeting required that the gentleman deputed by Bristol Corporation, the Society of Merchant Venturers, the Chamber of Commerce, the Dock Company, and the Bristol & Gloucestershire Rail-Road Company (already in being), should report on the 'expediency of promoting the formation of a Rail-Road from Bristol to London'. The meeting was to discuss such reports, and other information available on the subject. After this meeting, a small committee of four was deputed to make arrangements for a preliminary survey and estimate for a railway.

Such work necessitated the appointment of a suitable engineer. Of several candidates, the one who was already well-known in Bristol for his accepted design of a suspension bridge at Clifton Gorge, Isambard Kingdom Brunel — still only twenty-seven years of age — was appointed on 7th March 1833. His survey, which included alternative routes, was expeditiously carried out, and on Tuesday, 30th July 1833, at a meeting of representatives under the chairmanship of Mr Robert Bright (in the absence of the Mayor of Bristol), a company was launched with a view to obtaining the necessary parliamentary powers. Much work had been going on in the meantime to arouse the interest of a wide range of London businessmen in the project to strengthen the small group already working on the scheme. While the Bristol Committee had, for their part, appointed a remarkable young engineer for the projected railway, the London Committee engaged, as its secretary, a man who was to do as much for the emerging company, if not more. This man was Charles Alexander Saunders, an experienced business man of thirty-seven years of age, who was to devote the rest of his life to the service of the new company.

The first joint meeting of the two committees took place in London on 19th August 1833, when the name of the undertaking was changed from 'Bristol & London Railroad' to 'Great Western Railway'. Although Brunel had investigated routes both to the north and the south of the Berkshire and Wiltshire Downs, as did the surveyors for the M4 motorway some 150 years later, he preferred the northern route through the Vale of the White Horse. Both routes naturally raised the intense opposition of most land-owners. The projected line of about 120 miles was estimated to cost £2,805,330. The first prospectus was issued as a result of the London meeting. This document included alternative entry routes into London, and made mention of three possible branches: Didcot to Oxford; Swindon to Gloucester; and Chippenham to Bradford. The second of these three was to have great importance in the development of Swindon.

Saunders was indefatigable in making all the necessary arrangements. The most important was to obtain promises of financial support in order to get the bill to Parliament as quickly as possible. Since only about a quarter of the necessary capital could be guaranteed — instead of the statutory half — by October of 1833, the directors decided to seek authority for the London to Reading, and Bristol to Bath, sections only so that some progress could be made. Deposited in November 1833, the important examination in Parliamentary Committee of this bill did not commence until 16th April 1834 and lasted for 57 days. It was supported strongly by business interests, but equally strongly opposed, in particular, by the land-owners of the Home Counties. However, the Commons approved the bill, but it was defeated at the second reading in the House of Lords by 47 votes to 30. However, this lapse of time was to the eventual benefit of the Company, and a supplementary prospectus was issued which gave a much more detailed statement of the proposed route and works, together with better supporting financial information. Much was done, particularly by Saunders, to increase financial support. In his correspondence he showed increasing optimism, although he found it 'sad, harassing work'. By February 1835, the necessary additional capital needed to support the presentation of a new bill was promised. Again a difficult Commons Committee fight ensued and the third reading was not approved until 26th May. Trouble was experienced in the House of Lords, where it was referred to a committee chaired by Lord Wharncliffe, and some weeks of heated argument took place. The final reading in the Lords was eventually agreed to, and, at last, this Act, 5&6 William IV, Cap. 107 (Local & Personal Acts), Session 1835, received the Royal Assent on 31st August 1835. Soon afterwards, in 1836, the Bristol and Exeter Railway, and the Cheltenham & Great Western Union Railway, which had close ties with the GWR project, obtained their Acts.

What was to prove momentus to the newly formed GWR was the acceptance of Brunel's recommendation to adopt a gauge of 7 ft. 0¼ in., wider than any other then in use. It is clear from statements made at the time, and later to the Gauge Commissioners, that this was no hasty idea on the part of Brunel. It had been arranged with Saunders, who was aware of

Brunel's thinking on the matter, that a statement of the gauge of the projected railway should be left out of the Act. Agreement to accept this deliberate omission was surprisingly obtained from the Lords' Committee Chairman. The original Bill of 1834 is said to have stated that the line would be built to the 4 ft. 8½ in. gauge. If that Bill had gained the Royal Assent in 1834, there the matter would have rested. The detailed route embodied in the 1835 Act led to the realization of Brunel's dreams of a fine piece of railway engineering with almost level track, except for two specific inclines, and with minimum curvature over the whole London to Bristol route. The attraction of adding to this a wide gauge to obtain even greater stability was no doubt irresistible to his unique mind. It is quite possible that the decision to adopt the 7 ft. 0¼ in. broad gauge was one of the reasons for the final dropping of the proposed joint terminal facilities with the London & Birmingham Railway at Euston, as was originally intended. A deviation was sanctioned near Kensal Green to a new site for a terminus near the basin of the Paddington Canal in August 1836.

The Company, under Brunel's energetic leadership, very quickly started building, and both the London and Bristol Committees began active work on the London to Reading, and Bristol to Bath sections, respectively. It is not the task of this volume to record the history of this work and the many problems involved nor how they were surmounted. Suffice it to state that the first section to be opened for operation was Paddington to Taplow on 4th June 1838. Subsequent openings to the public were made to Twyford on 1st July 1839; Reading on 30th March 1840; Steventon (for Oxford) on 1st June; and Faringdon Road (later Uffington) on 20th July. Opened also in the same year was the Bristol to Bath section on 31st August, which involved a large amount of very heavy engineering work. The next opening in a westerly direction, and of importance to our subject, was the extension of the line from Steventon to a temporary terminus named Wootton Bassett Road. This was near the 80 mile post from (the original) Paddington Station, and was, in fact, about half-way between Swindon and Wootton Bassett at a place still called Hay Lane near what is now interchange 16 of the M4 motorway. As Faringdon Road had been the western terminus from London for about five months, so from 17th December 1840, Hay Lane at the eastern end of Studley Cutting, had its short period of fame. The Board of Trade Inspector of the time, Sir Frederick Smith, stated in his report that 'although Hay Lane Station is merely intended as a temporary terminus, the Company are forming it, in regard to sidings, switches, and other mechanical arrangements, in the same extensive and substantial manner as is their ordinary practice at permanent terminals!'

No doubt, because of the outlay required for this temporary station, the population of Swindon, when using the railway at this period, had either to make their way to Hay Lane, then travel back past their town towards London, or, more likely, drive to the first station up the line at Shrivenham. This is not because a station at Swindon was not proposed, but that it would not be built until the Cheltenham & GW Union Railway, already under somewhat slow construction, was ready to make the connection at the new junction. Hay Lane's five months of fame ended on 31st May 1841, when the line was opened to Chippenham, although it remained in the time-table until about August 1841, when the station at Wootton Bassett itself was ready. The only remaining portion to be opened was, of course, Bath to Chippenham, which included the then famous (or infamous, according to contemporary feelings on such matters), Box Tunnel. The opening of the whole route duly took place with little or no public ceremony on 30th June 1841. On the same day, the first section of the Bristol to Exeter line, also broad gauge, opened from Bristol to Bridgwater. In April 1840, the Cheltenham & GW Union Railway accepted leasing to the GWR, and the completed portion from Cirencester and Kemble to Swindon Junction was publicly opened on 31st May 1841. A temporary station was at that time provided at Swindon.

We have now come to the point where Swindon Junction was finally established and the commencement of the town's growth as a railway centre was about to begin. After outlining the early history of the town and the building of the railway which was to make it famous, we must now look back some five years to 1836. About this time, Brunel had turned his thoughts to the provision of the locomotives and rolling stock necessary to operate the services when the railway was opened. It is inevitable that a man of such imagination would try to break new ground in the design of locomotives, and he laid down particular conditions in his contracts, which were, with hindsight, self-defeating in character. The main problem appears to have been a strict limitation on the weight of locomotives in working order. This seems completely out of character for Brunel, who usually took the grand view of anything he undertook. It resulted in the delivery of locomotives with boilers too small to provide steam to meet the capacity of the cylinders fitted. There were also some designs which were very unorthodox and untried to say the least. These latter machines may have been of interest to him for that very reason. Whilst it is true that locomotive design was still in its infancy, the outcome of the Rainhill trials and development from that time had provided the basic criteria for an acceptable operational locomotive within the limitations which materials and engineering processes of the period allowed. Two locomotives which were accepted for

the GWR, however, were ones which had been built by Robert Stephenson to orthodox design. This was to prove fortuitous indeed for the GWR.

Before any of these new locomotives had been delivered, it was apparent to Brunel that the railway needed an officer to control the locomotive department, and authority was obtained from the directors in July 1837, to make the necessary appointment. It is not clear if Brunel had any particular man in mind at the time, although he must have been aware of candidates capable of filling such a post. It may have been advertised in some way and Daniel Gooch, a 20 year old engineer born in Bedlington in 1816, applied. He came from the same Northumbrian community that had produced men who were already famous in railway circles. A frequent visitor to his home was George Stephenson; and William Hedley, Timothy Hackworth and John Birkinshaw were all known to the family. Gooch's father worked at the Bedlington Ironworks where Birkinshaw was manager, and where the managing partner was Michael Longridge, later one of the partners in Robert Stephenson & Company.

Plate 2: Daniel Gooch, after receiving his baronetcy, from a drawing by Nye made in 1864.

British Rail

In his short but concentrated experience as an engineer up to this time, Gooch had been able to accommodate a very wide range of the engineering skills and processes of the day. The family moved to Tredegar in Monmouthshire when he was about 15 years old, and his father took a post at the iron works, and it was there that Gooch started his professional career. He commenced work in the moulding shop, moving later to the pattern shop, where a Mr Ellis was foreman. This gentleman's son, Thomas, was in charge of the mechanical department of the iron works, and a few years later was to build locomotives for the Sirhowy & Monmouthshire Tramroads. It is evident that his training at Tredegar was very broadly based, and he seems to have been treated as a privileged apprentice or even pupil, although receiving pay. After the early death of his father at Tredegar, he moved to the Vulcan Foundry near Warrington, which was run at that time by Robert Stephenson and Charles Tayleur of Liverpool. He went as a pupil to the locomotive manufactory, which was still in process of completion at the time of his arrival. Matthew Kirtley was engineman at this works, and here he learned much about engine building. However, Gooch's health broke down — he had already had health problems at the Tredegar works — causing him to leave the Vulcan Foundry, and after spending a short period with his brother, Thomas, on the London & Birmingham Railway, he undertook work as a draughtsman at the East Foundry, Dundee, early in 1835. This was under the managership of James Stirling, and one of his colleagues here was Archibald Sturrock. He stayed at this foundry for a year, moving, in January 1836, to the Newcastle works of Robert Stephenson.

In October 1836, Sir Robert Hawks offered Gooch the prospective position of partner at a new Gateshead locomotive works, which he accepted. Whilst placing orders for machinery for this venture, Gooch became acquainted with Whitworth. In November 1836 he visited the GWR Directors at Bristol, hoping to obtain future orders for broad gauge engines for his company. He should have met Brunel at that meeting, but the great man was elsewhere that day. This project for a new works at Gateshead fell through, however, and he asked his brother, Tom, by then engineer of the Manchester & Leeds Railway, for stop-gap employment and was given work in the Rochdale and Manchester offices of that company. It was from here that he heard of the post being created in the GWR.

Gooch's Mémoirs & Diary give a detailed account of his first encounter with Brunel, although it was written some thirty years after the event. He states that, at the end of July 1837, he heard that the post of Locomotive Engineer was to be created for the GWR, and he at once wrote to Brunel on 20th July. This historic letter is preserved in the GWR Museum at Swindon, and is reproduced as Appendix I to this volume. The appointment of Gooch, on 18th August 1837, was to prove one of the most momentous the GWR ever made, and equally so for Swindon.

At this time, no locomotives had been delivered and Gooch's first work on arrival was concerned with the preparation of plans for the engine houses and their equipment at Paddington and Maidenhead. He also took the opportunity to go to the various manufactories supplying locomotives to Brunel's orders, and was somewhat dismayed by what he discovered, mainly for the reasons discussed earlier. In November, the

Plate 3: *Vulcan*, the first locomotive to run on the Great Western track, as altered into a 'back tank' in 1846.

British Rail

first examples arrived by canal at West Drayton, after having come from Liverpool by sea to London. A suitable piece of track, about one and a half miles long, was completed there by December. Thus, the *Vulcan* (built by the Vulcan Foundry) was given a trial run on 28th December 1837, and became the first locomotive to run on GWR rails. Records show that another locomotive, one of the more orthodox ones already mentioned and named *North Star*, was also delivered in late November of the same year to the London side of the Thames at Maidenhead. Since no track was laid there until May 1838, there it had to stay. West Drayton, therefore, became for the time being, Gooch's operational establishment, with his own office, a temporary engine house, water supply, and other requirements.

As the time approached for opening the first section of line from Paddington to Maidenhead, (actually a temporary building just short of the Thames Bridge, and, therefore, more correctly, Taplow), Gooch found that the only locomotive on which he could really rely out of the ten then to hand was *North Star*, supplied by Robert Stephenson, and built ori-

ginally to the 5 ft. 6 in. gauge for the New Orleans Railway in North America. This locomotive, (together with a sister *Morning Star*, not delivered until January 1839), had been bought by the directors and altered to the broad gauge. The only other alteration, made before delivery to conform more closely to Brunel's specifications, was to increase the driving wheel diameter from 6 ft. 6 in. to 7 ft. 0 in. This was done on *North Star* only, but even this locomotive was not fully reliable, and gave Gooch problems. But at least it steamed reasonably well and was capable of hauling a train. This locomotive was therefore selected to head the directors' inaugural train on 31st May 1838. The public opening over the same stretch of line took place a few days later on 4th June. This time the locomotive *Aeolus* hauled the train, but did not function well. Troubles then began to accumulate for Gooch regarding his ability to run any service at all. But more importantly for Brunel, and by implication the Company, there was great concern over the unexpected rough riding of the trains. Arising from these complaints, the detractors at once started blaming the broad gauge for

Plate 4: *North Star* as it now resides in the Great Western Museum at Swindon. It was surprising how many original parts were found when rebuilt in 1924!.

Author's Collection

Plate 5: *Firefly*, the first GWR locomotive built to Gooch's own design.

British Rail

this short-coming, and almost immediately brought into question the correctness of the decision to adopt it. These were, in fact, the opening shots of a battle leading to the Gauge Commission in 1845, of which more can be read in later chapters.

Reverting to the locomotive situation, Gooch and his staff had to make enormous efforts to keep a service running, occasionally assisted by Brunel, when he had any time to spare. However, bowing to demands from shareholders for an enquiry into the state of the track, the directors required Gooch to make a report direct to them on the locomotive situation also, since only *North Star* and those already delivered from the Vulcan Foundry were capable of any reliable work. This put Gooch in a great dilemma having been appointed by Brunel and working under his direction. However, his report was made and, except for the receipt of an initial angry letter from Brunel, that great man no doubt realized that the criticisms made concerning the locomotives were well-founded, and future relationships between him and Gooch did not suffer. The direct result of this report to the Board was that Gooch received instruction, which had the full agreement of Brunel, to prepare drawings and specifications personally for future locomotives. With the wide training that he had received, and the experience gained in keeping the locomotives in service on the GWR, Gooch was well able to rise to the occasion. Great thought was put into the basic design and into items known to have an effect on reliability. Attention was also paid to standardization and interchangeability. He had

acquired by this time, as his chief draughtsman, T. R. Crampton who later became a great designer in his own right, particularly on the Continent. For accuracy, all drawings were lithographed, as distinct from the more usual hand copying, with its resultant omissions and errors. Furthermore, templates of selected parts were supplied with the drawings prepared under Gooch's control. The written specifications were extremely detailed so that there would be no excuses for not conforming to the strict contract clauses. Finally, there was to be a guarantee against bad materials and workmanship over the first 1,000 miles in full service.

Four basic locomotive designs were prepared in the following months of which the passenger engine types were obvious derivatives of the Stephenson 'Star' class. The largest passenger class had 7 ft. diameter single driving wheels and sixty-two were ordered with this 2-2-2 arrangement, being named the 'Firefly' class after the first locomotive to be delivered. They were primarily meant for the easily graded route from Paddington to Swindon. The second type, 'Sun' class, had 6 ft. driving wheels for use on the more heavily graded Swindon to Bristol section and feeder services. Twenty-one of these were ordered. The two goods types consisted of the 'Leo' 2-4-0 class, eighteen in number, with 5 ft. diameter coupled wheels, and the heavy 'Hercules' 0-6-0 locomotives, also with 5 ft. diameter driving wheels, with a boiler almost identical to the 'Firefly' class. Four of these were ordered. Delivery of all these machines was spread over the period 1840-2. Contracts were let to all the accepted locomotive builders of repute, presumably to obtain the maximum number capable of being delivered in a comparatively short time. As they arrived, together with those of the 'Brunel stable' which could be modified into reasonably reliable runners, the power position on the line began to improve.

About the time these orders were being placed, Gooch obtained authority to appoint an Assistant Superintendent, and he sent for his old colleague at the East Foundry, Dundee, Archibald Sturrock, to fill the position. This new post was required not only for the imminent opening of the GWR services, but because the directors, had, in addition, undertaken to provide locomotive power both for the Bristol & Exeter Railway for the first five years of its operation, and also the locomotives necessary to operate the Cheltenham & GW Union Railway. The arrival of the first of the Gooch designed locomotives, *Firefly*, took place on 12th March 1840 and it was an immediate success. It ran from Paddington to Reading thirteen days later with three vehicles in 46½ minutes, reaching a top speed of 56 m.p.h., confirming Gooch's ability as a designer, and the correctness of his methods of controlling his contracting companies.

A brief mention should be made here of the carriages used in the first few years of the GWR, although these were not the responsibility of Gooch. There appear to have been two types peculiar to the GWR. One was the posting carriage, a type of open saloon on four wheels, purporting to carry 18 persons, first class of course; and the carriage truck, also on four wheels, upon which could be mounted the private carriages of the 'quality' and in which they often rode en route. There were also examples of the standard type of four wheel first class carriage, with three compartments, and a second class open sided type of four compartments. Sundry other vehicles were used, including horse boxes. All these vehicles were, at that time, and for some years later, supplied by contractors, who no doubt had previously been in the stage-coach business. They were maintained at a depot near Paddington. There were also goods wagons (then referred to as 'waggons') of the open type, and tilt wagons, known later as 'bonnet-end trucks'. These were generally four-wheeled, but some of the open type were six-wheeled, the first in the country. It should be noted that in these early days, on being questioned by a Parliamentary Committee in 1839 concerning a third class of passenger, Saunders replied that perhaps the Company would later arrange to transport 'the very lowest orders of passengers'.

The foregoing shows how the locomotive department was expanding. When the railway had been planned, no more than servicing depots were allowed for in Brunel's estimate. No doubt the position was

Plate 6: Archibald Sturrock, first manager of Swindon Works, photographed in later life.

Author's Collection

the same on other similar undertakings, since it would have been wise to wait and see how the company fared before expending shareholders' capital on items other than the railway proper. Doubtless the provision of a more permanent and larger locomotive repair depot had been discussed from time to time. The matter apparently came to a head some time in the summer of 1840 for on 13th September 1840, we find the historic letter, as far as Swindon is concerned, being sent by Gooch to Brunel, setting out his views and arguments about where the new locomotive establishment should be situated. This letter is preserved amongst the railway archives at the Public Records Office and, because of its importance to our subject, is here quoted verbatim:

Bristol
13th September 1840

My dear Sir,
According to your wish I give you my views of the best site for our principal engine establishment, and in doing so I have studied the convenience of the Great Western Railway only, but also think the same point is

the only place adapted for the Cheltenham and Great Western. The point I refer to is the Junction at Swindon of the two lines.

The only objection I see to Swindon is the bad supply of water. There is also an apparent inequality of distance or duty for the engines to work — but which is very much equalized when the circumstances attending it are taken into account. I find the actual distances are as 76½ to 41 and the gradients are for the short distance of 41 miles a rise of 318 feet or 7.75 feet per mile, and for the 76½ miles a rise of 292 feet or 3.8 feet per mile. Swindon being the point at which these gradients change, the different gradients necessarily require a different class of engine, requiring for the Bristol end a more powerful one than for the London end.

That power can only be obtained conveniently by reducing the diameter of the Driving Wheels, therefore, supposing we work between Swindon and Bristol with 6 feet wheels, and between Swindon and London with 7 feet wheels, there will actually be very little difference between the work required of the two engines, when the additional gradients and curves, and the increased number of revolutions per mile which the small wheeled engine makes are taken into account. It would also divide the pilot engines very nearly equally, as Reading being the first Station where a pilot engine would be kept, say 36 miles, the next distance, to Swindon, would then be 41 miles, and on to Bristol another 41, and which I think would be sufficiently near for pilot engines to be constantly ready, and with this arrangement the watering stations would work very well. Steventon where plenty of water can be had, forming a central station between Reading and Swindon, and as our Oxford Traffic comes on there I should think it likely that all trains will stop there. A large station at Swindon would also enable us to keep our Bank engines for Wootton Bassett incline at Swindon instead of having a separate station for that purpose at the bottom of the incline, and in addition it would at any rate be necessary to have a considerable Station at Swindon to work the Cheltenham line, which would be saved if Swindon was our principal station.

It also has the great advantage of being on the side of a canal communicating with the whole of England, and by which we could get coal and coke, I should think at a moderate price. I am not sufficiently acquainted with the place to know how far we would be affected by the want of water, it might probably be collected in the neighbourhood, and as we have a great deal of side cutting they might be converted into reservoirs, and should even this fail us we have the canal. These reasons lead me to think Swindon by far the best point we have for a Central Engine Station. From the plans and sections there appear little or no difficulties with the nature of the ground for building upon, and by placing the station somewhere as shown in the enclosed sketch, it might be made in every respect very complete. I have not thought of the Bristol & Exeter line in the arrangement, as it is quite possible to work it very well by engines kept at Bristol as long as they are fit for work. In the same way we could work the additional Bath traffic, for when necessary they could always work their way to Swindon when any heavy repairs were required. The Engine House we are building at Bristol would be ample for any slight repairs that might be required during the time the engine was in working order, and that without any outlay of machinery beyond a few hundred pounds. I am not aware of any difficulties connected with Swindon more than the water.

I am, my dear Sir,
Yours very truly,
DANIEL GOOCH.

I. K. Brunel Esq.

We can see from this letter that the decision to select the site at Swindon was based on sound engineering and economic reasoning, as one would expect from Gooch. The accompanying sketch referred to shows a building to a round-house plan, set in a railway triangle, the GWR and Cheltenham & GW Union lines forming two sides of the triangle, a loop line to the west joining them up to make the third side. Although these ideas were not finally used in the new factory, the idea of having a western loop lingered on for many years. Shortly after the date of this letter, Brunel and Gooch made a visit of inspection to the site. They would have seen a green field area, bounded on the east by the Cheltenham line (no doubt still under construction), the almost completed line to the Hay Lane temporary terminus to the south, and an area of nearly level fields between, a slight fall being observable both to the south of the GWR main line, and northwards toward Cheltenham. It was perhaps on this visit that the apocryphal story of the sandwich left over from their lunch, took root! Whilst not deciding the site of the works, one can certainly picture Brunel throwing the remains of a sandwich with a remark such as 'so the entrance to the engine house will be about there'. With such tales history is often leavened. The correctness of Gooch's assessment of the suitability of the site is shown by its great development over subsequent years. Furthermore, his concern about the water supply, mentioned three times in the letter, was to prove only too well-founded. Accordingly, Brunel reported to the Board, which resolved in a minute dated 6th October 1840:

'That the Principal Locomotive Station & Repairing Shops be established at, or near, the Junction with the Cheltenham & GW Union Railway at Swindon'.

Some very hectic work must have resulted, under the leadership of Gooch, in providing schemes for the new establishment and preparing estimates. The latter would have carried great importance as the railway was not able, at that time, to be as financially generous as Brunel and Gooch would wish, due to the excessive building costs of the railway compared with the original estimates. However, the Director's report of February 1841 contains the following statement:-

'The final determination of working those two Railways* upon Lease has imposed upon the Directors the necessity of providing an increased stock of Locomotive Engines, Carriages, Waggons and other Plant adequate to the trade which may be reasonably expected.

It has also decided the Directors to provide an Engine Establishment at Swindon, commensurate with the wants of the Company, where a change of Engines may be advantageously made, and the trains stopped for the purpose of the passengers taking refreshment, as is the case at Wolverton on the London & Birmingham Railway. The Establishment there would also comprehend the large repairing shops for the Locomotive Department, and this circumstance rendered it necessary to arrange for the building of cottages, etc., for the residence of many persons employed in the service of the Company.

The Directors have, under these circumstances, made an arrangement with responsible Builders for the erection of Refreshment Rooms and Cottages, without the employment of any Capital from the Company. The profits of the refreshment business are to remunerate them for all the outlay in the accommodation required at Swindon by passengers, consequent upon the trains stopping at that place. The Company are to provide the land for the cottages, and to secure to the Builders a fixed rent upon lease, which rent will of course be re-imbursed by the tenants of the cottages. The only increased demand, therefore, upon the Company for capital at Swindon, will be to defray the cost of that additional land, and of the Engine Establishment and Repairing Shops there, which are indispensably necessary'.

* *Bristol & Exeter and Cheltenham & G W Union Rlys*

The final authority to proceed appears in the Board Minutes of April/May 1841, when it voted the sum of £35,290, 'for the buildings to be erected at Swindon for the principal locomotive establishment of the Company'. It was made clear that the sum did not include offices, stores, furnaces, and wheel shop, which were apparently to be financed otherwise. Also the works were to be constructed at the same time as the station refreshment rooms and 300 cottages. The financial arrangements for these matters will be dealt with as they arise.

History was to pass Swindon by no longer.

Chapter Two

The First Twenty Years~1841–1861
The New Swindon Manufactory

The decision to start a new industry, in particular a development of the 'green field' type, has a deep effect on the town or area in which it is to be located. In our own time, there has been so much development of this type that much expertise in forecasting the possible results is available. But, even so, we are only too well aware that often things do not turn out in the way that the planners foresaw. How much more difficult it must have been for Gooch to decide how to proceed in this great project at Swindon. However, we can make things a little easier to follow by splitting the narrative into two parts. One concerns the factual building and equipping of the new factory, the provision of people to operate it, and its early work. This will be the subject of the present chapter. The second is the social implications and results of the project, which will be dealt with in the next chapter.

It could be said that, in 1840, it was in many ways simple to start a new industry. As far as railway undertakings were concerned, if there was a relevant line of print in one of the annual supplementary applications for Parliamentary powers, then the purchasing of land, the dissuasion of any local opposition, and the preparation of drawings without bureaucratic planning restrictions, were all under the control of the Company officers. Thus the scheme proceeded entirely as a measure of their several skills, ability and drive. That Gooch in particular was entirely suited to this situation, there can be no doubt. Also by this time Brunel had attracted to him a group of very able civil engineers to whom he could delegate control of the many projects in which, by this time, he was becoming involved. What is equally important, these men were able and willing to do this work in such a way that, looking back, it is difficult to discern that it was not all done by Brunel himself.

To whom did he delegate the provision of the necessary plans and drawings for the Swindon establishment? By great good fortune we can suggest who this was with near certainty. It is in the nature of things that drawings of buildings and plant of very old establishments deteriorate in time, or are redrawn, completely superseding the old drawings, which are then usually scrapped. Whilst this has obviously happened to the Swindon drawings records, a small amount of the original work has been retained and is still part of the works records — albeit now under archival safety. They were retained for two basic reasons. The first is that many of them are the only ones showing original sewers, storm water and early water supply layouts in detail and were kept for continuous reference. The other reason was that the foundation of some of the shops and offices of the new factory were types not used in later additions — the inverted arch being the main example — and were retained for the detail shown, in case repairs or alterations were required in the future. Inevitably a few other odd drawings also became attached to this collection. It was not the practice to include in drawings the 'drawn by' and 'checked by' legend of later times and none of them is signed. They are ink tracings on a very frail type of tracing paper, with the notes in handwriting, and they were sent for mounting on to linen backing to Wm. Howard of 23, Gt. Russell Street, London. But on the linen back of the most important of these drawings is the rubber stamp in indelible ink of 'T. H. Bertram'. Also some of those not so stamped have notes in handwriting, which compares with that on the stamped drawings. So it was T. H. Bertram, one of Brunel's senior staff, then working under the principal assistant, J. W. Hammond, presumably at the Parliament Street offices, who prepared, no doubt in consultation with Gooch, drawings for, first, the engine house, and, later, the other new buildings for Swindon Works.

If further proof is needed, this can be found on 'Swindon Station Drawing No. 3' (note there was no railway station at Swindon at the time, only the locomotive station), where the main office at the south end on the first floor is marked 'Mr Bertram's Office'. This infers that Bertram became, in effect, the Swindon District Engineer, certainly during the period of building the Works. Also interesting is that the assistant's room next to Bertram's is marked 'Mr Owen's Office'. This is most likely to be W. G. Owen. If this argument is accepted, Swindon was built under the control of men who were both to be Chief Engineer to the GWR, with Bertram also 'acting' during Brunel's last illness and holding office until early 1860. In passing, the author had the pleasure of tenure of Mr Owen's office for the last ten years of his service at Swindon, and it is the only office still in its original condition in the whole Works. Perhaps it should be allowed to remain so.

One other interesting facet of the decision to build at Swindon comes to light. Whilst Gooch gives all the engineering and operating reasons for his choice of site, there is one which surprisingly is not mentioned in view of the tight financial position the GWR was in at the time. This is that the land required was already railway owned, albeit not by the GWR, but

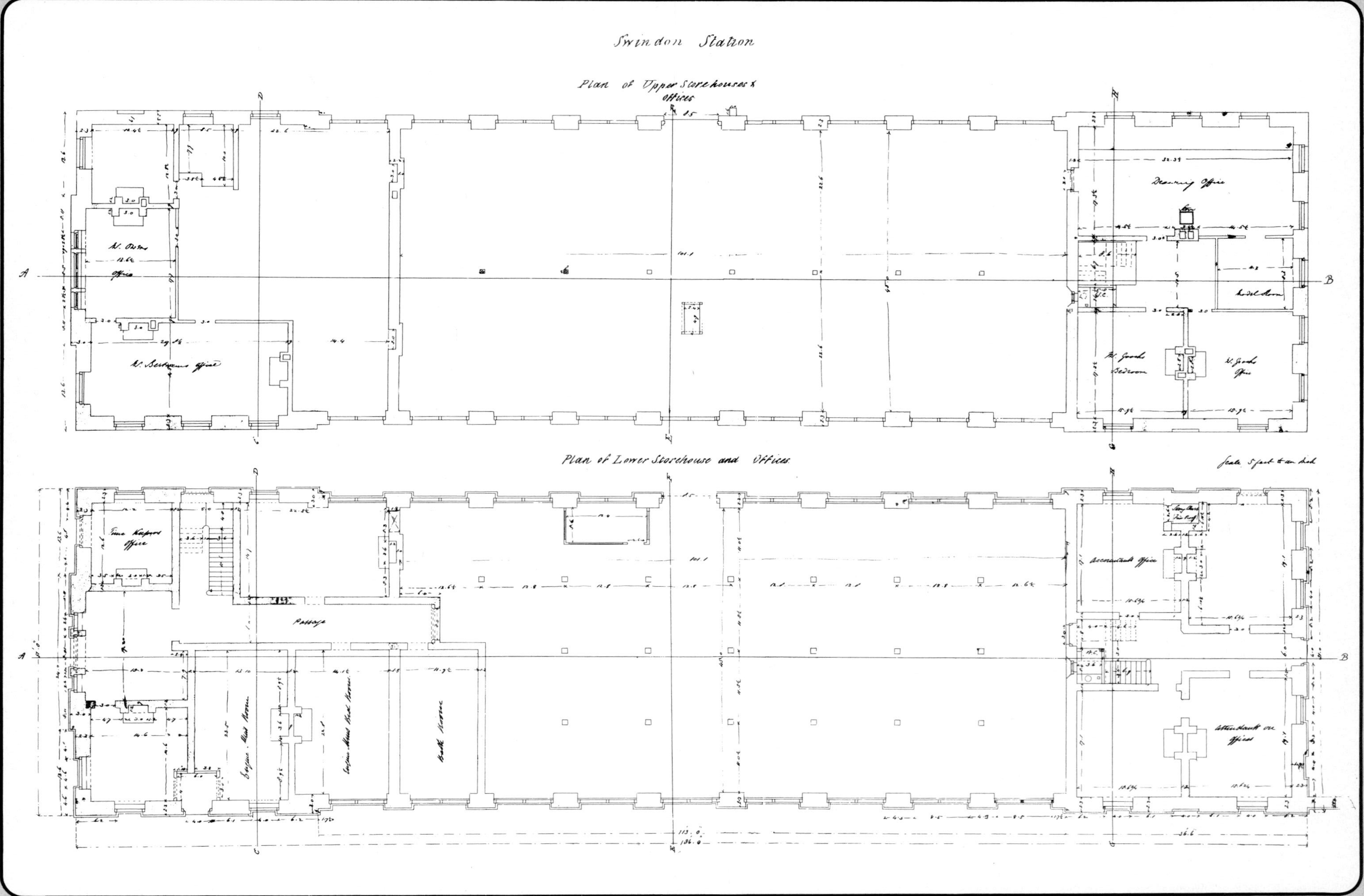

Swindon Station

Plan of Upper Storehouse Offices

Plan of Lower Storehouse and Offices

Plate 7: Reproduction of 'Swindon Drawing No. 3', showing plans of the office block. Bertram's office is at the lower left-hand corner of the 1st floor (upper) plan. Gooch's office and bedroom are on the same

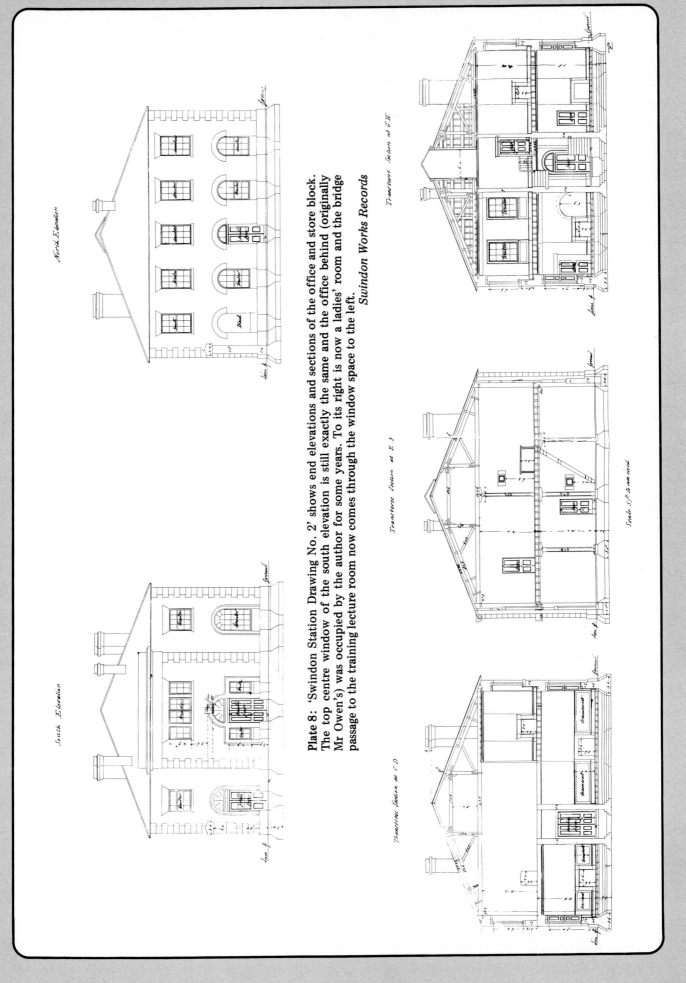

North Elevation

South Elevation

Transverse Section at C D

Transverse Section at G H

Transverse Section at E F

Scale 5/8 an inch

Swindon Works Records

Plate 8: 'Swindon Station Drawing No. 2' shows end elevations and sections of the office and store block. The top centre window of the south elevation is still exactly the same and the office behind (originally Mr Owen's) was occupied by the author for some years. To its right is now a ladies' room and the bridge passage to the training lecture room now comes through the window space to the left.

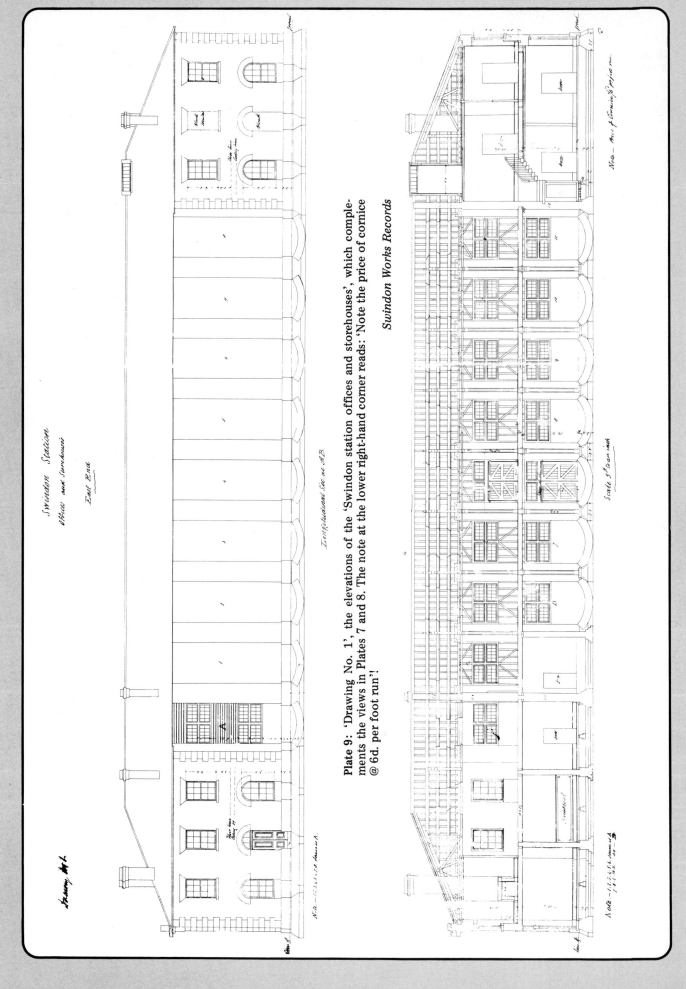

Plate 9: 'Drawing No. 1', the elevations of the 'Swindon station offices and storehouses', which complements the views in Plates 7 and 8. The note at the lower right-hand corner reads: 'Note the price of cornice @ 6d. per foot run'!

Swindon Works Records

by the Cheltenham & GW Union Company! Why this large piece of land had been purchased by such a financially hard-pressed undertaking is not clear, unless they had been faced with an 'all or nothing' condition of sale, which the original land owner could have imposed, knowing that the junction had to be made at that point. The other possibility is that it may have been thought expedient to rail connect the third side of the junction triangle, as already noted. Such a line was shown in Gooch's sketch accompanying his letter of recommendation to Brunel. Be that as it may, this parcel of land had already been purchased from a Mr Sheppard, whose name is still kept alive in Sheppard Street which connects the London Street on the estate to the station. The Cheltenham & GW Union Company were willing to convey this land to the GWR providing that there was agreement to provide necessary station and engine house facilities for working their line and was transferred by a conveyance dated 11th November 1841. A small portion of the area required at the south-west corner had also been purchased by the GWR from Thomas Vilett, one of the main landowners in the area, on 26th April of the same year.

As already inferred, the Company was by this time having financial difficulties. Brunel's estimate of some £2.8 million had been covered in the Act of Incorporation with an authorised capital by share and loan of £3.33 million. But by August 1838, £4.25 million had already been expended on the line itself, apart from rolling stock and other items. Faced with more expenditure for completion of the line, extra rolling stock, the provision of large items such as coke ovens, and the Swindon project, the total would reach around £6.25 million. It is not within the scope of this book to discuss these problems, but suffice it to say that they were overcome. As far as Swindon was concerned, it is evident that the utmost control had to be kept on what was to be provided, and at the minimum cost.

From amongst all the options open to Gooch and Bertram, what then did they decide to provide? Before listing these, the reader should be reminded that the processes which any heavy industry then required, particularly those specific to railway locomotive work, were very different from those required in this century. Indeed, they were different from what would be required about thirty years later. The main bought-in materials were wrought and cast iron together with non-ferrous metals and timber. It follows then that most of the manufacturing in wrought iron would be undertaken by smithing work of a wide variety. Cast iron items needed founding and similar facilities would be required for some of the brass or bronze items. A proportion of metal parts would need machining, although only sliding and rotating surfaces then merited this attention as most other final forming was carried out by smiths.

Therefore, a turnery was needed. The provision of a foundry also required the preparation of patterns, and this could be combined with general carpentry. Coppersmithing, particularly for steam pipes and fittings, would need a shop of its own, as would the production of laminated springs. Grinding was used fairly widely at that time for some of the forming processes and a shop would be provided for this activity. There remain the two specialist locomotive activities of boilers and wheels. These trades needed their own shops, the latter with the specific activities of wheel smiths, and tyre making. Other support shops had to be considered including an erecting shop as a bay from the repairing section of the engine house, and a steam hammer shop for the heaviest smithing activities. Also considered necessary were shops for tenders, trucks and truck painting, and a saw pit. Although Gooch may have wished for a wider range of activities at the outset, it must be realized that the remit of the Factory as planned was the maintenance and repair of locomotives and apparently the same activities for 'trucks'.

These then were the production requirements to be planned for, together with the necessary supporting services. The final layout agreed upon and built is shown in *Plate 10*. We will now study in more detail the way in which the buildings were erected, and the activities which were to be carried on in them. Helpful details can also be seen in the ink and colour wash 'bird's-eye' view of the Works dated 1849, which is to be seen in the GWR Museum at Swindon, and on the copy still at the Works and reproduced in *Plate 11*.

The engine house and engine repair shop were needed first, and work on these must have commenced in 1841. The engine house running parallel to the main line was some 490 ft. long and 72 ft. wide overall, and housed four through stabling roads. Internal width was 67 ft. 8 in. and the stabling tracks were in pairs at 13 ft. 2½ in. centres. The south bay was about 9 ft. narrower than the north bay. The south wall was of timber construction with timber columns at 12 ft. centres and about 17 ft. from rail level to the underside of the timber roof trusses of simple design. There was also a row of similar timber posts along the approximate centre of the building giving intermediate support to these trusses. Between the support posts of the south wall were timber panels of windows or louvres. These posts were joined and bolted at ground level to tapered hardwood piles 12 ft. deep driven into the clay subsoil. The internal tracks were mounted on longitudinal brick foundations with an inverted arch cross support, giving a shallow pit of maximum depth of 2 ft. below rail level. There were large square 'pagoda' type smoke vents over the tracks every 24 ft.

The ends were in masonry with a short return on the south side at each end in plain classic form. On a

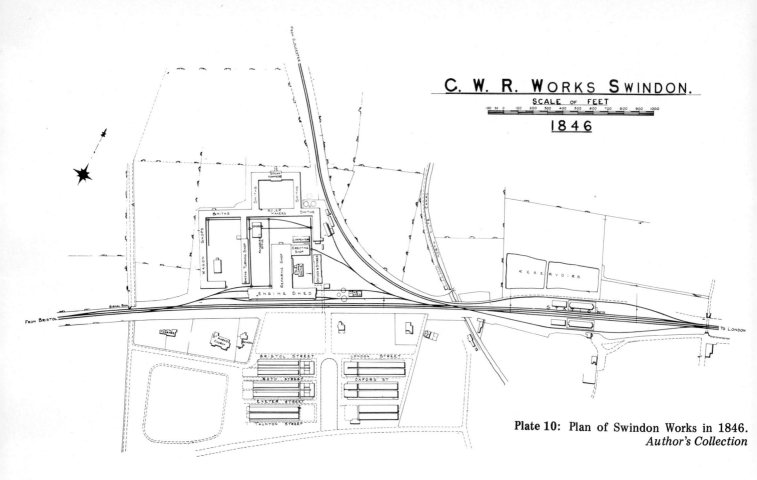

Plate 10: Plan of Swindon Works in 1846.
Author's Collection

Plate 11: Reproduction of an aquatint of Swindon Works and the New Town in 1849. The station and line to Paddington are in the top middle distance.
Swindon Works Records

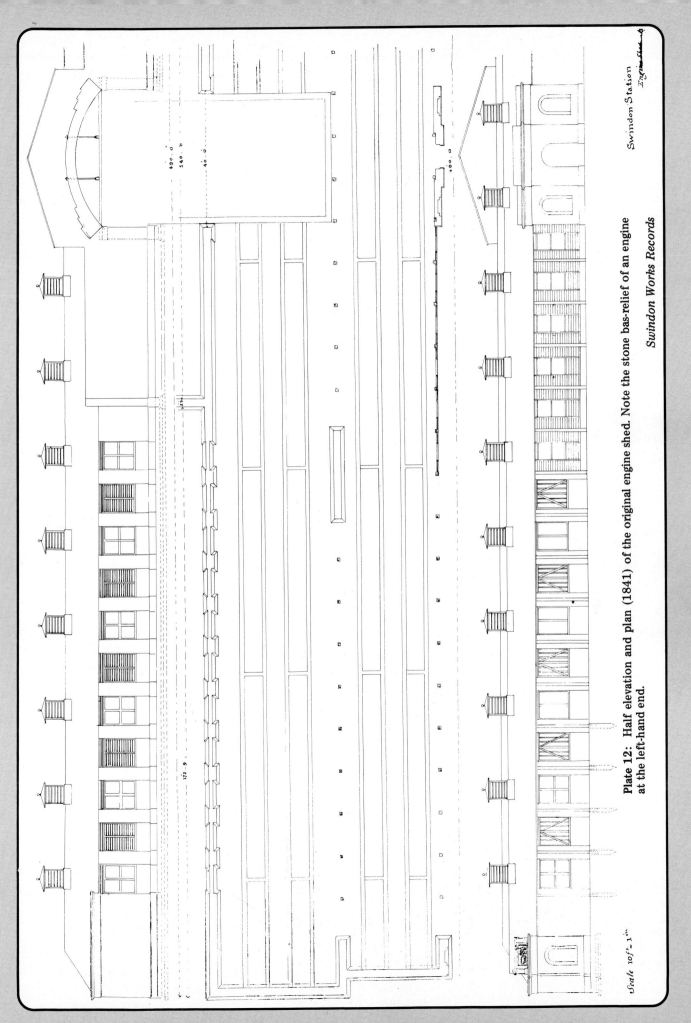

Plate 12: Half elevation and plan (1841) of the original engine shed. Note the stone bas-relief of an engine at the left-hand end.

Swindon Works Records

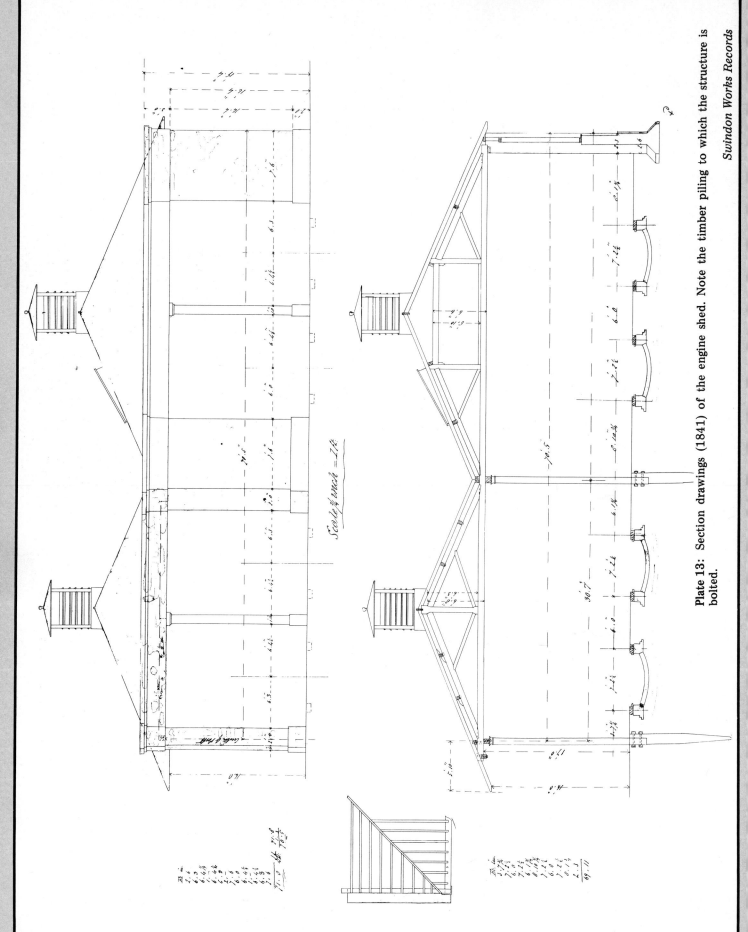

Plate 13: Section drawings (1841) of the engine shed. Note the timber piling to which the structure is bolted.

Swindon Works Records

Plate 14: Broad gauge locomotive, *Tartar* of the 'Rover' class, photographed in about 1878 and showing, in the top left-hand corner, the east end bas-relief still in its original position on the engine shed. The main office block extension of the previous decade shows its original two storey form.

Author's Collection

pediment formed above these return walls at both the London and Bristol ends, were handsome carved stone reliefs of a 2-2-2 locomotive and tender. These panels, each about 6ft. by 3ft., are the same ones which still adorn the outer walls above the entrance of the Main Office block and are seen by many people as they travel past by train today. They will be referred to again later in this book, but are shown in some detail on the original drawing of this building *(Plate 12)*. At the centre of the south wall was a matching stone entrance of the same classic design which was purely decorative. Inside the building on the opposite side was a large arched opening of 40 ft. clearance, which opened on to the main repair shop of the engine depot. The north wall of the long shed was of stone construction but with similar timber panels between the stone pillars. The roof was of timber rafters and purlins with slate covering.

This building must have been finished sufficiently to be used when the line was opened throughout from London to Bristol, and, when completed, could stable 48 engines and tenders. Originally there were no end doors, although these were added later. The main engine repairing house running northwards from this building was a grand structure of stone walls and had a fine timber interior. It is shown with great attention to detail in Bourne's famous illustration of 1845 *(Plate 17)*. Particularly attractive is the double rise roof forming the central span, which was 51 ft. out of a total of 140ft. between walls. It was thought that no drawing of this building still existed but looking through an old folio of untitled and, therefore, unidentified tracings the author discovered that one of these, yellow with age, and in pieces from being folded so long, was obviously most of the plan and elevation details of this early building. These fragments were carefully pieced together and a new tracing prepared, and is reproduced in *Plate 18*. No touching up of any kind has been done and judging by the handwriting it is most likely to be by T. H. Bertram.

The length of this building was 290ft., and as

Plate 17: 'Swindon Engine House 1845', one of Bourne's famous prints of the GWR.

British Rail

Plate 15 (top left): The original engine shed during demolition on 7th November 1929. Note the details of timber trusses, tops of timber piles to the left and grooves for timber louvres referred to in the text.

British Rail

Plate 16 (bottom left): The original engine shed, prior to demolition on 28th October 1929.

British Rail

stated, all interior columns and trusses were of timber except the centre span which was of wrought iron with timber principals. Bourne's print does make it look higher than the actual 21 ft. to the springing of the central arch. This allowed for about 20 productive repair bays on either side of the building, assuming that some were used as access roads. Since each bay was 44 ft. 6 in. wide, it would be possible with locomotives of the time to have two per bay if required, giving a capacity of up to eighty at one time. Shown in *Plate 18* is a secondary row of supports to an intermediate truss over the side bays, but from Bourne's print it is plain that these were omitted and a stronger roof truss substituted. Such a secondary row of columns would have been very inconvenient. Some years later the main timber columns were replaced by cast iron, retaining the unusual central double rise roof. These iron columns still exist in this part of the now extended shop, and in later days they supported the new roofs and overhead cranes in the side bays. One other interesting point to be seen in the drawing is the legend 'standing room for engines and tenders' in the central bay. It is presumed that at this time it had not been decided how to move the locomotives in and out of the shop, but it is plain from *Plate 12* (engine house plan) that a 'traversing frame', or traverser as it would now be called, was envisaged by Gooch, and provision is made in this drawing for a suitable pit to house it. Locomotives could be fed from the two northerly tracks of the engine house. Again it has been possible to prepare a new tracing from original untitled drawing fragments of this device, and the important sections are shown in *Plate 19*. The surprising thing about this traverser is that it was double tracked. It is plain that the distances between the two carrying tracks is exactly the same as the spacing of the two feeder tracks in the engine house so that a locomotive could be taken from, or delivered to, either track without additional movement. The traverser is so well designed that one could wish that modern ones had some of its advantages. Although of necessity it is of the deep pit design, as materials available would then allow little else, its support on four tracks, three wheels to a track, and the provision of additional side wall tracks with steadying wheels, would allow for very smooth movement with no crabbing. As it was hand-operated, through reduction gearing, this was advantageous. The details on Bourne's print are identical with this drawing. It was later replaced by a steam driven appliance of the shallow pit variety, the deep accident prone pit being thus eliminated. It is interesting to note that the west wall of the repairing shop still exists as the dividing wall between the present No. 19 & No. 20 shops of the modern Works and is the oldest masonry of Swindon Works still in use. This portion of the engine house was not completed at the time of the opening of the whole line from London to Bristol, for in Brunel's report, appended to the 14th half-yearly meeting of the 18th August 1842, it says that only a portion was in use at that date.

The erecting shop, which nowadays would be more correctly named the 'lifting shop', was at right angles to the engine repair shop, and joined to it at the north end of the east wall. A central track served both westwards to the traverser, and in the opposite direction out into the works sidings via a small turntable. There was standage for eighteen engines. We are fortunate that a photograph of this shop, looking west, was taken in about 1907 when the building had hardly altered, except that mixed gauge had been added, *(Plate 21)*. Of great interest in this picture is the timber and wrought iron overhead crane which was originally hand-operated, including the pumps for a hydraulic lift, the drawing of which is reproduced in *Plate 22*. The hydraulic equipment was made by Messrs. Napier. However, by 1907, it is evident that some electric power was available for the hydraulic lift and possibly for the travel and traverse. It is a little puzzling how the locomotives were moved through 90 degrees with only a single lift available, but it must have been achieved with manual help. This is the shop where Gooch built his first locomotive at Swindon in 1846. Also of note in the photograph is the power counter-shafting transmitting to buildings on either side, and the construction of the roof and trusses. This shop was nearly 10 ft.

higher than the engine repair shop. The coke shed and the turntables to the east of the engine shed would also have been on the priority list for early completion. All these buildings can be identified in the layout of the new Works in *Plate 10*.

Our attention must now be given to the other workshops which were still to be completed, and it is apparent from Board reports that little time could have been wasted, as most of the Works were operating by October 1842, which was only 17 months after the Board minute authorizing the project. One building which no doubt was hurried along is the office and stores block at the south-east corner. These are detailed on the 'Swindon Station Drawings' already referred to, and housed on the ground floor are the enginemen's (mess) room, bedroom, (!) and bathroom (!!). These men would be operating the trains. Upstairs were the offices of Bertram and Owen, who no doubt would wish to be working at site as soon as possible. At its north end on the same floor was Gooch's Swindon office, (he was never resident at Swindon), together with his bedroom, the drawing office (presumably where Crampton worked until his resignation in 1844), and the model room. There was also accommodation for accountants, clerks, and stores on both floors and the all important time-keeper's office *(Plate 7)*. This particular building was later extended at different times.

The building housing the 'turning shops' was higher than the others, having an upper floor, and still exists with its intermediate floor removed. It is the only building now left in the Works with an original timber trussed roof. The second floor was also used during its life for turning and fitting, and was for many years the tool room. The main area was equipped with some of Whitworth's early machine tools, including lathes, and a slotting machine which at the time was believed to be the largest ever made. Lighter lathes and other machine tools were housed on the upper floor. One machine which is definitely known to have been installed soon after, presumably in the turning shop, was a cylinder boring machine. It was constructed at Swindon, as was the case with many other machines. This particular boring machine, with later additions, lasted the whole life of steam locomotives and was disposed of with other old machines during the 1960s when it was still working to the high degree of accuracy required. South of this machine shop was a smithy, presumably for items needing final machining, and placed here to ease the transport problems. Including this particular smithy, there were in the whole Factory, some 180 separate hearths for the various types of work. The original plans show that much thought went into the equipping of these hearths, as all these shops were provided with underfloor brickwork ducts, having branches to each forge through which air was constantly passed from blowing machines at strategic points. A simple

Plate 18: Reconstructed drawing of the original proposals for the locomotive repair shop (engine house).
Author's Collection

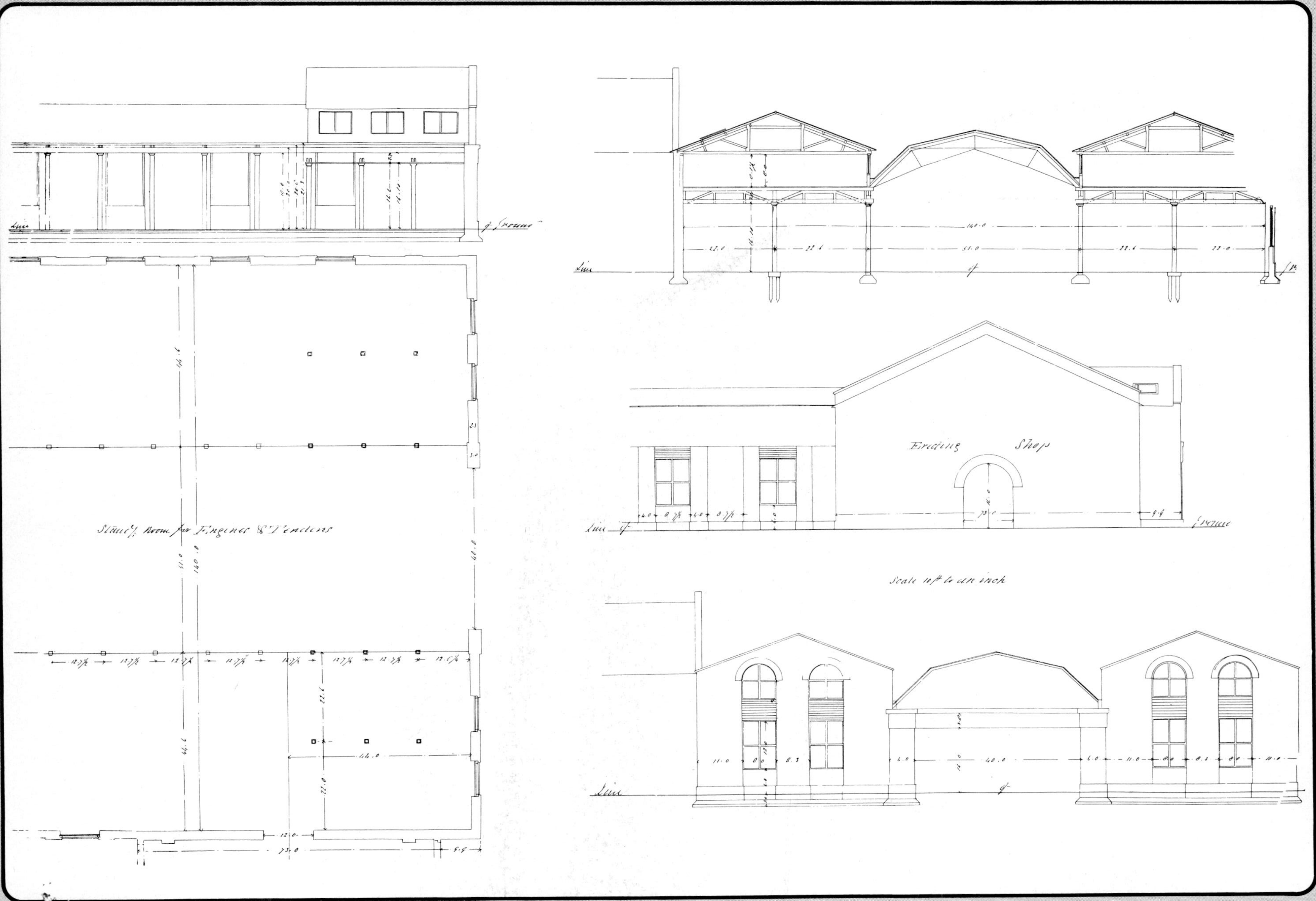

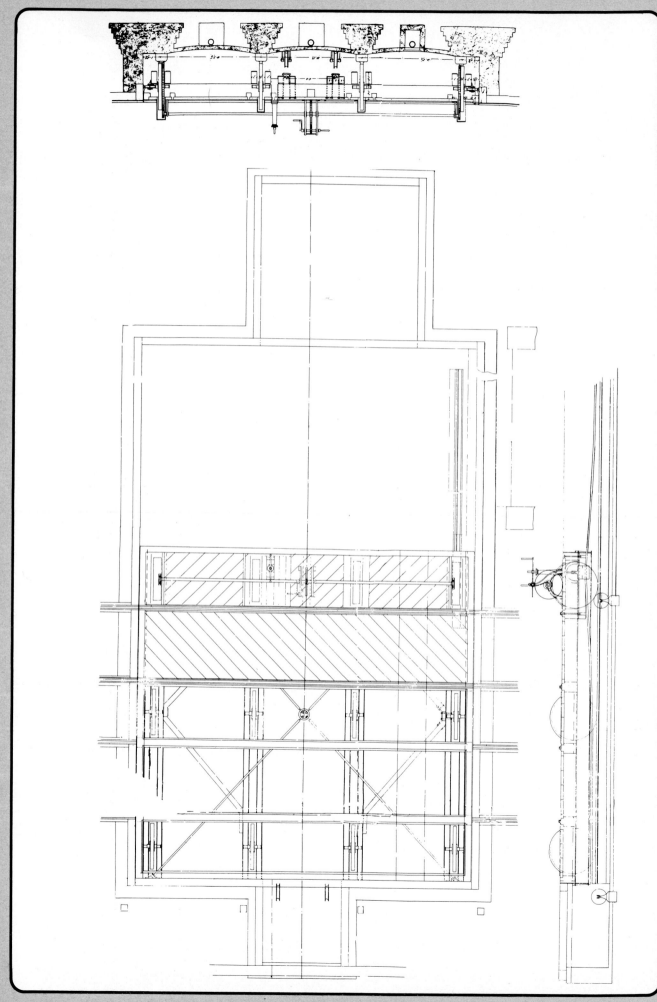

Plate 19: Reconstructed drawing of the 'traverser frame' serving the engine shed and repair shop. *Author's Collection*

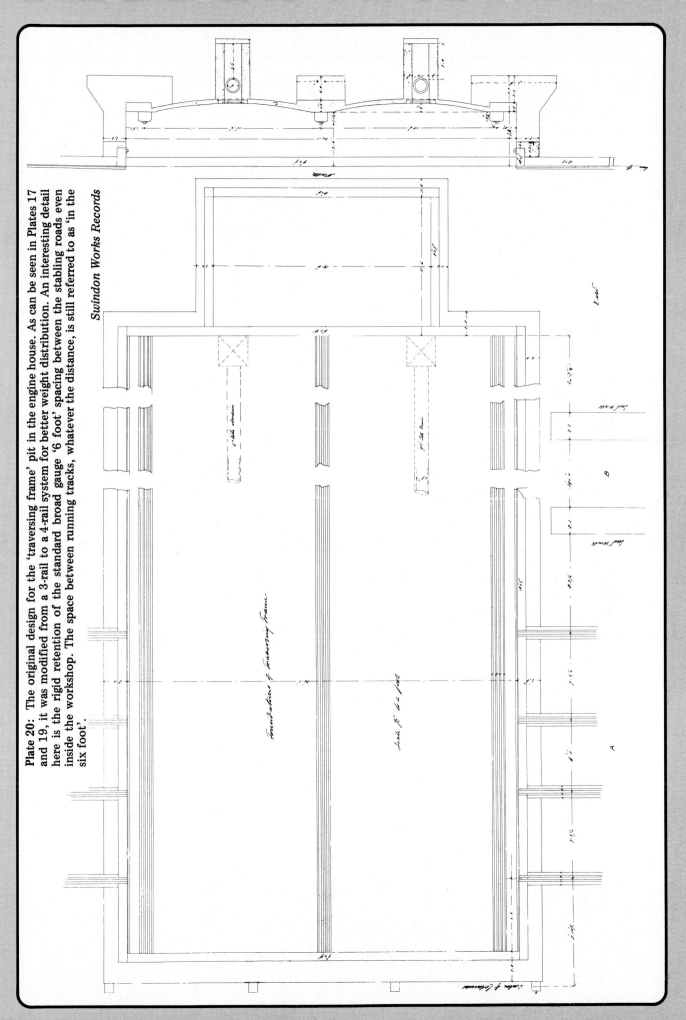

Plate 20: The original design for the 'traversing frame' pit in the engine house. As can be seen in Plates 17 and 19, it was modified from a 3-rail to a 4-rail system for better weight distribution. An interesting detail here is the rigid retention of the standard broad gauge '6 foot' spacing between the stabling roads even inside the workshop. The space between running tracks, whatever the distance, is still referred to as 'in the six foot'.

Swindon Works Records

Plate 21: A 1907 photograph of the original erecting shop. Note the thickness of the stone walls, and the original overhead hydraulic lift crane (now electrified). Gooch's *Great Western* was built here.

British Rail

Plate 22: An 1842 drawing of the overhead crane in the erecting shop. Note the hand levers for operating the hydraulic lift pump. Compare this with the previous photograph.

Swindon Works Records

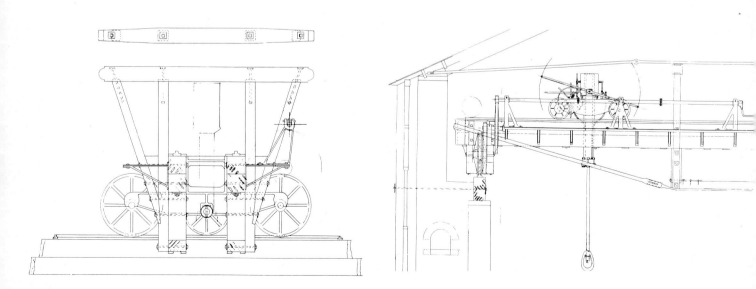

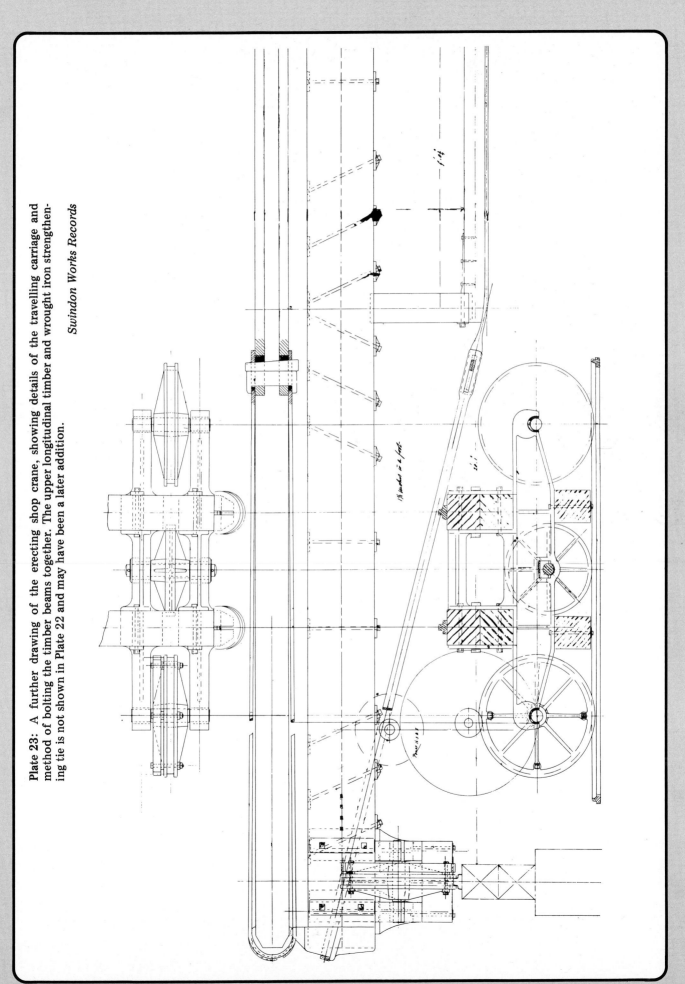

Plate 23: A further drawing of the erecting shop crane, showing details of the travelling carriage and method of bolting the timber beams together. The upper longitudinal timber and wrought iron strengthening tie is not shown in Plate 22 and may have been a later addition.

Swindon Works Records

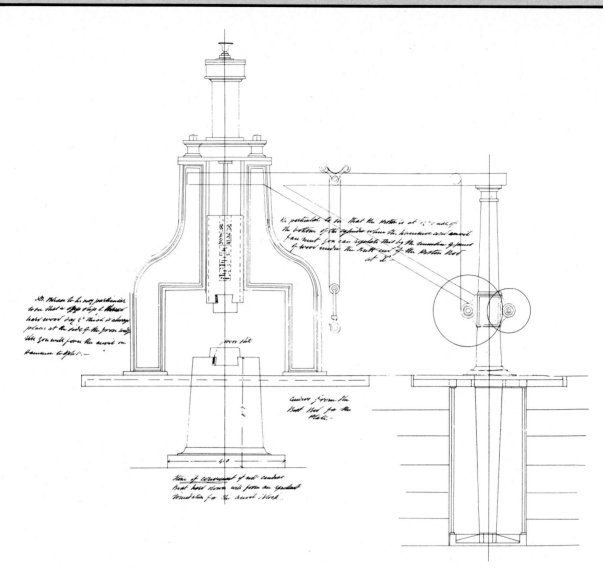

Plate 24: Reconstruction of the original installation drawing of the first Nasmyth steam hammer.

Author's Collection

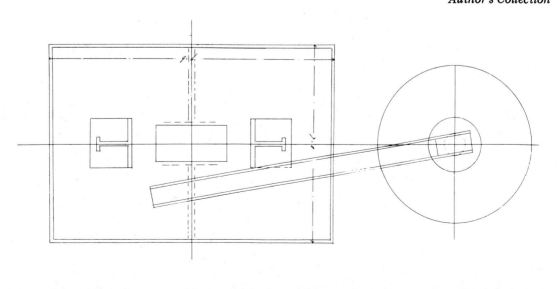

Plate 25 (right): The original boiler shop of 1842, prior to demolition in 1965. Note the yellow pine timber roof trusses, massive stone arch supports for the earlier overhead crane and the clerestory windows above what was, later, the locomotive 'G' millwrights' shop.

gate valve controlled the air flow for forcing each fire. These ducts were all installed with the foundation work and some still exist, unused, in a few of the remaining old shops. The largest shop in the northern row of buildings was the steam hammer section, and here were soon installed very large machines supplied by Nasmyth. An original sketch exists of one of these hammers. *(Plate 24)*. This is most probably the installation drawing, and has the following notes concerning foundations for the anvil block:-

'Stone if convenient, if not cinders beat hard down will form an excellent Foundation for the anvil block'.

Especially prepared iron faces were dovetailed into the hammer face and the anvil block (tup), and the notes on these also state:-

'Be particular to see that the piston is at 1½in. clear of the bottom of the cylinder when the hammer and anvil face meet you can regulate this by the number of pieces of wood under the butt end of the piston rod at 4in.'.

Also:- 'N.B. Please be very particular to see that a slip

of hard wood say ½in. thick is always placed at the side of the iron wedge else you will force the anvil on hammer to split'.

All these notes are given verbatim. There is no punctuation. A hand-operated slewing crane provided support for the large forgings to be worked.

The wheel smith's shop was where the forged T-sections of wrought iron were hearth-welded together to form a spoked wheel, a boss being welded to all the spoke sections at the centre. This was a very skilled and heavy operation. The tyres were also welded from four quadrants of material and shrunk on to these wheel centres. In 1840 before the Works was built, Gooch had taken out a patent for 'the steeling of rails and tyres'. This was done by welding a steel slab on to a wrought iron base. Although never adopted for rails because of cost, it was used for wheels and this was the method used originally at Swindon for all locomotive and tender wheels. 'Best Shear Steel' was the material specified, but this was so hard that it could not subsequently be turned to profile. This was overcome by the provision of a pro-

file grinding machine instead of a wheel lathe, to produce the necessary profiled tyres to the requisite diameter. Journal turning and possibly crank axle turning could have been conveniently grouped with this activity.

Details of the first foundry are almost non-existent. From the plan, the building does appear to be split into two areas, one about 55 ft. by 42 ft., and the other 40 ft. by 20 ft. and it is supposed that these formed the ferrous and non-ferrous sections respectively. The coppersmith's shop and a raw material store was also incorporated in this block. Strangely, no chimneys of any sort appear either on the early plan or the 1849 picture of the Works. Only one large roof ventilator can be seen on the latter. The carpenter's shop and the grinding shop formed another block to the north of the erecting shop, and here the patterns would have been prepared for the foundry.

The boiler shop was strategically placed between the smithing and forging activities and the locomotive repairing and erecting shops. This was a higher building than those adjoining, and must have housed an overhead crane, no doubt similar to the one in the erecting shop, but of a lesser span. Here were housed the plate rolls and other equipment required in plate preparation for boiler work. One other building on the east side of the complex was built to similar outside dimensions as the office block already described. 'Fitting' is named on the early plans for its ground floor, although there was a track up the centre with a midway turntable giving rail access to the yard. The 1849 picture, however, does show a number of locomotive wheels leaning against the wall of the building and complete wheelsets standing on the access roads. This could have been where wheels were pressed on to the axles and where the profile grinding and crank and journal turning was carried out. The upper floor may well have been used for additional office space, as it certainly was later.

There remain the fairly extensive 'truck shops' forming the west boundary of the new factory, and the 'tender shop'. The latter is self explanatory, but the former is more nebulous, as again little or no record of wagon activity remains on which to base much inference. Certainly there is mention of iron frames being prepared by Gooch, some apparently to accept carriage bodies supplied by other manufacturers. Rail access to these shops is also not clearly defined. However the simplest suggestion may well be the correct one. The primitive wagons of the period could well have been manhandled within the shops. There they could be split and dealt with separately as frame and body and reassembled outside in the yard. A separate truck painting shop was provided.

This then concludes the description of the main facilities installed during 1841/2. There remain to be discussed the supporting services. Primarily there was

the power needed for the machinery. This was obtained from two separate power houses on the east and west sides of the main quadrangle of buildings. Each site had its own water tank, boiler house and engine house. Live steam activities, such as steam hammers may also have been piped from these although the first Nasmyth hammer was fed from the boiler of the locomotive *Apollo* (Tayleur 1838). The steam engines supplying power to the machines via long runs of belt-driven counter-shafting were of two makes. One type with 21 in. diameter cylinders was by Stothert of Bristol, the other with 30 in. cylinders by Harvey & Co. It is known that two engines existed in the house adjacent to the turnery and it can be presumed that the same arrangement applied in the other house. Indeed, standby machines would have been a necessity in those days. But how the various makes of engine were distributed is not clear. The other form of power required was gas. This was manufactured in a bench of four handfired horizontal retorts from each of which led a 5 in. diameter pipe into a 12 in. diameter range. Presumably the raw gas was then 'cleaned' in the other buildings provided, and it was then fed into two (later three) 40 ft. diameter gas-holders. Mains are shown on the early plan going to points in the works including the tyre, smiths, and turning shops, the engine house and coke shed, the office block and to the housing estate. The small diameter distribution pipes from these points are not recorded. It is obvious however that the gas was used for lighting as well as production. Its use in the village will be discussed later.

Main drainage was a single system consisting of brick culverts of about 3 ft. internal diameter fed by smaller ones. There were three water-closet blocks provided in the Works and a drawing of one still exists. Drainage from this led into a form of cesspit which then drained into the main sewer. Storm water was collected into the same system as well as any other waste liquids. These sewers would have been laid before any other building took place over them and some of the original outfalls are still in use today but for storm water only. The trunk sewer, after passing through the Works, went via the cottage estate and westwards towards the area of (the later) Westcott Place and could, therefore, well have extended to the Swinbrook or Ray River. The arrangements for the water supply to the Works (which was of concern to Gooch in his original letter of recommendation) will be dealt with later when discussing the new housing estate being built in association with the works. One other original building which is still in existence was the Locomotive Works Manager's office attached to which was a store. Various other stores were provided, as were several scrap areas. No doubt in the early days when the railway network was incomplete, the cost of heavy materials was far outweighed by delivery charges. This would make the re-use of

Plate 26: This building is in line with, and to the north of, the office block already illustrated. Apart from new fenestration, it has altered little and still presents a handsome stone facade. The east boiler house portion was removed many years ago. It is easily identified in Plate 11 with the wheel sets stacked outside. It is now used entirely as office accommodation.

Swindon Works Records

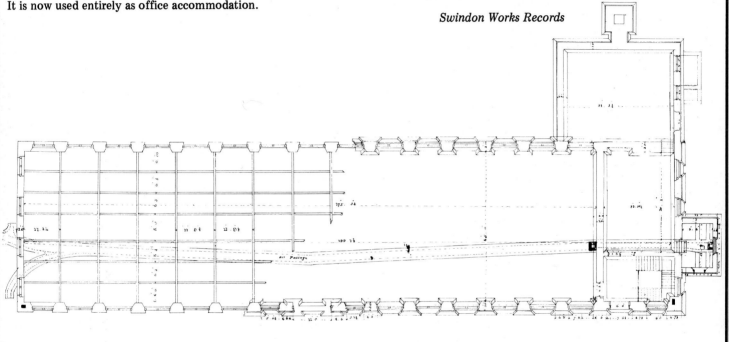

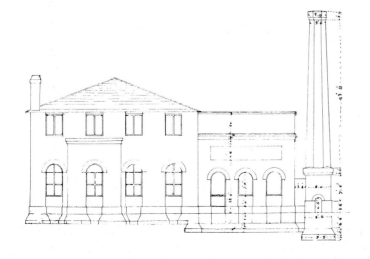

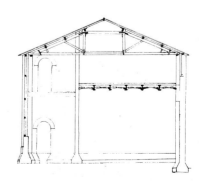

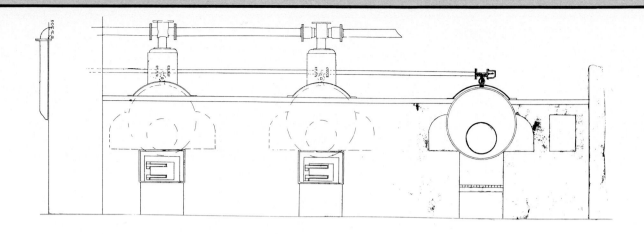

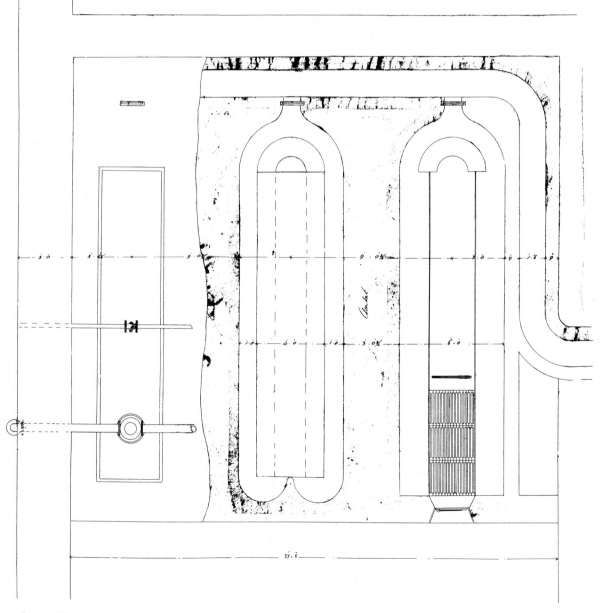

Plates **27 to 31** give details of the east boiler and engine houses, together with the blowing house and ducting system for the air blast to the forge and smiths' shops.

Plate 27: The boiler house, containing three underfed, three-pass shell boilers of four feet diameter, set in fire brick mountings.

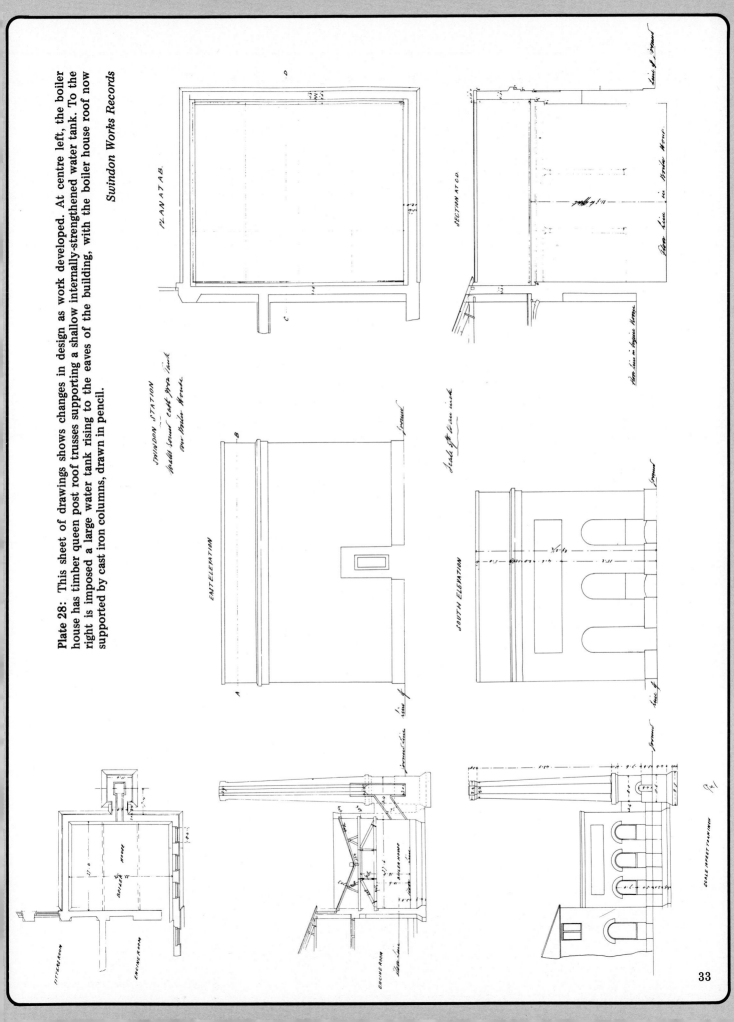

Plate 28: This sheet of drawings shows changes in design as work developed. At centre left, the boiler house has timber queen post roof trusses supporting a shallow internally-strengthened water tank. To the right is imposed a large water tank rising to the eaves of the building, with the boiler house roof now supported by cast iron columns, drawn in pencil.

Swindon Works Records

PLAN AT AB.

SECTION AT CD.

SWINDON STATION

North Vessel Cast Iron Tank over Boiler House.

ENT ELEVATION

Scale of one inch

SOUTH ELEVATION

SCALE INFEET FRAMING

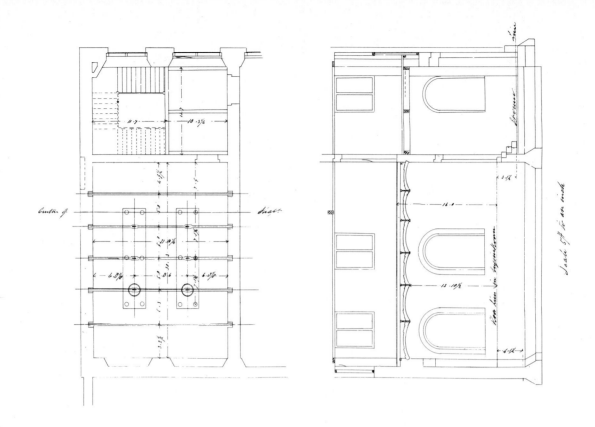

Plate 29: General arrangement of the boiler and engine house showing the stationary engine beds. Drawing projections were made, in those days, to suit the whim of the designer, and have to be carefully worked out!

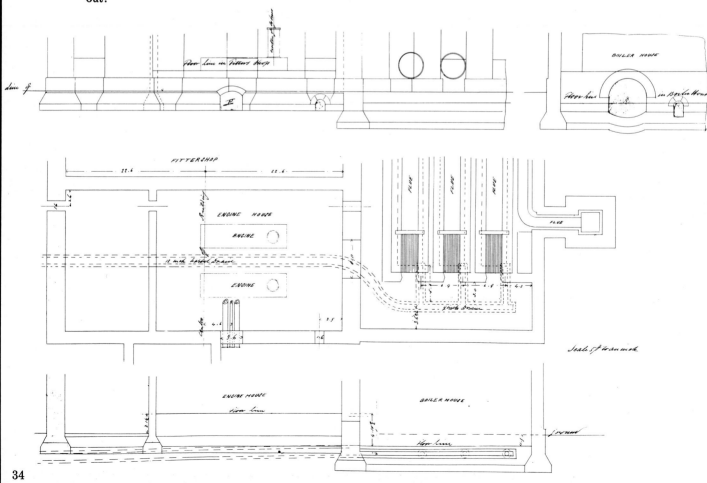

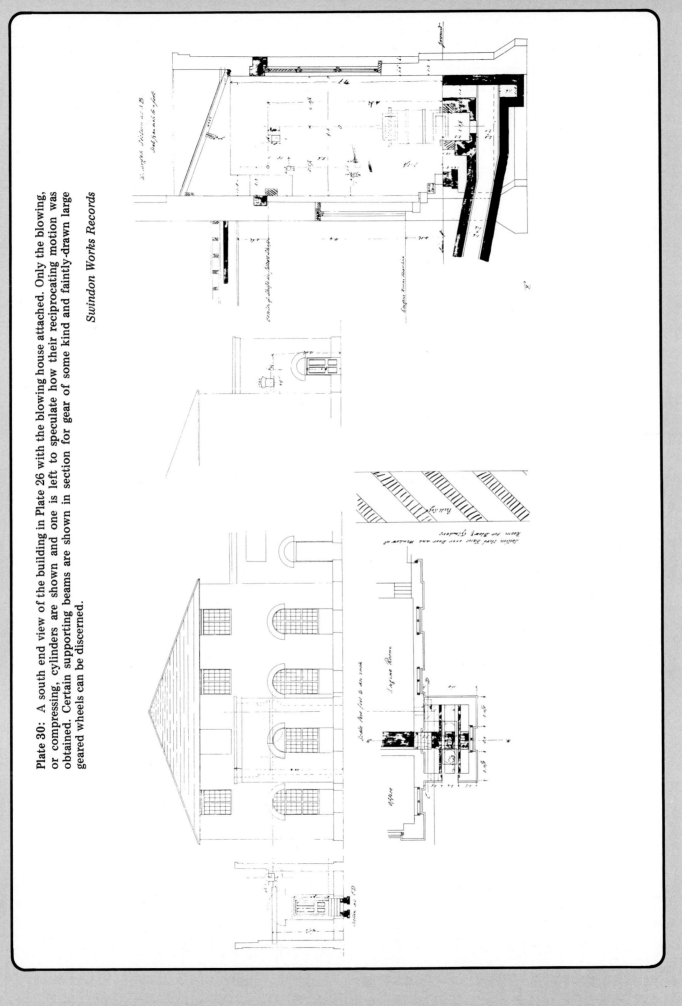

Plate 30: A south end view of the building in Plate 26 with the blowing house attached. Only the blowing, or compressing, cylinders are shown and one is left to speculate how their reciprocating motion was obtained. Certain supporting beams are shown in section for gear of some kind and faintly-drawn large geared wheels can be discerned.

Swindon Works Records

Plate 31: The compressing cylinders are clearly shown on this drawing, together with details of the brick underfloor ducting laid beneath the fitting, or more likely, the wheel shop on the ground floor of the building shown in Plate 26. The ducting rose to the surface to supply the forge shop hearths.

Swindon Works Records

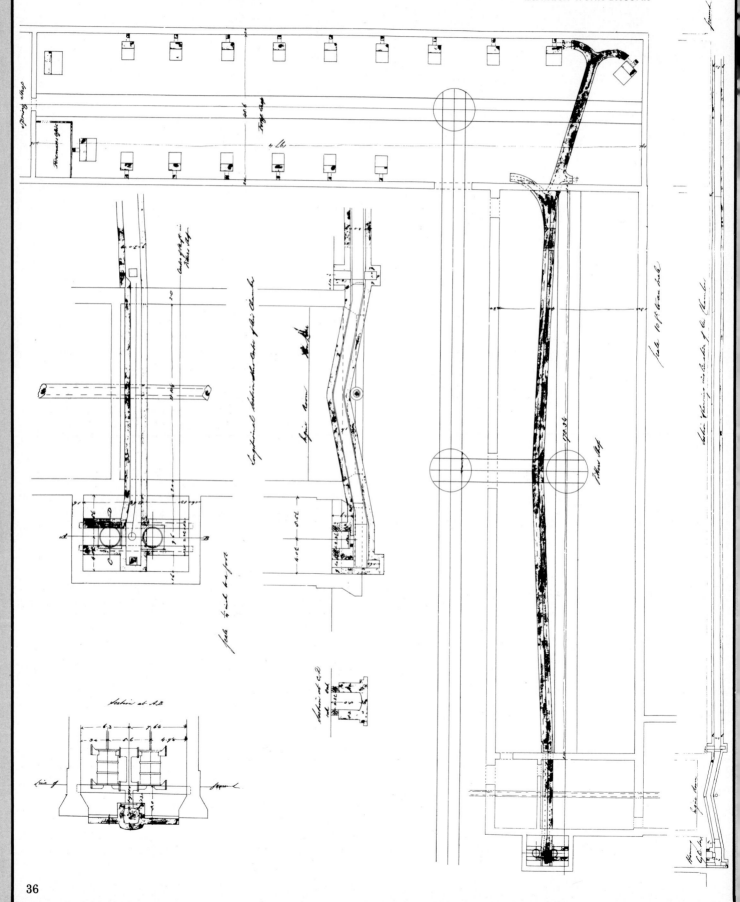

Plate 32: An 1842 drawing of workmen's closets.
Swindon Works Records

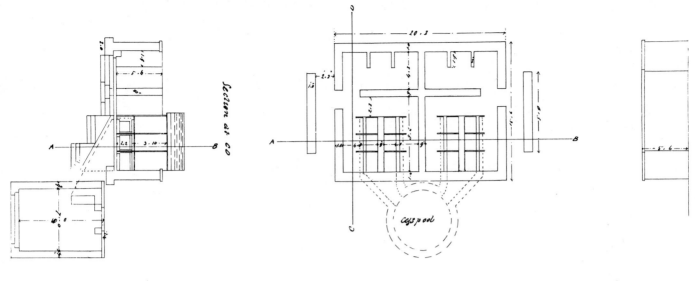

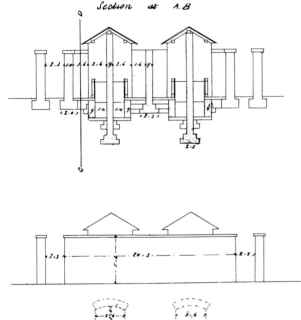

metals, in particular, very necessary.

The reader may well ask where the economy came in building the new Works. A study of the view of the new Works *(Plate 11)* answers the question. It can be discerned that standardization of buildings was the key. All the walls of the buildings were to the same basic design whether they were single or double-storeyed. The system of building used — the 'pillar and panel' method — may have been new then, but it has certainly been re-adopted in the last thirty years for houses. The pillars or columns, with centres at 11 ft. 7¼ in. intervals, were used throughout for the single-storey shops and these column spacings were the same or slightly larger for those with two floors. On these columns rested the roof trusses, which were generally of simple timber queen-post form, carrying a slated and timber-lined roof of low pitch. If the

building was of two storeys, the trusses were of the same type but of heavier construction, as these buildings were invariably of wider span. The spaces between the columns were filled either by timber frames with windows and slatting or more usually by a stone infill which was built to sill level with timber slatting and windows above. For the higher buildings, the timber framing was carried from the ground-floor sill level up to the soffit. Windows were provided at both floor levels with an additional intermediate timber-slatted area. The windows themselves were generally centre-hung and swivelled 'bottom out' for ventilation. Divided into four main sections, these quarter-lights were further divided by vertical glazing bars housing long narrow panes of cast glass which were translucent only. It is certain that much of the glass in those old buildings which still remain is original, even though the window frames may have been renewed over the years. All the single storey buildings were approximately 45 ft. 6 in. wide internally and a standard truss could be used throughout, again showing a great sense of economy, since nearly 150 of these were required for buildings of this span. The only complication was the adoption of hip ends to a few of these buildings. It is possible that some of the single storey shops built towards the end of 1842 had wrought iron trusses rather than timber, and one building still in use has these including multiple trusses to support these hip ends. Possibly this material was used only in those buildings which had this roof form.

The building material of all the original factory was of limestone, most of which came from the boring of the Box Tunnel or from cuttings in that area. It, therefore, would have required only transport costs for its acquisition. It was generally laid in the cheaper random rubble form, although in a few places coursed rubble was adopted if the stone available was suitable. No red brick was used, but blue engineering brick was used for arch work. Most arches were, however, out

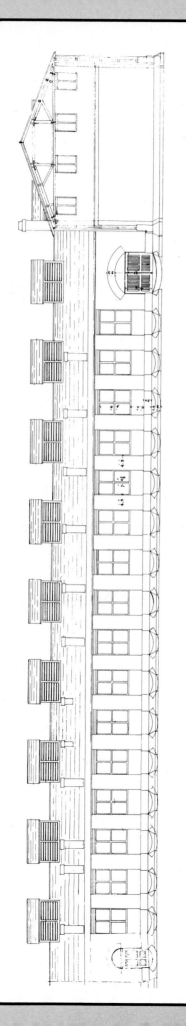

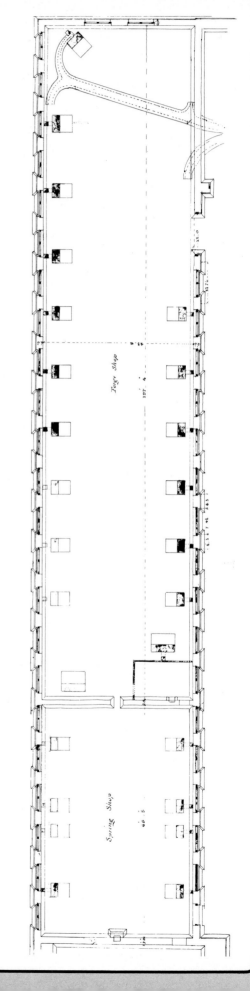

Plate 33: An 1842 drawing of the forge and smiths' shop. Note the inverted arches supporting stone columns in 'pillar and panel' construction, the underfloor air blast ducting and roof trusses. The left-hand end of this building was finally built in a different form.

Swindon Works Records

of sight as they were of the inverted type used as a foundation for the stone support columns. With the advantage of a heavy blue clay subsoil, this method of providing foundations was superior both in type and cost to the more usual method of deep footings of stone or brick. Where the clay is near the surface, these arches are almost entirely above ground and a few examples can still be seen where later additional buildings have not hidden them. Where the clay was deeper, normal footings for the columns were sometimes adopted, usually of stone laid in mortar. *Plate 33* shows most of the special details discussed. Those buildings of this period which remain today are as stable as when they were built and their design has made them very adaptable over the years. For example, it would be very simple to knock out the light panels to form new doorways or to use the stone columns for keying in new walls at right angles.

The new Factory is reported to have come into full operation on 3rd January 1843. It was under the management of Archibald Sturrock, who was already Assistant Locomotive Superintendent to Gooch and had moved to Swindon sometime in 1841. To him would have fallen the task of recruiting the skilled staff without whom the new installation was useless. A word should be said here about the titles given to the various appointments. It was only some time after the Nationalization of the railways that some semblance of uniformity was achieved in this matter within the railway industry. Things were much more complex in the early days, because often a man held more than one appointment as we find Sturrock did. Another difficulty arises from the way in which work was carried out in the early days. Owing to the shortage of qualified men, suitable supervisory and other key staff were probably only prepared to move to Swindon on their own conditions. We find these people referred to either as 'foreman' or as 'contractor'. The former title means what we understand today, except that the post implied total control of the staff he employed, including 'hiring and firing'. It was, therefore, much more a 'management' post than in later times. The term 'contractor' refers to a person who contracted to do certain work for the Company, and for which he claimed the right of first choice of the work available. For this he was paid an agreed sum by the Works Manager and he employed such other men as he thought fit as his own private employees. A certain John Fawcett was the first of such contractors to Sturrock for all wheel and tyre repairs — a highly skilled activity. This man set out at some later date details of most of the senior staff at the Factory from 1843 to December 1865, although individual dates of appointment are not recorded. This list was found by Mr F. F. Foord, one of the senior clerks in 1904, who prepared a fair copy and is to be found in Appendix II of this volume. This document does give some 'succession' problems when studied, however.

The assistant managers under Sturrock were Dougal Mack and Edward Snell. The first, from his name, could well have come from the Dundee Foundry. The second name is one which appears, like several others, as a 'family' name on the GWR. A study of the relevant part of the 'Victoria History of Wiltshire' shows that the area was not a barren desert as far as the basic artisan skills were concerned, and no doubt many local men came seeking work in what was perhaps the most modern factory in the country as far as plant and inventiveness was concerned. But the specialist locomotive builders would almost certainly have been recruited from the northern part of the country where most of their development had taken place.

A document preserved at the Public Records Office gives the establishment early in 1843 as follows:

Foremen	6
Clerks (Time Office & Stores)	14
Enginemen	48
Firemen	50
Stationary Enginemen	3
Cleaners, Coke men Labourers etc.	65
Fitters & Erectors	55
Turners	10
Contractors	60
Men at machines	7
Carpenters and plumbers	6
Coppersmiths	2
Brass Foundryman	1
Blacksmiths	14
Springmakers	2
Strikers	14
Boilermakers & Wheelmakers	4
Painters	2
General Labourers	25
Boys	35

This gives a total of 6 foremen and 417 other staff. It is assumed that the 60 contractors quoted include all the staff working under this system. A split between 'Works' and 'running shed' can be estimated at 320 to 103, but some duties may have been common to both activities.

This then is the staff which Sturrock managed to gather around him, and descendants of some of these men are still employed at Swindon. There is no doubt that the Works was a 'model' one in which to seek employment and for the times high wages were paid to attract the right people. Working hours also were not exceptionally long. Although it has been inferred in some quarters that a full six day week of 61½ hours was worked at the start in 1843, the author inclines to the view that, if this is so, it was for a very short period only, and the Saturday afternoon shift was soon dropped to give 57½ hours per week, split as follows:-

Breakfast Shift. . . . .6.00 a.m. — 8.15 a.m.
Breakfast Break

Morning Shift . . . . 9.00 a.m. — 1.00 p.m.
Dinner Break
Afternoon Shift . . . .2.00 p.m. — 6.00 p.m.
(not Saturday)

These hours lasted until 1866 when they were reduced to 56½ hours per week, by finishing at 12 noon on Saturdays. This reduction of one hour in the working week created great comment at the time and implies that, if an earlier reduction from 61½ to 57½ hours had taken place, it would have merited much more documentation and publicity. None has been traced.

The first work carried out in the new Factory was the day to day maintenance and periodic servicing of the locomotive fleet, similar to the modern maintenance depot with full lifting facilities, but with the additional advantage of ability to supply new or repaired parts, including boilers. There would also have been modifications where practicable to the early Brunel locomotives, although some of these were never capable of regular work. We do know of experiments carried out by Brunel to burn coal instead of expensive coke, although the problem was not to be solved successfully for nearly another decade. We also know that in 1844 Gooch carried out trials with corrugated copper fireboxes with a view to increasing the heating surface area. Two locomotives were so equipped but this resulted in little more than strengthening the fireboxes. During this period also, Gooch designed his own link motion to replace the more usual gab motion then in fairly general use. We can assume that this development took place in his Swindon drawing office and was possibly tried out on a locomotive. But by and large these first two or three years were most useful in 'working up' the new Factory. It must also be remembered that the Gauge Commission was set up in 1845 and that the energies of the chief officers of the Company were very much taken up in the many technical sessions and the long series of practical tests run with broad and narrow gauge trains. The broad gauge locomotives for these trials were being prepared at Swindon. The outcome was perhaps inevitable and the Gauge Act was passed in 1846 making certain that any new Railway Act must define its gauge, thus ensuring that all main line railways in future would be to the narrow gauge. However, the GWR was able to carry on with broad gauge within its defined operational area as it thought fit. The Commission admitted the obvious superiority in performance and capabilities of the broad gauge, due, in large part, to Gooch's practical efforts and no doubt Brunel's personality. But it did leave the GWR with problems which it continued to face for another 46 years. At this time Gooch's salary was increased to £1,000 per annum for his special services and he also received a £500 gratuity from the directors, who acknowledged in an appropriate Board minute the high state of efficiency of the locomotive department.

It must have been in late 1845 that a change took place in Swindon's policy. In February 1846, a new locomotive, the 0-6-0 'Premier', for freight work emerged from the Works. This was the first of the '1st Lot Goods' of 12 engines. The boilers were purchased from outside sources to the usual strict specification. Thus, it was not the first engine to be built entirely at Swindon, but it does show that the decision had been made to build there as well as repair. The cylinders were 16 in. diameter by 24 in. stroke and the coupled driving wheels were 5 ft. diameter. They were a great improvement on previous locomotives for this class of work.

Meanwhile, the Board had expected further trouble from the gauge controversy in 1846 and were intent on keeping their lead in engine power and efficiency to support their case. Accordingly, early in January 1846, they required Gooch to produce a 'colossal locomotive working with all speed'. It is not quite clear whether this meant a fast locomotive or that they wanted it in a hurry! Perhaps they meant both, and they certainly got it. Gooch and his designers no doubt had the basic ideas already in their minds for their next step in passenger locomotive design and were able to quickly produce drawings of sufficient detail for Sturrock to commence manufacture. The latter officer and his comparatively new staff must have put in herculean efforts, for this new locomotive was actually built and steamed by the end of April 1846, an unbelievable 13 weeks from the date of order! This shows that the organization of the Works was, by this time, of a very high order indeed. This new engine, appropriately named *Great Western*, was of the 2-2-2 wheel arrangement with 18 in. by 24 in. cylinders, 8 ft. driving wheels and 4 ft. 6 in. carrying wheels. The boiler was pressed to 100 p.s.i., but still carried a 'gothic' firebox.

No time was lost in shewing what *Great Western* could achieve for on 1st June 1846, it ran with a train of unrecorded weight from Paddington to Exeter via Bristol and the B & E Railway, a distance of 194 miles, in 208 minutes, and returned the same day in 211 minutes. These times presumably included stops. Also Gooch records in his mémoirs that on 13th June 1846, it hauled a 100 ton passenger train, which was heavy for that period, from Paddington to Bristol. The 77 miles to Swindon were covered, start to stop, in 78 minutes, and Bristol was reached in 132 minutes including stops. Brunel, Charles Russell, the GWR Chairman, and other directors travelled on this train.

The locomotive was found wanting in one respect. There was excessive weight on the leading axle and, shortly after these recorded journeys, this was proved by its fracturing in service at Shrivenham. The frame

Plate 34: *Great Western*, the first locomotive built entirely at Swindon, from a drawing by the late E. W. Twining.

The late E. W. Twining

was then lengthened by some 3 ft. and two front carrying axles substituted, making the wheel arrangement 4-2-2, although purists would argue this should be 2-2-2-2 as the leading pairs of wheels were fixed, not bogied. This engine became the prototype of all the broad gauge express passenger locomotives up to withdrawal in 1892. Six more locomotives were immediately ordered by the Board as the '1st Lot Passenger' or 'Prince' class and 22 more followed in three successive 'lots' built at Swindon up to 1851. In these 'lots', the 'gothic' firebox was superseded by a round-topped type and incorporated a mid-feather to improve heat transfer. This feature was to be used by other designers up to the final days of steam. The boiler was domeless and metal clad and the safety valves were surrounded by a polished bonnet. The driving axle was fitted with an additional central bearing, giving this crucial component no less than five bearings, since there were already two to each wheel in the double frame.

These 22 Swindon-built locomotives (plus 7 further ones supplied by Rothwell & Company in 1854—5) formed the great class of '8 ft. Singles' of Gooch's broad gauge. There were many improvements on the *Great Western* and the 'Prince' class, which, although more truly a 'class' as we would term it today, did have variations, although not of the larger interchangeable items. The first of the set, *Iron Duke* was

so named because it ran its trial trip from Swindon on that great man's birthday, 29th April 1847. The most famous was perhaps *Lord of the Isles* of the '4th Lot Passenger' which was shown at the Great Exhibition of 1851. This was to have been named *Charles Russell* after the Chairman; but that gentleman declined the honour and the final name was thought more suitable, considering who was patron of the Exhibition! History was to repeat itself in 1927. *Lord of the Isles* remained in service for 33 years before being withdrawn for preservation with 789,000 miles to its credit. During this time it kept its original boiler, a tribute to its manufacture and maintenance.

Further 0-6-0 goods locomotives of the 'Pyracmon' class, with round-topped fireboxes were built during 1847—8 as well as a class of 4-4-0 saddle tank locomotives in 1849 for the steep gradients of the South Devon Railway after the failure of the ill-fated atmospheric system. There is no doubt that the locomotives produced at Swindon were world leaders and that is what they were meant to be. Even in 1845 the GWR was running the fastest trains in the world to prove the superiority of the broad gauge with start to stop averages of over 40 m.p.h. even with the primitive signalling arrangements of the time. These were the 4½ hour Exeter expresses with six stops including the 10 minute refreshment room halt at Swindon. In

1847, a further acceleration of 13 minutes was made, reaching Bristol in 2½ hours, and, with an additional stop at Bridgwater, Exeter was reached in 4 hours 25 minutes inclusive. The racing stretch was generally Paddington to Didcot or Swindon to Didcot. The former fifty two and seven eighths miles was booked for 55 minutes, an average speed of 57 m.p.h., and it is recorded that the locomotive *Great Britain* covered this stretch on 14th May 1848, in 47½ minutes, an average start to stop speed of almost 68 m.p.h! The driver on this occasion was Michael Almond, who was later to be locomotive foreman at Paddington. On that occasion he was caught out by Gooch who by chance was travelling on the train and who admonished him in a kindly way. Incidentally, it was this fast down train, the 9.45 a.m. from Paddington, which was soon to be nicknamed the 'Flying Dutchman' after the horse which won the St. Leger and Derby races in 1849. The running and timing of these trains was done mainly on the initiative of Gooch, and certainly he credits himself with all truthfulness in his mémoirs as being the 'Father of the Express Train'.

It was complete faith in these locomotives for their design, workmanship and maintenance, that enabled the GWR management to run this great train service. Gooch was extremely scientific in his approach and had, by 1848, already carried out some important investigations into train resistances under varying conditions which were unsurpassed until the turn of the century. It was in connection with the problems of taking adequate cylinder indicator diagrams, which was difficult enough a century later, that Gooch designed and built at Swindon a dynamometer car, certainly the first of its kind. We know that the traction spring of the dynamometer itself was of five plate construction and about 7 ft. 6 in. long, the plates being carefully tapered with ½ in. spacers at the centre. Recording gear led from this to a moving paper roll provided with a time recorder. Also graphed was the wind velocity and direction, which was transmitted from suitable equipment on the vehicle roof. In addition he invented a new form of cylinder indicator which produced a continuous diagram on paper rolls. Thus commenced at Swindon a long history of locomotive testing which was to add so much to locomotive knowledge and design over some 120 years.

From the commencement of locomotive operations Gooch kept very detailed records of the performance of each locomotive. This included mileages covered 'light' and in traffic; weekly costs of fuel, lubricants and cleaning materials; and running shed and works repair costs. Also recorded were the monthly working expenses of depots, and, in the early days, the permanent allocations of individual locomotives and their driver's name. From June 1848, many of Gooch's enquiries which were made by letter to his

Plate 35: *Pyracmon*, one of the first batch of goods locomotives built entirely at Swindon, as illustrated in *Practical Management of Locomotives* by J. Sewell, 1848.

Author's Collection

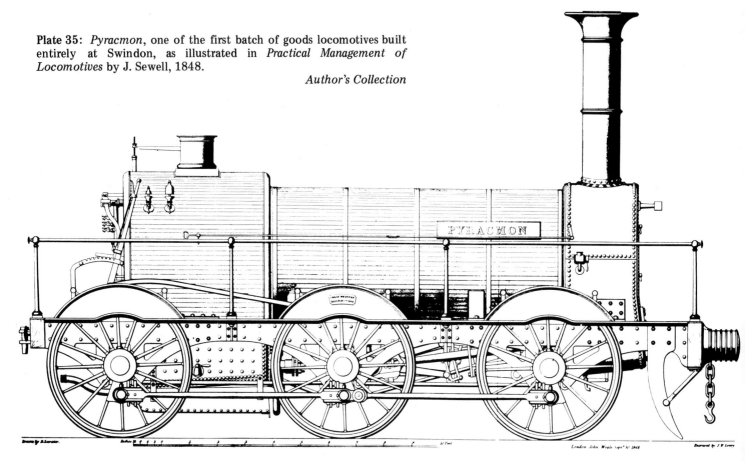

Area Foremen about their monthly results were re-copied on to the plain sheets interleaving each set of depot costs. These are often tart and to the point, as these examples show:

> To Mr Luxmore (Paddington)
> 'Be good enough to give your particular attention to the number of delays to trains by broken (sic) engines they have greatly increased of late'.

> And

> To Mr Rotton (Oxford)
> 'The consumption of fuel at Oxford has increased very much from 34 to 41 lbs per mile — how do you account for it'?

An example from these records gives the following locomotive costs per mile for the six months ending as quoted:

Sun	Dec. 1843	16.49d	June 1850	9.31d
Great Western			June 1852	7.25d
Vulcan	June 1848	15.68d	June 1852	7.76d
Pyracmon	Dec. 1847	12.28d	June 1852	8.95d

Such detailed records must have been invaluable for the purposes of comparison when the modification of locomotives or driving methods was considered as a result of the dynamometer and other investigations now capable of being carried out scientifically.

This great time of development was clouded by a period of depression which had near disastrous reper-cussions at Swindon. The railway mania of the mid-1840s had induced the GWR and other com-panies to take over or fight off many other undertakings, which either threatened their absolute control over particular territories or were likely to open up new feeder traffic. Many of the undertakings so leased or absorbed were poorly financed and necessitated the provision of large sums of capital. As is the case today, the funding of such capital was an expensive business, and as a result the Company was forced into a period of retrenchment. Furthermore, there was a general depression of trade in the country with the inevitable stagnation of traffic and con-sequently diminishing receipts. This affected all the other railways too. The immediate effect on the GWR was a reduction from a dividend of 8 per cent, which had remained steady for some years, to 7 per cent. But, more importantly, by mid-1848 the value of £100 (nominal) shares had dropped from a £146 stock market quotation in 1847 down to £95. It is a matter of history that at this difficult time there was a serious move between the Boards of the Great Western, London & North Western and London & South Western Railways for a sanction by Parliament for a permanent amalgamation. To put a final seal on matters the failure of the George Hudson railway empire in the middle of 1849 completed the loss of confidence in railways as an investment.

Consequently, sweeping economies were sought by the Board in all departments, including salaries, but dividends again fell to 6 per cent per annum in February 1849, and 4 per cent in August of the same year. As one of the largest departments, the locomo-tive establishment was a prime target for a very large share of the cuts. Finally, to add to the problems at Swindon, the agreement to supply locomotives to run the Bristol & Exeter Railway came to an end, resulting in a considerable surplus of locomotive stock and consequent loss of repair work. It comes as some surprise to find that the Swindon staff, which in 1843 had been approximately 450, including officials, had risen to 1,800 in 1847. This rise had been needed for the increase in repair work due to the rapid extension of the system and by the 'build at Swindon' policy instituted by Gooch and suppor-ted by the Board. The cuts were drastic and 1,800 staff was suddenly reduced to 600 in late 1847. The remaining staff were on short time working of an average 45 hours per week. The feelings of Gooch and Sturrock can be imagined, having worked hard to build up this specialist work force, though strangely, Gooch does not refer to the drastic measures in his mémoirs. He only rages at the suggestion that his own salary should be reduced which he, like other senior officers, strongly opposed.

The problems at Swindon were twofold. Firstly, it was in the middle of the large passenger locomotive building programme and we find that only seven 8 ft. Singles were completed in 1848, three in 1849, four in 1850, and only two 4-4-0 locomotives built in 1849. (No more of this last class were delivered until 1854, and these from R. & W. Hawthorn's, not Swindon). Consequently, much of the machinery must have become idle in the Works proper, and it is assumed that the 600 men remaining, which almost certainly included approximately 150 drivers and firemen, concentrated on the daily running of the locomotives, day to day maintenance and limited heavier repairs. Secondly came the social problem since dismissals in those days meant penury. Further-more, such men were housed mainly in railway cottages for which they paid regular rents to the Company. No doubt there were some who moved away to other work and were lost to Swindon for ever.

Gooch was also concerned about the problems of health in the community, which could arise from con-ditions of want, and this is discussed in the next chapter.

It is not clear how long this serious state of affairs lasted at Swindon. Although occurring suddenly, it seems that there was a gradual return to normality over two or three years. Great efforts were made by Gooch to make use of the resources of manpower and equipment available by undertaking railway work other than locomotives and wagons, such as bridge girders and permanent way fittings, although not without some opposition.

The final certificate for the building of the Works had been passed by the general committee of the Board on 4th April 1844, for the sum of £46,805. After this, not surprisingly, no mention of further financial outlay at Swindon appears in the minute books for a long period. The extension of the GWR northwards had, however, been progressing throughout this time. By 1853, it was evident that further facilities at Swindon were required, and a sum of £25,000 was voted for this purpose. Work did not start in earnest until May 1854 when Gooch, engaged in the ceremony of foundation stone laying, spoke of good relationships between staff and Board. Also in 1854 further cottages to complete the railway village were authorized at £5,000. Exactly which factory buildings were added at this time is difficult to ascertain, as there is a gap in the continuity plans of the Works between 1846 and 1870. When one eliminates later buildings whose opening dates are known, little is left over. The new shops would most probably have been additions to the northerly smithing shops, an eastward addition of one bay to the original engine repair shop, and additions to the gas works. The major part of the Works Manager's office block was rebuilt, offices replacing the stores area.

In 1850, Archibald Sturrock left the GWR on his appointment as Locomotive Superintendent of the Great Northern Railway, which he then served for 16 years until his retirement in 1866. He was only 50 when he left the Great Northern Railway and enjoyed 42 years in retirement. He died at the ripe old age of 93 on 1st January 1909, and was thus one of the longest surviving of the original band of railway locomotive engineers. Sturrock was succeeded at Swindon by Minard C. Rea, who had until that time been Locomotive Superintendent of the Bristol & Exeter Railway and was, therefore, well acquainted with the locomotives he was to care for in his new post. (Some doubt has been raised whether this officer's name was more correctly spelled Rae. Documentary evidence available from signatures in GWR correspondence, now at the Public Records Office, give conclusive proof, however. It is possible that confusion arose with the name of Swindon's first medical officer (spelt Rae), who was in the GWR's service at the same time).

Consolidation of the Works proceeded during this time, but an event which at first had no noticeable effect on Swindon, but was to do so shortly, was the amalgamation of the GWR with the Shrewsbury & Chester and the Shrewsbury & Birmingham Railways. By 1852 the GWR was operating as far north as Birmingham on the broad gauge, and, in 1854, after much skirmishing and in-fighting with the London & North Western Railway, it took these two railways into amalgamation. These were narrow gauge systems

and it was a condition of the agreement that the broad gauge should not be extended north of Wolverhampton.

So the GWR at last became a two gauge organization and the combined stock of 56 narrow gauge locomotives came into their ownership. With them came a remarkable man who was already 38 years old. This was Joseph Armstrong who had grown up amongst the railway pioneers at Newburn on Tyne, and George Stephenson and Timothy Hackworth were family acquaintances. He was to introduce to the GWR a family who served it for 100 years, and we shall study his career in more detail later. After the amalgamation, he was appointed, in 1854, as Assistant Superintendent to Gooch, taking charge of the newly formed Northern Division of the GWR centred at Wolverhampton. He thus had control of all the narrow gauge locomotives now acquired and also the daily running of the broad gauge locomotives as far south as Oxford. The new Southern Division comprised the rest of the broad gauge system with the headquarters at London and heavy maintenance at Swindon Works.

The acquisition of the narrow gauge railway posed problems to Gooch as it was desirable to provide the new Northern Division with a stud of well-designed and standardized locomotives. The policy of manufacturing locomotives there was to be initiated at Wolverhampton, Stafford Road, but this could not take place until alterations and extensions had been carried out. Having designed some narrow gauge 2-2-2 passenger and 0-6-0 goods locomotives, Gooch decided to put the passenger classes out to contractors but to build most of the goods types himself. These latter had, therefore, to be built at Swindon and pits and tracks within the Works were adapted where necessary for this purpose. The first narrow gauge locomotive to emerge from Swindon was No. 57 in May 1855. This was the first of 12 built in 1855/6 as the '1st Goods Lot'. As it was to be 17 years before narrow gauge rails reached Swindon, they were conveyed to Wolverhampton on broad gauge flat wagons specially made for the purpose. It has often been inferred that the men at Swindon looked upon these narrow gauge intruders with something beneath contempt. Be that as it may, between 1855 and 1861, 32 locomotives of this wheel arrangement of the 1st, 2nd, 3rd and 4th Goods Lots and two tank locomotives provided a good workload for Swindon after a particularly difficult time. It is likely that, after building, many of these locomotives never returned to Swindon, since they would have been maintained in the Northern Division. Wolverhampton turned out its first home-built locomotives in 1859 after works extensions which had commenced the previous year. These were to Armstrong's design, although no doubt many parameters were laid down by Gooch, particularly where boilers were concerned. The year 1859 saw commencement of the withdrawal of broad gauge train working from Wolverhampton in favour of the narrow gauge. This was systematically extended as far south as Oxford, while other narrow gauge lines were beginning to come into the fold. During this period of narrow gauge building, only 8 broad gauge passenger locomotives were built at Swindon, emerging in the latter half of 1856. They were the 'Victoria' class ('5th Lot Passenger').

The first great Chairman of the GWR, Charles Russell, resigned in 1855 and was succeeded temporarily by the Rt. Hon. Spencer Walpole, M.P. He in turn was replaced by Viscount Barrington in 1856. During this period, for various reasons, a number of factions arose in the board room and amongst the shareholders. The principal officers of the Company often found great difficulty in steering the GWR the way in which they as professional railwaymen knew it should go. In May 1857 another Chairman took office, the Hon. Frederick Ponsonby, who did some good work in restoring equilibrium. But in February 1859 we find him succeeded by Lord Shelburne.

On 15th September 1859 Brunel died, having literally burned himself out with work. For some time he had been ailing, and his GWR work had been under-

taken by T. H. Bertram, who now assumed the full duties of engineer on the railway until April 1860, when he retired. Another change took place at Swindon in 1857. During the previous year a rather sharp note is recorded after one of the directors had visited Swindon and found that the Manager, M. C. Rea was away ill, and indeed had been for some time and that 'his work is being done by Fraser'. This would be the John Fraser on the 1843/65 list (App. II). Although Gooch must have been aware of this situation, he probably had not reported it to the Board. Perhaps even senior staff were not paid sick leave and this was a kindness on Gooch's part! Rea died at Swindon on 18th June 1857 from consumption, and is buried in St. Mark's churchyard there. (Two brothers of his were already buried there, and his mother followed not long afterwards.) He was replaced as manager by none other than Gooch's youngest brother William, who had been working on the South Devon Railway contract for supplying locomotive power from the GWR. From Gooch's memoirs it appears that some more seeds of discontent were sown, as he was under the impression from the Board that William was to be groomed to take over from himself when he decided to leave the railway service. In fact William had accepted a lower

Plate 36: Locomotive No. 57, the first narrow gauge engine built at Swindon in May 1855. Seen here in its final condition in the early years of this century, it was withdrawn in November 1912.

British Rail

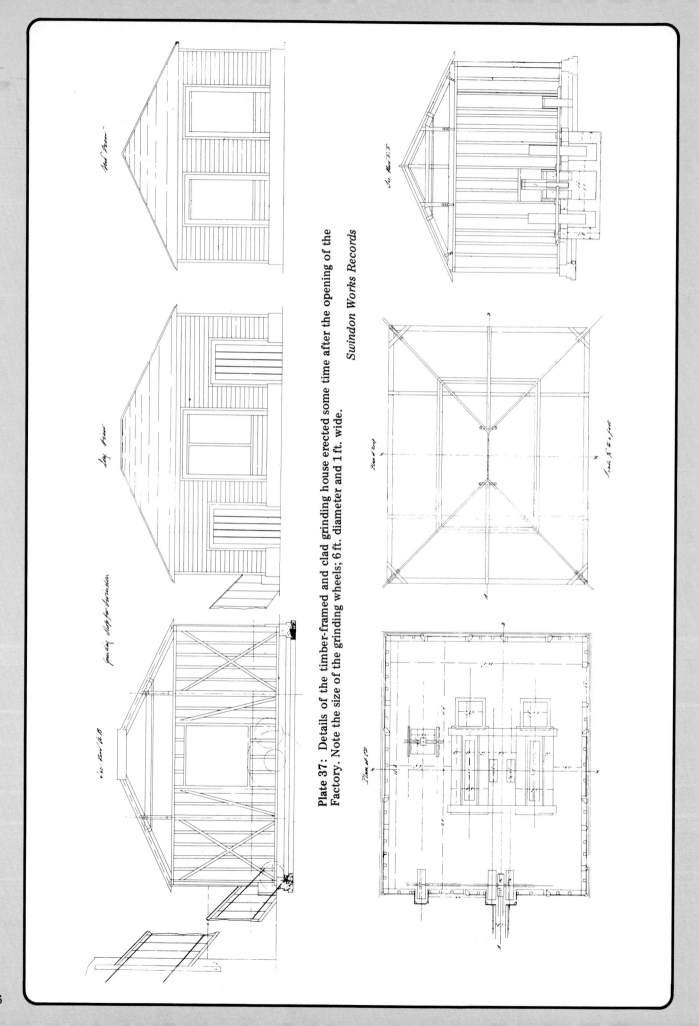

Plate 37: Details of the timber-framed and clad grinding house erected some time after the opening of the Factory. Note the size of the grinding wheels; 6ft. diameter and 1ft. wide.

Swindon Works Records

Plate 38: A view of the then west yard of the Works photographed from St. Mark's Church bell tower in 1860. Part of the upper room of the two storey building is shown in Plates 43 and 122.

British Rail

Plate 39: A view taken from St. Mark's Church bell tower 122 years later in April 1982. Retained buildings are easily identified.

D. Bird

salary to come to Swindon with this in view.

In February 1860 the directors in the half-yearly report recommended that a rolling mill should be added to the Swindon Works 'for the working up of the worn and damaged iron, in order to be converted, with the aid of fresh material of the very best quality, into new rails, which would possess a longer and therefore more economical existence than any which have yet been manufactured for them'. The types of bridge rails used by Brunel mounted on longitudinal timbers were certainly not so liable to vertical fracture with serious consequences, as were those used for rails mounted unsupported between cross sleepers. But track maintenance was very expensive, mainly due to the unequal performance of rails of varying quality supplied by different firms. A sum of £20,000 plus interest was voted for this project, which was to be paid off over a period of fourteen years by imposing on the using departments an annual charge of £2,000 over and above the actual material and manufacturing costs of the rails.

Although the Board authorized the commencement of this project in April 1860, Gooch records that full production did not commence in the new mill, which finally cost £25,000 for buildings and equipment, until May 1861. To operate this new plant, specialized labour had again to be imported, this time from the iron-making valleys of South Wales. We find from the works staff list 1845/65 (App. II) that the rolling mill was designed, constructed and managed by a Mr Thomas Ellis, also mentioning 'his' Welsh workmen. The reader will recall (from Chapter I) that Gooch, at about the age of 15 had worked in the Tredegar Iron Works where the foreman in the pattern shop was a Mr Ellis. That gentleman's son was also named Thomas and was Chief Engineer at the iron works. In 1847/8 he was building locomotives for the Sirhowy & Monmouthshire Tramways. It was not this Thomas Ellis who now came to Swindon, but did Gooch send to the place where he started his professional career for help in this project? Although not an uncommon name it could well have been another relative who had the necessary expertise required for rolling mill operation and who was recommended for the post. Whoever this man was, it is recorded in the Swindon Advertiser in April 1861, that, as the first newly-rolled rail left the mill, Thomas Ellis was grabbed by 'his Welsh workmen' placed in a chair and carried around the whole works in celebration.

Having reviewed the engineering history of Swindon until this date, it is clear that more than engineering problems faced Gooch's management staff during this twenty years of rapid development. That things were often difficult can be seen in the next chapter, but their solution was to be advantageous both to the Company and its employees at Swindon.

The new Works had served its apprenticeship and was on the eve of its coming of age.

Chapter Three

1841~1861 The Social Scene

We must now turn our thoughts back to 1841 and study the social implications of the coming of the railway on the small market town and its inhabitants. In 1831 the population was only 1,742. There was to be only a slight increase during the next decade, and by 1841, after the railway had already arrived, the census figures are given as 2,459 including 507 GWR workers. The latter presumably included those employed on building the factory and village, as well as engine drivers and firemen and the staff employed at the temporary station. These figures imply an Old Swindon population of 1,952 in 1841. The living conditions would be no better than those in other country towns. A report made in 1851 to the General Board of Health concerning the parish of Swindon paints a very sorry picture indeed of the state of cleanliness in the town. The conditions of such drainage and sanitation that did exist was deplorable. There were no sewers at all, merely open drains in the streets. The survey was carried out as a result of typhus epidemics due mainly to polluted water supplies. Admittedly some of these conditions in 1851 had worsened owing to the influx of so many families attracted to employment on the railway. The expectation of life in the parish of Swindon in 1840 was 29.8 years and had fallen to 25.7 years by 1849, and overcrowding must have been the main contributory factor.

Pigot's Directory for 1842 describes Swindon as a market town consisting of two principal streets. A corn mill was still working within 50 yards of a spring near the manor house (The Lawn). The quarries were quite active and business was created by the canal and the new railway about a mile further away. The main streets were lit by gas supplied from a company formed the previous year. The regular market dealt with corn weekly, fat and lean cattle fortnightly, and cheese monthly. There were also four fairs per annum; in early April, mid-May, mid-September and mid-December for all types of livestock and pedlary. Those in April and September were also hiring fairs. This then is the type of community which was to be suddenly swept into its own particular version of the Industrial Revolution but which never quite swamped the country influence, contrary to this sort of occurrence in the Midlands and areas further north.

There had already been an influx into the area of the navigators or 'navvies' building the railway during the years 1838—40. These were universally disliked wherever canals or railways were built because of their disruption to local life, eventually moving to another area as conditions required. The men employed by Messrs. J. & C. Rigby, the contractors for the Works, cottages and station, would naturally

include men of this type, but equally their staff would have been tempered by a large proportion of journeymen of the various building trades and skills. Whether these men were housed in huts at site, or sought temporary accommodation in Old Swindon, is not clear, but probably both. That they were numerous is apparent from the short time taken to complete the contract, this being well within 2 years, and most of it in 17 months. The building of the 300 cottages would have had the same priority as the engine house and repair shop, since accommodation had to be ready before anyone could be employed at Swindon permanently. The contractors would also have had a vested interest in finishing the refreshment rooms quickly, as it represented income to them under their agreement with the GWR to provide the cottages free in exchange for the 99 year lease of the catering services at the station.

Although not the earliest of its type, even on the railways, the new village was to be one of the best industrial housing estates of the period. It is thought to have been designed by Matthew (later Sir Matthew) Digby Wyatt and was very well built in Bath stone, most probably obtained from the cutting of Box Tunnel. It is well illustrated in *Plate 11* and consisted of three back to back rows of stone cottages with well proportioned doors and windows and with decorated stone chimneys. The rows ran east to west, but were split at the centre by an open space running north to south. The entrance road to the Works was at the north end of this area. The buildings facing on to this central area were of three storey construction and were used, in some cases, for shop and other commercial premises. Each house had its own privy adjoining a backway common to each block, where sewers were laid from the beginning. It can be assumed, therefore, that there was either a direct connection made from the privies or one made via a cesspit. The water supply to the Works and the village was obtained from the North Wilts Canal through a valve and was fed into two reservoirs immediately to the north of the passenger station. The sidings to the north of the present day station are still unofficially called the 'Water Sidings' by the staff. These reservoirs can be seen in *Plate 10*. From here water gravitated by pipe across the canal under the Cirencester (later Gloucester) line, by a syphon, to a well near the boiler house at the east end of the Works. From this well it was pumped via a filter house to the tanks provided above both the east and west boiler houses, and was thence fed to the Works and estate by gravity. In the village there were standpipes in the streets, but this supply was not intended for drinking water. It appears that for 23 years the

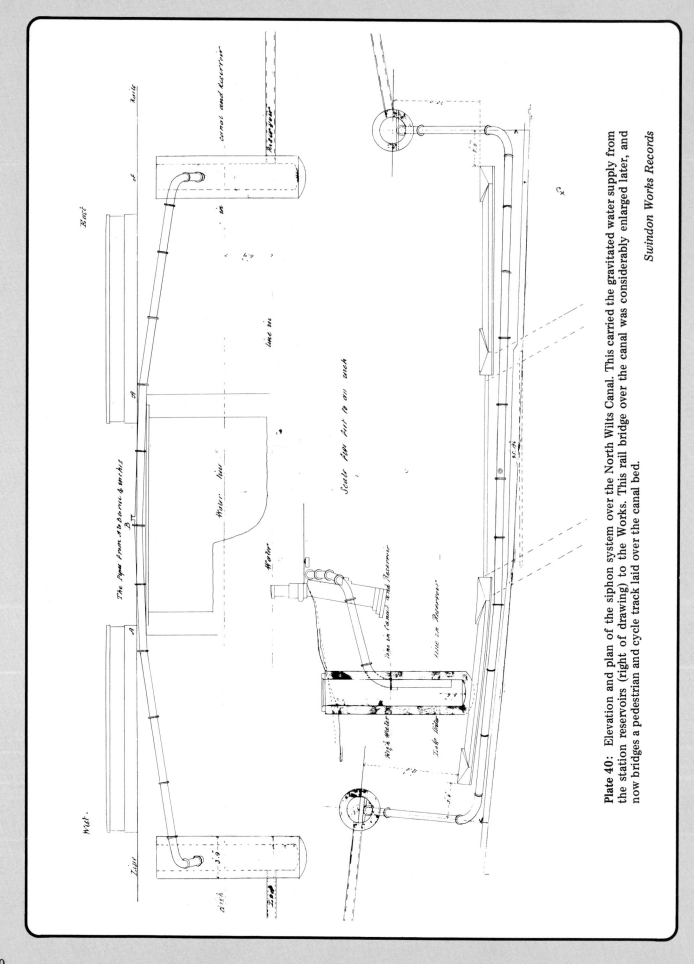

Plate 40: Elevation and plan of the siphon system over the North Wilts Canal. This carried the gravitated water supply from the station reservoirs (right of drawing) to the Works. This rail bridge over the canal was considerably enlarged later, and now bridges a pedestrian and cycle track laid over the canal bed.

Swindon Works Records

latter was sold by water carriers in the New Town, who brought supplies from the Wroughton Road spring two miles south of New Swindon. Not until after the Water Company was formed in the area in 1866 did the estate and the Works have a piped supply of drinking water. Doubtless the canal water was used for consumption at times and accounted for some of the ill health experienced. How the Works arranged for its internal drinking water is not known, although presumably it was obtained from the same source, possibly by small horse-drawn tank waggons. Reverting to the canal supply, by 1858 the charges for extraction were amounting to £200 per annum, but this supply was becoming limited. Other sources had to be sought and a series of ponds just north of the Works on the east side of the Gloucester line embankment were brought into use, subsequently referred to as the 'Back Cutting'. A steam pump house was installed and Gooch, assisted by Fraser, sank a well here to a depth of 142 ft. and was able to extract some 11,000 gallons per hour of good water to augment the supply. This well continued to ease the situation for a few years. Gas from the Works plant was also fed to the village and was used for street lighting. When it was installed in the houses for lighting and cooking purposes is unknown, although it is likely to have been at an early date. Streets were named after stations on the GWR and B&ER. Those at the eastern end of the village were called appropriately London, Oxford, Reading and Faringdon, and the western ones Bristol, Bath, Exeter and Taunton. The Bath Street was later altered to Bathampton Street to avoid confusion when 'The Sands' in Old Town was renamed Bath Road.

The different types of cottages were allocated according to status; the enginemen and artisans ranked above the unskilled men. There were houses towards the centre of the estate of a superior type for the foremen. Between London Street and Bristol Street and the railway was an open space. The portion on the Bristol Street side was used as a recreation and allotment area, whilst that on the London Street side was occupied by two identical houses built in country gentleman's style and laid out with formal gardens. The one nearer the station was for the stationmaster, and the other nearer the Works entrance was for the Works Manager and first occupied by Sturrock.

This was the nucleus of New Swindon which emerged during late 1841 and early 1842. There were a few houses already in the vicinity mainly connected with the North Wilts Canal Company, but apart from these and one or two agricultural houses and buildings, there was nothing but fields and cart tracks leading to Old Swindon. To these houses came the new railwaymen and their families. We have noted that the original establishment in 1843 was 423 men, and even assuming there was a proportionate number

of single men in addition to family groups such as brothers, or father and sons, there must have been at least 300 families ready to fill the houses as soon as they were completed. Knowing the rate of expansion to be over four times this working population in about five years, the ensuing overcrowding must have been a great problem. In a bid to improve this situation the Company commenced work on a 'barracks', as it was called, situated on one of the southerly corner sites of the cottage estate. The actual date of commencement is not certain but it was possibly in late 1846, since work was suspended as a result of the financial situation and the building stood uncompleted until at least 1849. It was intended to house the single men of the factory and thus relieve the pressure on accommodation in the village. The floors were portioned off into separate cubicles or small rooms. Communal cooking, washing and other necessary facilities were provided together with a bakehouse. The men therefore had to fend for themselves and the resultant lack of popularity led to under-use. In a bid to encourage occupation, a manager was appointed and presumably some services were provided, but this failed also and it then stood empty until 1860 when another use was found for it. Today, this much altered building houses the GWR Museum.

It is inevitable that speculative builders were quickly on the scene in these circumstances, and a number of streets of 'two up two down' type houses began to appear around the village to meet the demand. These would have been built for about £65 to £70 each, and no doubt were within the reach of some of the artisans and enginemen who were earning perhaps 25 to 30 shillings per week. Much of this housing development, although of local plain red brick, was built with bay windows and small front and rear gardens and was much better than much industrial housing of the period.

Concern in those days was also always felt for the spiritual needs of work people, perhaps, more than the temporal ones. As early as 1840 when the new town was only in the planning stage the Bristol directors had urged that a piece of the Company's land at Swindon be set aside for the erection of a church in which a number of 'sittings' could be available for the staff. These gentlemen had been urged in this matter particularly by the clergy and parishioners of the Bristol parish of S.S. Philip & Jacob (still a lively church known affectionately as 'Pip & Jay' today). The proprietors of the railway had argued, no doubt correctly, that subscribed capital could not be used for such purposes.

One of the London directors, G. H. Gibbs, however, had died in August 1842 and in his will was a bequest of £500 to assist in the provision of a church and school at New Swindon. Using this as a starting point the directors made an appeal shortly afterwards to

Plate 41: New Swindon in 1847. A locally published view of the junction at Swindon looking west to Bristol. The Station House is to the left and the Works Manager's House is in the middle distance. Also note the cottage estate, St. Mark's Church, the engine shed and coke house to the right. The engine *Fire Brand* entered service in May 1840 and ceased work in April 1866.

British Rail

Plate 42: A very early photograph of the first GWR School at Swindon, built in 1845 and demolished in 1879. St. Mark's Church stands behind.

Author's Collection

the proprietors and others particularly in Swindon, to which there was such a response, that the necessary funds were subscribed by 1843. Amongst the donations was a piece of land of about ¾ of an acre offered by Colonel T. Vilett, one of the major landowners in the area. This land was just to the west of the village and the plot ran parallel to the main line. At the same time the Company purchased a small parcel of adjoining land for the school. The Company received an additional gift from Colonel Vilett of a large piece of land south of the church site, for the use of the community as a cricket ground and amenity area. The latter two conveyances are dated 8th June 1844 and the donated church and vicarage land was conveyed at the Company's expense to H. M. Church Commissioners on 22nd March 1845. The church, finally costing £6,000 and dedicated to St. Mark, was designed, it is thought, by the young Gilbert (later Sir Gilbert) Scott, and was consecrated in April 1845. The area it was to serve was originally a 'Perpetual Curacy' or chapelry, before becoming a parish in its own right. The stipend of the first incumbent, the Rev. Joseph Mansfield, was paid by the Company until he left in 1850, after which a permanent endowment was made by H. M. Commissioners. The stipend was £120 per annum. The parish was legally constituted on 21st January 1846. The Rev. Mansfield was in Swindon some time before the church and vicarage was ready, and it is understood that a room in the Works was used for services.

The school was completed in 1845 and can be seen, as originally built, standing directly behind St. Mark's Church in *Plate 11*, and a very early photograph of it is illustrated in *Plate 42*. The school was built with a schoolmaster's house attached and provided with a play yard complete with maypole. Although all these original buildings disappeared by 1880, the socket in the ground into which this maypole fitted remained in position until well within living memory. The Company appointed a schoolmaster who was to serve the new community in a very great way. He was Alexander James Braid, and to him fell the task of organizing the new school. His wife and daughter also taught. Fortunately a copy of the school regulations was amongst the Paddington papers (now at the Public Records Office), and, although these are for 1859, some 14 years after the school opened, they are unlikely to have altered much. The school was fee-paying for the families of employees, although at a later date other children were admitted if there was capacity. The fees — 4d or 2d according to age in 1859 — were paid weekly on Monday mornings before lessons commenced for the week. These amounts were slightly increased shortly afterwards, but any family with four children already at school could send 'Quintus, Sextus and Septimus' etc. free. The syllabus contained the usual 'reading, 'riting and 'rithmatic', together with history and geography.

Scripture was taught by the St. Mark's clergy, but an attempt to make Church attendance compulsory for the pupils by the Rev. Mansfield was halted by Charles Saunders, the Company Secretary, on behalf of the directors, who firmly held that this was a matter purely for the parents. Girls were taught needlework in addition, and were exempt from corporal punishment. Five hours of schooling per day, including playtimes, was the norm, with two weeks holiday at Christmas and three weeks in the summer. There were also the usual short breaks at Easter and Whitsun, and no charge was made for the remaining part of these weeks. An interesting item of equipment was an iron ball (no doubt cast in the Works), with which the boys could play. It is doubtful if any safety officer would allow it today!

We must not assume that all we have said about religion and education meant that the community was necessarily of a quiet and sober nature. As we shall see shortly, the opposite was very often the case. But it must be remembered that the artisans, in particular, were working in what was probably the most up to date and forward-looking industry in the country. Although they were not educated men in the way which we understand the term today, they were extremely skilled and intelligent men and needed to be literate and numerate in order to carry out their various trades. They were high-spirited too, and the local lock-up was often found to be too small. Outdoor sport was avidly followed during all possible daylight hours, despite a long day in work.

In September 1843 a small number of men in the Works grouped together to set up a library. Who or what this group consisted of is not recorded, but it is most likely that they were artisans working together to further their technical education. Some of the books could have been purchased by individuals and pooled for general use, some given by friends and possibly Gooch, Sturrock and other officers were amongst these. By March 1844 there were 15 members of this group and the library had grown to 130 volumes. It is interesting to note that the first rate-supported library in the country was not to open until 1852 in Salford, so this was a very forward looking action by these men. Such a movement deserved nurturing, and, no doubt spurred on by Gooch, on 8th January 1844 the 'GWR Mechanics Institution' was established. The aims were set out as being 'for the purpose of disseminating useful knowledge and encouraging rational amusement amongst all classes of people employed by the GWR at Swindon'. Assistance was forthcoming from the Company and a suitable room was made available in the Works for the new organization to carry on its activities. The author has been unable to find any reference to the location of the room but, by process of elimination, the most likely place appears to have been the whole or part of the floor above the

Plate 43: This upper floor room in the original Works, later the tool room and latterly a bolt store, is almost certainly the first room made available to the Mechanics Institution for theatricals, dancing etc.

British Rail

shop discussed in the last chapter, where it is thought that the wheels and wheelsets were produced. That the new organization was fulfilling a need is an understatement. After all, there was no organized social life in the New Town, and this new organization was capable of providing, by virtue of its aims, just what was wanted by the inhabitants. At the end of 1844 membership had risen to 129 and the library had a stock of 522 books. Starting in this modest way it moved from strength to strength. It was perhaps natural that the schoolmaster, Alexander Braid, should be connected with this organization. Indeed, the library may have been kept at the school, but it was a stroke of genius on someone's part that Braid should be appointed secretary of the new Society. This gentleman was to use his very great academic and organizational talents to expand these small beginnings into a full educational and social service for New Swindon.

Very soon after the formation of the institution the activities were widened by a portion of the floor above the turnery being made available for dancing and theatricals, and only a year or so later the free-standing shop, originally erected as the truck painting shop, was cleared and altered for a range of activities, the other room being retained for theatricals only. Therefore, by the time that the savage period of unemployment came in 1847, this organization had become a real focal point for the social life of the community.

The sudden changes brought about by the dismissals at Swindon naturally had a catastrophic effect. People were possibly no more provident with their earnings then than is often the case today and, although earning high rates of pay for the times, they would have saved little in the comparatively short period they had been in employment. As far as the railway officers were concerned, their main problem was the health of this close-knit and overcrowded community. Outbreaks of typhus, smallpox and similar diseases were accepted as the norm, and indeed there were many cases of typhus in Old Swindon at this time. Already a Provident Society had been formed by the Company in 1838, but this was only available to the operating staff. In 1843, the GWR Locomotive Department Sick Fund came into being for assistance during illness and for the payment of funeral expenses. In the following year this was extended to become the GWR Locomotive & Carriage Department Sick Fund Society.

As well as the former benefits there was also provision for a small pension. Membership was a condition of employment and contributions could be made through the paybill or directly to the Society, weekly. There were different classes of membership and benefits varied accordingly. Men leaving the service were able to continue as 'outmembers'. The Works Manager was President ex-officio, and there was some financial assistance to the funds from the directors. The committee of management drawn from the membership were also trustees and the funds were suitably invested. This was the first form of social assistance at Swindon. A Mr Rae occupied the post of Works Surgeon and presumably dealt with accidents there, but possibly had private patients amongst the staff if they wished and could afford to employ his services. There were other medical men in private practice in the area. In fact, there are four surgeons listed in Pigot's 1842 Directory for Old Swindon, who may also have been available in New Swindon. Gooch's alarm at the prospect of a sickness of epidemic proportions due to the unemployment situation was such that he wrote to the secretary, Charles Saunders, and his deep concern is apparent in his letter sent during November 1847, quoted here in full. However, it must be prefaced by saying that some months earlier it had been proposed that a small number of larger houses should be built at the west end of the cottage estate for officers now at Swindon, including one for Mr Rae, although nothing had yet been started:-

'My Dear Sir,
The serious distress that will be occasioned amongst our workmen at Swindon by discharging so many and putting the rest upon short time induces me to hope the Directors will grant a request the men have made to me, namely to assist the men to pay the Doctor for attending all the families of the men, both in and out of work, for the bulk of those discharged have been determined to remain in the neighbourhood of Swindon in hopes of better times, as there is no chance of employment if they go elsewhere, and many have been very lately induced to come to Swindon at considerable expense to them in removing their families from a distance.

Those men who are to be retained in the Company's service have very generously offered to assist the unfortunate men in any way in their power, and one of the plans is to arrange with Mr Rae, Surgeon, to attend the whole for a small weekly payment by each man. This arrangement I have no doubt I will be able to bring about if I can get some assistance from the Directors. What I would beg of them to do is to allow Mr Rae to live in the Cottages house-free in consideration of his attending all the accidents that occur in the Works for nothing.

The attendance in these cases is at present on a footing that I think the Directors will not consider just either to the Surgeon or the men. In all private establishments the Doctor's bill for attendance on accidents is paid by the Employers: up to the present time at Swindon this has not been done, as I have not felt myself authorised to pay the Doctor and have only done so in one or two cases, where he has been money out of pocket for bandages etc. There is little doubt we are liable for the Doctor's first attendance on the case, as we are the party who called him in. The result in a great many cases is that the Doctor is not paid at all from the inability of the injured man to do so, and in others he is paid by a subscription amongst the other men. The London & North Western pay a Surgeon at Crewe £50 per annum and give him a good house, for which he attends all their accidents. There is more than one accident on the average per week for which Mr Rae is sent to attend in the Works, or the man is carried to him, and many of them very serious ones.

What I hope the Directors will allow me to do is either to give me authority for accidents as they occur, or that they will give Mr Rae £30 per year to take them all, or what is nearly the same thing, to give him his house free of rent. If this is done I feel convinced it will be considered a great boon by the men and will enable me to make a better arrangement with the Doctor for them.

It must not be forgotten that our men at Swindon are not in the same position as those employed in working the line who have no difference in their wages made from the bad times, but the men at Swindon in addition to the assistance they will be called upon to give to those thrown out of work entirely, are themselves only allowed to work three-quarters of their wages. I am sure if the Directors would themselves visit Swindon and hear the many distressing cases I heard yesterday they would at once grant what I so earnestly request and in all possibility much more. I believe with the good feeling now existing at Swindon the men will do much good amongst their unfortunate fellow workmen.

I enclose you a note which will show you only one out of at least 50 cases as bad or worse. It is not a gift to the Doctor I ask but that the men may be relieved from the cost of numerous accidents, leaving them still to support their own sick, which, I fear, will be a heavy matter this winter as amongst other misfortunes we have some very bad cases of smallpox in the village. I have to meet some of the men Thursday evening, and shall be glad to tell them their request and mine is agreed to. Your own kind assistance in this matter will much oblige.

Yours very truly,
DAN. GOOCH.'

This proposal was agreed to almost immediately and Gooch and the local officers lost no time in implementing their side of the proposals, for in December 1847 the Medical Fund Society was instituted among the men still in employment, with Archibald Sturrock as their President. The officers and committee were elected in the same way as for the Sick Fund Society, with the vice chairman and treasurer being chosen from the committee. Among the original rules is set out 'That the object of the Medical Fund is to provide medicine and attendance to the men employed in the Works of the Great Western Railway at Swindon and their wives and families; and in order to carry out the regulations of the Company that all men employed at this establishment shall subscribe a rateable portion of their wages towards a general fund, the following rules for giving effect to this regulation have been determined on'. As rightly stated in its volume 'A Century of Medical Service 1847—1947' published by the Society, there is no record of any such regulation in the Company's documents, but one suspects that Gooch introduced this wording in order to properly support as a moral obligation, his side of the bargain which he had made in his letter to the directors. Thus was formed what was to be perhaps the greatest social service to the community at Swindon.

The financial arrangements embodied in the Medical Fund makes the Works at Swindon perhaps the very first industrial organization to require membership of a health fund a condition of employment. Whether this claim is valid or not, it was certainly a very enlightened move for its period even though not made with completely altruistic motives on Gooch's part. The expanding history of this great Society will be dealt with chronologically. The contributions at the outset were on a sliding scale varying from 1½d per week for a youth earning less than ten shillings per week up to a maxmimum of 4d per week for a married man earning more than £1 weekly. That the early days of the society were not easy is apparent in the attitude of other members of the medical profession in the area, and even the Vicar of St. Mark's, on the grounds of denial of freedom of choice of medical staff. Mr Rae had an assistant named Rogers but, as the Society could not afford to pay for more professional help, Gooch made it clear that the arrangement had to work within the financial and other limits already agreed with the Board. Mr Rae received a capitation fee for his services, but from this he had to supply all medicaments and dressings, so it would not appear to be a sinecure. Mr Rae died in 1853 and was succeeded by a very competent surgeon Dr. Hind who served until 1859. This gentleman was very active in the preventive side of his work and made urgent representations in 1853 about the filthy state of the new town.

Although the railway village was equipped with drainage, it would seem that its upkeep was almost non-existent, and no doubt with the rough state of the roads and lack of control of what entered the sewers in the Works itself, the system became virtually useless. Not surprisingly an outbreak of typhus occurred in 1853 and Dr. Hind feared that this might foreshadow cholera. At the time, the cleaning of the streets and drains was in the hands of a Bath contractor who was sharply reminded of his shortcomings, but it must be remembered that the new town now included an increasing area of speculatively built houses where drainage of any type was limited. There was not any formal local authority to which an appeal could be made. The only likely body was the Old Swindon Board of Guardians and they felt that the problem was not of their making. Not until 1864 was a local board of health formed. Furthermore, in epidemics such as typhus, the illness could strike either high or low of those persons living or working in the locality.

The Medical Fund Committee were very active in 1853 and in the following year, and succeeded, within the voluntary limits of their service, in eradicating or at least improving the main causes of insanitary conditions such as the slaughter houses, pig sties, those privies not connected to drains, and sewage fed into the canal from which factory and household water was pumped. Better water filters were used, and the improvement and extension of road paving was undertaken. Things eventually improved as a result of their efforts and the minute books became virtually free of complaints. A minute from 1859 is worth recording, however. It refers to the appointment of an official at the princely sum of £1. 5s. 0d. per annum, called the 'Keeper of Lime, Brushes, and Invalid Chair'. The issue of lime for cleansing purposes was no doubt instituted by Dr. Hind early in his appointment in order that families could cleanse their walls, floors and drains etc., and no doubt this appointment put it on a regular footing. From that time on, lime could be obtained by all members of the fund, on application at the lime house, for cleansing and whitening purposes, right up until the time of the formation of the National Health Service. The mention of 'the invalid chair' also denotes an extension of services, which was to continue throughout the life of the Society. Perhaps, most important in the later 'fifties were the subscriptions to famous hospitals in London, Bath and other places to which the surgeon could refer members for specialist services. It became apparent that Dr. Hind was overworked, and perhaps overstretched himself at about this time, so much so that he was unable to cope to the satisfaction of the fund, and he resigned his position in 1859. The Society was most fortunate in appointing in September of the same year Dr. G. Swinhoe who served as Senior Medical Officer with great distinction well into the 20th century, and we shall see later what great strides the Medical Fund was to take.

Reverting now to the activities of the Mechanics Institution, one can now get in better perspective the conditions under which it flourished. There is no doubt that the principle of living hard and playing hard was accepted as natural by many. Details of the early phenomenal growth of the organization are

NEW SWINDON MECHANICS' INSTITUTION.

THE FOLLOWING

LECTURES

WILL BE DELIVERED AT

The School Room, New Swindon.

First—On Thursday, March 18th, 1847,

By PHILIP HENRY HATCH, Esq.,

Lecturer at the London Mechanics' Institution and various other Metropolitan and Provincial Literary and Scientific Institutions.

SYLLABUS.

ON THE GENIUS OF BOZ.—The New Movement. Comic Philanthropists. Dickens a Social Reformer. The important questions introduced in his works. Old English Sports and Customs. Duelling. Capital Punishment and Prison Discipline. The elements of Modern Tragedy. Sentiment and Pathos. The true Province of the Pathetic. The juvenility of Laughter. Advantages and utility of Satire illustrated. Boz's Humorous Delineations Graphic Phrases and mode of Sketching Character.
ILLUSTRATIONS.—"Christmas at Dingley Dell." "Oliver Twist." "Little Nell." "The Murderer Sikes." "Mrs. Todger's Boarding-House." "Kate Nickleby." "The Ghost." "The Kettle." "Captain Boldwig and Mr. Pickwick." "The Four Sisters."

Second—On Thursday, April 1st, 1847,

By Mr. K. GARDINER.

SYLLABUS.

ON THE RISE AND PROGRESS OF LANGUAGE.—Introduction. Definition of Language. Articulation. Description of the Voice and on what it depends. Origin of Language. Structure and Composition of Words. Pronunciation of Words. Different Styles of Speech. Written Language. Discovery of Letters. Methods of Writing. Materials for Writing. Conclusion.

Third—On Thursday, April 15th, 1847,

By HENRY M. NOAD, Esq.,

(Whose Lectures on Magnetic Electricity gave so much satisfaction.)

ON THE MINERAL ACIDS.—SULPHURIC, NITRIC, AND MURIATIC.—Their Preparation. Qualities and Extensive Uses in the Arts.
NOTE.—This Lecture is the first of a series of four which Mr. NOAD has engaged to deliver on the third Thursdays in April, June, August, and October in this year.

Tickets of Admission to be had of Mr. ANN, of Swindon ; Mr. BRAID, the Secretary of the Institution ; and from any Member of the Council.

PRICE OF ADMISSION.

.ecture, Reserved Seats, 1s.—Persons employed in the Works, not Members of the Institution, 6d., who may take wi Lady on the Payment of 3d.—Members of the Institution admitted Free, and with the privilege of taking in one Lady F e

THE BAND WILL BE IN ATTENDANCE AS USUAL.

Doors open at SEVEN o'Clock. Lecture commences at a Quarter to EIGHT.

ALEXANDER JAMES BRAID, Secy.

SWINDON MECHANICS' INSTITUTION.

SYALLABUS OF A COURSE OF SIX

LECTURES

TO BE DELIVERED IN THE

SCHOOL ROOM, NEW SWINDON,

On ALTERNATE MONDAYS, at Seven o'Clock in the Evening.

LECTURE 1st, December 8th,

By Dr. RYAN,

Of the Royal Polytechnic Institution, London,

On HEAT.—Its Sources--Effects and Phenomena--Latent and Sensible Heat--Vaporization and Boutigny's Experiments.

LECTURE 2nd, December 22nd,

By Dr. RYAN, on PNEUMATIC CHEMISTRY.—The Chemical Composition of Air—The Pressure and Elasticity of the Atmosphere—Combustion—Respiration---Ventilation.

LECTURE 3rd, January 5th,

The subject of this Lecture will be announced at the previous Lecture.

LECTURE 4th, January 19th,

BY EDWD. COWPER, ESQ.,

Lecturer on the Mechanical Arts, at King's College, London,

On PAPER MAKING.—Papyrus--Paper from Linen Rag--Cutting the Rag---Grinding into Pulp--- Bleaching---Making by hand---the Mould, &c.---Making by Machinery--Pulp Strainer---Fourdrinier's Machine---Dickinson's Machine---Sizing--Cutting---Silk thread in postage Envelopes.

LECTURE 5th, February 2nd,

By EDWARD COWPER, Esq., on PRINTING AND PRINTING MACHINERY.---The first printed Books---The common Printing Press--Stanhope Press--First idea of Printing with Machinery---Nicholson Steam Printing Machines---Koenig---Donkin---Applegath and Cowper---Napier---Rich--Book Machines The Times Newspaper Machine.

LECTURE 6th, February 16th,

The subject of this Lecture will be announced in the previous Lectures.

The Swindon Great Western Band will be in attendance to play some favourite Airs before and after the Lectures.

Tickets of Admission to be had of Mr. ANN, of Swindon ; Mr. BRAID, the Secretary of the Institution ; and from any Member of the Council.—Price of Admission, Reserved Seats for the Course of Lectures, 5s.—For a single Lecture 1s.—Persons employed in the Works, not Members of the Institution for a single Lecture 6d., who may take with them a Lady on the payment of 3d.—Members of the Institution admitted Free, and with the privilege of taking in one Lady Free.

DORE, PRINTER, SWINDON.

Plates 44 and 45: Mechanics Institution handbills of 1847/8 advertising various lecture series for adult education classes.
Author's Collection

sparse, but what is available gives a clear view of the organizational flair of the secretary, Alexander Braid. We have copies of handbills for 1847 and 1848 giving details of courses of lectures held in the railway schoolroom. Two of the lectures advertised on the earlier handbill are of a literary nature: one by Philip H. Hatch, Esq., a lecturer from the London Mechanics Institution, on 'The Genius of Boz' included discussion of the work of Dickens as a social reformer and the value of the famous illustrations in his books in strengthening the impact of his aims. Another by Mr K. Gardiner was on 'The Rise and Progress of Language' and discussed its use in writing and speaking. A third lecture by Henry Noad, Esq., ('whose lectures on magnetic electricity gave so much satisfaction'), was 'The Mineral Acids — sulphuric, nitric and muriatic - their preparation, qualities and extensive uses'. Admittance to these lectures for members was free, and one lady could be taken without payment. Reserved seats for non-members were one shilling if unconnected with the Works; if a Works employee, but a non-member, seats were sixpence plus threepence more if accompanied by a lady. Doors opened at seven for a quarter to eight and 'The Band will be in attendance as usual'. The other handbill advertises two lectures of a series of three by Dr. Ryan of the Royal Polytechnic Institution, London. The first was on 'Heat — its sources, effects and phenomena' and discussed latent and sensible heat, also vaporization and Boutigny's Experiments. The second was on 'Pneumatic Chemistry' covering the composition of air, pressure and elasticity of the atmosphere, combusion, respiration and ventilation. There were also two lectures given by Mr Edward Cowper, lecturer in mechanical arts at Kings College, London. These two dealt in detail with 'Papermaking' and the allied subjects of 'Printing and Printing Machinery'. It is again announced that 'The Swindon Great Western Band will be in attendance to play some favourite airs before and after the lectures'.

Plate 46 (above): An early, but undated, photograph (thought to be about 1855) of the Mechanics Institution Band.

British Rail

Plate 47 (left): Mechanics Institution handbill for a concert in 1847. A full evening's entertainment was guaranteed!

Author's Collection

One can see that the subjects of lectures were of an educationally high order, and confirms the previous remarks about the intellectual standard of the artisans already resident in Swindon. It is known that these lectures were supported to the limits of the available accommodation. Another interesting item is the reference to a band as early as 1847, and must have been one of the first activities started. Attendance at lectures and readings could well have been good advertisement for the music classes and the concerts. An early photograph of this band in about 1855 has survived and is illustrated in *Plate 46.* A copy of the handbill for a 'Musical Entertainment' is reproduced in *Plate 47,* and in common with the times must have made a very full evening's entertainment! In fact, by about 1850, there were at least four separate instrumental groups. The major one was the band already referred to. A copy of the rules is still in existence, and they show that the members were under strict control. Practices were held twice a week and the following fines were imposed:

For being late at practice 1d
For being absent 2d
For being absent and music not sent 3d

For discipline in rehearsal:-

For not keeping quiet when requested 2d
For playing another man's instrument 2d

(One would have thought this latter would be encouraged!)

And now for the heinous crimes:-

Entering the band room in a
    state of intoxication . . . . 2 shillings!
Using the instrument in a public house . . . .5 shillings!!

This latter fine could be almost half a week's wages for a labourer, but one wonders who made the fateful decision to fine, and how difficult it was to collect! There was a separate band for dances, appropriately known as the Quadrille Band, and a Drum & Fife Band, which no doubt was connected with a Volunteer Army Force. Finally there was a group of handbell ringers. In the latter organization if the conductor was abused during practice there was instant dismissal from the group!

This widening range of educational and social activities made an increase to premises vital, added to which the workshops already on loan were available only as a result of the reduction in the workload, and they would soon be required again for their proper use. In addition, the school was in constant use from morning until night. It is plain that Gooch discussed this matter with Sturrock and the committee at some length. Saunders duly reported to the board meeting of 1st September 1853 that Gooch had delivered to him the prospectus of a scheme promoted at Swindon for establishing new buildings for the Mechanics Institution and also a market. The proposals provided for lecture and reading rooms and other amenities suitable to the activities, and to include a large room where employees could take their breakfasts and dinners on workdays. Facilities for families to bath were included. Seven years previously, in 1846, the Chairman, Charles Russell, had asked Gooch about the facilities for bathing at Swindon because of the 'present mania for baths and washhouses'. The Market too was badly needed because of the lack of shops in the New Town. Needless to say it was a time of great prosperity for the shopkeepers of Old Town, but the problems were very real for the railway housewives negotiating steep muddy paths to and from these shops over a mile away for their heavy weekly purchases.

The submission suggested that railway land — (a portion of that left clear between the east and west blocks of the railway village) — be made available on suitable terms and that authority be given to raise £3,000 in shares at Swindon to finance the project. The Board approved the plan with the following minute:-

'That this board will consent to demise the land necessary for the proposed buildings at New Swindon for a nominal yearly rent of 3 shillings per annum upon a lease to be renewable for ever'.

Conditions were made that the design of the buildings should have prior approval from the Board and that the special objects for which they were to be erected were to be exclusively followed out and used for no other purpose, except with express permission of the Board. No sale or sub-lease could be made to other parties on pain or forfeiture of the lease. The Company were prepared to pay the new organization £100 per annum for the provision of the amenities for the employees to continue indefinitely to offset the loss of the rooms that had already been made available free in the Factory. Brunel was asked to prepare a plan of the site available and Saunders was to take the necessary action to put the plan into effect as soon as the capital was raised.

And so the New Swindon Improvement Company was formed. On 8th December 1853 the Deed of Settlement of this Company was approved including the statement:-

'That the objects or purposes of the said Company shall be the providing of accommodation for the inhabitants of New Swindon in the County of Wilts and the vicinity by the establishment there of Baths, Reading, Lecture and Refreshment Rooms, a Market and shops and for other local Purposes'.

The lease of the land was filed in the deeds office Paddington on 3rd October 1854, but the foundation stone was laid on Wednesday, 24th May 1854, amid great ceremony and Masonic rites. Earlier in the day the Methuen Lodge No. 914 had met with a great number of dignitaries of other provinces, including the architect, Edward Roberts, from a London Lodge. These worthies, among whom Gooch and most of the management were included, formed a procession wearing full regalia, and were joined in a similar way by the Manchester Unity of Odd Fellows, the Ancient Order of Foresters, the Directors and Councillors of the Mechanics Institution and the New Swindon Improvement Company. They processed from the Works, past St. Mark's Church, around the cricket ground, and back through the estate to the new site, where, after coins of the realm had been duly placed in a cavity, the foundation stone was laid by Lord Methuen. A banquet followed for over 1,000 people in two large marquees on the cricket ground. In such a way were things done in those days. *Plate 48* shows the Mechanics Institution as originally built.

Plate 48: The Mechanics Institute, built by the New Swindon Improvement Company, shortly after opening in 1855.

British Rail

Plate 49: The market building, opened in 1854, but shown here as photographed towards the end of its life in the late 1880s.

British Rail

The upper floor of the building comprised the main assembly hall 76 ft. by 40 ft. which also had a stage 50 ft. by 25 ft. The ground floor housed the reading room 50 ft. x 25 ft. below the stage area, the library, a coffee room, the men's messroom and the council and housekeeper's rooms. Hot and cold baths were also provided, replacing similar amenities existing within the Works and later in Reading Street on the cottage estate. Heating was by a boiler flued up one of the turrets of the building. The baths existed here only until 1864, the messrooms until 1877. The large hall gave greater scope to the amateur theatrical and choral classes with which the orchestral groups also appeared. An educational board was formed in connection with the Society of Arts and all kinds of adult education flourished. It opened on Monday, 1st May 1855, with a presentation by the Amateur Theatrical Society of two plays apparently well known to audiences of the time: 'Rent Day' and 'Binks the Bagman'. The band was, of course, in attendance.

The market building is illustrated in *Plate 49*. This photograph was taken in about 1890 shortly before its demolition. It was opened on 3rd November 1854, and consisted of 34 stalls bisected by a single gangway. Some stalls faced inwards to a central fountain and some outwards to the surrounding roofed walkway. Like many new undertakings, only eleven stalls were hired at the time of opening and these consisted of three butchers, one 'meat salesman', one 'Porkman', two greengrocers, one general draper, a fishmonger, a boot and shoe dealer, and a provision dealer. On opening, a wide range of goods was available from 'halfpenny herrings and sheeps' trotters to poultry and oxbeef'. Both the institute and market were erected by the firm of Streeter from Bath.

At last the new community had convenient shopping facilities. The outside verandah of the market was to become a regular meeting place and a local 'Speaker's Corner'. There was also the celebrated 'Hole in the Wall' through which certain beverages were purveyed, seemingly for many years without the appropriate licence! This market served the community for some forty years.

The Mechanics Institution was also instrumental in starting what was to become an institution in itself. In 1849, it organized an outing by train for about 500 of its members to spend a day in Oxford. The railway company very generously provided free railway travel for this event, which was naturally repeated annually, coming to be known as the 'trip'. This name stuck and in later years the Works annual holiday (unpaid of course), with its free 'Mechanics' pass, gained the regular name of 'trip', and today the annual holidays are referred to amongst the railway community and others in Swindon, by the same name. This was also the beginning, so far as the GWR was concerned, of the system of 'free passes' for employees and their families. Further day outings took place annually, the one in July 1854 being to the Crystal Palace (by then re-erected at Sydenham after the 1851 Great Exhibition), and in 1855 over 1,600 people again took advantage of a 'trip' to London. With the new buildings available, the activities could expand both in range and style. The Amateur Theatrical Society were putting on plays and concerts about every eight weeks, but not without some setbacks, for in 1856 it is reported that the company 'butchered' a play called 'The Innkeeper of Aberville'. To add to the troubles, on the same evening a singer of comic songs who appeared immediately afterwards could not properly remember even the first two verses of his number and ran off the stage in confusion! But the reporter wryly records that it did not matter much as it was performed before the smallest audience seen there for some time. About this time the wish was expressed that entertainments would start promptly, as it was so tiresome waiting three quarters of an hour after the appointed time, and the consequent late finish meant going home after the street lights had been extinguished! Annual appearances were being made by the famous Victorian actor, George Grossmith, who gave lecture readings on Dickens' books, choosing a different one each year. The subject of debates would be daunting to us today if the two examples advertised in the local weekly paper are a guide:-

'The execution of Charles I — was it justified?'
'Was Cranmer's conduct in accordance with his priestly office?'

Such debates apparently drew large numbers of participants. The Mechanics Institution had come a long way since its inception in 1843 with 15 members for, at the Annual General Meeting in 1855, it was reported to have a membership of 634, of whom 622 were from New Swindon. The library contained 2,542 volumes, with annual issues totalling 18,798 in that year.

The cricket ground, mentioned earlier, was situated immediately south of St. Mark's Church and was presented by Colonel Vilett. From the shape of this land on the property plan it was possibly a complete farm field, which had been then levelled, trees planted around it and a perimeter path laid down. This cricket ground was maintained by the Works and, as its name implies, was used primarily for this game. The original changing rooms were of a temporary nature, situated on the north side, and there are records of matches played there in early issues of the Swindon Advertiser in 1854/5. It was later to be known as the GWR Park under a separate committee formed in 1873, but prior to that period it is not clear how it was controlled.

The spiritual life of the New Town was not left to the Anglicans at St. Mark's. There were early steps by the various dissenting churches to promote evangelism in the area, working in the early days from the centres already existing in Old Swindon. In 1849 the Baptists opened a church in New Swindon near the railway village in Bridge Street and in the same year the Primitive Methodists built a church in the lane then becoming known as Regent Street, which later developed into Swindon's main shopping street. This church was strategically placed half-way between Old and New Swindon. There were other small 'mission' churches also. Apparently all churches had good congregations, church-going was the accepted practice in those times for 'respectable' families.

A further recession, although not as bad as ten years previously, occurred in 1857. This was again due to a drop in traffic on the line of some 35,000 train miles per year. Short-time working was again introduced for a period. The Works closed on Friday night until the start of the 9 a.m. morning shift on Monday.

Also in April 1860, was founded the 11th (New Swindon) Rifle Volunteers, with officers from the works staff led by Captains W. F. Gooch and Fraser. An armoury was provided in one of the cottages which was later to become part of the Medical Fund Hospital. In August 1859 the Board minuted that the funds set aside to support the school and church were now becoming exhausted, and that new provision would soon be required. This may have been a political move to test the possibility of a school board being formed, although this did not in fact occur for several years.

The arrival of the Welsh workmen in 1860/61 to staff the new rolling mills posed a serious problem for W. F. Gooch, then Works Manager. The newcomers naturally brought their families with them, which immediately raised the question of housing, as, despite rapid private building, the area was badly overcrowded. Furthermore, they were almost certainly moving from 'tied' company houses of the ironmasters in Wales, and, therefore, had no finance to assist them. Lastly, they were to all intents and purposes at that time 'foreigners'. It occurred to the management that the 'barracks' were completely under-used and, as a stop-gap measure, hasty steps were taken to commence internal alterations to this building. 'Flats' were formed by re-arranging the many separate batchelor rooms (one report says there were about a hundred of such small rooms), into groups of three or four-roomed units. This was done

in time for about twenty families to move in on arrival. Of course, the communal washing, cooking, bakehouse, and other amenities of the original building were unaltered, and many are the stories of the not so neighbourly squabbles that were the inevitable outcome of such an arrangement. As well as the twenty wives, there must have been about 50 or 60 children, so it is not surprising to find it reported that W. F. Gooch had almost daily to make personal visits there to settle domestic arguments. No doubt the husbands were carpeted also! The contractor for the mill, Thomas Ellis, solved the problem for his staff. The exact arrangements are not easily traceable but the most likely is that he negotiated for one of the benevolent societies to underwrite in effect a block mortgage. Whatever the method, the result can be seen to this day in the second and less recognised railway village of New Swindon. This is the block of two streets of stone cottages on the south side of what is now Faringdon Road known originally and inevitably as 'Cambria Buildings', facing on to the park. The rear row of cottages is still known as Cambria Place, and a small Baptist chapel was built in the centre of this block. The history of this small church, originally Welsh-speaking, confirms the likely origin of the group of workmen. When later in the 19th century this church was joined with the larger Baptist church in New Swindon, an outstanding debt on a loan was paid off to the Monmouthshire Baptist Association, in which county Tredegar then stood, and from where most of the rolling mills' staff are thought to have originated. In many ways this small estate is as remarkable as the railway village proper, even if only for the way in which it came into being, and it is hoped that care will be taken to preserve it as carefully as the local authority has its older neighbour.

It is appropriate here to look ahead to 1867, for in the latter part of this year, the 'barracks', emptied of its Welsh occupants, was sold to a body known as the New Swindon Wesleyan Chapel who converted it essentially to the form it is seen in now as the GWR Museum. It became the centre for this denomination in New Swindon for some ninety years, being opened as a church in 1869. It was, together with St. Mark's to have great influence on the life of New Swindon, which we have studied in some detail in this chapter. But changes were looming on the horizon which would again prove momentous to Swindon, and we must now look at the larger canvas of the GWR as a whole to set the scene for the next act in the drama.

Chapter Four

1861~1877 The Turbulent Years

The next sixteen years at Swindon Works were to be arguably the most turbulent, yet also the most progressive, in its long history. The GWR Company had weathered many storms, both financial and political, and it was now having to face up squarely to the problems of the break of gauge, particularly where carriage of freight was concerned. It had already accepted the narrow gauge (NG) by absorbing into its organization a group of NG railways; and more were to follow. One result of this amalgamation was the addition of a third rail to the broad gauge (BG) between Reading and Paddington by January 1861, which allowed NG trains to run from Paddington through to Chester and beyond. Relations with the BG railways with which it was closely associated, particularly the Bristol & Exeter, the South Devon and the South Wales, were not always easy, and the same can be said of some of the other large 'foreign' railways, particularly the London & South Western, London & North Western, and Midland with which it found itself in successive situations of friction or agreement. Many of the old group of directors and officers had gone or were soon to go, and policy changes were inevitable.

Over these twenty years Swindon had struggled into being, only to be knocked back by retrenchment just as its operations were becoming firmly established. The return to normality after the period of recession was slow, and, although there had been some extensions in 1854, a Works plan of 1861, if available, would not have shown much variation, except for the addition of the rolling mills, from one of 1843. Certain problems had been surmounted, however, particularly in adapting the Works to build as well as repair locomotives. But even if every effort had been made it is doubtful whether more than ten new locomotives could have been built per year with the equipment and space available. This figure could not meet the replacement rate then becoming imminently necessary, let alone the work which could arise from the expansion of the Company's operations. In at least one respect it was ready for an increase in activities because the manpower position was now greatly to its advantage owing to the quick increase in local population. Taking Swindon and the adjoining area of Stratton St. Margaret together, the population figures over three decades show the trend:-

Year	1841	1851	1861	1871
Swindon	2,459	4,879	6,856	11,720
Stratton St. Margaret	1,565	1,725	1,642	2,527
TOTAL	4,024	6,604	8,498	14,247
Percentage increase over previous 10 years	-	64%	29%	68%

People were still being attracted to the area to find railway work but, more importantly, many families had been settled there for a generation and sons were now automatically offering themselves for employment, partly because a family tradition of railway service was taking shape, but mostly because Swindon was a one industry town.

As in the period 1855—61, further orders were now placed for a total of twenty two NG locomotives for the years 1862, 1864 and 1865. These were to meet the expansion of freight traffic in the Northern Division. More were also wanted as a result of the acquisition in 1863 of the West Midland Railway (which had been formed in 1860 from the Oxford, Worcester & Wolverhampton; the Newport, Abergavenny & Hereford; and the Hereford & Worcester Railways).Earlier relations with the first member of this group had been very troublesome over the broad gauge running powers on its line north of Oxford. Although there was strong Parliamentary opposition, this Amalgamation Act became effective from 1st August 1863 and, as a result, six directors from the WMR gained seats on the GWR Board. Policy changes now occurred which would not previously have been considered. Acquisition of the WMR gave the GWR another works at Worcester; a new Worcester Division was formed and Armstrong's responsibilities as far south as Oxford were restricted to Leamington in the process. It also brought into GWR stock a further mixed bag of one hundred and thirty NG locomotives. E. Wilson, the WMR Locomotive Superintendent, stayed on at Worcester for a short while as Divisional Superintendent.

Coincidentally, matters came to a head with the BG South Wales Railway (SWR). Leased and operated by the GWR, this line ran from Gloucester to New Milford in West Wales and carried through BG traffic from Paddington and the West Country, and had a major portion of the country's Irish traffic through its port at Milford Haven. Its disadvantage was that the increasing coal traffic from the expanding South Wales coalfields was difficult to win, since the railways in those valleys were all NG because of the terrain they served. Also, the break of gauge transhipment costs was a deterrent to seizing the long-haul traffic from coastal shipping. Consequently, the SWR Board made it clear that conversion from BG to NG was most desirable. It did not help the situation by having its line from Landore (Swansea) to Milford laid with the sleeperless Barlow rail. Although originally cheap to lay and theoretically easy to alter gauge, it was not a very satisfactory track for the increasing train loads. The amalgamation of the SWR took place on the same date and under similar conditions as that of the WMR, putting these problems firmly into the lap of the GWR Board.

In the previous year Gooch had designed BG locomotives for the new Metropolitan Railway, an 'underground' railway built on the 'cut and cover' method. This ran from Paddington to Farringdon in the City and to the new meat market of Smithfield. The GWR was to provide the rolling stock and work the line. These locomotives exercised Gooch's ingenuity, as they needed 'to consume their own smoke' using the terms of the day, and were the first in the country fitted with condensing apparatus for working in the tunnels. In his scientific researches Gooch had some years previously made tests to see how far a locomotive could run without a blast through or over the fire; he was thus acquainted with the problems. The result was a BG 2-4-0 with outside cylinders — an arrangement necessary to allow the water tanks and condensing equipment to be placed under the boiler. Ten of them were built at Swindon in 1863/4 and twelve built privately by Messrs Kitson and the Vulcan Foundry. They were the last locomotives to be designed by Gooch.

As has been intimated, Gooch was becoming very unhappy in his relationship with the Board. Whilst some longer serving members of the Board were still in office, together with a few of his old officer colleagues, particularly Charles Saunders, he was reasonably content, although there had been periods of conflict. As one of the country's foremost engineers, he also undertook considerable private professional work. He was a colliery owner in his own right and on behalf of others. In 1860 he became a director of the Company owning Brunel's huge steamship the *Great Eastern*, which was already well launched on its short chequered career. In the same year, he voyaged in her to America on a sales promotion trip. He had considered severing his connection with the GWR for some time, as seemed apparent, in 1857, from his moves to place his brother at Swindon with a view to future succession to the post of Locomotive Superintendent. However, his health was not good and, in January 1863, soon after the Metropolitan Railway was opened, he suffered a collapse and was advised to take a trip abroad. He left for Italy in mid March. While returning through Switzerland he had an urgent message from the ageing Saunders to return as soon as possible because of trouble over the working of the Metropolitan, resulting in the withdrawal of the GWR stock from the line. Gooch was also appalled at the appointment, in 1863, of Richard Potter, as GWR chairman, formerly chairman of the WMR. He also had no confidence in the new directors now appointed from both the WMR and SWR, with whom he had repeatedly crossed swords in the past. The feeling was apparently

mutual and, during the first meeting he attended of this reconstituted Board, Gooch walked out and never again attended. Before leaving for Italy he had joined Whitworth in forming, at Manchester, a 'gun company' mainly so that he could later place one of his sons, but also as a new interest for himself when he retired from the railway. In 1864, he also joined the company which was about to make another attempt to lay a transatlantic telegraph cable and, on their behalf, was able to purchase the *Great Eastern* for a very low sum. He was already the largest bond owner of the ship. Gooch's old friend and colleague, Charles Saunders, retired from the GWR after the amalgamation with the WMR and SWR, and this left him with little cause to remain with the Company, although there is no doubt of his continued feelings of loyalty to it. Eventually, in late March 1864, he finally decided to resign, but not before discussing the matter of a likely successor with Potter. He was not surprised to find that the chances of his brother being appointed to his post were nil, but amazed to find that they would not even consider Armstrong from Wolverhampton. It transpired that the WMR caucus on the Board had already made soundings to Sacré of the Manchester, Sheffield & Lincoln Railway. Gooch was so incensed that he wrote personal letters to all his old Board friends. As a result Potter was outvoted and Joseph Armstrong received the appointment to Gooch's great satisfaction. Although his notice did not expire until 6th October, he ceased working for the GWR on 7th September 1864, after 27 years service. It was obviously not possible for his brother William to stay at Swindon as manager under the circumstances, so Gooch formed a company to purchase the Vulcan Foundry, placing William there as Managing Director. Another notable loss at that time was the retirement of J. Gibson who had been the Carriage Superintendent at Paddington for 18 years since 1846. This is the man who is remembered for the 'Gibson Ring' method of securing railway tyres to wheel centres, a method which is still in general use in this country and abroad. It was decided by the Board that Joseph Armstrong should occupy both posts and he received from the Board his appointment as the first Locomotive Carriage & Wagon Superintendent of the GWR in June 1864.

We can now examine in more detail the life and career of Armstrong. Born in the same year as Gooch at Bewcastle, Cumberland, in 1816, he was 48 years old on his appointment. Educated in Newcastle, he became intimately connected as a lad with Stephenson's Wylam engines and started work at an early age under Robert Hawthorn, the engineer of Walbottle Colliery, Newburn on Tyne, where his family were now living. This Robert Hawthorn was the father of Robert and William Hawthorn who later formed the famous locomotive works of that name in

Plate 50: Joseph Armstrong — Locomotive, Carriage & Wagon Superintendent (1864–1877).

British Rail

Newcastle. Armstrong also became acquainted with Timothy Hackworth, and it is thought that through this association came his first chance to drive locomotives on the Stockton & Darlington Railway. By 1836 he was working as a driver on the Liverpool & Manchester Railway, later moving to the Hull & Selby Railway where his interest in this company was the greatly improved locomotives of George Gray. He was soon promoted to foreman at Hull running shed and repair shops. Gray moved to the London & Brighton line as superintendent in 1845 and Armstrong followed him but did not stay after Gray moved again. His experience secured him the position of Assistant Locomotive Superintendent of the Shrewsbury & Chester Railway at Saltney, Chester, in 1847 under Edward Jeffreys, becoming superintendent when that engineer left in 1852. In 1853 he took over control of the combined stock of the Shrewsbury & Chester, and Shrewsbury & Birmingham lines, moving to Wolverhampton. When these two companies were amalgamated with the GWR in 1854, he became assistant to Gooch and Northern Division Superintendent.

Armstrong was thus a very experienced railway engineer by the time of his appointment in 1864 to the new post of LC&W Superintendent of the GWR. He had strong family and professional connections

with the northern narrow gauge group of railwaymen. In his ten years at Wolverhampton he had gathered around him a team of men upon whom he could rely. He was also, like his mentor Timothy Hackworth of Shildon, a dedicated Wesleyan Methodist, being a circuit lay preacher and class leader during all his adult years. Consequently his inherent attitude to the social and moral conditions of the time was very enlightened, as was his relationship with his fellow men, whether employer or employee. The decision to make his headquarters at Swindon was inevitable if he was to weld together successfully the locomotive, carriage and wagon departments, and he moved at the latter end of 1864 into the house which had been built for Sturrock. It would be very interesting to have details of the personal remit he received from the Board on his appointment. Policy changes were planned both for the GWR in general and also within the new combined department. It seems certain that the broad gauge fraternity at Swindon, who had remained as aloof as possible from their narrow gauge colleagues, would begin to wonder what had hit them in the next few months.

Since it was not until 7th September that Gooch attended his office for the last time, Armstrong used the period from June to September in effecting a gradual transfer of power from Gooch, and to assess the new situation. Quite a vacuum in top management had resulted from the resignations and it was imperative to fill some vacancies as quickly as possible. The first appointment made was perhaps indicative of what was going to happen to the management policy at Swindon. The man who would have appeared as the obvious choice for manager at Swindon was John Fraser who had already acted as manager when Rea was ill in 1856/7, but was passed over when W. F. Gooch was appointed after Rea's death. He had subsequently become Locomotive Superintendent of the South Wales Railway and was therefore well qualified. Armstrong, however, now selected him as his Carriage & Wagon Superintendent in place of Gibson, although the post was no longer a principal officer of the Company, but a senior assistant to Armstrong. It can be construed that this was a move to clear the Swindon pitch for Armstrong's own Wolverhampton-trained protégés. Conversely it may have been the better post for Fraser, since Armstrong's permanent residence at Swindon would inevitably mean the curbing of any future Works Manager's freedom of action. In order to maintain immediate continuity at Swindon, another assistant at the Works, F. A. Bucknall, was appointed manager, but apparently only in a temporary capacity for a few months. His name does not appear at all in the Fawcett List (App. II). We know that in 1856 Bucknall was locomotive foreman for the Wilts & Somerset lines, and in 1862 was stationed at Weymouth as district foreman (or

Plate 51: Samuel Carlton — Locomotive Works Manager (1864—1896).

Author's Collection

superintendent) of the Wilts & Somerset & East Somerset area, which comprised the lines from Chippenham (Thingley Junction) to Westbury and Salisbury and to Yeovil and Weymouth and other branches. He moved to Swindon as an assistant at the Works before Fraser left for South Wales.

Armstrong's permanent choice for the post of Works Manager fell on Samuel Carlton. There is no doubt that this caused surprise at Swindon where the narrow gauge faction was found to be in the ascendancy. Carlton hailed from Liverpool, being born there in 1829, and apprenticed at the Liverpool (Edge Hill) & Crewe Works of the L&NWR. After ten years there he took a post with Pearson & Co., Marine Engineers, at Liverpool. He later moved to the Vulcan Foundry at Warrington, and in 1855 joined the GWR at Wolverhampton under Armstrong, later becoming foreman of the fitting, erecting and machine shops. This was the post he vacated on his appointment to Swindon.

Meanwhile the country had entered upon another period of wild railway speculation, which reached its climax in about 1865. Unlike the 1840s when the public were enticed into supporting over-optimistic ventures, now it was many of the railway companies themselves who were developing schemes for new lines all over the country. The GWR was in a very

vulnerable position, with the broad gauge given as the reason for building new lines into their territory to avoid break of gauge transhipments. Fighting such cases cost a great deal, and the financial situation was still very delicate. The GWR itself considered a new line; a South Wales & GW Direct Railway. This proposed a mixed gauge line from the main line at Wootton Bassett to Chepstow, crossing the River Severn near Oldbury Sands by means of a 2¼ mile bridge, and Parliamentary consent was obtained. The crossing would have been just north of where the Severn Bridge carrying the M4 motorway stands today. The same year a less publicised project was proposed by Charles Richardson, a GWR civil engineer, for a South Wales Junction Railway utilizing a tunnel under the Severn between Rogiet and Pilning, but there was little support, and the Bill was withdrawn.

Under the financial stringencies in force, any immediate large expenditure at Swindon could not be expected but the recently formed locomotive committee of the Board was required:-

> 'to make enquiry and take such action as may be found necessary in connexion with the recommendation that Workshops at Swindon be altered at a cost of about £12,000 and new and improved machinery be provided at a cost of about £10,000'.

It must be assumed that Armstrong had already had a look around Swindon and wished to use these modest authorizations for immediate necessities. The apogee of the BG had been reached with about 400 locomotives in service, whilst already the NG stock was approaching similar numbers. The new equipment was required for this changing pattern, but we do know that some of the alterations carried out now were more concerned with the safety and welfare of the staff within the Works, including improvements to ventilation, cleanliness and lighting. An extension to the steam hammer shop was made early in 1865, and a fitting shop added to the west side of the original repairing shop. Having obtained authority for the 'shell' of this new shop, Armstrong systematically proceeded to develop it by annual purchases of machinery and equipment, so that it became the principal machining and fitting centre for the Works. To power the machinery a further steam engine of 153 h.p. was installed. It operated at 80 p.s.i. and turned at 120 r.p.m. Its flywheel was 10 ft. in diameter. The shop was to be known as the 'R' shop following the system introduced to denote locomotive shops with letters of the alphabet. The carriage and wagon shops were later to use numbers to distinguish them.

In the middle of 1865 an announcement was made that was to cause great public debate. This was the proposal to establish a new Carriage & Wagon Works for the whole system at Oxford. As a BG organization, the GWR had not previously had its own carriage works, only the maintenance shops at Paddington under Gibson. New stock was obtained from outside suppliers. Acquisition of the S&CR and S&BR had also given them Saltney Works near Chester, repair shops at Coleham, Shrewsbury, and the OW&W Worcester Works. New NG carriage orders had been placed at Saltney and particularly at Worcester, but there was a disastrous fire at the latter works on 12th November 1864 when eighteen new carriages were also lost in the conflagration. The Oxford City Corporation were very eager to lease land for the project, albeit land that was flooded by the Thames nearly every year! The site was 22 acres of Cripley Meadow west of the station, but there was a strong and powerful outcry from the University, who saw the proposal as a commercial invasion of their preserves, and did not want their city invaded by a mob of 'mere mechanics'. The dons took the war into the railway camp, sending a deputation to Paddington, and there appeared amusing articles and cartoons in 'Punch'. The Board, under Potter's chairmanship, would not be diverted from their opinion that Oxford was the best site, based on its position as the boundary between the BG and NG sections of the railway. Other towns offered to have the new works: Reading, Abingdon, Banbury and Warwick. Swindon also made its feelings felt, the initiative in this case coming from the tradesmen of the Old Town, supported by the local gentry. A 'memorial', or petition as we would now call it, was prepared by them and carried 172 signatures, about 90% of these being in some form of business or trade in the town. The document reads:-

'To the Directors of the Great Western Railway Company.

The Memorial of the Inhabitants of Swindon Wilts Sheweth;

That your Memorialists having heard of the intended removal of the Carriage Department of your Company from Paddington they beg respectfully to represent that New Swindon presents an eligible site for establishing the works in as much as your Locomotive Department is now established, the extensive character of which with the large population consisting chiefly of the Artisans and Labourers already located there, seem to point out the desirable position which New Swindon affords of having the Locomotive and Carriage Departments in the same locality.

At New Swindon provision has already been made for a numerous Population and can readily be extended to meet any increase, there are numerous places of Public Worship, Schools, an excellent Mechanics Institute and Library, an extensive public recreation ground, and Market both at Old and New Swindon. The Town of New Swindon is well drained and lighted, and arrangements are being made to supply pure water to the whole of the District.

It is believed that if any land is required beyond the quantity now held in hand by the company it can be procured at a reasonable rate contiguous to the Factory at New Swindon, and also that the Cottages and accommodation for the work people would be amply provided.

Your Memorialists therefore pray that the Directors will be pleased to take into consideration the favourable position afforded at New Swindon for the establishment of the Carriage Department there'.

It is not surprising that the first signatures on the petition were two large landowners in the area, followed by the principal solicitors and a bank manager! The West Midland faction on the Board led by the chairman, however, were determined to have the new establishment within their former territory. The excuse for not considering Swindon was that there was no narrow gauge connection. Whilst true, the gauge had been mixed from Oxford to Paddington since October 1861 and there was already a long term plan for similar conversions over a large portion of the system. So the short distance from Didcot to Swindon was really no problem at all.

The new Board had considerably upset the financial equilibrium of the Company during their short period of power at Paddington with a policy of larger financial outlay to obtain greater returns. They had amassed capital projects of nearly £3 million, including the South Wales Direct line referred to earlier. The Oxford Carriage Works project was to cost about £80,000, nearly twice the actual cost of the original Locomotive Works at Swindon. (There had been no appreciable devaluation of the currency). Potter was now in a difficult position, and having other interests outside the railway, pressure of business was given as the reason for tendering his resignation in September 1865. He left the directors with the unenviable task of finding someone with the ability and will to attempt to rescue the Company.

Since leaving the GWR in September 1864 Gooch had worked with Whitworth at their armaments company and taken great interest in the revived Atlantic cable project. He was asked to stand for Parliament as a Conservative, for the Cricklade constituency which included Swindon and he was in little doubt that his standing at Swindon would ensure his election. Parliament was dissolved early in 1865 and he started his canvassing in March. He commenced early as he wished to be on the *SS Great Eastern* to take control of the telegraph cable laying, boarding the ship on 10th July. Three days later he heard he had won a Parliamentary seat. The cable laying proceeded well until 2nd August when, about 1,000 miles west of Ireland, the cable parted and after fruitless attempts to reclaim it from the sea bed the ship returned home. He was greatly surprised on arrival to find an approach being made for him to assume the chairmanship of the GWR. After the resignation of Potter no other director had been willing to assume the heavy responsibilities that the post now entailed. Gooch's first reaction was a definite refusal but he was approached not only by the old GWR directors but also many of the officers and senior staff who had great faith in him. Gooch himself says that the latter had lost all confidence in the direction of the Company, which was visibly sliding into disorganization and discontent. Gooch must have appreciated the irony of the situation, having left the service only a year previously under a cloud and now being looked to as the Company's saviour. This strong bargaining position enabled him to lay down his own terms for freedom of action, and with this assurance, special arrangements were made for his appointment as director. He was elected Chairman on 2nd November 1865, starting his second career on the GWR, which through many trials and difficulties was to last until his death in 1889.

On taking office Gooch examined closely the financial situation of the Company and was profoundly shocked by what he found. The previous chairman's commitment to expansionist policies required huge expenditure to be met for which no financial support had been obtained. In addition to the items already mentioned, some £½ million had been allocated for new rolling stock, with some orders already placed, and an undefined amount for the rebuilding of some large stations. Gooch's immediate reaction was to call a halt to every proposal that had not gone too far so that a systematic review might be made and a programme prepared which would meet the Company's immediate needs and for which finance could be arranged. This last was to be done with unhurried care and consideration. He was, of course, still involved in the arrangements to manufacture and lay a new cable across the ocean, and other business undertakings. He took his seat in Parliament on 6th February 1866 and chaired his first half yearly meeting of the GWR shareholders on 2nd March. He received a very warm welcome at this meeting and was able to obtain formal support for suspending the costly schemes which had been envisaged. Steps were quickly taken to disentangle the GWR from the agreement to lease land for a carriage works at Oxford, and that matter was then allowed to rest for the time being. Having taken such immediate steps as he felt necessary to avoid bankruptcy of the Company, he again joined the *Great Eastern* steamship sailing at the end of June, and on 27th July he was able to send the first telegraph message from Newfoundland after successfully laying the new cable. Also by 8th September and by dint of some very resourceful work, he and his team had located and raised the earlier broken cable from a very great depth, spliced it to a new length and successfully brought a second cable ashore at Newfoundland. Gooch was awarded a baronetcy by Queen Victoria for his part in this great achievement, and this was gazetted on 13th November 1866.

He, therefore, missed the next half yearly meeting of the Company but returned home to even greater

financial troubles, which had arisen in September after the failure of the merchant bankers Overend Gurney & Co., with whom many railways were connected. In the ensuing panic other banks and financial houses failed and with them in particular went large railway contractors. The London, Chatham & Dover Railway fell into receiver's hands. The Great Eastern, the Brighton and other companies found themselves in great difficulties. as did the GWR when premature rumours circulated of their inability to meet debenture payments. Ensuing Stock Exchange distrust severely embarrassed the Company. Over £14 million was now held by the Company in debentures and loans, and interest rates had risen to 8.7 per cent, so liquid capital had to be raised quickly to meet these payments and thus avoid bankruptcy. Gooch was tireless in his efforts to meet these immediate commitments. An appeal was made to the Bank of England who refused assistance, so Gooch, with the approval of the proprietors, took the brave and unprecedented step of approaching the Government. The Chancellor of the Exchequer at that time was Benjamin Disraeli, and Gooch's letter of 11th March, together with Disraeli's reply of 13th March, is preserved. It is apparent that Gooch, accompanied by two directors, presented the letter personally but Disraeli was not politically prepared to take Parliamentary action to grant a government supported loan of £1 million to a large public company, whatever may have been the national consequences of its collapse. If forthcoming, such a loan could have produced a form of nationalization of the company by virtue of the direct financial interest the government would have had in the running of the GWR.

No doubt because of Gooch's obvious determination to save the Company, the Board was able to come to an understanding with the debenture holders, either by obtaining renewals or paying their commitments out of revenue. The cash flow, due to the huge size of the GWR was thus able to save them, and the total current net revenue was just enough to balance the books. Those smaller companies who did not have this level of business were unable to weather the storm. By keeping a strict control on expenditure (and a cool head), Gooch managed to hold the Company's creditors at bay and enabled the grave situation to be gradually overcome. The Board was reduced from 25 to 16 directors, and this pruning also helped Gooch to restore the balance of strength which existed before the amalgamation of the WMR and SWR. Most of this new Board were to serve for the next 20 years.

Thus, by the end of 1867, equilibrium had been re-established, but rigid economy still reigned, with drastic cuts in train services, and larger intervals between maintenance of rolling stock and buildings. The GWR now began to earn an adverse reputation for service that was to tarnish its image for a long time. Despite this, business generally was on the increase, and difficulties were encountered in meeting traffic requirements. The proposal to convert the SWR from BG to NG was set aside for the time being, but it was recognized that it could not be held off for long. An essential pre-requisite for such a conversion was the provision of sufficient new rolling stock, and the decision now had to be made concerning the new carriage works, particularly after the loss, by fire at Worcester, of vital stop-gap capacity. Gooch was now able at the half yearly meeting of proprietors in March 1868 to propose a carriage works at Swindon for an outlay of only £26,000. This was not a snap decision but had been discussed by the Board during their financial troubles in the previous year, and they had provisionally approved a plan for new shops at Swindon with standings for 100 carriages and 50 wagons. This item was minuted on 16th October 1867 with a 'shot' estimate of £21,000. Such was the optimism in adversity of the new board of directors under Gooch's leadership.

It is very apparent that Joseph Armstrong had contributed a great deal with advice in these matters, and he was aware of the gigantic task that was ahead in re-equipping the railway at the earliest possible date. Planning for a new stock of locomotives required a long lead time because of the design problems involved. The programme for new carriages was mainly a matter of preparation of the site and building the necessary workshops. To assist him in these problems, Armstrong again sent north for two able men in their different spheres, but of widely different personalities. One was William Dean, the other Thomas Gethin Clayton. The former was to devote the rest of his career and life to the GWR, the latter, after a short and effective period at Swindon, was to serve, in an equally distinguished way, the Midland Railway at Derby.

William Dean, who was to undertake the design and provision of the new NG locomotives as principal assistant to Armstrong, was born in 1840 and educated privately. His father was manager of a London soap works. Apprenticed under Armstrong at Wolverhampton in 1855, he took part from the start in the building of locomotives there, gaining a very wide experience and at the same time carrying off many prizes in mathematics and engineering science offered by the Society of Arts. Completing his apprenticeship in 1863, and, after a short period in the drawing office, Armstrong appointed him as his assistant. When Joseph Armstrong moved to Swindon in 1864, his brother George replaced him as Superintendent of the Northern Division, and Dean remained there as assistant and manager of the Stafford Road Works. In June 1868 he moved to Swindon as principal assistant at the early age of 28. He brought with him as his confidential clerk, W. H. Stanier, who

Plate 52: William Dean — Locomotive, Carriage & Wagon Superintendent (1877—1902).

British Rail

was eventually to be assistant to the General Manager of the GWR, and to be followed in the railway service by an even more eminent son, Sir William A. Stanier, F.R.S. Dean, apart from his work, was also to devote himself to the welfare of the people of Swindon as keenly as his superior, and for a much longer period, as we shall see later.

Thomas Clayton was cast in an entirely different mould. He had worked at Wolverhampton originally as a pattern maker, and had a very unfortunate attitude to those who worked with and for him. He was, not to put too fine a point on it, overbearing in the extreme but he had, by sheer drive, ingenuity and experience, clawed himself up the promotion ladder. It was these latter attributes which now attracted Armstrong, and he was to use them to ensure that his new Carriage Works was completed strictly to his requirements and in the minimum of time so that the production of carriages and wagons could commence. The title of Clayton's new post was Superintendent, but in modern terms it was that of Project Manager.

One of the reasons for the disparity of estimates between the Oxford and Swindon proposals was due to Gooch working an old trick again. As with the original Locomotive Works, (where he was aware that the land in question was already railway owned), he

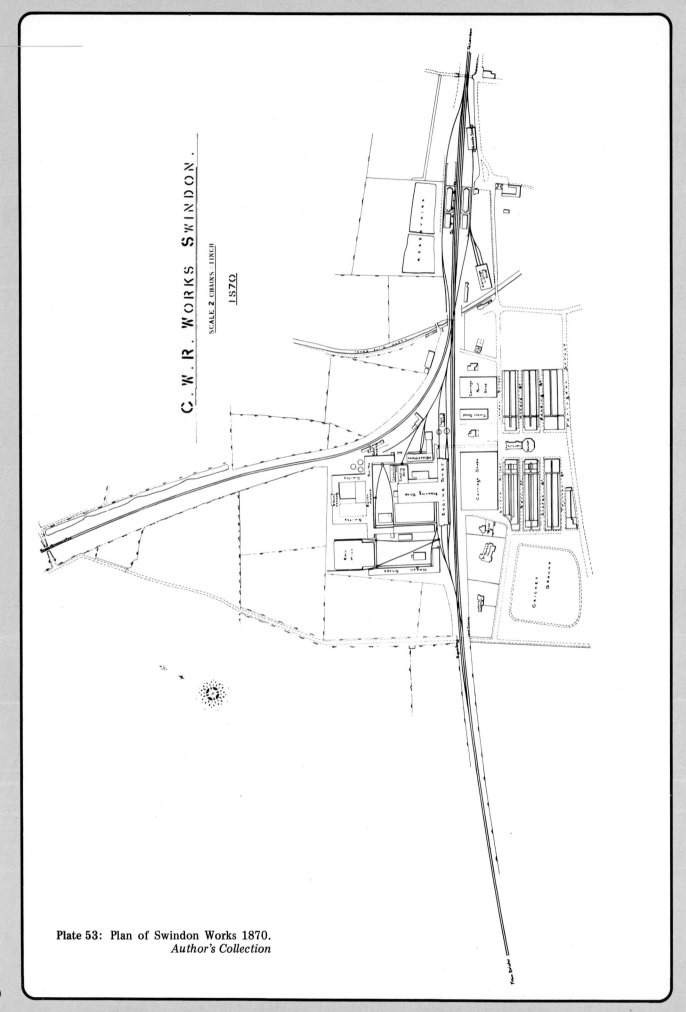

Plate 53: Plan of Swindon Works 1870.
Author's Collection

knew that the land to the south of the main line at Swindon, on which stood only two big houses for senior officers, was already GWR property. Therefore, no expensive and time-consuming land transactions were involved. The proposed new buildings would not, for the time being at least, encroach on these houses, and building must have started immediately. By the end of 1868, under Clayton's drive, the 420ft. x 265ft. building, the first in the Carriage Works, was ready to be internally equipped. Armstrong reported to the Board as early as 19th May 1869, that work was sufficiently forward at Swindon so that new orders for carriages could now be concentrated there in order that a workload would be available at the planned completion date. Comparison of the 1870 plan of the Works *(Plate 53)* with that of 1846 *(Plate 10)* makes these and ensuing developments clear. Additional authorizations were made for equipment during 1869, including the first steam fire engine. In 1870 new development spread to the area between the two managers' houses already referred to. At this time the directors authorized a new house to be built for Armstrong and future L&CW superintendents. It was completed in 1873 and stood in its own grounds south of the main line and west of the Works, on land purchased from the Rolleston family. It was named 'Newburn' by Armstrong, after the home of his childhood and the place closely connected with the early history of railways. Some time in 1869, no doubt shortly after the report to the Board concerning the progress of the new shops, Armstrong received authority to proceed with the construction at the Company's Works of the first large composite order placed by the GWR up to that time:-

	£
16 Locomotives	25,000
76 Carriages	26,800
460 Wagons	38,400
130 pairs of spare wheelsets	2,140
Tarpaulin sheets to the value of	3,000

Not all of the work could yet be done at Swindon — some of it was still going to Wolverhampton and Worcester — but it was a foretaste of the great activity to come to Swindon in the next few years. Armstrong must have pointed out at once the shortcomings of the 1843 Locomotive Works for such a change in workload, because a rolling programme of additions and improvements to buildings and a corresponding purchase of new machinery and equipment was also put in hand. These moves also illustrate Gooch's success in improving the financial situation of the Company. Indeed it is reported in April 1868 that dividends were again being paid in cash, only 2½ years after he was appointed Chairman. The Board was thus able to agree to this programme for the Locomotive Works, which was initiated as soon as the

new Carriage Works was in a suitably advanced state. More land was required for this, and the very large sum of £16,000 was paid for two parcels of land to the west and north of the existing works. The individual costs of these two plots is not known. The conveyance of the larger northerly one from the Reverend S. Bellas was completed by November 1871. However, the smaller and more important piece, between the west face of the Works and Rodbourne Lane, was under negotiation from the Rolleston Estate trustees until September 1873. Knowledge of later dealings with the same trustees implies some very difficult negotiations to obtain an acceptable price for land which was essential for the Company to acquire. Although similar problems were to arise later, it then became the general policy to purchase land which might be wanted for future extensions when the opportunity arose. A possible forerunner of this policy occurred in August 1868 when a large roughly triangular piece of land, immediately to the south of the station, was purchased. Whilst a small portion over which the east and west station approach roads ran was retained and eventually dedicated to the public, the major portion was sold by the Company, in December 1869, to Joseph Armstrong and a legal associate. This land may have been the subject of ideas for a southward rather than northward extension of the Carriage Works at some future date, which was later found unpractical.

The completion of the first major portion of the new Carriage Works is a suitable point to look again at the changes taking place in the community. We have heard how Armstrong had a very strong sense of responsibility for those people over whom fate had placed him. In 1864, soon after his arrival, the New Swindon Local Board had been formed, and during much of its life, until the Urban District succeeded it some 30 years later, Armstrong and his successor in the post at Swindon were either members or chairmen. Generally at least half, and often more, of the board complement of 12 members, were railwaymen. This is not surprising in itself, but it is evidence of the encouragement given to the men at Swindon to take a vital part in organizing and controlling their own environment. Under the guidance of the chief officers at Swindon, and often with the help from the Board at Paddington, this willingness to be involved in social and civil affairs by staff has, down through the years, made an immeasurable contribution to the community life of the town. A later indication of this is that, out of 81 Mayoral appointments, 40 have been undertaken by acting or retired railwaymen since the borough's incorporation in 1900. Armstrong was untiring in his work to make the rapidly growing town a better place to live in by supporting all the organizations already there, such as the Mechanics Institution, Medical Fund, Sick Fund Society and

Plate 54: The west end of Clayton's original carriage shop, built in 1868, but seen here about ten years later. This part of the shop later became a sawmill and the area which it occupied is now one of the car-parks for the Works.

British Rail

many others. One very practical undertaking was in encouraging the founding of the New Swindon Permanent Benefit Building & Investment Society in 1868. Gooch was persuaded to become President. Armstrong was one of the three trustees, and at least four of the directors at its formation were members of the Works management, including Samuel Carlton. The secretary appointed was William Hall, the long-serving locomotive accountant at the Works, and he carried on this work after his retirement from the railway in 1891. Public confidence was great and hundreds of the community joined very quickly, eventually becoming owners of the many houses that were built in the new streets generally to the south and east of the Works. The Society gave great impetus to the building trade and was, perhaps, the reason why Armstrong purchased the land referred to earlier, as his colleague in the deal was also a trustee of the Society. Two of the

streets built on this land, possibly with the Society's help, were named Carlton and Haydon, after members of the Works management. Others were named after towns served by the GWR not covered by the estate; Gloucester, Cheltenham and Weymouth. Gooch Street also appeared at the time, although the land for this was just east of that concerned in this particular purchase. Armstrong Street, south of Gooch Street, was to appear later. Systematically the surrounding farmland was converted to housing development and at last the conditions of over-crowding in the town began to ease. Even so, the progress of house-building was unable to eradicate these problems entirely for a considerable time. With the population almost doubling between 1861 and 1871, and continuing to increase by some 800—1,000 per year until the end of the 19th century, housing was to be a constant problem. In 1874, it was not unusual for three families to occupy a six roomed house, and rents were high. Many families were forced to live in villages up to 6 miles away from the Factory, with the inevitably long walks to and from work each day. Four other building societies were soon operating in the district; the Oxford, Reading, West Wilts and Ramsbury Societies. From available records it is known that by 1876 the New Swindon Permanent Society had assisted in building 209 houses on which a total of £33,635 had been advanced.

In 1866, Armstrong assisted in the formation of the Swindon Water Works Company to give both Old & New Swindon a safe water supply, although for the first year or so there was trouble with poor quality mains and the railway village was not served until 1867. The GWR was the largest user of this water and guaranteed the financial success of the project. The supply was piped from a new reservoir built into the escarpment of the downs at Wroughton some four miles to the south of the railway. The cost of the waterworks was £13,660.

On 31st May 1869 an event took place which was dear to Armstrong's heart. This was the consecration of the new Wesleyan Chapel, extensively altered from the former 'Barracks', and there was a whole week of special services and meetings to celebrate the event. It is not generally known, however, that prior to the purchase of the barracks for this purpose, a parcel of land of approximately the same area had been conveyed to the trustees of the New Swindon Chapel. This transfer had taken place on 1st December 1865, the site being opposite the cottages in London Street and between the two managers' houses referred to earlier, in one of which, Armstrong resided. This land was repurchased by the GWR in 1867 when the new Carriage Works were under discussion and the final site sold in lieu on 9th November 1867. It is also recorded, in 1869, that about 5,000 people took advantage of the Mechanics Institute annual trip. Many of them stayed away for a week's holiday — a sure sign of their growing prosperity.

The New Swindon Educational Board came into being soon after the formation of the local board, although the schools in New Swindon were still run by the GWR. Indeed, there was great pressure on the space available, with the original school overflowing, and this is made clear in reports in the later 1860s of the Educational Board's prize giving ceremonies. Some alleviation was gained by using rooms in the Mechanics Institute, and a further building was erected in Bristol Street close to the original school to ease the pressure. The original drawings of this building were destroyed together with much other material some years ago, but it is thought to have been completed by 1871. Even this addition was unable to cope with the rapid rise in school population, and in 1873 the much larger College Street schools were opened in the centre of the business area of New

Swindon. This was built entirely by the GWR, but taken over later when a properly constituted school board for the County was formed in 1877. Only the infants and girls were transferred to College Street; the boys remained at Bristol Street. A drill hall for the Rifle Corps had been built on the 'Cricket Ground' early in 1871, at a cost of £1,500, £1,200 of this being found by the GWR to replace the armoury in Taunton Street and even this was now pressed into use for boys until a new boys' school in Sanford Street, adjacent to the College Street schools, was completed for the new schools board in 1881. The Bristol Street schools were now closed. The old school and house were demolished to make way for a new road wagon shop. The newer extension was converted to become the works laboratory in 1883, and served in that capacity until 1978 when adjacent buildings were used for this purpose.

In 1868 an event especially affecting children was commenced by the Mechanics Institution. This was the annual 'Juvenile Fete' or 'Children's Fete' as it was later called, which was to become one of the largest of its kind in the country. In a few years it had established a pattern which remained largely unaltered until the outbreak of World War II (The development of this great social occasion in the Swindon calendar will be dealt with in greater detail in a subsequent chapter).

In 1869 another great event took place with the opening of the Medical Fund Society's new swimming baths. These were in a building, still in use just north of the Gloucester line junction, which now forms part of the diesel locomotive servicing depot. The Society could now boast the ownership of washing, Turkish, swimming and shower baths. Their washing and Turkish baths were first sited near the Mechanics Institute, and then until 1868 on a site at the back (i.e. the Faringdon Road side) of the 'Barracks' until the building was taken over by the Wesleyans. The new swimming bath adjoined the North Wilts Canal, but it is presumed that the necessary water came from the reservoirs via the filter house, and not direct from the canal.

In 1871 the committee recorded their opinion that a cottage hospital for the community was a necessity. Nine years previously, Gooch and the Medical Officer, Dr. Swinhoe, had been asked their views on this subject by the Board, but now Armstrong laid definite proposals before the directors. These were modest, and envisaged taking over the ex-armoury and cottage adjoining. A grant of £130 for alteration, and a £20 annual subsidy was all that was requested. The directors granted this, together with a second cottage for a dispensary; a third cottage was added later. The work was finished in 1871 resulting in a four bed ward, operating room, surgery, bathroom, nurses' accommodation, and a mortuary. It

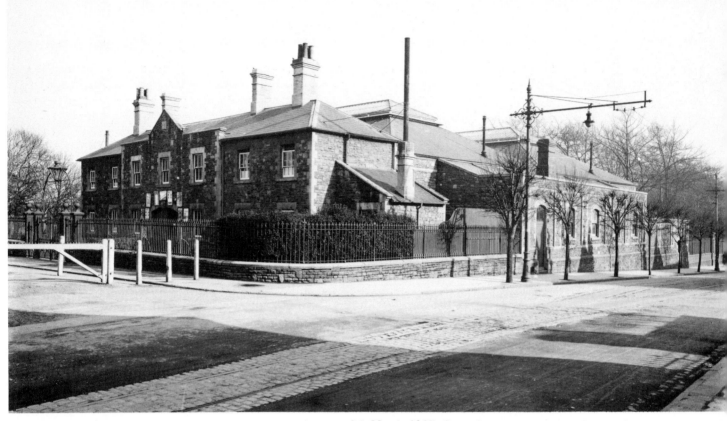

Plate 55: The 1871 drill hall, still in its original form on 9th March 1927. On at least two occasions it served as an overflow school building.

British Rail

Plate 56: A view of the original Medical Fund swimming baths, taken from the station, in about 1887.

D. Bird

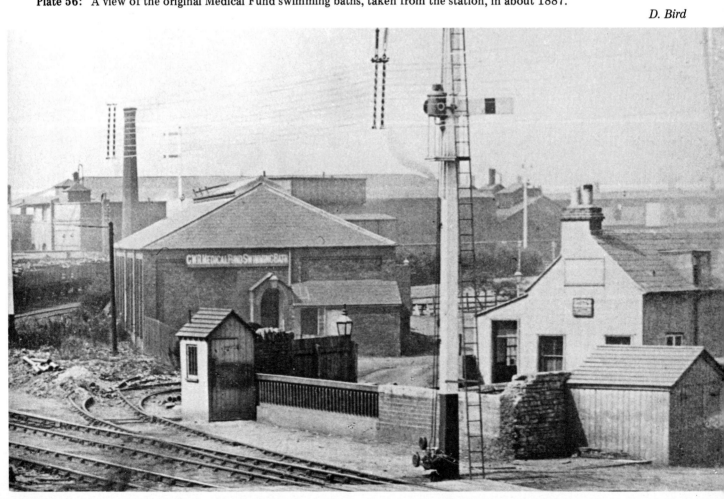

was formally opened in 1872 with a boost that was quite unexpected. At the half-yearly meeting of the proprietors on 29th February 1872 a resolution was passed that a testimonial of 5,000 guineas (£5,250) be made to Sir Daniel Gooch in recognition of his successful efforts in stabilizing the Company's affairs. Indeed at that meeting a dividend of 5 per cent was announced, a great achievement indeed. Gooch's immediate reaction was to donate £1,000 of this testimonial to an endowment fund for the hospital, and the Medical Fund Society provided the same amount. Thus with a £2,000 endowment, the future of the hospital was assured. The Society registered in 1873 under the Friendly Societies Act and thus finalized its stability. It was by then a flourishing institution with two surgeons and two qualified assistants, as well as the accident hospital — a full medical 'cradle to grave' service for the GWR community.

One last social undertaking of this period was the formation, by Armstrong with himself as chairman, of the 'New Swindon Park Committee'. The first meeting took place on 1st May 1873 and was necessitated by the lack of co-ordination in the running of the former 'Cricket Field'. The rapid rise in population (11,720 in 1871) had obviously put great pressure on its use, and better control was required. The committee was virtually the top management team at Swindon Works. The 'gardener' was to be provided with a uniform and to be sworn in as a special constable, if possible, and his wages raised to 20 shillings (£1) per week, although 'in future he is not to be allowed to sell flowers or cuttings on his own account'. The committee was to formulate rules and endeavour to amalgamate the various cricket clubs. Subsequent minutes of meetings show a much tighter control of the activities and running of what now became the GWR Park, and charges were made to the various organizations for its use where appropriate. They were also expected to arrange for entrance charges to games and other events, such monies being made payable to the Park Committee!

Returning to the subject of the new Carriage Works, two further buildings, a timber shed and paint shop,

Plate 57: The Medical Fund Society Hospital, opened in 1872, as it still looked in 1916.

British Rail

were built further east between London Street and the main line, and flanked by the managers' houses. These latter shops were authorized in 1870 and 1871, but late in 1869 improvements were put in hand inside the recently completed 1868 carriage shop.

There had, for a long period, been much concern that men entering the Works had to walk across the main line, a very hazardous undertaking in darkness or inclement weather. Indeed, there had been many serious accidents and fatalities at this crossing. The new carriage shops were, of necessity, built with floor levels corresponding to that of the main line. There was a difference of about 10 ft. between the main line rail level and London Street, due to a gradual fall in the land. Armstrong took advantage of this and constructed a pedestrian subway beneath the track from the street northwards to the main office block which had had a new east wing added in 1870. It was some 300 ft. long and 15 ft. wide, but had only 7 ft. head clearance. It should be recorded, however, that the Company had little option but to provide some alternative way of crossing the track, as this matter of safety had been raised in Parliament by a local MP, and pressure was thus put upon the Board. Ideal for safe pedestrian traffic, this new 'tunnel entrance', as it has been called ever since, was opened on 5th February 1870. Later it was to cause access problems when the motor van and lorry appeared. As a safety measure it was to prove a boon over the years, and its uniqueness has engendered quite an affection in generations of railwaymen and visitors alike. The roof of the tunnel, over which a large traverser was to operate for many years, was supported by large half fish-belly cast iron girders. The lower flanges were used as springings for intervening brick arches. The whole structure was built for £800. The floor could not be lowered later to give more head clearance, as the main outfall of the Works sewers passed just below the paved surface. One other carriage building, which came into use in 1868 and was enlarged a few years later, was a carriage lifting shop on a site just south of the station and on the east side of the canal. Presumably this was used in the early days as a repair shop only.

Another structure which was to become a landmark, and erected in 1870, was the high level water tank in Bristol Street. This is a graceful cast-iron structure rising to a height of about 70 ft. and surmounted, until recently, with a double tank of 41,000 gallons capacity. It was selected by Sir John Betjeman, that great enthusiast and authority on architecture and Victoriana, as one of the most interesting structures in the district. The original tank, alas, has had to be replaced recently with a utilitarian box-shaped fibre-glass monstrosity which completely ruins the sense of balance originally obtained by the whole structure. This tank, completed in 1871, originally took water from the new water company, and ever since has pro-

Plate 58: The water tower, erected in 1870, much admired by Sir John Betjeman. The Bristol Street School extension stands to the left of it.

British Rail

vided the high pressure needed for all the higher buildings which were to appear in the works in later times. The water problem at Swindon was now becoming difficult. One will recall that Gooch's only reservations when recommending the site concerned the water supply, referring to the matter three times in his letter to Brunel *(see Page 8)*. Already in the previous chapter we have noted the provision of the 'back cutting' ponds to improve water availability and even the supply now available from the embryo Swindon Water Works Company did no more than assist in meeting the Factory requirements. With even larger extensions to the Factory imminent the position could only deteriorate. When the line to Circencester had been opened, a station and a loco-motive water supply had been provided at Kemble, some 13 miles from Swindon. This water was obtained from a well near the station and raised by means of a horse-driven pump. In 1872, Armstrong installed a steam pump there and arranged for special trains of rectangular water tanks on wagon frames to run regularly between Kemble and Swindon Works, thence to be pumped into the storage tanks to augment the supply. This service also provided a useful 'running-in' duty for repaired locomotives. This Kemble supply is not thought to have commenced before the NG conversion of the line, but the arrangement was to continue for about 30 years.

1872 saw the start of progressive authorizations enabling Armstrong to convert the Works into a large production factory which was to be almost completely self-supporting. For buildings alone between 1872 and 1876, the large sum of £76,000 was allocated. This did not include the acquisition of the land already under negotiation or the equipment to furnish the shops when completed. These extensions are listed below in order of date authority, as this is doubtless related to their priority. Where expenditure was later increased, this has been included in the total sum quoted:-

Shop	Date Authorized	Vote (£)
New Iron Foundry	18th December 1872	8,500
New Tender Shop	18th December 1872	5,000
New Boiler Shop	19th March 1873	9,000
New Engine Repairing Shop	6th May 1874	12,000
New Brass Foundry Stores, Brass Finishers Shop, Grinders & Machine Shop	7th October 1874	15,000
Equipment for various new shops	13th March 1875	5,000
Enlargement of carriage painting shop	17th November 1875	3,500
New Engine Painting Shop	19th January 1876	6,500
New Gas Works	2nd February 1876	10,000
Additional carriage shops	15th March 1876	10,000
	Total	84,500

In addition, a number of smaller sums were voted for general machinery and special items such as a NG locomotive weighbridge, shop boilers, special founda-tions and walls etc., amounted to a further £13,000 over the three years 1874—76. One can imagine the activity of the small number of managers, including Armstrong himself, who contributed to the planning and preparing of estimates by providing the detailed information required by the Board to support the various submissions. Of special note is that of the five months November 1875 to March 1876, when four major schemes were presented and approved. It is a great pity that all the documentary evidence of this great period of activity was destroyed about 15 or 20 years ago by well-meaning, but misguided, policies of only retaining information still likely to be of use to the Works in the future.

The expenditure specific to the Carriage Works listed here virtually completed the buildings on the south side of the main line as they existed until 1963, including two of the three timber sheds beyond St. Mark's Church and Rodbourne Road. All the main buildings in this group were of stone, but by now this was obtained from the south side of the railway at Foxes' Wood between Keynsham and Bristol, and this quarry remained the stone supply for Swindon as long as was required. It was during this period that the well known large curtain walls joining the various faces of the new shops bordering London Street and Bristol Street were completed. These walls led to the

Plate 59: Working 'inside'. These south walls of the carriage shops, photographed in 1920, facing on to London Street, and the tunnel entrance, helped to give rise to this local expression.

British Rail

term 'he works inside' given to those employed in the Factory. This colloquial term is still used today, although newcomers to the town have often to be assured that it does not refer to certain H. M. residences, such as Dartmoor or Wormwood Scrubbs. When completed and rearranged internally, the three blocks formed a systematic production flow commencing in the west, where the sawmill supplied wrought timber for the assembly of carriage and wagon bodies. Then followed the supplying and fixing of internal fitments (finishing), and the final painting of the vehicles at the east end. The iron frames and wheels at that time came from the Locomotive Works. Most of this complex of buildings was erected under the energetic but fearsome superintendency of Clayton.

It was now that the Lot system, first introduced for carriages and wagons in August 1867 using alphabet codings, was revised and numbers introduced. Whilst the early records state that most of the orders were now placed at Swindon (early exceptions being Lots 5, 6, 7, 8 & 9), it is not certain that they were all actually built there. There would have been a period when both the new shop itself, and the additional skilled staff were 'working up'. It is likely, but not certain, that the new staff when taken on may have worked temporarily in the truck shop of the original Factory until the new carriage shop was capable of use. Work would have been of the simplest kind to start with. Indeed, Lots 1, 2, 3 & 4 were for low wagons, cattle wagons, horse boxes and carriage trucks. The early carriage designs were of the simple slab side and flat end variety, and, perhaps, incorporated additional embellishments as skills and facilities improved. If difficulties arose during this period, it is likely that some Lots or part-Lots would have been transferred to Worcester or Saltney, but this would not have been recorded. However, more sophisticated carriage designs were in hand, and Lot 57 comprising 15 NG 1st/2nd class composite six-wheeled vehicles finished in May 1872 was the first of the new generation of carriages from the completed shop. The previous Lot 56 for 1st class vehicles was in the same category, but was not completed until January 1873.

It is not thought that Clayton had control of this early output, but that it was managed by Samuel Carlton of the Locomotive Works, who was, in any case, providing the frames and wheels. Furthermore, although a successful 'driver' and 'troubleshooter' in modern parlance, Clayton was not cast in the mould of the type of senior officer encouraged by the Board, who was more likely to be autocratic but with a strong social sense. The selection of this type of officer was prevalent throughout the life of the GWR with only very few exceptions. Whatever the situation, in 1873, he was offered, and accepted, the newly created post of Carriage & Wagon

Superintendent to the Midland Railway at Derby at a salary of £700 per annum. His brief there was to reorganize the Midland's existing rolling stock, to design and build new stock, and lastly, to plan, design and build a new set of shops at Derby, as he had done at Swindon, and follow up with a new stock replacement programme. His experience eminently suited him for this new job, and he served the MR with distinction from 1st July 1873 until December 1901. Some of the finest coaching stock then in existence was produced under his management at Derby.

It was a few months after Clayton's departure before the first official Carriage & Wagon Works Manager was appointed. Consideration may well have been given to a single management structure at Swindon, but the better course prevailed of setting up a separate one. Again Armstrong turned to his old Northern Division to fill the post. It was the only GWR area able to supply the specialized experience. The choice fell on James Holden, manager of the Saltney Carriage Works at Chester. Holden was another scion of an old railway family, having been apprenticed under his uncle, Edward Fletcher, then Locomotive Superintendent of the York, Newcastle & Berwick Railway, at their Gateshead Works. He had

Plate 60: James Holden, Assistant Locomotive Carriage & Wagon Superintendent (1873—1885). He later became Locomotive Superintendent of the Great Eastern Railway.

R. C. H. Nash

joined the GWR at Saltney in 1865 and was appointed manager there on 2nd November 1870. His promotion to Swindon as C&W Works Manager is dated 18th June 1873, but it is believed that he did not finally settle at Swindon until the first weeks of 1874. He, too, in the fullness of time was to rise to high office there and elsewhere.

There is one group of shops whose origin is a little hazy. These are the first wagon shops built to the north of the station and east of the North Wilts Canal. The GWR had owned a large plot here since 1841, when it was purchased from a certain James Prince and others. The only portion used had been for the feeder reservoirs for the Works' water supply, but shops for brake equipment, smithing and wagon building appeared here, in the author's opinion, soon after 1873. There is a small sum of £1,500 for 'sheds for wagon repairs' mentioned within a larger vote on 29th September 1869 and this must have been used as an 'anchor' authorization to which could be attached any surpluses from other sources — a very common procedure. A smiths' shop must have been in use in 1875, as a 'steam hammer for wagon work' was purchased then. This cheaply built group of buildings was to be the nucleus of the huge expansion which began in earnest on this site about 15 or 20 years later.

All the new locomotive shops of this time were built between the original west boundary of the Works and Rodbourne Road, which ran northwards along the west side of the GWR Park, and passed over the main line via a level crossing guarded by disc and crossbar signals. Authority was now obtained to construct a road underpass at a cost of £3,170 but this was not proceeded with until 1888, possibly for reasons which will be discussed later. There was as much concern about accidents at this crossing as there was for the pedestrian crossings at the Works and the station. The new iron foundry, which was later to be twice extended, ran parallel to the main line eastwards from Rodbourne Road. It was of stone construction similar to the Carriage Works with a very elegant elevation due, in particular, to the system of fenestration. This style was reproduced in later extensions, and is to be seen to advantage when passing in the train between London and Bristol. It is regularly inspected by architectural students. The inside consisted of two 40 ft. span bays, supported in the centre on cast-iron columns, and provided in both bays with overhead cranes. The cupolas were on the north wall of the foundry. The original section was about 190 ft. long, with a high glazed roof supported by wrought iron trusses still in use today. Additional light was obtained by a row of clerestory windows running continuously down each side. This new shop promoted the development of modern casting techniques which were required particularly for the complicated combined cylinder, valve and steam chest units.

The new boiler and NG engine shops built to the north of this foundry also had a north/south row of subsidiary shops attached to their east side for machining, fitting and brass finishing activities. At the extreme south end was a new brass foundry. Further north again was the separate tender shop and locomotive paint shop. For the first time red brick was used for these new workshops, though the 'panel' method of construction was still used. This time, however, the inset brick panels were surmounted by freestone decorated arches, which helped to lighten the appearance of the large areas of wall. The tidy appearance of this arrangement is apparent to people using Rodbourne Road, as the main bulk of this new block faces it. Also in red brick, was the boundary wall continuing roughly northwards from the new tender and paint shops. Blue brick was used here as an architectural relief. The provision of new brass and iron foundries allowed the old foundry, situated east of the original BG erecting shop, to be demolished. A new NG engine shed was also now provided, north of the Works and to the east of the Gloucester branch. BG locomotives were provided with a single road lean-to shed on the west wall of this new depot, and this was kept in use for them until 1892. This allowed the gradual take-over of the old long running shed *(Plate 16)* for repair purposes. The space between this and the BG erecting shop, now cleared, was completely filled by a new extension to the erecting shop, which was built in stone to match the original buildings. All these additions can be seen by comparing the 1870 layout of the Works *(Plate 53)*, with that of 1880 *(Plate 63)*. Finally, more capacity was provided for forging work by the provision of a drop hammer shop near the steam hammer section which, by now, had expanded considerably.

Thus in the space of about six years, Armstrong had more than doubled the shop floor space which he had found when he arrived at Swindon, simultaneously taking advantage of the great improvements in machine tools and processes that had developed over the previous twenty years. In 1872 came the provision of a works 'hooter'. Prior to this, a large hand bell had been rung to denote starting and finishing times, but this was obviously inadequate for the extended works. A very large steam hooter (or whistle), similar to those fitted to steam ships, was mounted on the roof of the 1864 fitting and machine (R) shop over its steam engine power house. The range of this device was about 12—15 miles, and was sounded first at 5.20 a.m. to allow suitable walking time from the surrounding villages. The installation was officially licensed (and indeed still is, through the transfers of authority) by the New Swindon Local Board, and was deemed a great asset by everyone in the district, including the agricultural community. There was, however, one objector, Lord Bolingbroke, who had his seat at Lydiard Tregoze some 2½ miles

Plate 61: The locomotive paint shop (later L2 shop) authorized in 1876, pictured soon after opening.

British Rail

Plate 62: The much admired south elevation of the old iron foundry, extended twice, but preserving the same architectural features. The shop is now devoted to diesel engine repairs.

Author's Collection

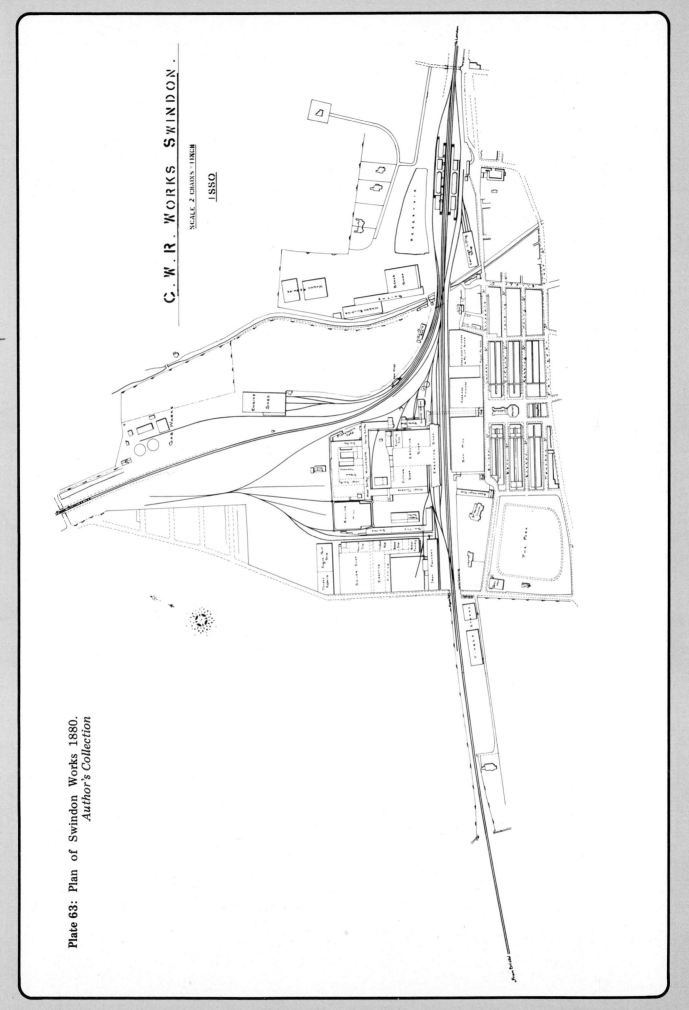

Plate 63: Plan of Swindon Works 1880.
Author's Collection

G.W.R. WORKS SWINDON.

SCALE 2 CHAINS = 1 INCH

1880

away. He had been confined to his bed with an illness, and objected to being awakened at the unearthly hour of 5.20 a.m. He forced an enquiry to be held which took place in June 1873, under an inspector of Local Government Boards. The local Chamber of Commerce supported the hooter unanimously. There was a petition signed by 4,360 railway workmen of the GWR, and one of 2,328 from business and agricultural groups in the surrounding area. There was only one against — the noble lord — and he did not attend the hearing, sending his doctor instead. This called forth wry comments from the inspector. From evidence given by James Haydon, one of the assistant managers, experiments had been made to improve the range of a small experimental hooter used since about 1867 and the tone and range had, in consequence, altered. As well as waking his lordship too early, it was also said to disturb his nesting pheasants! Not surprisingly the inspector ruled in favour of the GWR, and the hooter, although in a different position, still blows today at fixed times (but not at 5.20a.m.) and is still used almost subconsciously by large numbers of the town's population. Another facet of the walking time and the 5.20 a.m. hooter, is that the GWR in these early years of existence at Swindon had many footpaths from certain villages and hamlets re-routed and straightened to the Works, on the basis of 'as the crow flies'. These realignments were carried out at the expense of the GWR, and were protected by legal 'in perpetuity' clauses. It is feared that many of these rights have been overlooked in recent years of development, but no doubt the legal documents for such paths are still in existence.

The narrow gauge did not reach Swindon until the year when much of the first large-scale conversion was carried out in 1872. This programme had started in 1869 on the Hereford to Grange Court (Gloucester) and the Oxford to Wolverhampton routes, a total of some 110 miles, but only small sections were completed in 1870 and 1871. Then, in 1872, the whole South Wales route from Swindon to Milford via Gloucester and its branches were converted. The 'Up' line received attention first, whilst a minimal BG service was continued on the 'Down' line. After the 'Up' line had been converted, a similar restricted NG service ran on this line whilst the remaining BG 'Down' line was dealt with. There had, of course, been mixed gauge access from Oxford and Didcot to Paddington since 1861, but after that any delivery of NG locomotives or rolling stock on special vehicles was only necessary over the short distance from Swindon Works to Didcot. Nevertheless, this had been a very heavy traffic, particularly since about 1867 when Armstrong's new stock building programme began to roll. Much new stock was naturally needed for the extension of NG services over the routes now being converted. The BG stock,

when withdrawn, was stored in sidings wherever they could be found and in some cases, particularly adjacent to the Berks & Hants line, vehicles were actually run off the track fanwise into fields hired for the purpose until they could be called in for conversion or scrapping. In the year of the conversion of the South Wales line, a Bill was deposited in Parliament for the construction of a Severn Tunnel Railway from Pilning station, on the east side of the estuary, to a point on the SWR near Portskewett. The cost was estimated at £750,000. Having received the necessary sanction, work was commenced in March 1873 at Sudbrook on this great, but difficult, undertaking which was to take 16 years to complete.

The last of the major undertakings at Swindon in this period was the provision of a new gasworks. Supplies, until now, had come from the plant built with the Works in 1842. This had been extended to the limits of space available, but it was quite inadequate for the increasing demands now arising. The site selected was land which had been purchased in September 1874, immediately to the north of the new engine shed, taking in the whole width of the land between the Gloucester branch and the North Wilts Canal. A comprehensive set of buildings, comprising horizontal retort house, purifier house, scrubbers etc., was erected, including two gas holders and two houses for resident staff. New supply mains were provided to the Works alongside the track. The previous gasworks had achieved a capacity of about 40,000 cubic feet per day, but the new plant was capable from the start of 250,000 cubic feet per day with adequate room for later extension. At this time gas metering was introduced for the first time to households on the estate, and to other users such as the Mechanics Institute and Medical Fund. This is the first known reference to gas being used to light houses, but it is clear that it had already been the practice for some time. It is not certain whether gas was laid to the houses when new in 1843. However, before the introduction of meters, charges had been made on the basis of the number of burners installed, and this was before the introduction of the luminous asbestos gas mantle. Complaints now came from some tenants claiming 'incorrect' readings of their new meters, due, no doubt, to their former wasteful use of gas. Although the financial sanction for the new plant was not made by the Board until 15th March 1876, the gas was on line by June of that same year, so it was obvious that agreement to proceed had been made earlier so that the new plant would be ready to meet the requirements of the additional shops as they were occupied. This plant was to be extended considerably during its life, and latterly was purported to be the largest private gas works in the world. With the exception of a small sum for resiting the permanent way points and crossings shop to a more convenient position in 1877, all other financial authorizations

Plate 64: The 1874 gasworks adjoining the Gloucester branch, photographed just after opening.

Plate 65: Further extensions at the gasworks were made in 1891 to the horizontal retort branch (centre) and the building on the right, in 1892.

Plate 66: The steam-driven surface traverser, which replaced Gooch's double-tracked pit traverser, in the engine repair shop. The original roof can still be seen in position, but the timber columns have been replaced by cast iron units which still remain in use today.

were for additional works machinery and equipment. At this time points and crossings were also manufactured at Reading, but it is thought that after this rebuilding of the Swindon shop, the work was gradually concentrated there and continued until 1963, although outside contractors were often used when it was convenient.

An interesting item, approved by the Board in July 1877, was the insurance cover obtained for the Works to the sum of £100,000, placed with the National Insurance Company of Ireland. This policy was still in force in 1890 and illustrates the unwillingness of the GWR to accept financial self-liability as was the common practice in the 20th century.

We can now see how Armstrong had, in a few short years, transformed Swindon Works from what was no more than a large repair installation into a very efficient and self-supporting engineering works capable of economic production of locomotives, carriages and wagons and the periodic heavy repair of such stock to meet the greater part of the total requirements of the GWR.

Wolverhampton (Stafford Road), under the strict rule of his brother, George Armstrong, had ably assisted in the large locomotive building programme, and Worcester and Saltney shops had gradually been transformed into useful repair shops serving specific geographical areas. All this had been done starting from a position of near bankruptcy. However, careful decisions had been made to provide capital for projects which could be shown to have long-term economic merit. When the individual projects were approaching completion, they were at once put into use to work them up and to train the large number of new artisans employed.

In 1870/71, just as the expansion of the Locomotive Works was starting, there was a great deal of agitation amongst the GWR workmen for a reduction in the hours worked and also an increase in the rate paid. The former request was coupled with the national problem of extremely long hours still worked in many industries, particularly in the northern part of the country, and viewed as a social, rather than a financial, injustice. The outcome was the adoption on 1st January 1872 of the 'nine hour day' which was also being accepted in other areas. Its application at Swindon would be more correctly called the 54 hour week (of 5½ days), and was arranged as follows:-

Breakfast shift	6.00a.m. – 8.15a.m.	Monday
Morning shift	9.00a.m. – 1.00p.m.	to
Afternoon shift	2.00p.m. – 5.30p.m.	Friday

On Saturday, the half day ended at 12 noon. These hours were to last for 47 years until 1919. A ten per cent increase in pay was refused. At this time, the basic rate for labourers was 18 shillings per week rising to £2 or more for skilled men, but these rates

were high when compared with the notoriously low wages then paid to agricultural workers in the area. Payment of wages to date had been made fortnightly, but from 4th February 1872 it was made weekly.

For Swindon, this was also the beginning of the end of the broad gauge building period, since the imminent large conversion to narrow gauge could not be undertaken without a huge programme of new NG stock construction. Until August 1863, only 57 NG locomotives out of a total stock of 301 had been built by the Company (and only 44 of these at Swindon), but from then on nearly all locomotives were to be produced within the Company at Swindon and Wolverhampton. There were naturally some stock additions accruing from absorbed railways. About 140 had come on to the list in that way by 1877, particularly from the B&ER amalgamation in 1867. The position is best illustrated in the following table:-

	1864	1877	Stock +/-
BG locomotive stock	360	297	– 63
NG locomotive stock	342	1,351	+ 1,009
Total stock	**702**	**1,648**	**+ 946**

Of the huge increase in NG locomotives, Armstrong built about 600 at Swindon, and his brother contributed over 250 more from Wolverhampton in 13 years. For Swindon this meant 60–70 per year from the time the extended Factory was able to produce at a reasonable rate in about 1869. The measure of activity becomes phenomenal when taking into account the joint efforts of the two brothers from 1869 when the new numbered Lots for carriages and wagons commenced. We find that new stock built from 1869 until mid-1877 consisted of 1,963 carriages, passenger brake vans, horse boxes etc. and 10,173 wagons of all types! And all this came from one absolutely new works, while the others were still adapting to different circumstances. This huge new workload takes no account of the heavy repair programmes over the years, including rebuilds and BG/NG conversions. Although new production and repair rates were to be higher in later years, this would be when far greater improvements in shops, facilities and increases in staff had been made. This level of activity must rate as the highest ever achieved at Swindon, all under great difficulties, bearing in mind that it also included the building and equipping of new workshops in both locomotive and carriage departments using internal labour.

In locomotive design, it is not surprising that Armstrong's main concern was with simplicity, and orthodox practice became the order of the day. He did ensure, however, that his new NG locomotives were equally as powerful as their larger BG counterparts. He could not, of course, emulate their large boiler capacity, but the NG boilers were on very generous lines for the times and generally were provided with about 20% more heating surface than the NG locomotives produced by his contemporaries. There was also a great deal of standardization of parts. He did not generally provide cabs for his enginemen, being convinced from his days on the footplate that such protection led to drowsiness. Conditions had changed, however, and this policy was quickly reversed by his immediate successor. All his locomotives were of various six wheel arrangements, and this period saw the beginning of the replacement of the single-wheeler express locomotive by the 2-4-0 form, giving greater adhesion for the increasingly heavy trains.

Joseph Armstrong had presided over his enormous responsibilities with great ability. His only interest was in the great Company which he served, but his basic humanity meant that such service included total dedication to the welfare of the huge staff of 13,000 which he controlled throughout the system, including all the engine drivers, firemen, depot and other outdoor machinery staff. He saw this work as a specific part of his service to the Company, and his appointment as president or chairman of the many societies was never nominal, but always fully committed. As far as New Swindon was concerned, the only epithet which suits his position is that of patriarch. His firm but straight dealing was respected, as was his example to others in taking such an active role in all forms of local government, social service, and general welfare of the community. He came to Swindon when it was, in effect, still struggling with its own Industrial Revolution and in a few short years he transformed it into a model factory and town, with all the amenities that could then be expected. Furthermore, the notoriety of early railway towns for licentious living and drunkenness was no longer now applicable in this well ordered community. Richard Jefferies, the local author, writing in this period says that there was now little incidence of violent crime, drunkenness and immorality, and pays particular note to the higher intelligence of the employees. He records that 'where one book is read in agricultural districts, fifty are read in the vicinity of the factory'.

The strain on the constitution of such sustained effort and devotion to duty had the inevitable result, and Armstrong's health began to fail. Although pressed to lessen his activities, he steadfastly refused. He suffered a seizure during a meeting at Newport in the first part of 1877 and was eventually persuaded by the Board and his family to take a complete rest. He left for an extended 3 month holiday, but having got as far as Matlock, Derbyshire, where he was to undergo hydropathic treatment, he was again taken seriously ill with nervous exhaustion, and died early on the morning of 5th June 1877, at the age of 61. The reaction in Swindon to his death is most clearly transmitted from the treatment it received in the 'Swindon Advertiser', from where most of the infor-

mation concerning the event and subsequent funeral has been taken. Leaders and main articles on the subject took pride of place in four successive issues. Even allowing for the Victorian attitude to death and bereavement, the sense of loss which the death of Armstrong brought to the town and the GWR was very deeply felt. In the newspapers his work for the welfare of the community is given great prominence, as is his personality, including his charitable nature, and his acts of help and goodwill to the poor and needy. He is said to have lived only for his family and the GWR, and research into his life shows the truth of this. It can be compared favourably with that which Samuel Smiles wrote concerning George Stephenson.

Whilst there had been a large respectful following at the funeral of M. C. Rea about 20 years before, which was again to be seen much later in 1896 on the death of Samuel Carlton, there is no doubt that the public demonstration at Armstrong's funeral was never to be repeated in Swindon. It took place on Saturday 9th June 1877, at 2p.m. Action taken by Swindonians and others was entirely spontaneous and not at the wish of the family. All business in Old and New Swindon closed from 1.00p.m. until 3.00p.m. and the Works closed at 9.00a.m. after the breakfast shift. About 1,500 employees, all attired in black, met in the GWR Park at 1.00p.m. grouping under their respective shop foremen, 22 groups in all. From here they proceeded to line the route from the carriage entrance of Newburn House to St. Mark's Church, two deep on both sides of the route. Behind them gathered a crowd estimated at 5,000 to 6,000. The path from the church gate to the porch was lined by 170 volunteers of the Rifle Corps and the local police superintendent and 25 constables were in attendance. As we are aware, Armstrong was a Methodist and for some long time had been working, with others, for the provision of a non-denominational burial ground for the town, as part of his strong feeling for liberty in religious thought. This new cemetery was not yet completed, however, and the necessary dispensation had to be obtained for his interment in St. Mark's Churchyard.

A temporary platform had been built adjoining the main line at Newburn House where special trains from Paddington, Wolverhampton and from further north were terminated. There was also a deputation from the London, Brighton & South Coast Railway. The weather was fine, and the ceremony included Masonic courtesies, although the whole funeral was of the simplest possible character. The cortège was led by the vicar of St. Mark's and superintendent minister of the Methodist Circuit, together with almost all the Anglican and Free Church ministers of the town, with the Chief Medical Officer, Dr. Swinhoe. The coffin was followed by three of his four sons, and Sir Daniel Gooch headed the directors and chief officers of the GWR. There followed William Stroudley from the LB&SCR, virtually all the divisional and district locomotive superintendents, and many of the other divisional officers. The contingent from Wolverhampton under the local officers numbered about 100. Also represented were the numerous organizations with which he had identified himself, and many tradesmen of the area. In all, the cortège numbered nearly 900 people. Twelve of his Wesleyan associates bore the coffin to a grave in the south-east corner of the churchyard, over which was later erected a porphyry column, still seen by those passing by in Church Place.

There was a spontaneous move from all quarters for some form of memorial, and subscription lists were opened. The general opinion was that the memory of such a man should not be perpetuated by the more usual forms of statuary or garden of remembrance. The best solution possible was found, when the large sum collected was handed over for the provision of a new vessel for the Royal National Lifeboat Institution. This new boat, when launched, was named *Joseph Armstrong*, and sent to the storm and rock-bound coast of the Lizard Peninsula, where it was stationed at the little Cornish village of Cadgwith. It remained there for many years in service to mankind, which would have been in accord with his sincere wishes. This Swindon connection with Cadgwith was perpetuated for many years, as it became the choice of some of the senior Swindon officers as a holiday haunt. The last Works Manager to follow this tradition was R. A. G. Hannington, who died in 1937. When he built a new house in Mill Lane, Okus, Swindon in the early 1930s, he named it Cadgwith, and the house still bore this name until recently.

But the only true way of assessing Joseph Armstrong's great work at Swindon is by the use of that same inscription which is to be found above Sir Christopher Wren's tomb in St. Paul's Cathedral:-

'SI MONUMENTUM REQUIRIS, CIRCUMSPICE'

Chapter Five

1877 to the Century's Turn
Life with the Slumbering Giant

By chance, the death of Joseph Armstrong was coincidental with the beginning of a new phase in the life of the GWR. This phase, which was to continue for most of the 25 years now to be reviewed, only showed changes towards normality in the late 1880s. The establishment and town at Swindon being so much a part of the GWR in entirety, could not be dissociated with the state of torpor which now spread throughout the system. Although quite out of keeping with every other period of the life of the GWR, the reasons can be identified, and because of their affect on the development and work at Swindon, they should be examined first.

The reader will recall the adverse economic situation of the Company which led to Gooch's election to the chair, and the simultaneous loss of confidence in railway investment generally in the years 1864—1868. This crisis had been successfully weathered by the Company, and during 1870—77 there had again been large expenditure by the Company, particularly on major gauge conversions. At Swindon itself it was necessary to re-equip and extend, in order to provide the large amount of new NG locomotives and rolling stock to operate the converted lines, and to meet increasing traffic demands. However, whilst this process was still in being, the country was sliding into a period known to economists as the 'Great Depression'. This is usually placed between the years 1873—96, although the boundary dates are somewhat arbitrary. Furthermore, like all such periods, it was not just a gradual decline followed by steady recovery, but contained short periods where the process was much more acute. In particular, there was a false boom lasting a few months, commencing in 1883, followed by an equally rapid collapse, and not until the first three or four years of the next decade can it be said that the country's economy stabilized and moved into a growth situation.

This is the general background in which the situation at Swindon over this period must be viewed. But if one expects to find a period of extended gloom in the town, nothing is further from the truth, although this cannot be said of the GWR as a company. This strange situation has intrigued some historians of our economic development, who have advanced various theories and reasons for the comparative stability of the Works during this time. The Works, as modernized under Armstrong, was a highly valuable asset of the Company, and its management was now so cleverly manipulated that maximum value was obtained from it. The outcome was the maintenance

of a high level of efficiency, thus giving reasonable stability to the town during this difficult period. The accounting methods then in force were far less sophisticated than in later years, and because of this, manoeuvreing of financial resources within the Company could be readily expedited. The control of the Company was largely in the sole hands of the chairman, Daniel Gooch, and, great businessman and engineer that he was, strict direction was kept on each of his departmental officers. There is no doubt that Gooch saw the railway first and foremost as an engineering concern, without which there was no business, and it is therefore natural that his priorities usually leaned in that direction. But let us not lose sight of the magnitude of the operations. Whatever the state of the economy in general, the railways were in a steady growth situation during all this period, and at the time of his death, in 1889, Gooch was in personal control of a huge enterprise with an authorized capital of over £80,000,000.

The death of Armstrong dealt a heavy blow to the Board, as his great achievements had been accompanied by a high level of financial efficiency, and this had been recognized by them in Board minutes. The choice of a successor was really in no doubt, since William Dean had been appointed to the post of principal assistant some years previously, although the presence of Joseph's brother, George Armstrong, in charge of the Northern Division at Wolverhampton, must have posed some queries. Although Armstrong's funeral had taken place on 9th June, it was not until the afternoon of 26th June 1877 that Dean received a personal letter from Frederick Saunders, Charles Saunders' nephew and successor to the post of secretary to the Company, acquainting him of the Board's appointment. Dean was still only 37 years of age and had, under Armstrong's careful guidance, become quite a formidable personality, cast very much in the same mould as his predecessor in his concern for the welfare of the staff under him. Gooch, in his diaries, showed some personal concern at the situation which arose in this important department in new hands. He remarks 'I hope he will do well'.

To Dean, the situation posed its own problems, although his future relationship with George Armstrong, at Wolverhampton, must have been uppermost in his deliberations. Already 55 years of age, George had stamped his rugged personality on the Northern Division & Works under his control, and there were noticeable variations from Swindon practice, in particular the external fittings and finish of

Plate 67: The houses in the Wagon Works, which replaced those on the south of the line, awaiting demolition prior to World War I. In the foreground is Station House, then Marlow House. Compare details with those shown in New Swindon 1847 (Plate 41). The semi-detached Clifton House and Woodlands in the distance served as offices for another 25 years.

British Rail

locomotives and rolling stock. His elder brother, Joseph, had always firmly controlled the basic design features of rolling stock built at Wolverhampton however, and it is evident that Dean felt that if this situation could be maintained satisfactorily, it would be in the best interests of them both and the Company in general. George was, therefore, left in control with only a light rein from Swindon, and the two men worked successfully and in apparent harmony for about 20 years, with George not retiring until he was 75, in 1897. His great contribution was the continued training of selected engineers to fill high office in the company as they matured, thus carrying on what had already become a tradition and was to continue until the partial eclipse of Wolverhampton during Churchward's regime. An example of the quirks in local practice was that Swindon locomotive classes were always ordered in

Lots of 10 or multiples, whilst in the Northern Works, Lots were always in dozens until 1893. Shortly after his appointment, Dean and his family took over residence at 'Newburn' whilst Armstrong's widow and her family moved to 'Woodlands', one of a pair of semi-detached but commodious residences, (the other was named 'Clifton House'), which had been built adjacent to Marlow House and Station Villa. Those latter houses had recently replaced the two original management houses built at Swindon on land now invaded by the new Carriage Works. The new houses were on land to the north of the station, and were, also, in due course, to be overrun by wagon works extensions, although 'Woodlands' and 'Clifton House' survived as offices until the early 1930s. Dean, like Churchward after him, left no diary or mémoirs, and therefore facts regarding his private life are virtually unrecorded. It is evident from many sources, however, that he took a great part in public affairs as did his predecessor, by assuming most of the presidencies or chairmanships now vacant, and applying himself to them, plus some extra ones, with extreme vigour.

We should now examine the position vis-à-vis the BG section of the railway. The Bristol & Exeter Railway had eventually been amalgamated into the GWR in 1876, before Armstrong's death, and was followed by the South Devon and West Cornwall railways in 1878. The latter was originally a NG line, a third rail to provide BG had been laid in 1866 completing the BG line throughout from Paddington to Penzance. Although other small undertakings were involved, only one large one, the Cornwall Railway (Plymouth–Truro), remained nominally separate until 1889, although it had been leased and worked jointly by the GWR, B&ER and SDR from its opening in 1852. Thus, by the early days of Dean's accession, he had control of virtually all the BG locomotives still running, as the smaller factories of the amalgamating companies were relegated to running depots or light repair works, such as Newton Abbot. The book stock of BG locomotives had risen again from about 180 to 339 in 1876, but the number was to fall every year until the final abolition of the BG in 1892. Dean's BG work was, therefore, the modification of the additional stock to conform, where possible, with Swindon practice, but scrappings were inevitable in the process. It is a pity that, at this time, the opportunity was not taken to design and build at least one new class of express BG locomotive of new design, to show what could be achieved, but the traffic operation of the Company, since 1864, had been under the control of G. N. Tyrell as Superintendent of the Line. To say his approach to everything was cautious is no exaggeration, and he heartily disliked any speed over 40 m.p.h! During the early days of the strict economies imposed, by Gooch, to save the Company, such an approach was perhaps acceptable, but this unprogressive outlook became the norm, and it was indeed unfortunate that his tenancy of this important post lasted no less than 24 years, until his retirement, at the age of 72, in June 1888. As an old railway servant he had great influence and managed to oppose almost all plans put up by his divisional officers to improve the train services. Only the monopolistic situation of the GWR in its area made it possible for the Company to survive the depths of public antipathy which it engendered, with its low level of service, lack of attention to carriage comfort, the conditions of stations and all those other items which make up the public image of such a company. It may well be asked why Gooch did not force the issue in these matters, but it must be understood that although now solvent, during these years of depression the Company's finances were still finely

balanced, and he was becoming more cautious in his old age, (he was 61 at the time of Dean's appointment), having another 12 years of service ahead. Furthermore, he had embarked on the great project of the Severn Tunnel which was to be a continuous financial drain on resources, although of everlasting value to the GWR when completed.

Dean's only contribution then to the BG situation was to continue the policy instituted, in 1876, by Armstrong, of building standard NG locomotives, but fitting them with lengthened axles and wheels outside the frames to meet short term BG requirements. These were the 'Convertibles' and were to be a feature of Dean's term of office; not necessarily new locomotives, but often existing classes withdrawn for short term modification to BG. Such an arrangement destroyed any chance of producing a machine which could exploit BG capabilities to the full, and in any case, such a situation would not have been countenanced by Tyrell.

James Holden, who had been appointed to Swindon Carriage and Wagon Works on 18th June 1873, was appointed Dean's assistant on 17th April 1878, but in doing so an abnormal situation arose, in that he retained his post as Carriage and Wagon Works Manager. Until Holden left the GWR in 1885, the Carriage Works retained only an assistant manager, located in the new offices built in 1878 as part of the new brake shop north of the station. The impression is gained that there was still indecision as to the necessity of having separate management structures for the two groups of work. W. H. Stanier, who had been brought from Wolverhampton to Swindon by Dean in April 1871, became chief clerk, and later in the period, his post was redesignated office assistant to the LC&W Superintendent. Stanier was also very active in local affairs. He became much involved in the formation and building of the new Sanford Street Congregational Church in 1877 in the New Town area, this being an offshoot from the already well established church of the same denomination in the Old Town. He was also deeply engaged in management of the Sick Fund & Medical Fund, and was to be a member of the school board for 23 years, 16 as chairman, until the formation of the Borough of Swindon.

It is not surprising to find that after the authorization of £10,000 for additional carriage shops by the Board on 15th March 1876, twelve years were to elapse before any large sum was again voted for Swindon Works. During this period there were small sums allotted annually for the purchase of machinery, also some early purchasing of parcels of land to the site north of the station with later extensions in mind. Locomotive building, which had until recently reached such high figures, now settled down over the next six years to a more steady output, both from Swindon and Wolverhampton, and new building was in the order of 40 and 18 per year from the respective works, although there were 'highs' and 'lows'. Much rationalization appears to have taken place with the inevitable withdrawal of locomotives from service, so that between 1877 and 1883 the net total NG stock of the GWR was only rising at the rate of about 40 locomotives per year. A similar trend can be seen by examining the carriage and wagon Lots authorized during this period. It is clear that a policy of concentration of work on the largest, and therefore most economic centres, was being systematically followed. Also apparent is that much work was being carried out on the 'revenue' account, as distinct from the 'capital' account needing nominal proprietors' sanction. All rolling stock, by its very nature, has large portions replaced during heavy repairs, and this is particularly so with locomotives. The boiler and wheels wear quickly compared with other parts, and 'repair' often really means 'replacement', so that over a period, little may remain of the original machine except perhaps the frames, leaving the Company's stock in virtually 'new' condition. This form of repair expenditure eliminated the need for a depreciation account, 'new' stock being only authorized to meet known additional expansions in traffic.

A study of the Locomotive Carriage & Wagon department's half-yearly accounts for the years 1881–1887 inclusive, shows how the finance was skilfully manipulated to avoid, as nearly as possible, the dissolution of the skilled workforce that had been gathered, and to gain the maximum benefit from the large sums of money invested at Swindon in the years just prior to this period. We find that by December 1881 the capital stock of locomotives was 1,553, but already there was an excess of 156 (10.05%) available for traffic. By the end of 1887, whilst the capital stock had risen to 1,600 there was an excess of 267, or 16.69% over nominal. Further investigation shows that convenient round figures every half year were debited to the 'locomotive renewals' account, ranging from £35,000 for the last 6 months of 1881 and gradually decreasing to £22,000 for the last half of 1887. Therefore, over the seven year period, some £382,000 for locomotive 'renewal' was taken from the revenue account, whilst in the same period only £94,000 was allocated from capital account.

A similar picture emerges from the carriage and wagon statements, although the scope for financial adjustments in this sphere was not so wide because of the shorter life of their main timber components. Nevertheless, we find for the same period that the capital carriage and wagon stock of 38,330 vehicles, already in excess by 1,104 (2.88%) in 1881, had, by 1887, risen to 41,912 with an excess of 2,824 (6.71%). There was, therefore, an annual 'renewal' programme financed from revenue, declining from £88,000 per annum in 1881 to £66,000 per annum by 1887. The capital account does show the effect of

the depression, particularly the relapse in 1883/4, when after half year authorizations ranging from £30,000 to £120,000 for new stock in 1881/2/3 and early 1884, there was a complete halt in capital account authorizations until the last half of 1887, when £70,000 was again voted for carriages.

From all these figures the reader may well say — so what? The hard facts are that all this rebuilding and replacement took place when the annual train mileage on the GWR was almost static, only slightly increasing from 29.5 million miles in 1881 to 30.5 million in 1887, and, in fact, falling, in 1885, to under 29 million miles!

It can be deduced from the foregoing that as long as the proprietors were receiving what they considered a reasonable annual return on their investment, they were happy to know that the railway stock was being kept in good order, and did not question too closely how this was accomplished. Since the salaries of the officers and supporting supervisory and clerical staff also came from the revenue account, the chairman was able to organize a good holding situation for the Works through difficult periods. Whilst all the figures just quoted refer basically to all rolling stock work on the GWR, by far the largest share of work came to Swindon, with only Wolverhampton gaining enough to keep its locomotive activity viable. When the 'chips were down' after the economic relapse in 1884, Dean took suitable action, and in October of the same year reported that he had organized a general laying off of wages staff, in line with the temporary drop in train mileage — but everywhere except Swindon! So, as in later times, the smaller and less efficient works suffered, whilst the large highly organized main works flourished.

The pressure on Swindon, at this time, was not for great innovation, but trains were getting heavier and the 2-4-0 type locomotive was becoming more common on passenger work, although the large diameter 'single wheeler' still held pride of place heading the principal expresses. However, during Dean's term of office, the majority of locomotives designed by him were of the 2-4-0 and 0-6-0 varieties, either in tender or tank engine form. He did, however, embark on some experimentation, and the conditions allowed for better evaluation of single units, an opportunity not afforded Armstrong. Dean appears to have turned his thoughts to his first experimental locomotive very soon after appointment, although it did not appear until 1880. It was his habit to allot the lowest available numbers for experimental types, and this appeared appropriately as No. 1. It was a double framed 4-4-0 tank with a rather peculiar suspension arrangement to the leading truck. This did not prove successful, and was soon modified to the 2-4-0T arrangement. It does show Dean's great interest, however, in the value of suspension gear design, and its effect on smooth running and much of his future

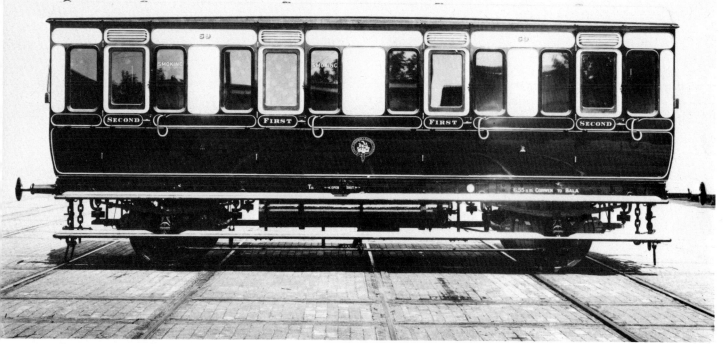

Plate 68: Narrow gauge carriage No. 59, typical of the early Dean period, was 26 ft. 10 in. long. Built in 1879, it is seen here as it looked in 1900.

British Rail

work on rolling stock lay in this field. His second foray was with a 4-2-4 express tank locomotive, no doubt bearing in mind the success of the B&ER in this field, although in BG, under their superintendent J. Pearson. Two were to be built, the second with Joy's valve gear, but the first, No. 9, was a very unstable runner and was rebuilt as a 2-2-2 tender locomotive after three years. No. 10 appeared in similar form two years later, but still with Joy's gear. His other project was in the use of compounding, now becoming popular on the continent, and also under F. W. Webb on the L&NWR. For this experiment, however, he chose a tandem arrangement of high and low pressure cylinders beneath the boiler of 15 in. and 23 in. diameter respectively, with a 21 in. stroke. The first, No. 7, appeared in February 1886, followed shortly afterwards by No. 8 of different dimensions. No great success was attained with these either, but one does feel that, perhaps, the idea, which had theoretical support, was not engineered too successfully. With his experimental work Dean appears to have wanted to put too many new ideas into one machine, and there is little doubt that this point was noted by at least one of a group of young engineers on his staff, now rising to prominence.

Dean's first major additions to the express passenger 2-2-2 locomotive stock were a reflection of Gooch's style with sandwich frames. With their 18 in. by 24 in. cylinders and 7 ft. diameter driving wheels, their performance was excellent. Appearing as Nos. 157—166

in 1879, many of them gave over thirty years service, and No. 165, withdrawn in January 1915, was not only the last of its type, but also the last of the 2-2-2 wheel arrangement to run a train on the GWR, a type which dated back to Stephenson. In 1891/2 there was a later batch of the same wheel arrangement but with 20 in. by 24 in. cylinders and 7 ft. 8½ in. diameter driving wheels. The increased dimensions required the provision of a larger boiler for this '3001' class. There were 30 in this class and ten of them were built from the beginning as 'Convertibles' to augment urgently needed BG motive power, reverting to NG after the 1892 conversion *(see Plate 72)*. The boiler was quite long compared to the diameter and also had a raised casing over the firebox for the first time on new builds. The extra weight this long configuration imposed at the front end made for unsteady running, and subsequent locomotives in the class (3031 onwards), appeared in the 4-2-2 arrangement, and eventually all the earlier locomotives were so modified. The result was an extremely elegant design indeed, becoming known as the 'Achilles' class after the name of the first 4-2-2 to appear, No. 3031.

The main 2-4-0 classes were the 2201 of 1881/2 and subsequent 3232 series of 1892/3, with slightly larger cylinders and heating surface. These were for use mainly on secondary services, and in South Wales and on the Weymouth branch. In 1889 appeared the 3206 series of 2-4-0 to become well known as the

Mileage, Locomotive Expenditure, and Traffic Receipts: "Great Western" compared with other Railways, Half-year ending Dec. 31st 1885.

	Great Western £	G.W. Per Train Mile d	London & North Western £	L&NW d	Midland £	Mid. d	Great Northern £	G.N. d	North Eastern £	N.E. d	Taff Vale £	T.V. d	Lancashire and Yorkshire £	L&Y d	London South Western £	L.S.W. d	Great Eastern £	G.E. d	Metropolitan £	Met. d	Metrop.n District £	M.D. d
Number of Engines (capital £)	1582	16	2323	25	1732	16	768		1506	19	161	38	909	16	539	11	673	10	67	20	48	18
Loco. Expenditure.																						
Running:-																						
Salaries, Office Expenses, & Gen.l Superintendce	11,033	2.51	21,286	2.82	12,172		3,997		9,938	3.18	1,543	3.79	5,508	3.12	2,755	2.80	3,399	2.67	776		616	
Contribution to Enginemen & Firemen's Fund	600																					
Wages connected with the working of Engines	164,291		236,381	2.92	228,250	3.19	96,336		161,685		23,086	5.75	101,783	3.12	61,928	2.80	87,818	2.69	10,604	2.80	7,911	2.97
Coal and Coke	76,501	1.47	139,331	1.66	116,074	1.60	67,124		96,876	1.91	13,945	3.27	57,483	1.76	78,327	3.11	71,692	2.17	13,101	3.46	10,269	3.07
Water	13,345	.20	4,389	.08	12,597	.08	1,826		13,191	.26	2,144	.33	7,944	.33	7,859	.22	7,168	.18	1,671	.44	1,719	.53
Oil, Tallow, and other Stores	12,863	.19	27,865	.33	24,052	.33	13,814		14,187	.28	3,359		16,103	.44	16,031	.49	6,684	.26	1,186	.31	1,055	.31
Total "Running"	266,959	4.39	601,961	4.84	381,391	5.26	185,733		285,916.5	5.64	42,531	10.50	183,313	5.63	165,616	6.84	177,422	5.40	26,562	7.01	23,044	6.89
Repairs:-																						
Wages	107,446	1.66	87,268	1.06	86,171	1.18	39,555		123,103	2.23	11,690	2.91	47,138	1.44	37,251	1.54	50,639	1.54	1,918	1.29	3,716	1.11
Materials	67,072	1.07	96,492	1.13	88,860	1.22	30,683		81,170	1.60	7,930	1.96	38,860		31,992	1.32	32,173	.99	5,244	1.38	3,112	.93
Total "Repairs"	174,517	2.67	183,762	2.19	174,581	2.44	70,062		204,515	4.93	19,610	4.89	107,083	3.29	69,243	2.86	82,810	2.57	10,162	2.68	6,858	2.05
General Charges:-																						
Repair of Workshops & Eng.e J.Tools	8,610	13	{15,782} Special		1,284	.01	3,686		9,618		2,134											
Gas	2,116	.06			4,317	.06			8,295		—											
Total "Gross Expenses"	484,360	7.42	628,794	7.51	573,701	7.92	263,460		509,816	10.06	65,851	16.3	249,901	9.82	237,644	9.82	263,631	8.03	37,500	9.90	30,578	9.13
Less, Power supplied for other Lines & for Switching	12,835				39,724		Dr. 639		8,295		2,112		23,577						424			
Total "Net Expenses"	471,525	7.40	615,185	7.51	533,977	7.63	264,099	7.21	501,581	10.12	63,109	16.0	272,327	9.04	237,644	9.82	263,631	8.03	37,011	8.03	—	
Per Centage on Traffic Receipts	11.94		12.05 / 11.79		13.99		14.71		16.21		19.14		14.45		15.81		—		12.29		—	
Train Miles:-																						
Passenger Trains	7,613,569	41 / 50.9	10,353,208	53.7	7,021,017	42.0	4,527,751	51.5	5,220,050	44.0	150,224	16.3	4,339,116	60.3	4,214,611	72.6	4,838,892	60.6	898,590		797,674	
Goods do.	7,717,820		9,280,511		9,756,735		4,258,695		6,663,973		742,810		2,847,398		1,689,263		2,959,710		—		—	
Total	15,291,162		19,633,719		16,778,732		8,786,446		11,884,023		923,034		7,186,516		5,803,930		7,498,592		898,590		797,674	
Total "Gross Train Miles"	15,658,848		20,068,730		17,372,303				12,156,839		963,203		7,808,704		5,803,920		7,877,606		908,792		802,112	
Traffic Receipts:-																						
Passenger	1,909,468		2,206,963		1,262,929		770,037		1,010,190		47,624		770,735		1,049,329		1,000,958					
Goods	2,029,601		3,007,221		2,551,892		1,003,728		2,083,007		282,379		1,112,900		450,415		795,830					
Total	3,939,070		5,214,185		3,814,821		1,773,765		3,093,197		330,003		1,893,635		1,499,774		1,796,788		301,573		207,300	

Plate 69: By national legislation, all railway accounts were compiled in the same way and were, therefore, comparable between companies. This page, from the locomotive & carriage departments' half-yearly statement at 31st December 1885, makes use of this facility. Of particular interest is the locomotive cost per

Plate 70: Locomotive No. 162 of Dean's '157' class. Built, in 1879, at Swindon and having 18 in. x 24 in. cylinders and 7 ft. driving wheels, it remained in service until October 1904, working mainly on the Southern Division of the GWR. A few of the class, including *Cobham* illustrated here, were named in the early 'nineties.

British Rail

Plate 71: Dean 'Single' No. 3009, *Flying Dutchman* built in March 1892. This is the form of the '3001' class as designed for the narrow gauge.

British Rail

Plate 72: Dean 'Single' No. 3024, *Storm King* built in July 1891 as a broad gauge 'Convertible', one of a batch re-entering service as narrow gauge in late 1892. Comparison, with the previous photograph, should be made to assess the minimal work required for conversion.

British Rail

Plate 73: Dean 'Single' No. 3032, *Agamemnon*, in the final elegant 4-2-2 arrangement of this class. In this form they became world famous for their beauty and performance. The author is proud to possess a set of the splasher crests in their original condition; two items from No. 3025 *St. George*, one from No. 3051, *Stormy Petrel*.

British Rail

'Barnums'. Still retaining sandwich frames, these however had the usual ash or oak flitch replaced by iron spacers, the remaining spaces being filled with teak pieces. These powerful engines had comparatively light wheel loadings, giving them wide route availability. It was this latter capability that made them suitable for hauling the special large circus trains around the country, of which Barnum & Bailey's was perhaps the most famous. There of course, is the origin of their nickname. Many locomotives had been built for goods workings to the 0-6-0 wheel arrangement, both at Swindon and Wolverhampton, and particularly the latter during Joseph Armstrong's early days at Swindon. They had been, almost without exception, of the saddle tank type, but tender engines of this arrangement with coupled wheels usually around 5ft. diameter were frequently built at Swindon from about the same time. This latter type became very numerous, but were of many types varying in detail. Indeed, the very first NG engine built at Swindon, (No. 57 in 1855), was to this arrangement, retaining its basic form throughout its life until its withdrawal 57 years later in 1912. By that time the railway had been supplied with the huge batch of 260 engines built to thirteen Lots between 1883 and 1899. These were

the famous 'Dean Goods' locomotives which became ubiquitous, together with their modified or rebuilt predecessors, over the whole system. They were so successful and numerous that Churchward found no necessity to add to the class or type.

Many served overseas during World War I, and many were to serve abroad again during the 1939—45 conflict, some of the same engines being selected for the second time. It was not until 1930 that Collett again built to this arrangement in the 2251 class, and even then, this was to fulfil a need for a lighter machine for lines of the constituent railways which had joined the GWR at the 1922 Grouping. An example of the 2301 class is shown in *Plate 74*. It was on such locomotive designs that Dean's reputation as a locomotive designer was based. Although trying out batches of new ideas from time to time, on one, or sometimes two experimental engines, his hallmark is to be found in the extreme simplicity, power, economy, ruggedness and easy maintenance of the major classes he designed, and among them are some of the finest engines ever to emanate from Swindon. A watershed in locomotive policy was reached in about 1896, and the circumstances and outcome will be discussed in due course. During the period 1877—1895 no less than 727 NG engines were completed

Plate 74: Dean goods locomotive No. 2449 of this famous class. From Lot 92 of 1893, this locomotive was not withdrawn until January 1953. It was one which did not see ROD service in the two World Wars.

British Rail

at Swindon Works, although about a third of these were saddle tanks of Armstrong's basic design with improvements.

The rate of activity just described is only a guide to the total work output over this period, and there was one particular item which was to appear consistently in annual expenditure over most of this time. There had been increasing pressure on all railways over the years of engineering development for more effective braking of trains. This had originally been limited by hardwood being the only acceptable material for brake blocks on the wheels. Brakes virtually never appeared on a locomotive, being fitted only to the tender, if there was one, and hand operated by the fireman. Some carriages and wagons were fitted similarly but demanded the presence of a brakeman on each vehicle so fitted. Apart from a call for a form of continuous brake, for passenger trains at least, it was necessary to develop suitable equipment for the engine itself. This latter was met by the provision of steam brakes, and the GWR was early in fitting these to their locomotives. The matter of continuous braking of trains was different however, and companies were reluctant to embark on any of the, as yet, unproven systems which began to appear. Already such devices were falling into the two main categories of pressure or vacuum operation. The GWR preferred the vacuum brake in principal, and in the light of the current performance of flexible piping and other subsidiary items, their first choice fell to the Sanders vacuum system. This was fitted to certain rolling stock in 1876, and was followed quickly by the improved Sanders-Bolitho design, and extensive trials of this were made. Dean was convinced, however, that the vacuum concept could be improved, and that this matter should be pursued before committing the company to a large outlay of capital which might not be finally justified. So in 1880 he entrusted this development work to the 24 year old Joe Armstrong, the third surviving son of Joseph Armstrong. 'Young Joe', as he was generally known, had been a pupil of his father at Swindon, but suffered from poor health. Indeed, he was on a long sea trip of recuperation when his father died. He, and a sister accompanying him, heard the sad news at Cape Town. Before he was able to recommence work, he was sent on another such trip to the Mediterranean. On his final return it was evident to Dean that Joe was the son who had inherited, to the greatest degree, his father's engineering talents, and was regarded by the family and the Works as something of a genius.

To assist 'Young Joe' in this task, Dean selected another young man of 23 years — George Jackson Churchward. This young man, born in 1857 at Stoke Gabriel in Devon, had early decided to take up engineering, and in 1873 was articled to John Wright

the Locomotive Carriage & Wagon Superintendent of the South Devon Railway at Newton Abbot. Wright had been selected for this post by Daniel Gooch. As early as 1875, Churchward, and another pupil at Newton Abbot, had designed and built a three-wheel steam road car, and he was still only 18! This vehicle finally found its way to the Science Museum in London. The GWR took over the working of the South Devon Railway on 1st February 1876, prior to full amalgamation in 1878, and Churchward went to Swindon to complete his articles. The Works register records his entry on the GWR books on 4th August 1877, when he was employed as a draughtsman, and here he spent his time, no doubt carefully watched by Dean, until his selection to assist Joe Armstrong. This joint work took about two years to complete, and the outcome was the GWR version of the vacuum brake, together with the combined steam and vacuum application valve. Although one cannot make any assumptions as to which man was responsible for any one of the special facets of this equipment, the generally held opinion is that Armstrong was the innovator and Churchward the one who turned the brilliant ideas into everyday reliable engineering. The main difference of this system to that finally adopted in 1903, was that the piston rod of the vacuum cylinder was anchored whilst the cylinder moved to apply the brakes. This method was reversed in the 1903 type. A fine model of this original design of cylinder is to be seen in the small museum maintained within Swindon Works.

To mark the completion of this project both men received promotion. Joe became assistant, to gain running experience, in the Swindon Locomotive Division, and within three years moved to the same position at the Wolverhampton Northern Division, a post which also included managership of the Wolverhampton Factory, under his uncle George. Since this was the post from which Dean had stepped to fame, it was evident to all that already Joe was becoming the 'heir apparent' to Dean. This move was to end in tragedy however, for on New Year's Eve 1887/8 he went down to Wolverhampton Works and running sheds to see how things were, and on his way back at 12.30 a.m. on 1st January 1888 was run down by a freight train and killed. He was just 31 years old. The GWR lost one of their most promising engineers, but made way for another, for Churchward, in his later days, told Joe Armstrong's nephew, R. J. Armstrong, that if Joe had lived, he (Churchward), would never have become Locomotive Superintendent, as Joe was far more clever than he was — a great tribute from a great man.

Reverting to the matter of continuous braking, as soon as Dean could report to the Board his satisfaction with the new GWR vacuum system, we find a large annual sum on the capital account being authorized, this being £20,000 per annum in 1880/1/2 followed by a lull during the financial relapse, then returning with £10,000 in 1886. The portion allocated to carriages was heavier in the earlier years, usually being £18,000. Since there was continuous new building in this period for all types of rolling stock, any new stock, whether built on capital or revenue account, would be fitted with continuous brakes, where appropriate, automatically, the special authorization being used only to equip existing stock. This injection of work into Swindon at this time must have been very welcome in maintaining a work load for the labour force. It is convenient, at this point to note other items of interest emanating from Swindon during these difficult years.

An activity which helped to keep many parts of the Factory busy was the manufacture, for internal use, of a wide range of machine tools financed from the revenue account. The Works machinery records, compiled later, included an inventory of machines currently in use and gives 'Swindon Works' in the makers columns for the major portion of machines installed during this 15 to 20 year period.

One large activity which grew up 'mysteriously', and which is almost forgotten today, is brickmaking. As intimated in Chapter Two, the Works is built on an extensive bed of blue clay from which can be made a good quality brick of distinctive colour. A brickworks was in existence about the middle of the eighteenth century, before the advent of canals, just below Swindon Hill where Queen's Park now stands, and although this is now gone there have been continuing brickyards scattered around the town, in particular near the village of Purton. It is likely that Armstrong was aware of this potential, and quite possibly brickmaking started in a small way during his tenure of office. It will be recalled that this was the period when the first brick buildings were erected in the works. The area where production started was on land immediately to the north of the new tender and engine paint shops (completed 1876), where bricks could have been produced at least to assist the current building programme. This brickyard was well established by 1884, with three large kilns in operation, clay being taken from the surrounding area and presumably refilled with railway ash and spoil from elsewhere, to bring the land back eventually to the required level, a process which was always in progress within the works boundaries. Soon after building the new narrow gauge engine shed, with its single track broad gauge shed attached just east of the Gloucester branch in 1871, Armstrong had purchased the rest of the land between the shed and the North Wilts Canal, an area of some 15/16 acres. This purchase from the Rolleston estate was completed in September 1873, with a view to later extensions to the engine shed or Factory. We find from the New Swindon Park correspondence that the southern portion of this had been set aside, for the time being, as

an additional cricket field to ease the pressure on the Park. The northern portion, however, would need considerable levelling before it could be used for building purposes, and it can be reasonably conjectured that the terracing of this area, by the removal and regrading of clay subsoil into suitable level lots, was the reason why a more permanent brickyard was opened on this site. No special financial provision was made for it by the Board and no doubt the project was seen to be self-financing. Works buildings for some years were, therefore, built mainly from home made bricks. There were three kilns originally, but this was extended to six some time between 1890 and 1900. This extension may have been as early as 1891, since on 13th August 1890 the Locomotive & Stores Committee of the Board authorized manufacture, as and when possible, of no less than 3,535,000 ordinary stock bricks to be used on the foundation and interior work for the widening of Brunel's famous Thames viaduct at Maidenhead. This was in conjunction with the quadrupling of the main line to Didcot, one of the final contributory factors leading to the demise of the broad gauge. So when one travels over the two outside tracks of this great viaduct, one is travelling over a large piece of Swindon! Brickmaking continued on this site until the Swindon engine shed was enlarged in 1908. The masons' yard for the Works was also established on this site by 1884. One other type of work gathered by Swindon at this time, was the provision of wrought iron bridge girders, and the manufacture of 80 tons of these, at £11 per ton, was ordered in August 1883, although doubtless smaller orders were being dealt with as they arose.

The committee of the Mechanics Institution was being kept busy expanding the scope of its social activities. Pressure on accommodation was such, that they had plans prepared for what amounted to a complete internal rebuild of the existing premises, and the erection of a new theatre on a southern extension which would have required demolition of the market, opened in 1854. The plans, dated 28th November 1878, show a theatre to accommodate no less than 1,867 people, including 84 standing places. It was to be arranged with stalls and pit seats numbering 816, a surrounding circle or gallery for 360 and a second gallery above for 607. This would have exceeded, by over 400 seats, the final capacity of the later Empire Theatre in the town! The proscenium arch was to be 35ft. wide, with a 45ft. depth of stage. This was indeed a noble scheme, but no doubt far too expensive to contemplate, as it is presumed that the market would have had to be replaced.

Much emphasis was, however, placed on further education, especially of engineering subjects, and more formal technical training of engineers was beginning to take shape. This had become possible because of the formation of the County School Board

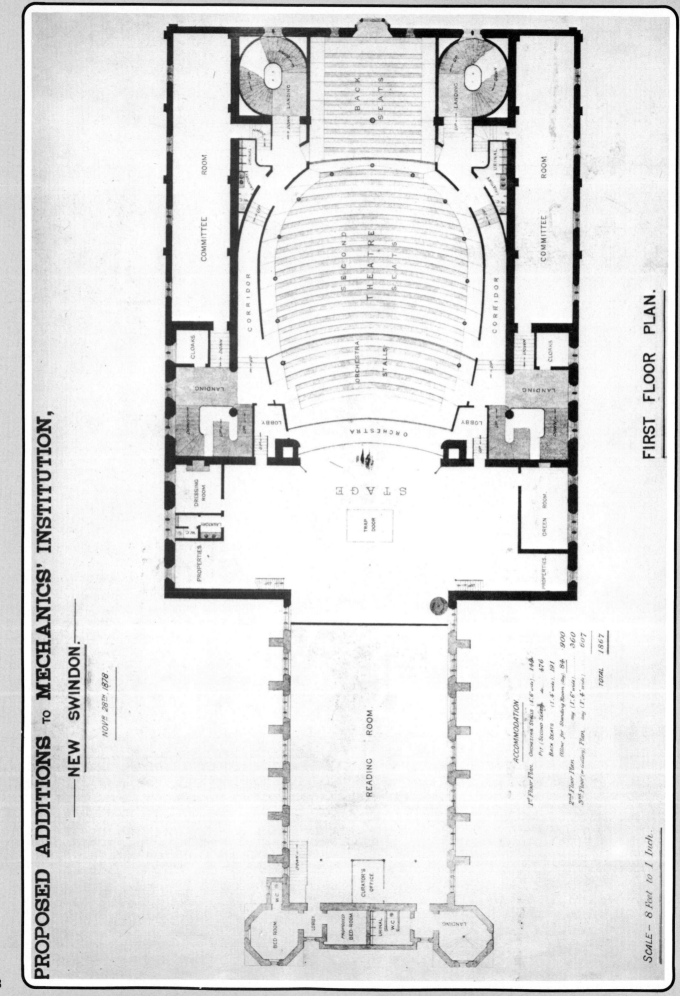

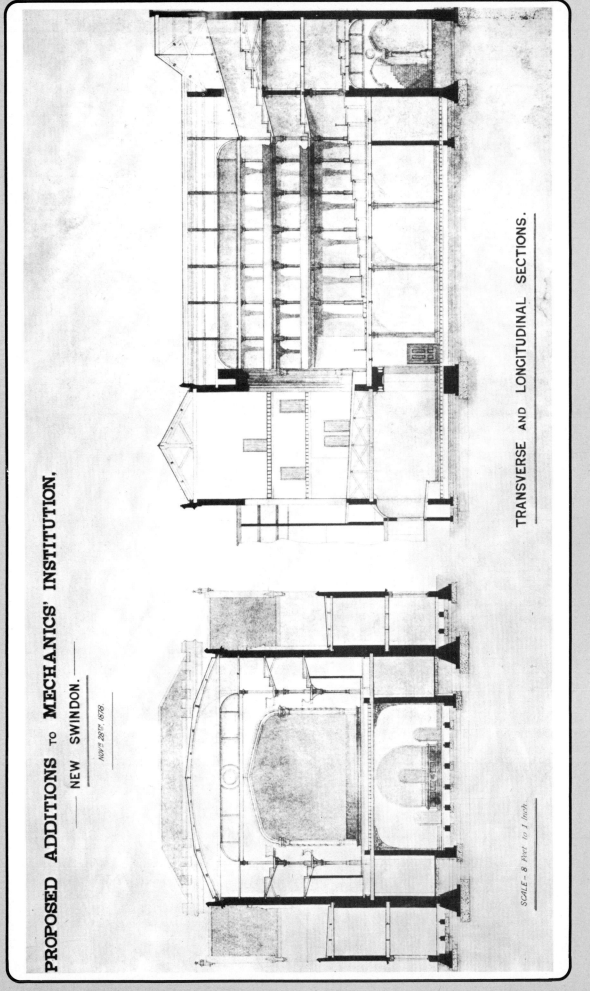

PROPOSED ADDITIONS TO **MECHANICS' INSTITUTION.**

—— NEW SWINDON. ——

NOVᴱ 28ᵀᴴ 1878.

SCALE - 8 Feet to 1 Inch.

TRANSVERSE AND LONGITUDINAL SECTIONS.

Plate 76: Sections of the proposed theatre. The heavy rake to the stage is very apparent together with its unusual 45 ft. depth. Note also the 'Palace of Varieties' type of balcony seating tiers.

British Rail

British Rail

in 1877, and the ensuing assumption by this board of control of elementary education for Old and New Swindon. The process took a few years, however, until more schools could be provided, but by about 1881, the Bristol Street schools were vacated, together with the drill hall overflow, and the GWR was no longer responsible for this work. Better concentration on adult classes was then possible.

A red-letter day in the life of the Anglican Church took place on 28th October 1880, when Lady Gooch laid the foundation stone of St. Paul's Church in the centre of the New Town. This was a further new parish carved out of that of Christ Church (Old Town), and the fairly young one of St. Mark's (New Town), and gives an indication of the expansion of the area. The first survey maps of Swindon were published in 1885, but older town plans, prepared by the railway about 1878, show that street extensions of Old and New Swindon were such that the two were now really joined, and rapid extension eastward was envisaged. An interesting sidelight on the work of the Medical Fund occurred in 1878 when one of the members, by the name of Harris, was run down by a train and lost both legs, his life being saved in the hospital. The Society provided him with a pair of socketed false legs, cleverly made in the carriage works, after which he was known locally as 'Peggy Harris'. This provision of false limbs became a permanent feature of the service, and manufacture of a wide range of such appliances became the norm, the last man to be engaged on this activity only retiring about 1970. However, in the years following the formation of the National Health Service, the work only consisted of repairs to limbs that the owners were more than content to continue using. Examples of this art are kept in the Works museum collection. In 1887 the Society set up its first dental clinic, together with a dental surgeon. This department was also to expand enormously in the ensuing years, which is not surprising as it is recorded that, in the few months from the surgeon's appointment until the end of 1887, he had carried out over 2,000 extractions! During this year an undertaker was appointed. Previous to this a hand bier had been available for the deceased persons' relatives and friends to use, but the undertaker was now provided with a grand horse-drawn hearse, or 'shillibeare', as it was called, after one of the London horse-bus contractors. For a member's funeral, the Society also provided, without charge, the horse, (complete with nodding black plumes), to draw the vehicle, although a charge was made for the horse if it was the funeral of a member's dependent. The author readily recalls this beautifully made vehicle, with its deeply engraved glass panels, wending its way, with measured tread, to the churchyards or cemeteries in the area.

The work of the Chief Medical Officer, Dr. G. M. Swinhoe, had greatly expanded, and the house on the estate which he had occupied was quite inadequate, so the Board put in hand the building of a suitable house, with consulting rooms, at the corner of Church Place and Faringdon Road. This building, known as 'Park House', was authorized in 1876, but was not ready for tenancy until December 1877. Dr. G. M. Swinhoe continued to live here until his death in 1907, after which it was taken over for the accommodation of the medical staff. It continued life as a medical examination centre until a few years ago. At the time of its building the membership of the Society was around 7,000 and still rapidly increasing.

In 1881, there appeared on the scene a rival company in the Swindon, Marlborough & Andover Railway (SM&A). This small concern, later to become the Midland & South Western Junction Railway (M&SWJ), was always a poor concern, and was inevitably looked upon with some hostility by the GWR as it cut right across its territory and joined rival companies to the north (MR), and south (L&SWR). The original Marlborough to Swindon section was planned to tunnel under Swindon Hill and join the GWR main line immediately east of the Junction station, but the tunnelling gave trouble, due to quicksands and a poor contractor, and had to be abandoned. A plan still exists showing the projected line from the station, and it would have cut right across what was already the expanding east side of Swindon on an embankment to the site of the proposed tunnel (now part of Queen's Park). An alternative route from the new Company's Swindon station (Swindon Town) on the south side of the hill was taken, crossing the GWR main line at Rushey Platt just west of the Works, with a connecting junction to the GWR at this point. A heavy toll was imposed by the GWR for this easement, and although reduced after appeal, was always a source of trouble to the M&SWJ. Services were eventually run from Swindon Junction to Swindon Town for three years until 1885, but this operation ceased until the GWR became the owner of the line in 1923. The new line's effect on Swindon was always, therefore, minimal, although it did provide a convenient north-south route between Birmingham and Southampton. There is little doubt that if the tunnel had been built and all the traffic had passed through Swindon Junction station, a very different history of this small railway may well have emerged. Its works were situated at Cirencester, and the rolling stock never had any connection with the GWR Works until 1923. One of the main offices of the company, however, was situated at Swindon Town, and one or two GW officers sought employment there. However, once the northern extension to Cheltenham was completed and the through route available, this small company, under the able direction of Sam (later Sir Sam) Fay, ran a very creditable service, which continued until World War I. Another line affecting Swindon emerging at this time, was the GWR Highworth branch. Leaving the main line a short distance east of the station, this short line of about 5½ miles was really a commuter line for the small market town of Highworth and the intervening villages. Known affectionately, by the local populace, as the 'Highworth Bunk', it survived until the time of the Beeching cuts. It was opened on 9th May 1883 for traffic, and in its earlier days carried a reasonable amount of cattle and milk traffic as well as passengers, before the days of the bus and car.

Of greater importance to Swindon Works, although much further away, was the completion and opening to full traffic, on 1st December 1886, of Gooch's great project the Severn Tunnel Railway. The great problems of financing and building this engineering work has been dealt with very adequately in other volumes, but the maintenance of the three main pumping stations at Sudbrook, Sea Wall and '5 Miles 4 Chains' was the responsibility of the Locomotive Works Manager at Swindon, and under the general control of the LC&W Superintendent. Indeed, the manager at Sudbrook ranked as an assistant to the Works Manager. The care and maintenance of the huge Cornish beam engines, supplied by Harvey of Camborne, boiler houses, rising mains and valves, ventilating fans and engines, all became an 'outstation' activity for the Works, providing a constant workload for the millwrights and other shops. However, a very interesting sidelight in connection with Severn Tunnel has recently come to light in the form of a slim correspondence bundle put at the disposal of the author. At that period all railway correspondence was written in longhand and so only the copies of Dean's letters are available, and any enclosures provided were not copied on to the correspondence bundle. Nevertheless, the subject matter is of extreme interest.

The earliest letter, dated 16th August 1892, less than six years after the opening of the tunnel, is from Dean to R. E. Crompton, the well-known electrical engineer. In it, Dean states that he had been 'instructed' by the GWR chairman and deputy chairman to put himself in communication with Crompton on the subject of electrical haulage for the Severn Tunnel Railway. One immediately senses that Dean was not enamoured with the idea, and this is possibly borne out by the way in which the matter proceeded. The start was quick enough, Crompton replying the next day suggesting dinner and discussions at his private residence the following week. Dean took certain gradient and other diagrams with him to the meeting and sent further information a few days later, undertaking to arrange certain traction tests in the near future. Crompton was then abroad for a short period, but on his return nothing seems to have happened. Indeed, not until 12th March 1893 does Crompton enquire how matters stand, including feelers as to

the use of electric welding in the Works in the future. Apologies are then made for the non appearance of the traction tests. (It must be remembered that the Gooch dynamometer carriage was the only one then available). On 28th April 1893, another contender, in the shape of Francis Fox of the still famous firm of consulting engineers, asked if he could undertake preparation of suitable proposals. Dean then apparently said, (unsupported by any available letter), that he had no intention of dealing with more than one interested party, this being clear from a letter to Dean from one of the directors on 8th May 1893. And there, surprisingly, (or was it?), the matter ended. Only one more letter is on file — six years later on 22nd February 1899, when the General Manager's office enquired if the proposals believed to have been made by Crompton for Severn Tunnel were available as no correspondence could be found at Paddington. There is no reply. As we shall see shortly there were good reasons for silence at this time, but it is interesting that this particular small file of correspondence survived — unofficially lost in a safe place perhaps. We may never know the full facts but here, as quickly as it was born, died the first proposal for main line electrification on the GWR.

One of the important introductions to the Works made by Dean was the provision of the chemical laboratory. Previous to this time W. H. Stanier had undertaken simple chemical tests at his home in The Sands (later Bath Road), in Old Town, on materials and other items, and later a small room at the tunnel entrance had been placed at his disposal for this work. The closing of the day schools at Bristol Street made possible the modification of this building, only erected a few years previously as a school extension, to become the Works chemical laboratory. The 1845 school and house were demolished at this time. Starting with a staff of two, the laboratory quickly expanded, and was augmented in the works by the installation of special equipment for materials and other mechanical testing, at a temporary site until a testing house proper could be established, where it still stands at the time of writing.

The problem of water supply was again becoming acute for two separate reasons. One was the basic inadequacy of the total supply available, and the other the small proportion of the total supply which was potable. Although the Swindon Water Company was increasing its output, albeit slowly, this was only just sufficient to keep pace with the increasing number of households in the town to be served, and the Works was not able to increase its intake from them as it would have wished. As a result, thoughts again turned to new wells. It was deduced from such geological information as existed, that water should be available if wells in the area were sunk deep enough, and it was decided that the first efforts should be made in the Works itself on the supposition that even if the well was expensive, the distribution costs would be minimal. Work appears to have commenced on a site at the north end of the Works some time in 1880, and by 1881 two 8ft. diameter wells had been sunk to a depth of about 250ft. These were brick lined and provided with cross headings at 170ft. and at 246ft. Metal linings were provided where the shafts passed through sand beds. A single shaft was to continue from this level at 10ft. diameter for a further 220ft. where it was proposed that the bore be reduced to 7ft. diameter. Core drilling continued down to an unprecedented 736ft! Water was found in quantity at a natural level of 88ft. below the cill, i.e. at 241ft. above ordnance datum (Newlyn mean sea level) but was very saline, although strangely, for such waters, an exceedingly small quantity of sulphates was present. Equally strange and annoying to the Works, was that it was soft water, in the large part of southern England where hard water is the norm. An analysis taken in August 1884 is here compared with a sample from a well at Purton station, only a few miles to the north and sunk in the more normal oolite beds of the Cotswold area. All figures are in grains per gallon of sample:-

	Swindon Works Well	Purton station Well
Total solid matter in solution	117.7	84.3
Chlorine in chlorides	36.4	7.7
Corresponding to NaCl	60.0	12.7
Hardness Temporary	1.4 degrees Clark	15.0 degrees Clark
Hardness Permanent	0.2 degrees Clark	23.6 degrees Clark
Hardness Total	1.6 degrees Clark	38.6 degrees Clark

The findings were under discussion for a considerable time, and geologists were approached. This resulted in official interest from the Museum of Practical Geology in Jermyn Street, London, who were keen to have core samples for their records as well as examples of rare ammonite and other fossils found in the drill-cores. Unlike other wells in the area, large beds of Oxford clay were penetrated as well as Forest marble, and the interest was such, that reference to the wells, with discussion, was made at a meeting of the Geological Society in March 1886, being published in their August 1886 Proceedings. None of this was helpful to the situation and no reason for, or way of, avoiding the saline waters was proposed and the wells were finally abandoned, although they are still in existence. They have been used in recent years by university projects concerned with the long-term chemical effects of saline waters

on metals. All that the Works gained from this, therefore, was to provide a new contribution to the geological map and data of the area! Succeeding efforts were then made at points along the Gloucester branch, but only trial bores were made to avoid high expense. None was very fruitful and eventually a second well was sunk at Kemble and this, at least, increased for the time being the amount available for the tanker trains, and with a deepening of this well in 1899, this was just sufficient to keep the Works and engine shed supplied.

The year 1884 was noteworthy for the purchase of a further 25 acres or so of land from a Mr Thomas Turner for £4,100, and it was clear that extensions to the C&W Works were in mind for the future, and by 1889 there appeared a new large wagon lifting shop (No. 21 C&W) on the middle of this site, and the opening of this facility greatly increased the wagon building and repair capacity. The land purchase included the house 'Eastcott Lodge' and outbuildings, from whence the land had been farmed. This house should not be confused with Eastcott Farm, which straddled what is now Corporation Street, adjacent to the Transport Depot. Two other land purchases were made four years later each of about 20 acres in extent, one costing only £200 per acre, but the other £400 per acre. The former area was to the north of that purchased from Thomas Turner, but the other was a new move for the GWR, being land to the west of Rodbourne Road and north of the main line. Both these purchases were from the estate of Thomas Vilett Rolleston, and the variation in land prices makes clear the importance of the more expensive site at £8,000, against the Carriage Works area at only £4,100. It also shows again that the GWR was dealing with astute agents who were plainly aware of the future planning of the Works, and able to use this knowledge to advantage in business negotiations. This particular land purchase foreshadows a milestone in the history of the GWR — the final withdrawal of the broad gauge lines.

Although the details of the final extinction of the BG on the GWR is not a subject for detailed study in this volume, and has indeed been well described elsewhere, the events prior to the final decision are important because of the resulting effects on Swindon. Since the large conversions of the SWR in 1872, and the almost equally large mileage of the Wilts & Somerset and other lines in 1874, small lengths of BG had been gradually eliminated yearly, until, by 1885, only the lines west of Exeter and Creech Junction to Chard were principally or entirely BG. The matter was finally brought to a head in 1885 when the Board of the Cornwall Railway minuted that the time had arrived, in their opinion, when NG should be adopted. The GWR General Manager, Grierson, was then required to report fully on the matter, doing so on 1st April 1886. There is no doubt that the directors were still loath to take this final step, doubtless for sentimental as well as hard financial reasons. The 'Great Depression' was only just showing signs of easing, but these trends might still turn out to be false. There is little doubt also that respect for their ageing chairman, Sir Daniel Gooch, who had shown lifelong faith in the broad gauge, weighed heavily on their conscience. The matter was laid on the table, however, but later, that great gentleman, at the very last general meeting over which he was to´preside in February 1889, intimated to the proprietors that the abolition could not be put off much longer. His death, on 15th October 1889, took from him the painful necessity of pronouncing the inevitable sentence. Sir Daniel was succeeded as chairman of the GWR by Frederick Saunders, the former secretary of the Company.

The final matter which made the conversion a necessity was the need to quadruple the main line between Taplow and Didcot, and the extra costs which would be incurred if the mixed gauge line to the west was to be retained could not be justified. Arising from this situation the new chairman and his deputy, in discussions with the chief officers decided, on 26th February 1891, that conversion should be completed in 1892. After a short period of uncertainty about the timing of the work, the definite date of May 1892 was agreed and the necessary planning and preparations put in hand. Further land was also purchased at Swindon, north of the line, and north-eastward between Cricklade Road and the station (Whitehouse Road), in 1891, including an extra 3 acres at £296 per acre to tidy up the transaction. As mentioned earlier, dealings were very protracted on some of these purchases, the trustees of the Rolleston Estate, Mr Shepherd, retaining the services of the firm of Maxwell & Tuke, civil engineers, surveyors and valuers in Manchester and Bury. Whilst no doubt acting in the interests of their clients, the asking price was, at the time, ridiculously high at £500 per acre, and it is clear from preserved correspondence that both sides became quite ruffled in the ensuing negotiations.

However, except for the 3 acres referred to, none of this cost went against the gauge conversion, so it is assumed that the GWR had every intention of enlarging the Factory on the sites in due course. Dean's main preparations at Swindon were twofold. Firstly, the provision of adequate siding accommodation for the BG stock to be stored whilst awaiting conversion or scrapping, and secondly, the costing and planning of the locomotive, carriage and wagon conversions and for the comparatively small replacement programme required. After much discussion it was clear that some 16 miles of sidings were required, some of which could already be found in the Works.

The estimates were to house:-

150 Locomotives at 36 ft. each
500 Carriages, Vans etc. at 36 ft. each
3,000 Wagons at 18 ft. each

Great efforts had to be made, in 1891, to get together any old flanged track available, and even by the end of 1891 they were considerably short, saved, in the end, by 350 tons found lying at St. Blazey. Much more difficult to find was the timber for sleepers, and appeals were sent to all quarters for anything that could be had — old solebars, headstocks, wagon sides and floors. Amusing reactions are apparent from the correspondence however. Some districts plainly used this chance to get rid of much stock that had embarrassed them for a long time, whilst other district officers would send nothing until they had an order in their possession. Naturally, the Works Manager, Samuel Carlton, was not even told that the all-line appeal for scrap materials had been made, and writes accusingly to his chief, Dean, asking why all this material was suddenly being dumped in his Works. The laying of all these sidings was touch and go, and even when a considerable amount was ready, no move had been made by the Civil Engineering & Signal departments to connect them to the main line as late as the end of February 1892, eleven weeks before the conversion. The land at the west end of the Works had to be levelled before any track could be laid and this meant considerable labour and transport. A total of £8,500 was allowed for all this preparation and tracklaying, excluding the cost of the secondhand track materials. Just to make matters a little more difficult, a public footpath crossed the line from Newburn House, and then over this land to the village of Shaw between Swindon and Purton. The right of way had to be maintained and the Works provided a brick-built pedestrian subway for a distance of about 780 ft. north-westerly to run under the ground now to be made up and levelled. Known as the Shaw subway, this was extended southerly in 1905, under the main line, to Dean Street. In 1914 a further access was made into the Works near the weighbridge. Completing the story of this subway, the Company was able to close it to the public at the north end in about 1920, and in 1941 this 'dead' portion, which still existed, was converted into an air raid shelter, a further entrance being made into the 'A' wheel shop. The southern section still provides an entrance to the Works.

In spite of all the difficulties, Samuel Carlton had everything ready in time for BG and convertible stock to be moved into both the Locomotive and the Carriage & Wagons Works before the fateful weekend of 21st/22nd May 1892. Men also had to be provided to assist in the actual conversion work, and these were transported to the West Country from all over the system, from as far as Chester and Crewe in the north, and New Milford in West Wales, with Swindon having to supply their quota. The locomotive department complement in the 'working notice' for the weekend was 168 men, these joining into one eventual train load with 204 from Chester, 24 from Honeybourne and 45 from Chipping Norton, to work in the Ashburton area. A further 77 men from Swindon joined a contingent of 337 from Weymouth, at Trowbridge, to work at Launceston and St. Austell. Although presumably these latter 77 men were from other departments at Swindon, the author has good reason to think that some, at least, were drawn from the Carriage Works.

During the week previous to the conversion, most remaining BG stock was brought to Swindon. The final trains from all the branches and main centres, such as Plymouth and Penzance, arrived between the early hours of Friday, 20th May, and Saturday, 21st May. The very last BG train to run consisted of vehicles required until the last minute. As this train passed each station between Penzance and Exeter, the station masters were given the necessary written authority to issue possession notices to the engineering department to start work. This train was necessarily double headed, and was due at Swindon at 9.45 a.m. on Saturday, 21st May, although it is said to have been rather late in arriving! Of course, east of Exeter was still mixed gauge, and there had been some latitude given for working any remaining BG stock with NG locomotives as empty stock specials, and these were arranged as required; but Saturday, 21st May, was the final date for these to run. Activity at the Swindon 'F' signal box controlling the entry into the main group of temporary sidings, must have been very hectic indeed in those last days of BG operation.

There are several statements to be found in contemporary correspondence of the estimated numbers of the various categories of rolling stock expected to be dealt with, but naturally none of these could be wholly accurate. Perhaps it is best to quote the report of Dean, to the Board, which was submitted some three months after the conversion, which gave the position at 31st July 1892.

	BG Stock at 31/12/91	Replaced by NG Stock	Converted 1/1/92 – 31/7/92	Still to be converted 31/7/92
Engines	196	69	34	93
Passenger Stock	347	26	285	36
Non-Passenger Stock	242	105	86	51
Freight Stock	3,302	2,026	767	509

All conversion work was completed by the middle of 1893. The preceeding figures for freight vehicles

do not include any private owner stock, but this did not constitute a large number, and belonged mainly to only two firms. Amongst the scrappings at this time were the great 4-2-2 Gooch 8 ft. Singles. As stated earlier, convertible locomotives, had, in general, been produced to keep the BG system at work, but there had been small groups of 'renewals' of these historic machines. The last three had all taken place under Dean — six in 1878, six in 1880 and the last three as late as 1888. By the time the last renewal took place it was thought that the drawing office should have correct records of these locomotives, but it was found necessary to call in the chargeman erector, William Cave, to provide virtually all the dimensions, as almost all had been continuously altered since the 1847 set of drawings was prepared. It would be interesting to know if Cave kept any notebooks, and if so, whether they are still in someone's keeping! The very last to be thus dealt with was *Tornado* emerging in July 1888. They were all supplied with cabs typical of current practice, but retained the original Gooch brasswork. Two famous engines had already been withdrawn for preservation, *North Star* and *Lord of the Isles*, but were to meet their doom some years later.

Special layouts were prepared in the carriage shops, south of the line, to deal with the passenger stock, which fell into three categories:-

   a) NG bodies on NG frames, but running on BG bogies
   b) NG bodies on BG frames
   c) Full BG vehicles

For condition (a), a pair of parallel roads, each provided with hydraulic bogie drops and traversing facilities at the lower level, made possible the dropping of BG bogies, traversing out to the parallel road where they were raised and run out, a NG pair of bogies replacing them. The reverse procedure placed these under the carriage body to which they were then lifted and secured. At least 20 carriages could be dealt with per day in this way, and occasionally this figure was well surpassed. For many years it had been realised that final conversion was inevitable, and for this purpose both frames and bodies had been so constructed that by releasing selected timber peggings, they could be parted longitudinally. Sections of the requisite width which had been 'designed into' the vehicles, were then removed from the particular longitudinal part of the body, and the two now equal halves re-pegged to become NG width, both body and frame. This was the method used for all the vehicles in group (c), and the frames only, in group (b). One can see from the preceeding table that the majority of wagons were replaced, but it is likely that such material, from these, particularly side and floor timbers, could be re-machined and used again. Convertible locomotives needed, in the main,

Plate 77: Broad gauge locomotives awaiting scrapping or conversion at Swindon Works in 1892. This less familiar picture is interesting, with the saddle tank locomotives and the inclusion of 'Newburn', at that time William Dean's residence, in the background.

British Rail

Plate 78: A rare picture of the special installation of sub-rail hydraulic lifts, used for conversion of narrow gauge-bodied broad gauge carriage stock for narrow gauge operation.

Author's Collection

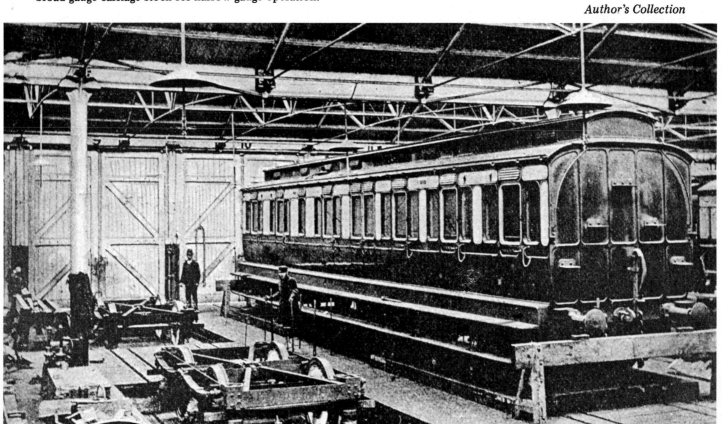

only shortening of axles and re-trimming of frames and skirting to suit wheels being inside rather than outside the frames. Opportunity was taken, however, to reboiler some at this time. An interesting sidelight on the narrowing of BG passenger bodies and frames, is, that this had been developed during the time, and possibly at the original instigation of James Holden the Carriage Works Manager from 1873 until 16th August 1885, when he resigned to become Locomotive Superintendent of the GER. As we have said previously, he was Dean's principal assistant also, from 17th April 1878, and could possibly have been responsible for keeping the conversion of vehicles under constant review. A few years later, when he was at Stratford, he used the reverse of this method when the GER wished to improve the comfort and capacity of some of their coaching stock, new timber sections and panels being added to vehicles 'split' in the same way in their workshops.

The death of Sir Daniel Gooch, on 15th October 1889, at the age of 73, marked the end of an era in the life of the GWR, which he had served, with only a few months break, from 1837, a period of 52 years. During this time his personality had become indelibly stamped into the whole life and organization of the Company, which had risen to be one of the largest in the world. Because he had never resided in Swindon, his loss there was, perhaps, not such a personal one, but keenly felt in an official sense. He had represented the Cricklade Division in Parliament, within which Swindon was still included, from 1865 to 1885, and was thus in touch with the whole community over and above that of the local GWR folk. We have seen that he never lost interest in the town he personally founded, frequently attending functions, and in constant touch with all that was happening. As chairman, the way he manipulated the financial control of the LC&W department to the advantage of Swindon is very clear, and whilst this was of general benefit to the proprietors, it also made clear his unwavering attitude to maintain the investment in manpower and plant he had initiated there, to the continuing gain of the community. On the debit side there is little doubt that his strict control of the Company's economy in general, so necessary in the first decade or so of his chairmanship, was carried on far too long, and was partly to blame for the rising unpopularity of the GWR in the period now under review. In his later years his conservative outlook on technical innovation became more obvious, although against this must be balanced his persistency and determination through the sixteen difficult years of building the Severn Tunnel, to see the project completed. His final assessment must be as one of the giants of the Victorian age, both as engineer and businessman, with the religious and moral outlook of the times which demanded justice at all times in his dealings with others whatever their

position in life. Swindon itself can never repay its debt to him. He was buried in the churchyard of Clewer, near Windsor, where his home was. The funeral was quiet, by request, and apart from family and close friends, the GWR was represented only by directors and chief officers. Although the broad gauge was to remain in truncated use for another 2½ years, it can be truly said that it died with its great protagonist, Daniel Gooch.

During the long period of depression, for reasons we have seen, Swindon slowly but firmly developed, helped by steady employment, and a resultant town expansion. At the same time, the great Company which it served appeared to its customers to be in a state of somnolence, with services declining, together with a visible lack of attention to those things which the travelling public and traders looked upon as forming a Company's 'image'. The combined population of Old and New Swindon, recorded as 11,770 in 1871, had, by 1881, reached 19,904. This rise was mainly due to the successive transfer of carriage work from the northern factories. There was also the closure of the B&ER Works at Bristol and other centres after the amalgamation, which brought further locomotive work to Swindon. Although few civic plans appear to have been made before the first large scale ordnance survey, published in 1886, the railway, or possibly the railway officers, serving on the New Swindon local Board, did produce one or two at an earlier date which have survived. These town plans may have been used for reference purposes, to pin-point the streets in which the employees lived. They may also have been used to accompany some early form of property register, when considering the further purchase of land for expansions. One of these is undated, but has been fairly accurately placed as 1879, and one can see that the Old and New Towns are just becoming connected at least by recognized roads, although at this stage few of these new roads were built upon. Such development took place during the 1880s, and was accompanied by new house building in the Rodbourne area, and also to the east of the station. Although modest in style, most if not all the new houses now built included drained sanitation, although laid on drinking water supplies were not so widespread. The Old Town still suffered from bad drainage, and although some attempts had been made to alleviate the situation, local newspaper and other reports show that epidemics of smallpox, scarlet and typhoid fever were still prevalent.

By 1891 the population had risen to 33,001 although there had been some minor boundary changes in previous years resulting in the inclusion of Coate, Even Swindon and Gorse Hill areas within the two local board boundaries. Even so, this was a rise of about 50 per cent in the administered population within a short period. The provision, or perhaps non-provision, of roads had been a constant problem for the local boards, neither wishing to spend money not directly concerning their own area. One great problem which has become more embarrassingly apparent in the 20th century as road traffic increased was the virtual division of the town into two parts by the railway. The main London to Bristol line passes through the main part of the town on low embankments, connecting a few higher spots in the natural terrain. As we know, Brunel achieved an almost level track over very long distances, and through this particular area, was not prepared to take the more natural average level of the ground, some 15 ft. below, to reduce expenditure at the cost of his track gradients. Therefore, the road north from Swindon to Cirencester was bridged at Gorse Hill, and a bridge of no more than accommodation standard was provided over the lane running northwards and just east of the station (now Corporation Street and Whitehouse Road). The other road from the New Town to Rodbourne Cheney, just west of the original Works, (Park Lane and Rodbourne Road), was provided with a level crossing controlled by disc and crossbar signals. This latter crossing had been a source of concern for many years. As early as 1875 Board sanction had been given for a pedestrian subway to be built at this site, but it had lapsed, possibly because of the death of Armstrong. Dean pressed for a subway suitable for horsedrawn traffic, but objections were raised by the agents for the Rolleston estate over the lowering of access from their fields to the proposed road. They were also not keen to sell the land required on both sides of the line, as it would mean breaking agreements with tenants. At least one fatal accident had occurred prior to 1875. Again a woman was killed on the crossing on 27th October 1881, and this put further pressures on the GWR in particular, from Parliamentary questions. Although by statute the railway was not required to consider other than pedestrians if a subway (or bridge) was provided, there appeared an item in the 1884 GWR Parliamentary Bill No. 1 for powers to construct a 20 ft. wide vehicle subway, after another fatal accident, to a boy, on 20th April 1883. By this time it had become possible to purchase the adjoining fields, when the sum of £500 per acre was asked, subsequently reduced to £400 after much haggling. It was still questioned whether a footbridge would suffice, but Dean was more acquainted with the local conditions and could foresee road traffic problems in the future. A traffic survey was carried out in 1883 over the crossing, when it was found that between 12 noon and 8 p.m. about 2,400 pedestrians, 200 vehicles, 70 horse riders, 10 cattle and 55 perambulators were using the crossing, (these figures are approximations). The Board was still concerned about the price of the land, and took the matter to arbitration. One senses that the landowner himself now took a personal interest in the case, no doubt feeling that public opinion might be damaging if the project were delayed further. As a result, we find, in April 1888 that, the price was dropped to £200 per acre, as long as the GWR paid the arbitration costs, and on 3rd October the project was authorized at a cost of £4,800. Only the costs of that portion of purchased land applicable to the project would have been included in this sum. Work started quickly, and despite the problems of track occupation and relaying of the Swindon Water Company's mains, it was opened for traffic at 7 p.m. on Thursday, 19th December 1889. The road level, when opened, was virtually the same as today's (raised) footpath under the bridges. Subsequently the road itself has had to be lowered twice, once for the tramway system when installed, and later to allow for increasing headroom to accommodate double decker bus and other road traffic.

On 16th April 1891, Dean received a proposal from Paddington that was to have benefits of a personal nature to the staff. This was the establishment of a savings bank under powers which had been conferred on the GWR in 1885. Draft rules were circulated to all departments for discussion. On 18th June 1891 a Board minute laid out the general conditions, which included that deposits of not less than one shilling (5p) be accepted, no one to deposit more than £50 in any one year, the rate of interest to be 3½ per cent, but any excess of holdings above £300 not to receive interest. The bank appears to have struggled into existence in a somewhat haphazard way later in 1891 and early 1892, each station or establishment making its own arrangements through their accounts department, as locally practicable. Dean was concerned about administration problems for the large concentration of staff, and sought the views of James Holden from Stratford, as the GER already had a bank in operation. Inevitably elsewhere, station masters did not want to undertake the extra work on behalf of locomotive department staff who happened to be resident in their area, and some acrimonious correspondence ensued. By January 1892 there were about 250 depositors in the Paddington area, and about 375 for the whole line, but it is clear that the scheme was growing fast. At Swindon the bank business was soon operated from the Works ticket office. W. H. Stanier co-ordinated the efforts, on behalf of Dean, for the department as a whole; safes and other equipment being provided as required. There were some doubts and rumours soon circulating that transactions were not private, but this was strongly denied, a suitable letter being inserted in the GWR Magazine by the Chief Accountant at Paddington. Inevitably, within a year or so, a special clerk was appointed as 'assistant receiver' for the bank at Swindon, a Mr Adams, and he was followed later, in 1903, by Mr Julius Edgar Noble. The 'receivership' was, of course, vested in the post of Chief Clerk. With the ability in due course to have regular deposits transferred via the paybill and other advantageous changes, the GWR Savings Bank developed strongly over the years.

Little has been said, until this time, about trade unions. The reasons are simply that such organizations had not been too successful in attracting members in enough quantity to become very effective in the Works. The earliest, and strongest one, was among the footplate staff, and they were early in the field, and rightly so, opposing excessively long hours of duty on the footplate. Representations were made to Armstrong shortly before his death and useful concessions in this respect granted, and this pattern continued during Dean's period of office. Within the Works however, things were different, although it is clear that some employees from the earliest days of the Factory were members of such unions as were then in existence. The Amalgamated Society of Engineers, Machinists, Millwrights, Smiths and Patternmakers was over 25 years old by the time Dean took office, having a countrywide membership of 44,578 by the end of 1876, with an annual income of about £146,000. Whilst we do not know the number of members of the Swindon No. 1 Branch, in 1877 their income was £793, so it could have been in the region of 240, and a second branch was being formed. By 1884 there were members in the Works of the United Society of Boilermakers & Iron Ship Builders, Amalgamated Society of Carpenters & Joiners, Society of Brass Founders of Bristol and the United Kingdom Railway Officers & Servants Association, the Association of Vehicle Builders and doubtless others as well. The author has been unable to find mention in the Swindon Advertiser or North Wilts Herald of union activities, although the odd mention may be tucked away in small paragraphs not spotted. Equally, local politics had their main basis in the district issues, and had little connection with those operating nationally. Indeed, from the newspapers one occasionally finds some odd pairings at local board level, in support or defence of a particular proposal.

One could perhaps place the beginnings of organized trade union activity in 1891, when the Swindon & District Trades Council was formed, the first full meeting being held on 19th January of that year at the Riflemans Hotel. This followed subsidiary meetings of the main unions with meaningful membership in the district. Representation on the Trades Council included individual unions later to become part of the National Union of Railwaymen. It is difficult to assess at this distance the real effect that this organization had on the Board of the GWR as far as their local staff is concerned, but it may be significant that new concessions and services were given to the staff in the next two or three years. The new organization however was quite poorly supported in its early years by union members, and it was not until after the turn of the century that it began to make itself felt. However, it was quite active when urban district councils succeeded to local boards in 1894.

One of the concessions from the directors, was the introduction of privilege tickets at one quarter of the full ordinary fare, and half this price for children under 12. The scheme had been announced on 15th January 1890, but was introduced a year later in February 1891. This was of great advantage to families visiting friends and relatives in other towns on the system, and for trips at weekends. Similar arrangements are still in force on British Rail. It was about this time too, that the enforced long breaks from work at Christmas and Easter were removed, and men did not have to go short of earnings during these two periods. The annual 'trip' shutdown was to remain unpaid, however, for many years to come. Nevertheless this holiday was growing in popularity each year. For instance, in 1892 the Works closed at 1 p.m. on Thursday, 7th July, and did not re-open until 9 a.m. (omitting the early 6 a.m. shift) on Thursday, 14th July. In some years this period was increased by extending the break until 9 a.m. on the Monday week following the closure. The official trip day was Friday, 8th July, in 1892, but it is not clear from old records how many trippers went for the day only, or stayed away for longer periods. But when one assesses the places to which they were travelling, a large number indeed must have been taking an extended holiday away of several days. It is interesting to examine the choice of destinations in that year, and compare it with the places which were the recognized resorts some forty years later. It must be remembered that the Mechanics Institute free pass was only available on the GWR, with special additions on some lines over which running powers were effective. Thus we get in the summary of areas:-

Destination Area	Adults	Children	Total
London	1,669	1,163	2,832
West of England (including Weston-super-Mare)	3,280	2,460	5,740
Weymouth	2,337	2,187	4,524
South Wales	1,637	1,322	2,959
North of England	1,314	879	2,193
Totals	10,237	8,011	18,248

Firstly it is clear that almost all members took tickets and travelled for at least one day. Secondly, a destination such as London does not necessarily mean the end of the journey, as forward trips paying full fare on other railways to, say, Southend or Margate are likely. Similar conditions applied at other railheads. So of the 2,832 going to the London area, 2,560 booked for Paddington, and the only other place of note in the detailed lists is Winchester with

147, another railhead. Similarly for the Weymouth group, 4,252 out of 4,524 went all the way, the next largest being 57 to Devizes! It is when we examine the West of England however that the change of holiday patterns really emerge. Weston-super-Mare and Weymouth are the nearest watering places to GWR Swindonians, and retained their popularity for decades. Out of the 5,740 West of England travellers, 1,972 opted for Weston-super-Mare, but the interest comes from the places further west available to the staff. The significant ones are Plymouth — 586; Teignmouth — 642 and Newton Abbot 1,583. The ones we would naturally expect to appear high on the list surprise us; Torquay — 172; Paignton — 65; even Barnstaple rates highly at 143, but Exmouth (via ferry at Starcross) only one! Coming to Cornwall, this must still have been considered 'foreign parts'; St. Ives — 2; Penzance — 91; Newquay —7; Falmouth — 14. There are of course in all these groups, small numbers to many lesser stations on the line. The remaining areas tell the same tale. For South Wales, there were 727 for New Milford (some possibly sailing to Ireland to see relatives); Swansea — 1,011; Cardiff — 294; but 310 for Tenby. In this group however, there were many Welsh families who were now settled for a generation or more at Swindon, and returning 'home' for a few days, e.g. Ebbw Vale — 7; Mountain Ash — 11; Aberdare — 33. By far the largest parties travelling north were to Birmingham— 400; Manchester — 350; Chester — 493 and Birkenhead — 555. Many of these trips were no doubt extended further. Wolverhampton naturally has a reasonable number at 86; but only Crewe — 50, and Oxford — 25, have numbers over 20. One last interesting point, the secretary of the Mechanics Institute did not even apply to Dean to approach the directors for the grant of the annual trip on 8th July, until 4th May, only nine weeks before. In that time all booking arrangements had to be made and trains, no doubt about 15 — 18 in number, had to be

Plate 79: The main hall or theatre of the Mechanics Institute as it was until the disastrous fire on Christmas Eve 1930. The beautiful pargetted ceiling was completely restored and remains the same today, but a modern proscenium arch replaced the one seen here.

British Rail

provided and manned. It is supposed that little or no booking of accommodation was done, indeed at the popular GWR resorts it was customary for landladies to be present at the arrival stations as the trains came in, canvassing for business. This custom carried over at a few places, although to a lesser extent, until about 1930.

By the middle of the 1880s, the market, built by the Swindon Improvement Company some thirty years before, had become fairly disreputable, and there were many moves to replace it. Other problems also beset the committee of the Mechanics Institution, mainly because of their success. They had, over the years, provided the sole means of technical and artistic further education, and by 1888 there were about 500 students, and numbers were still increasing. The original institute building was now literally 'bursting at the seams' and it was felt that a complete review of the situation must be made. Proposals, in 1890, were therefore made to the Board that the assets vested in the Swindon Improvement Company be transferred from official shareholders to a group of trustees. Much history had to be investigated at this time to clarify the original proposals, and what changes had taken place in the interim period. It was pointed out that the washing bath facilities had been removed to the Medical Fund Society in 1864 and the workmen's messing facilities rehoused in new rooms on Works premises in London Street in 1877. The state of the market was made clear, and as the space it occupied was now badly needed for extensions, this activity should be discontinued. The committee submitted that their sole object in future should be with educational matters and such social activities as could be included under this general heading. The basic proposals were agreed by the Board, and legal steps taken to liquidate the old company. The Institution secretary, F. G. O'Conor, was appointed liquidator, co-operating with the GWR Solicitor, R. R. Nelson. The original market licence from the Lord of the Manor, Mr Goddard, issued on 1st January 1855, could not be traced, but arrangements were made to reassign these rights to the New Swindon Local Board. This body proceeded to build a new market — originally in the open air, and later to be covered in on a site in Commercial Road. This was opened in 1892, lasting until about 1976.

Meanwhile the transfer deed was prepared and arrangements made to repay the outstanding loan of £1,400 to the GWR Company. The engrossed deed was approved by the Board in December 1890 and duly sealed, winding up the affairs of the Swindon Improvement Company on 31st December 1890. This step required publishing in the London Gazette, and this being done, the transfer became legal three months from the publication. Under the agreement, the £100 per year, which the GWR had paid as rent in lieu of premises earlier made available in the

Works prior to the original building being erected, was now continued as an annual subscription to the new organization. The new committee lost no time in preparing for their extensions and the work was entrusted to architects Brightwen Binyon of Ipswich, the contractors being Grimwood & Sons. Building operations commenced during 1891 much material being purchased from the Works itself, and the new extensions were opened by the deputy chairman of the GWR, Viscount Emlyn on 1st March 1893. It was at this time that the roads surrounding the institute building were renamed Emlyn Square. Prior to this, and before the original buildings were erected when it was a wide avenue, it had been known as High Street, New Swindon. An application was made to the Wiltshire County Council, who were now responsible for education matters, for a grant towards the cost of new technical school buildings. It is most likely that this was done during the planning stage as the county decided, no doubt correctly, that as the state had accepted the responsibilities of providing technical as well as elementary education, it would be better undertaken publicly rather than by a private organization. As a result a new Technical Education Council was set up for the area and assumed the management of such classes, although then, and for many decades later, the railway staff continued to fill most posts for lecturers and instructors on a part time basis, in addition to their main employment. Therefore, when the new buildings were completed, the Mechanics Institution Council offered facilities such as reading room, smoking room, billiards, bagatelle, chess and draughts, ladies' reading room and extra dressing rooms for the existing theatre and hall. Also included was a new lecture room, council room and secretary's office. Thus was set the final pattern of life of this organization. The result, for Swindon, of the decision by the county to take over technical education, was the provision and completion, by 1895, of the North Wilts Technical School in the new Victoria Road between Old and New Swindon, evening classes already being carried out in elementary school premises, and no longer at the Mechanics Institute. This important addition to the town's facilities was to lead to the provision of secondary education in the same new schools also in 1895. One of the first new boys entering this new organization was Frederick W. Hawksworth, a name not unknown to the GWR in later years!

It was possibly this change in direction of technical education which had a bearing on another organization being formed. How this actually came about, and whether it was one or more people who took the original initiative, is not clear from surviving minute books, correspondence and local press reports. The issue of the 'Swindon Advertiser' for Friday, 17th February 1893, states under the sub-heading 'Junior

Plate 80: The reading room of the Mechanics Institute. This facility was withdrawn a few years after World War II, although the room is still used for other purposes. Note the great range of daily and periodical newspapers and magazines which were always available.

British Rail

Engineering Society', that the first meeting of the society was held in the lecture hall of the Mechanics Institute on Friday, (presumably 10th February) when there was a good attendance of members and candidates for membership; Mr A. E. Leader was voted to the chair. This gentleman then proceeded to explain the circumstances which had led to the formation of the Society (not recorded). Officers and committee, which included young men already holding responsible positions for their age in the Works, were elected. The object of the Society was 'to bring together the engineering students of Swindon for mutual improvement, and for spreading knowledge among the members by the reading and discussion of papers on any subject pertaining to engineering science'. It was further stated that the committee hoped to arrange excursions during the summer months to places of engineering interest.

One suspects the hand of the now maturing G. J. Churchward behind these moves, although there is nothing to substantiate this. Certainly, it does not

appear to have been suggested by William Dean, for we find the secretary, E. G. Ireland, later to become a Divisional Superintendent on the GWR, writing to Dean on 3rd March 1893 informing him that the Society, 'knowing the interest you would take in such a movement' had elected him President. Apparently the chairman, A. E. Leader, had endeavoured to approach Dean without success, (such men were very inaccessible in those days), to obtain his consent, and therefore they anticipated his acceptance. No reply from Dean is with this correspondence, so it is presumed that he agreed verbally, and subsequently took an active and helpful interest in its proceedings, soon authorizing visits to such places as Severn Tunnel pumping station at Sudbrook, and having special train arrangement made. The address book notes 43 members joining in 1893, but this does not include the President and Vice Presidents, numbering seven, all being senior officers at Swindon. This lively Society met at least fortnightly, the first lecture being delivered by the chairman on 3rd March 1893, on the subject of 'Lubrication'. Quite soon the winter series of lectures fell into a pattern consisting of papers given alternately by men of the GWR and outsiders who were specialists in their subjects. 'Intermediate' papers were presented by the young men of the Society to encourage discussion on such items with which their work was bringing them into contact. Such an approach was ideal for the further training of young practical engineers, and it is regretted that such methods are not in vogue at the present time. On 23rd January 1894 they held their first 'Conversazione' in the large hall of the institute. Already with a membership of 80, this event staged a fine exhibition of many models and appliances, many of them working, and including microscopes, electric lighting appliances, and an electric fountain with 'glow' lamps. Many of the models and other examples of equipment were loaned by Works officers and were a great success with the ladies and other visitors. We read that during the first half of the evening the stage was 'brilliantly lighted by ten sixteen-candle-power electric lamps lit by a dynamo in the basement, the arrangements for the supply of the current being most satisfactorily carried out under the personal supervision of Mr E. J. Ticknell'. The gallery was tastefully arranged for refreshments! After an overture from the band led by Mr W. D. James, an address was given by Mr Story-Maskelyne, a local worthy, scientist and Member of Parliament. Then followed a full musical programme by members and their sisters, lady friends and wives, ending with dancing, or as the press usually expressed it — 'indulgence in the terpsicorean art'. This annual 'Conversazione' was to become, for many years, one of the biggest social gatherings in New Swindon. Some years later, this Society was renamed the 'GWR Swindon Engineering Society'.

Moves were being made nationally to reorganize local boards into urban district councils, and these discussions again engendered speculation about merging the Old and New Towns into one authority. There was much opposition to this. The Old Town was still in a much worse condition for services than New Swindon, although some services, such as education, were common to both. In 1890 the New Town local board decided to provide new public offices at a cost of £10,000, in advance of the urban district council reorganization which took place eventually in 1894. These new buildings, to be known later as the Town Hall, were opened on 21st October 1891. Talks on amalgamation did not stop however, and a further move was made by the Wilts County Council in 1893, to no avail. New Swindon themselves tried again, early in 1896, after becoming an urban district. But in 1897 it was incorporation rather than amalgamation which at last turned public opinion in Old Town and the possibility of early attainment of county borough status, (one that has ever since

eluded Swindon), that led to firm discussions. Certainly the two UDCs were now working more closely together. In the year of Queen Victoria's Golden Jubilee, 1887, a new establishment, the Victoria Hospital consisting of 12 beds, had been opened in Old Town, and at the time of the Diamond Jubilee in 1897, the two bodies jointly sponsored an endowment fund for the hospital, which had already doubled in size. Finally a draft charter of incorporation was produced in March 1899 and finalized on 20th January 1900, to take effect from 9th November of that year. The Charter Mayor, by reason of having the maximum number of votes cast in the election for councillors, was G. J. Churchward, who had chaired the New Swindon UDC.

Another sign of the growth of the railway town was a new project of the Medical Fund to centralize most of their activities into one new building. In January 1888, we find the Chief Medical Officer writing to Dean showing his concern for the dispensing and other services, and asking for discussions on the subject. As a result, the Works Manager, Samuel Carlton, was instructed to carry out certain improvements at the house still used as a dispensary, as a short term measure, and by 1889 W. H. Stanier was in contact with Paddington and examining existing agreements between the Society and the Company. Finally, in August 1889, the directors agreed to lend capital at 2 per cent to cover the cost of new swimming baths, and to erect a new dispensary totally at the Company's cost. Land for such a project, situated almost opposite the hospital in Faringdon Road, had been purchased from Major Rolleston by the Society in 1885. It was a condition that this land now be conveyed to the Company. A grant of £2,000 was requested for the dispensary, and the total cost of the new buildings, including this, was £7,500. After other financial adjustments, a loan of £4,500 at 2 per cent interest was requested, capital to be repaid at £225 per annum. It was further requested that the Works carry out the building and that the stone be supplied free from the Foxes Wood Quarries. The committee and trustees must have thought they had the measure of the directors! Building by the Works was, however, refused, but Dean was allowed to undertake the ironwork at a 'reasonable price'. There were by now over 9,000 registered members, so the new amenities were desperately needed and orders were soon placed for materials and equipment for the project, and by the latter part of 1890 work was well in hand. A subway was built under the Cottage Estate, from the carriage shops to the new buildings, to supply water, steam and other services. This small subway still exists and although no longer used, has to be pumped out occasionally. The new large and small swimming baths, dispensary, consulting rooms and other amenities and offices were duly opened in 1892, and became another great asset to the Society and to the

Plate 81: The Medical Fund Society's consulting rooms, dispensary and swimming baths erected in 1892, but photographed in 1920, after Turkish and other baths had been added at the rear in 1899.

British Rail

Plate 82: The dispensary of the Medical Fund Society as seen in 1920.

British Rail

welfare of the railway community in general. A further advantage of the baths was that in winter months they could be floored over to become large assembly and dance halls. In 1899 the new buildings were extended to include washing, Turkish and Russian baths, thus completing the rationalization of activities on the one main site. Incidentally, a hair-dressing establishment was also opened on the new premises, but strangely this never became very popular although it struggled on until 1918.

We will now look into what the Works were engaged upon during the last decade of the 19th century. When G. N. Tyrell at last resigned as Superintendent of the Line in June 1888 after his long reign of 24 years, he left behind a legacy of slow and poor services over most of the system. Whilst there had been reason for caution in earlier days, to conserve the Company's financial solvency, such a state of affairs had become habit. His successor, N. J. Burlinson, however, had a much more realistic and vigorous approach, and with increasing financial stability, started at once to lead the GWR back into

righteous paths, laying the foundations, for others to build upon, of a railway service comparable with any in the world. The decisions he was to make had a great effect on Swindon. We have already discussed the final demise of the BG in 1892 over which he presided in operating matters, and have discussed the special work that this imposed in both the Locomotive & Carriage & Wagon Works. Burlinson was also very much aware of the decrepit state of the NG carriage stock in general and was soon in correspondence with Dean on the matter. At this time, the American railways had made considerable strides in the field of passenger comfort necessitated, in their case, by the long distance hauls their extensive country required. This had led to the introduction of Mr Pullman's cars for day and night travel, with interior heating, lavatory accommodation and restaurant facilities. A few examples of this type of vehicle had been introduced into this country, notably by the Midland Railway and there was an increasing demand for all these facilities where appropriate. As far as the GWR was concerned, their

Plate 83: A recently discovered photograph, taken inside the GWR Hospital (circa 1895). The two men standing are Drs. G. R. and A. C. Swinhoe, sons of the Medical Superintendent, Dr. G. M. Swinhoe. The matron is seated in front of them. The nine patients may have comprised the total number of males under care at that time.

R. C. H. Nash

first essay into sleeping carriages had appeared in the last days of Armstrong in 1877 and had lavatories fitted. Dean produced, in 1881, a much better design. Incidentally, these latter vehicles were the first to be built as NG bodies mounted on BG frames, an arrangement which was to be necessarily a feature of the period. Lavatory accommodation began to appear as a facility to some first class passengers lucky enough to choose the right compartments in the carriage, as they were usually built on the 'diagonal system', that is, so partitioned that entry from compartments on either side could be made. Some family saloons were also fitted. Dean's main contribution to passenger comfort however was in the design of new suspension, and much was done, in this direction, under his guidance. Train heating still relied on the 'foot-warmer' supplied at small cost at the various stations, although a variety of new methods were used for experiment. Even by 1890 the introduction of steam heating ('for winter only') was still in the experimental stage, the type with the steam supply coming from the locomotive boiler being the only one favoured by the GWR.

It was the use of these amenities and engineering improvements, with the encouragement of Burlinson, that Dean produced his famous Lots 551, 552, 553 and 580. The four vehicles built in these Lots proved to be a landmark in the history of British passenger trains, as they formed the first fully corridored train to enter service in this country. Individual carriages and the Pullmans on some railways had offered this facility for single vehicles only, but the fully corridored type of formation was to become the standard for all express and other main line trains. The orders for the first three Lots, taken from the carriage body shop records, were issued in the middle of 1890, although that for Lot 580 did not reach that shop until 28th February 1891, and was not completed there until 14th November. No doubt there were running trials in the intervening time, and perhaps some discussion of the final make-up or 'consist' of the train and it did not enter revenue service until 7th March 1892, working on the Paddington to Birkenhead route. The sobriquet 'Birkenhead Stock' therefore became attached to it, and for a time only the one set was available, travelling one way on each day. The train was steam-heated, and a small number of locomotives was modified to provide this service. Needless to say the experiment was entirely successful, and it is not surprising to find Burlinson writing to Dean on 7th November 1892 after a meeting with him a few days previously, suggesting changes to improve the next batch of similar vehicles, two sets for the 'Cornishman' express, and a balancing set for the Birkenhead service. There is also record of one of the Directors, Col. the Hon. C. E. Edgcumbe, sending in his own suggestions to Dean regarding the ventilation of smoking compartments. These sets

were introduced in 1893, and subsequently similar stock was put in hand for the South Wales and other services. Some of these later vehicles were somewhat longer than the original 50 ft. 'Birkenheads', being 56 ft. long, and others 52 ft. We find that the estimated cost of the new 'Birkenhead' set, now of 5 vehicles, (Brake Third; Third; First; Second; Brake Third;), was £5,280 for the complete set, and that for the 10.15 a.m. 'Cornishman' trains of four vehicles each, (Brake Third; First/Third Composite; Third; Brake Second), the cost was £4,060 each set! A 'Falmouth Coupé' vehicle was also included with these latter sets in service. The 'South Wales Corridor' sets appeared in service in 1896, and a very heavy carriage building programme developed. It was over this productive period in the Carriage Works that G. J. Churchward presided as manager, having assumed the chief responsibility when Holden left in 1885. Some authorities have opined that, being basically a 'locomotive' man, he must have been somewhat frustrated holding this post for ten years until December 1895. The author feels that such suggestions overlook the fact that all the senior managerial staff, and the two Works Managers in particular, were all more appropriately assistants to the LC&W Superintendent, and undertook all types of work allocated them by their chief, as well as the day to day oversight in the designated posts. The hand of Churchward is most clearly apparent in carriage development at the time, in that he undoubtedly developed from Dean's basic ideas much of the detailed design work, incorporating, at the same time, practical production design for a wide range of carriage improvements. He would also have worked at other projects, and locomotive boiler design was no doubt one of these, during the same period. There was now a rising generation of excellent carriage designers who were later to hold high office, such as L. R. Thomas, T. O. Hogarth, F. Marillier and Surrey Warner, the latter to go to the L&SWR as their Carriage Superintendent in 1906. Churchward's complete mastery of his subject is seen from his paper, *Modern Railway Carriages* which is still regarded as a 'classic' on its subject, which he gave to the Junior Engineering Society on 9th January 1896. Copies of this paper are now rare, and the author's own copy is greatly treasured. A measure of its value is that it is still used as a reference work eighty years later!

In a comparatively short period the quality of passenger comfort and service increased rapidly, and at last the giant that had slumbered quietly through nearly two decades began to awaken — and what an awakening it was to be. Apart from the end of the period of depression in the country, the final removal of the broad gauge and the energy of the new and rising senior officers began to retrieve that good name which had become more than tarnished. The measure of the great improvement to passenger comfort, is the

Plate 84: 'Birkenhead' four carriage corridor train with luggage van and Dean 'Single' No. 3003.

building of about 740 new carriages between the years 1894 and 1899. This was a greater annual rate than Churchward was to attain a decade later. There did remain, however, one obstacle to better services in the West of England — the enforced ten minute refreshment stop at Swindon Junction. The reasons for this being imposed were discussed in Chapter Two, and the reader will recall that in return for relieving the financially hard pressed Company from building the necessary 300 new workmen's cottages at Swindon and the refreshment rooms at the new station there, the contractors, J. & C. Rigby, had been granted a 99 year lease of the catering in these refreshment rooms from Christmas 1841, at the nominal rent of one penny per annum. The lease stated that:-

'All trains carrying passengers, not being Goods trains or "trains to be sent express" for special purposes, and except trains not under the control of the GWR Company, which shall pass the Swindon station either up or down, shall, save in case of emergency or unusual delay arising from accidents, stop there for refreshment of passengers for a reasonable period of about ten minutes.'

It should also be remembered that in the early days of the train service, 1841—45, the normal running time from Paddington to Swindon was usually 2½ to 3 hours, so a few minutes stop for other reasons was essential! Therefore, at the time of granting the lease, the conditions would not have appeared unreasonable to the directors. Now is the appropriate time to review the repercussions of this decision. As well as separate dining rooms for each class on both platforms, there were, on the upper floors, extended dining and entertainment rooms, and a small number of guest rooms connected across the main lines by a covered footbridge.

Messrs. Rigby, being civil engineers and not in the catering business, at once re-let the lease to Mr Griffiths, who controlled the Queens Hotel at Cheltenham, for a premium of £6,000 and a rent of £1,100 per annum. About this time the establishment appears as the 'Queens Hotel' and this name was probably initiated by Griffiths after his Cheltenham establishment. No doubt in these early years it was well run, but in 1848 Rigbys sold out their lease entirely to a Mr Phillips for £20,000, thus making a gross sum of £33,700 out of the transaction over seven years. Whilst Rigbys, to whom the GWR was a valued customer, held the lease, one would have expected there to be some control of the establishment to the advantage of the railway, but once the lease had been let to a tenant or disposed of completely to a third party, the GWR was powerless in this respect. Railway historians are well aware of Brunel's remarks, during one of his visits, regarding the quality of the coffee to Mr Player who was managing the establishment, and of other recorded remarks by travellers regarding the quality of food and drink on offer. Even whilst Rigbys still officially held the lease, there were some complaints on the services Mr Griffiths' staff were giving, but more importantly, Saunders and Gooch, as early as 1845, decided to take full advantage of the capacity of their new locomotives. When they introduced greatly accelerated services in 1845, they tried, on a few trains, to maximise on time saving, by reducing the stop at Swindon to one minute. Mr Griffiths of Cheltenham, through Rigbys, objected to this action naturally, and failing to obtain satisfaction from Saunders, filed a Bill in Chancery to compel the ten minute stop, in May 1845. Rigby and Griffiths had to wait until the following January before judgement was given in their favour, the court deciding that a 'train sent express' referred only to a private special train. The ten minute stop was therefore re-introduced. The new owner, Mr Phillips enjoyed his lease for 24 years before another attempt was made to encroach upon the ten minute stop. This time it was the Postmaster General who set things off by ordering, that from 1st November 1871, one train each way between Paddington and Bristol be designated 'mail train', and only five minutes was to be allotted to Swindon for exchange of mails. The Company was only too willing to comply, but naturally Mr. Phillips, aware of the previous court ruling, again took the matter to Chancery, but this time the case was lost, with the ruling that mail trains were not under the control of the Company. Possibly because he thought further inroads may be made on his monopoly, Phillips sold out in April 1875 to a Mr G. Moss, with the transfer price this time being £45,000. For the next five years a great change for the better was effected at the refreshment rooms, and they were now purported to be amongst the best. During this earlier period of its life a 'Queens Hotel tap' had been opened across the road from the station, as the 'public' part of the premises, and this inn still retains the name 'Queens Hotel'. That is not to be confused with the 'Queens Arms Hotel' on the corner of Corporation Street and Station Road East, later to be renamed the 'White House Hotel'. Possibly because of the better service given by Moss, the rooms were not so profitable, and were sold to Mr. Chater in

June 1880 at a discount figure of £35,000. But to the surprise of all parties, only one year later Chater was able to sell himself out to H. G. Lake for no less than £70,000 — a good profit in one year! After a short time in control himself, Lake sub-let to a company, who made what they could from the business, with dire results to the travelling public. Apart from the ill effects of the poor refreshment service, the GWR could not let this great incubus affect their services much longer, and removal of the BG and the need to recast their whole train service from 1893 onwards, made it imperative that the lease be bought out. This was eventually done towards the end of 1895, for what was then the huge sum of £100,000, which was liquidated by an annual charge to revenue until 1920. If this had not been done, we would have had to wait until Christmas 1941 for relief! The first train to run through Swindon, under the new arrangement, was the 10.45 a.m. ex-Paddington on 1st October, although the lease was not officially terminated until 12th November 1895. So ended the saga of this unwittingly bad decision made by the directors in 1841. The reputation of the rooms soon improved, and in the next decade they were to receive, on more than one occasion, Royal patronage, although this was to be incognito and of a very discreet nature!

On Holden's departure in 1885 for the GER, Dean did not appoint a successor to the position of chief assistant. He regularized Churchward's post of Assistant Carriage Works Manager to that of Manager. The general Works management pattern was still probably what it had been for some time, viz. Locomotive Works Manager, S. Carlton; Rolling Mills Manager, W. Ellis; (presumably the son of the original T. Ellis), Carriage Works Manager, G. J. Churchward; Wagon Works Manager, L. R. Thomas; Timber Manager (or Inspector), T. Hogarth. In addition there was a senior assistant of long standing at the Locomotive Works, named James Haydon, who ranked financially in the group. There was also the Chief Clerk, W. H. Stanier; Chief Accountant, H. J. Birch; the Outdoor Assistant to the L&CW Superintendent, T. Simpson; the Chief Draughtsman, W. H. Waister; and junior officers in charge of the gasworks and stores. From staff records one can assume that Carlton had overall control of Haydon and Ellis, whilst Churchward had oversight of Thomas and Hogarth. Dean was, therefore, working with three principal engineering assistants, Carlton, Churchward and Simpson, and with his chief clerk, Stanier, also technically inclined, he felt this was sufficient. Some of the team, however, were ageing, and on Monday, 23rd March 1896, Samuel Carlton died, in his 67th year, after an extended period of ill health. He had been Works Manager since 1864, having been appointed from Wolverhampton by Armstrong. During his long period at Swindon he had, like other GWR officers, served the community to his utmost

Plate 85: Passing Swindon on 1st October 1895, is the 10.45 ex-Paddington. This was the first train to pass Swindon after the removal of the refreshment room stop.

British Rail

ability, taking a prominent part in local board affairs, and serving on the controlling boards or committees of the Mechanics Institution, Medical Fund Society, New Swindon Gas Company, Swindon Waterworks, Parks Committee, New Swindon Permanent Building Society and many other activities. Due to his failing health, he had found it necessary to reduce his outside activities during the last five or six years of his life, although he maintained great interest until the end. He was extremely inventive and held many patents for railway devices, and was a great 'production' engineer, using modern terms.

His funeral, which took place the following Saturday, was almost as impressive as that of Armstrong's earlier. At least 800 men from the Works lined the route of the cortege from his home, Marlow House, to St. Mark's Church, and many more came to pay their last respects. The body was conveyed on a hand bier, eight foremen from the Works being bearers. About 500 people, on foot, followed the twelve carriages. Numerous officials from Paddington and elsewhere attended, including almost every Divisional and District Superintendent. After the service, the cortege proceeded around the park and Cambria Place to the cemetery, which Armstrong had done so much to inaugurate. Undeterred by

extremely bad weather, crowds, braving driving hail and high winds, lined the route the whole way.

G. J. Churchward had been moved, in 1895, from his post as Carriage Works Manager to that of Assistant Locomotive Works Manager, presumably because of the continued illness of Carlton, and he was now appointed manager in his place from 25th March 1896. This placed him, in effect, but not in name, as senior assistant to Dean, and from this date one can begin to discern his hand clearly in the matter of locomotive design. At the time of this appointment, there had been no major extension to the Factory at Swindon for about 20 years, although progressive improvements had been made to equipment and layout to meet the gradual increase in the volume of work which Swindon had been fortunate enough to obtain. That they had maintained efficiency can be seen from comparable costs of other major railways which were computed on exactly the same basis. Over the years 1881—87, the gross running cost of locomotives per train mile on the GWR averaged 7.56d (3.15p), and this was only bettered by the GNR at 7.28d (3.03p). Out of this gross cost of 7.56d, the repair costs at main Works was only 2.8d (1.7p). Similarly for carriages the cost per train mile averaged 2.53d (1.05p), and this low figure was only equalled by the GNR. Other items of interest are the installation of the first 20 telephones, authorized on 20th December 1893, and the employment of female labour. When the latter actually commenced is difficult to ascertain with any accuracy. We do find that in October 1890, however, the 'Third Annual Tea' for female staff, was held, there being about 100 attending. Knowing the propensity at this period for this sort of gathering, it might be assumed that employment of women on suitable work started in 1886 or thereabouts. Since they came under the control of foreman M. W. Harvie, it is clear that they were employed in the trimming (upholstery) shop, and certainly in the laundry, opened in November 1893, employing 9 or 10 ladies only at first, but to expand later. Those employed were the widows or daughters of former male employees who had died, or dependants of those badly injured. Again this was an example of the Board's sense of social responsibility for such people. At the function mentioned, tea was followed by a concert (including songs by Mr Harvie!), and a dance. Whether the 100 attendance refers only to the female employees is not clear, for, in the following year, this figure had risen to 230, which would be rather high if only referring to those employed.

In 1896 large purchases of land were made west of the area which had been used for the reception sidings for BG stock in 1892. This extended the GWR land westwards to the M&SWJR embankment and the River Ray, from the existing boundary of the Swinbrook which flowed roughly northward near Newburn House. Only two more small parcels of land immediately to the north of the new acquisitions were to be made later. These large purchases therefore generally encompassed what was to be the final westward boundaries of the establishment for nearly 80 years. Obviously such a large outlay would not have been made without something in view, although this was not to become clear for another year or two. So within some few months of his appointment, Churchward was making great plans for the future of the Locomotive Works. Improvements were already in hand at the gasworks, with mechanical charging and withdrawing equipment for the retorts, and on 10th June 1896, Dean received authority to construct a new carriage shop at a cost of £14,000 on the main wagon works site north of the station. There had been a smaller grant of £10,000 in 1892 for a 'carriage shed' on this site, and it is believed that this had been used at the start for seasonal storage of vehicles. It now became part of a larger group of shops where it was possible to concentrate all carriage repairs, and retain the older buildings south of the main line, to be re-laid out for new work only, on a continuous flow basis from west to east. This had obviously been planned by Churchward whilst carriage manager. A month later, on 22nd July 1896, a larger sum of £21,000 was made available

for modernizing the 'B' group of locomotive repair shops which included the original repair and erecting shops of 1841. This was when this group of shops was completely re-roofed, and provision made for better overhead crane facilities. Other small improvements were made in other areas within this authorization. In proposing the case for these two votes from the Board, Dean made it clear that no Works extensions of note had been made since 1876 and 1874 respectively, since when there had been a large increase to the rolling stock, and the locomotive stock had increased by over 1,000. The work was to be carried out by Works staff, and materials issued through the stores organization.

Another landmark put in hand in 1896 was a new pattern stores, built on the west side of Rodbourne Road, and surmounted by the now familiar large 225,000 gallon capacity water storage tank. A year later, a new stamping shop was provided in the C&W Works area (No. 18 C&W Shop). This shop was to supply items for both Works and for stores stock. In June 1898 authority was given for an additional carriage shed 'for storing carriages and carrying out painting and small repairs'. This was built to the north of the new carriage lifting shops just completed and was soon to be incorporated into that group. A running saga within the history of the Works of providing such storage accommodation continued, with an inevitable takeover for repair work, and the summer-use stock having to remain out in the open repeatedly! Even more significant, however, is that between January 1896 and December 1899 the large total of £68,231 was authorized for new machine tools and equipment at Swindon. This represents a major re-tooling of both Works and was preparing them for a period of high development and increased production. It must be remembered, too, that the last decade of the 19th century saw great development in machine tools in particular. This was when the earliest cam-operated automatic lathes came on to the market and the GWR was one of the first to install examples of these in the re-equipped 'R' machine shop in 1899, when rebuilt at a cost of £12,000. These were also the years when pneumatic hand tools became available and the first rivetting guns on a new compressed air system were introduced in 1896. An example of the first of these hand tools is still preserved in the Works.

The last of Dean's experimental locomotives, No. 36, appeared in August 1896. This was a massive 4-6-0 freight engine, the first of this wheel arrangement to appear south of the border, the only previous example being the 'Jones Goods' of the Highland Railway. A typical Dean design, with its double frame and large domed boiler and the classical outline always expected from his work, it nevertheless had many innovations. These were particularly apparent in the long boiler, which was fitted with 'Serve' tubes,

Plate 86: Experimental locomotive No. 36, the first GWR 4-6-0 of 1896, nicknamed *The Crocodile*.

British Rail

Plate 87: The exhibits prepared in the old paint shop for shipment to the Columbian Exhibition in Chicago in 1893. Note the locomotive steam brake controller on the right.

British Rail

and had the first wide firebox in the country. The inner frames were terminated short to accommodate this feature. It was fitted with water feed pumps and live and exhaust steam injectors. It was almost twice as powerful as existing 0-6-0 freight locomotives, and served the whole of its ten year life working heavy coal trains on the heavily graded Severn Tunnel line between Rogerstone Yard, Newport and Swindon. It is not unnatural that it received a nickname — 'the Crocodile', although this was very unfair considering its elegant outline.

One item which should be related here is an earlier visit of a GWR locomotive to America. All those with railway interests are very much aware of the visit of the locomotives *King George V* and the rebuilt *North Star* to the Baltimore & Ohio Centenary Exhibition in 1927, but not so many are aware of an earlier visit in 1893. This was the year of the Columbian Exhibition held that year in Chicago. The GWR was invited to send their, now withdrawn, BG locomotive *Lord of the Isles* which had remained in preservation since June 1884, with *North Star* (in its later form) as its stable mate. A Works personality, chargeman erector Benjamin J. Hale, was selected to travel with it and act as public relations officer. The locomotive was given the usual beauty treatment and shipped from Liverpool in January 1893 on the White Star *SS Tauric*. The crossing was very rough indeed and took 15 days, being unloaded at New York on 14th February. It was set up at the exhibition in Chicago in the place of honour and accorded the title, 'the greatest locomotive in England'. Hale appears not only to have enjoyed himself immensely, but also encouraged much interest in visiting the 'old country'. He was given ample supplies of current books and pamphlets on the GWR and England in general. During the visit he met a certain J. E. P. Wicks, who had worked previously in the locomotive offices at Swindon, but was now chief cashier to the Pullman Car Company. He also met W. Llewellyn who had been apprenticed at Swindon, and was then leading hand in an electrical and mining machine shop. The locomotive eventually left for New York on 14th December, and sailed on 1st January 1895, arriving at Liverpool on 11th January. Ben Hale then built up exhibits of *North Star* and *Lord of the Isles* for exhibition at Earls Court. He also represented the Company with the latter locomotive at Cardiff. He was appointed foreman in 1894. Later, in 1912, he became chief foreman of the machine shop, retiring in 1932.

From 1896 onwards the preponderance of locomotives appearing were those of the increasingly widespread 4-4-0 type for express passenger and mixed traffic work. Although chronologically, these should be dealt with in this chapter, for reasons now to be explained they are best considered in the next, when we are detailing the development in locomotive design instituted by Churchward.

William Dean had been born in 1840, and was only 28 when Armstrong brought him to Swindon in 1868, and placed upon him the heavy responsibility of providing the designs for the new range of locomotives then envisaged. The high rate of activity under Armstrong, until his premature death in 1877, has been described. So Dean was only in his 38th year when he took responsibility for what was, without doubt, the biggest and most onerous engineering post in the country, and possibly in Europe. He had steered his department skilfully through the tortuous periods of the succeeding years, always making sure that sufficient finance was available to ensure the adequate programme of maintenance. This policy had been enhanced by the design and building of simple locomotives which were highly reliable and inexpensive. His relationship with George Armstrong, to whom he had originally been junior, was not particularly easy, but his policy of a 'loose rein' helped. George Armstrong would not consider retirement until 1897 when he was 75 years old, and he died four years later on 11th July 1901. He was succeeded, after a short period under W. H. Waister, by J. A. Robinson, Divisional Locomotive Superintendent at Bristol, and brother of J. G. Robinson of Great Central Railway fame. During Dean's earlier years too, there had been increasing difficulties with the footplate staff in particular. This was not peculiar to the GWR, the main reason for dissatisfaction being the long hours and working conditions, which, in these days, would not be tolerated. These were the early years of firms coping with the stronger union attitudes, and much needed to be learned on both sides. To anyone in a position such as Dean's with a huge organization to run virtually single handed, and only a handful of assistants to take day to day control, the extra pressures on his time were tremendous. He was the only person with whom other departmental officers were prepared to discuss mutual concerns, and many hours must have been spent travelling betwixt Paddington and other centres.

This heavy and unremitting work-load, possibly increased by his decision not to replace Holden, with another principal assistant, took its inevitable toll, but tragically for him. There was a gradual, but irreversible, reduction of his mental faculties, the most obvious being an increased loss of memory for day to day details. When this began to be apparent is not clear, but a study of Churchward's financial advancement from staff records may give some indication, coupled with the actual design changes on locomotives now coming into use. One can see Churchward's ideas emerging almost as soon as he took over managership of the Locomotive Works in

1896. He was made chief assistant to Dean also, on 27th July 1897, but received no increase in salary until December of that year. It is clear from this period that Dean was leaving more to Churchward than would normally be expected. The ensuing years were handled by the Board, and Churchward in particular, with the utmost tact and discretion, showing not only their honour for this great man, but the utmost care for his welfare. The vital clue, in the author's opinion, comes on 31st July 1899 when Churchward's salary was suddenly increased by a third, but he still remained as chief assistant. It must be remembered that the salaries of chief officers like Dean were very high indeed, and bore no comparison with that of immediate assistants. It must have been at this time that the directors entrusted Churchward to take virtual control at Swindon, but simultaneously making it appear as if Dean was still at the helm. Whether much pressure was put on Dean to retire is not known, but if so it was done unobtrusively, as he remained nominally in charge until June 1902. Most employees in the Works were aware of the situation and many were the difficulties which arose as a result of Dean's daily visits to his workshops, but loyalty and tact were prevalent in putting everything to rights later. Eventually the Company purchased a house for him at 10 Terlingham Gardens, Folkestone, and after holding his important post for exactly 25 years, he was persuaded to retire there in June 1902. Added to the pressure of his work was the anxiety of his private life. His first wife, whom he married in 1865, died soon after the birth of their third child, and the wife of his second marriage in 1878, died in 1889. Both his daughters predeceased

him, one in infancy in 1870, and the other in 1893. His only son was an officer in the Royal Navy. Dean died on 24th September 1905 at Folkestone and was buried there, privately, a few days later, with only single representatives of both directors and officers at Paddington attending. Churchward attended from Swindon, as did J. Holden from the GER, and D. E. Marsh, who had trained and worked under him at Swindon, later moving to the GNR at Doncaster, but by this time L&CW Superintendent of the LB&SCR. The vicar of Rodbourne Cheney, where Dean had regularly worshipped, was also present. His loss in Swindon did not go unnoticed, but was accepted with the same understanding as had been his last difficult months in the Works.

The years just before the turn of the century were to be a watershed in the life of the GWR. Its long years of financial struggle were now much eased, the politics of the railway mania period were gone, and the organization had been welded firmly into an entity under Gooch's guidance. A succession of highly competent railway engineers made it their business to provide the necessary tools to run an efficient business, and the GWR now had a top management in all branches which was already arousing the sleeping giant of the last 20 years into full wakefulness, which was to place it suddenly on the stage as leader of world land transport. But they also had in one particular man something just a little bit extra. This was George Jackson Churchward who was to prove himself, in the space of only a few years, one of three or four of the world's greatest steam locomotive engineers.

Chapter Six

1897~1914 The Glorious Years

Although discussion of locomotive development could have continued in the previous chapter, until the time of Dean's retirement, it is more appropriate, knowing the circumstances of his last years, to recommence the review from the year 1897 in order to place the astounding developments, which were to take place, in their proper perspective. As we have seen, Churchward moved to the Locomotive Works as Assistant Manager in 1895 during the last illness of Carlton, and succeeded him as Works Manager on 25th March 1896. His succession to the top post was now inevitable, and this was duly acknowledged in his additional appointment, on 27th July 1897, as Chief Assistant to Dean, a post which had lain vacant for 12 years. There is little doubt that Churchward had a hand in certain developments to locomotives in the period immediately previous to his move to the Locomotive Works, particularly with items appertaining to boilers. The 'Duke' class of Lot 102, express passenger locomotives of the 4-4-0 wheel arrangement appearing in 1896, are usually referred to as the last pure Dean design, but the locomotives were provided with an extended smokebox containing spark arrestors, a practice that was then largely American, and one must suspect that this was proposed by Churchward, who had made a thorough study of American locomotive design. Other items on this class may also have been fitted at his suggestion. The succeeding 'Badminton' class, with numbers following on where the 'Dukes' left off, and commencing with No. 3292, were already on order and drawings issued for them to be fitted with a raised round topped firebox. Apparently, quite late in the proceedings, Churchward had the boiler design changed to the Belpaire type. How this late change was agreed with Dean we shall perhaps never know, but one thing is clear, to complete the locomotive in time, the boiler designs must have already been to hand, or in a very advanced state. The provision of the vastly different flanging blocks for this type of firebox would also have been difficult to provide within this time, if some previous work had not already been done. Whilst these points must remain supposition, they do make engineering sense and support the theory of much previous work put in on boilers by Churchward to convince him that this change should be made. The boiler barrel of this, and other early numbers of the class, also carried Serve tubes, already fitted to No. 36, the freight 4-6-0 locomotive. The 'Badminton' class had 6ft. 8½in. driving wheels as against the 5ft. 8in. wheels of the 'Dukes' and were capable of high speeds, incorporating many new items in detail design. In the following year, an order was issued for a further 20 'Duke' class mainly for use in Devon

Plate 88: George Jackson Churchward, CBE, Locomotive Carriage & Wagon Superintendent 1902—1916. Chief Mechanical Engineer 1916—1921.

British Rail

and Cornwall, where Brunel's beautiful timber trestle viaducts were now being replaced and heavier locomotives being used. Fifteen of these retained the flush round topped firebox as carried on the previous batch, but four had Belpaire fireboxes and pressed to 180p.s.i. rather than 160p.s.i. as previously. The last numbered locomotive of the batch, which incidentally appeared first, carried a very different boiler indeed. It had a Belpaire box, but this was lengthened by 20 per cent. The boiler still carried a dome, but although the boiler barrel itself was still parallel and the sides of the firebox straight, this was to be the prototype of the first of the new standard range which Churchward was to produce. The locomotive upon which it was placed was No. 3312 *Bulldog*.

Plate 89: The experimental 4-6-0, No. 2601 (nicknamed *Kruger*). Note the combustion chamber forward of the firebox and the saddle-mounted sand-box.

British Rail

Plate 90: No. 2602 (nicknamed *Mrs Kruger*), the second of the experimental class, but in 2-6-0 form as were the remainder of the series.

British Rail

The 'Badminton' class was being built at the same time as these additions to the 'Duke' class, and one of the 'Badmintons', No. 3293 *Waterford*, was fitted with a similarly large boiler to *Bulldog*, except now the dome was replaced by safety valves within the GWR brass 'bonnet'. This change was made possible by placing the steam collector in the top of the new large firebox crown, and a similarly modified boiler was also fitted to the new locomotive No. 3352 *Camel*. This engine became the prototype of what was latterly known as the 'Bulldog' class, i.e. 5ft. 4in. diameter wheeled 4-4-0 locomotives carrying the standard No. 2 boiler. The steaming propensities of these two engines were closely followed by Churchward and compared with other types in use. A year later, in 1900, the 'Atbara' class of 6ft. 8½in. 4-4-0 engines also appeared with the same type of boiler.

Excellent as the large class of 'Dean Goods' were, the introduction of No. 36 had shown the advantage of more powerful engines to haul the ever increasing coal traffic, from South Wales, in longer trains to give better track utilization, particularly through the Severn Tunnel and up the long gradient on the English side. This was another chance for Churchward to try out more of his boiler theories. As a result, there appeared one of the ugliest locomotives ever seen on the GWR. Using much the same arrangement below the running plate as the elegant looking No. 36, it was surmounted with a massive high-pitched boiler, which not only had a Belpaire firebox, but also a combustion chamber extension stretching 3ft. 6in. forward of it. The 10ft. 6in. long barrel was surmounted by a large sandbox in the form of a saddle just behind the smokebox. The now standard 4ft. 7½in. diameter freight engine wheels were driven from 19in. diameter cylinders with the stroke increased to 28in. More importantly, for the first time on the GWR, piston valves were used, albeit of the simple plug type, but much experience was to be gained from this innovation. Originally pressed to 200p.s.i., the boiler was subsequently reduced to 180p.s.i. Since the Boer War was now in progress, it is not surprising that No. 2601 was nicknamed *Kruger*.

From the experience gained from No. 2601 and the steaming capabilities of *Waterford* and *Camel*, a second experimental freight locomotive, No. 33, was developed with 4ft. 7½in. diameter wheels in a 2-6-0 arrangement and with the parallel standard No. 2 boiler. This proved to be very successful and was eventually adopted as an extra standard type, the 'Aberdare' 26XX class.

The success of the leading pony truck on No. 33 led to the remaining 9 'Krugers' being built with the 2-6-0 arrangement, but retaining the same ugly boilers. These boilers were very unreliable however; perhaps there was too much innovation at one time, a

fault of Dean's. If so, it was a fault Churchward was never to make again. The boiler pressure had to be further reduced to 165p.s.i., and although nominally of higher rating than the 'Aberdares', they were unable to match them in service and they only had a short life until withdrawn in 1907. By some quirk of circumstance however, the 'Kruger' boilers were retained in stock and utilized for stationary steam raising purposes working at a nominal 100p.s.i. In this form, they were very successful indeed, and enjoyed long service, both in Swindon Works and at other depots on the system. In fact, the last locomotive type stationary boiler in use in Swindon Works in 1965 was of this type. How much of the original boiler still existed cannot be surmised, but the railway certainly got more than adequate value from them.

A shortened version of the *Camel* domeless Belpaire boiler was provided for an experimental 2-4-2 tank locomotive with radial axleboxes at each end, an arrangement much used on the LNWR and other lines at the time. Again this locomotive had piston valves of a design varying from those on the 'Krugers'. The engine was also fitted with water pick up apparatus. Later renumbered 3600 in the class series, this type of piston valve was not repeated, some locomotives reverting to slide valves, but others to the better 'semi-plug' piston valves.

Although not going into detail which other volumes, specifically studying the development of locomotives designed by Churchward, can do, enough has been said to illustrate the way in which his many new ideas were being worked out and tested in service. The work already discussed had been spread over nearly four years. During this time the railway traffic was still being worked by 4-4-0 and 4-2-0 express locomotives and most of the freight by six coupled machines. But all these experiments were being watched simultaneously, so that balanced judgement could be made by comparative performance data. Churchward's philosophy was that the major area for improvement lay in the total steam circuit, and it was here that efficiency of the steam locomotive was based. When new and acceptable parameters could be applied to this part of the locomotive, the time would be ripe for improvements beneath the 'running plate'. For without a steam circuit of high efficiency to feed the engine proper, there was little to be gained from improvements to the valve gear, compounding and similar matters.

In his *Outline of Great Western Locomotive Practice 1837–1947*, the late Harry Holcroft relates that in 1901, whilst he was still an apprentice at Wolverhampton, the Dean single wheeler, No. 3021 *Wigmore Castle*, appeared at Stafford Road depot with wooden templates fixed outside the frames adjacent to the front bogie representing outside cylinders. Similar reports are to be found from other

Plate 91: Locomotive No. 100, (later *William Dean*) as originally built in 1902.

British Rail

sources of the sighting of this locomotive at other places on the GWR. It was very evident that something was afoot, and that clearances for the use of outside cylinders (virtually heresy to GWR practice), were now being considered. Much speculation transpired amongst those interested in such matters, but it is questionable if many guessed aright except those working within the ivory towers of the Swindon drawing offices. It was several months before curiosity was satisfied, but in February 1902 another prototype rolled out of the Factory. This was No. 100, a huge 4-6-0 passenger engine which discarded virtually all GWR traditional styles and ideas of the pre-1895 era. Although to our eyes today, it can be accepted as a handsome design, at the time it had few admirers, particularly amongst GWR supporters. The two outside cylinders were 18 in. diameter but with the stroke now extended to the extraordinary length of 30 in., an increase foreshadowed in the 'Kruger' 2601. Of the traditional ornamentation there was none, and in outline angular, but it was a prototype and as such, these considerations were best left until the design had been proved or modified. Again it was the boiler which drew most attention. The steel Belpaire firebox was now 9 ft. long and with a 14 ft.

8 in. by 5 ft. diameter domeless and parallel barrel. Piston valves were again fitted, but only 6½ in. diameter, (later increased to 7½ in.) This type of valve was still not mechanically satisfactory but problems surrounding it were being systematically solved. With a power rating some 25 per cent above everything else in passenger service, it was an indication of what was to come in the near future. It was fitted with vacuum brakes to all wheels including bogie, the outcome of a decision made by Churchward following the comparative ineffectiveness of steam brakes in emergency application, highlighted in the Slough accident of 1900. Another outcome of this accident was the change, in 1903, from a sliding vacuum cylinder to a fixed cylinder on trunnions operating through a moving piston, and fitted with accelerating valves to admit air direct in emergency conditions.

This locomotive emerged for service whilst Dean was still officially in office, although it is apparent that he had little or nothing to do with its design. Eventually retiring some three months later, it was named *Dean* by Churchward, no doubt with approval by the Board — a very sincere and pleasing tribute to the great man as he left the service of the GWR after 47 years.

This original nameplate was later amended, in more

than one form, to *William Dean*, and the locomotive was re-boilered after 16 months service. The original boiler, working at 200 p.s.i. was the prototype of what was to be the outstanding one of the series, the standard No. 1. Before this change, however, another locomotive appeared in March 1903, No. 98, properly recognized as the first true Churchward standard locomotive; it was a milestone in design. On this, the standard No. 1 boiler had acquired a cone form on its rear ring, which shape was to be further developed later, in order to obtain better heat transference in the hottest part of the boiler. Incredibly there were two further experimental types being built at the same time and emerging soon after; No. 97, a large freight 2-8-0; and No. 99, a 2-6-2 side tank locomotive. In all these three were to be incorporated most of the results of the experiments and trials, many of which had been under critical review for up to five years, and which Churchward and his staff had now brought to fruition. They were also remarkable in that, although they were three separate and distinct types, Nos. 98 and 97 carried the same standard No. 1 boiler, whilst No. 99 had the standard No. 2. All the cylinder castings were identical. A new casting pattern had been designed so that a pair could be bolted back to back, after suitable machining, to stretch the correct width of the locomotive and forming, in the centre, a machinable saddle mounting for the boiler. They were machined to nominal 18 in. diameter by 30 in. stroke, but with enough metal to offer slight variations to the bore. Provision was made for piston valves no less than 10 in. diameter to accept the American style semi-plug type which had proved to be the best solution to wear and lubrication problems. A further American introduction was the use of bar frame extensions forward of the main plate frames to accommodate the new outside cylinder arrangement with the required running wheel clearances. Finally, most of the Stephenson motion gear was common, the only general difference being in the lengths of the actuating rods due to the varying wheel centres of the three locomotives. Many other items of equipment were, of course, already standard or became so on this batch of prototypes.

As early as January 1901, the drawing office had produced a remarkable single sheet depicting no less than six standard types of locomotive. Each one of these carried 18 in. by 30 in. cylinders, although at this time only 8½ in. diameter piston valves were contemplated. Furthermore, these piston valves were specified to have very long travel and large double port openings. There were only two boiler types required, equating to the standard Nos. 1 and 2 shortly to appear, yet the range of locomotives was two 4-6-0 types, express and mixed traffic; one 2-8-0 freight; a 4-4-2 tank for heavy suburban work; a 4-4-0 for lighter express work; and lastly, a general duties 2-6-2 tank. There were only three driving wheel sizes

and one diameter (3 ft. 3 in.) for carrying wheels, whether pony, radial or bogie. Only one of these standard types did not appear during Churchward's term of office. The new Superintendent-elect proceeded with his plans for a stock of locomotives to meet the new demands on the railway now becoming evident, but in a way which was to produce the utmost economy to the GWR in operation and maintenance costs. From this point of view it was fortuitous that circumstances allowed him to start preparations for this great change of direction in locomotive policy some five years before the departure of Dean. Without this period of time it may not have been possible to initiate the new ideas and allow sufficient development time, together with reasonable time for single prototype locomotives for proper assessment. The possible result may have been the necessity of ordering batches 'straight off the drawing board', a situation which has dogged many a chief officer even up to the present times.

There were other great problems which were noted by Churchward when he was transferred from the Carriage Works in 1895, notably the increasing inadequacy of the facilities at Swindon. There was little he could do immediately, although, as we have seen, one authorization of £21,000 was made, in 1896, for additional engine repair facilities. There were other political matters not made public at the time which, perhaps, cautioned him to bide his time. The end of the broad gauge had raised the question of locomotive building and repair policy. There was much support on the Board to expand Wolverhampton, which had always been a 'narrow gauge' works, to become the major locomotive works, Swindon assuming similar responsibility for carriages and wagons. From the point of view of labour, material and fuel availability there was much to commend it. However, it was also agreed, but had not been proved, that work reductions at Swindon would cause permanent loss of valuable labour. Against the Wolverhampton proposals was the difficulty of finding suitable land for expansion, and this was a problem that might well increase, as the area was already being developed residentially. As far as Swindon was concerned, it was argued that timber was more easily available there as the main C & W material. Land was also easier to obtain and needed little preparation for building. The reality of the situation is highlighted in correspondence dealing with the land purchases west of Rodbourne Road at Swindon for the BG reception sidings. In this, Dean asserts that, after conversion and scrapping is completed, the area could be used 'for new carriage sheds'. As long as George Armstrong was at Wolverhampton he continued trying to purchase the necessary part of Dunstall Hill which would need to have its top sliced off to create suitable level ground, although the opposition and price was too excessive.

Plate 92: No. 98 (later No. 2998), the next development of the two cylinder 4-6-0, but again an experimental locomotive. It is seen as outshopped in September 1903.

British Rail

Plate 93: No. 97 (later No. 2800), the first 2-8-0 in the country, built in June 1903.

British Rail

Plate 94: No. 99 (later No. 3100), the prototype of the 31XX class, also of 1903.

Plate 95: The remarkable sheet of standard engine diagrams prepared in 1901 by Churchward using only two types of boiler. Only 'Class B' (centre left) was not produced in Churchward's time.

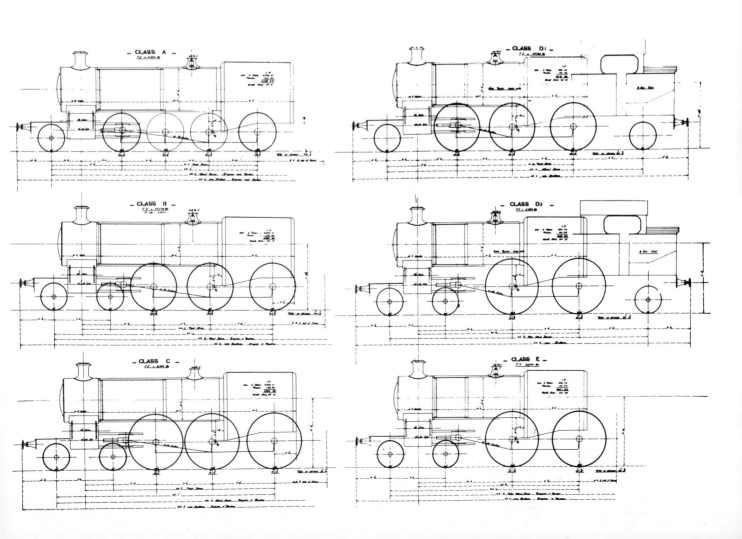

It was in this situation that the small development only was authorized, in 1896, and by that time Churchward was already looking at the situation from a different viewpoint, and to Swindon's advantage. The case for extension of locomotive activities generally could not be denied. In plain financial terms the reasons were obvious. In the 20 years, 1880–1899, out of £117,800 authorized for new and improved shops and major plant at Swindon, only £40,000 was specifically for locomotive shops, an average of £2,000 per annum. Expenditure on machinery for the Works as a whole had also been meagre in the first 15 years of the period, except for that built in the Works, only showing significant improvement after Churchward's arrival. During the same period, the locomotive stock had risen by about 52.5 per cent, and no major work had been undertaken at Wolverhampton either. Churchward doubtless foresaw the large locomotive building requirement before him, which, by his own reckoning, meant the building of larger and heavier locomotives and the existing shops would be unable to handle these. Doubtless with Dean's approval, he set about designing a new set of shops on the land now available at the west end of the Factory, and was able to prepare a convincing case for the Board. After somewhat prolonged discussions this project was authorized, on 27th June 1900, at the cost of £33,000, and was to become the first part of the famous 'A' shop. It was to be a single building almost square in shape, 480 ft. by 486 ft. between walls, an area of 233,400 sq. ft. or 5.36 acres (2.12 hectares approximately). Designed and built by Swindon staff, it was the first building in the Works of which the structural work was entirely of steel; wrought and cast iron being the previous materials. All walls were of the distinctive red Cattybrook smooth faced bricks, made to the full 9 in. by 4½ in. by 3 in. dimensions, causing matching problems when future alterations were made. Sills and other items were picked out in blue engineering brick. Internal natural lighting was excellent by north light saw tooth ridge roofing mounted on Warren girders and with supporting columns kept to a minimum. Walls were pierced with the maximum amount of windows conducive to structural strength. The authority was for 'a lifting and machine shop' and it was laid out with the machine and fitting shop 480 ft. by 165 ft. along the north wall. To the south of this was the 415 ft. by 306 ft. erecting shop of four bays, each pair served by a traverser and with a stock area between. Each lifting bay was provided with twin crab electro-hydraulic cranes at 50 tons capacity per crane, with pit accommodation beneath of 20 per bay, making 80 pit roads in all. Adjoining the east side of the erecting shop was a power house, and an area to be developed as a testing plant totalling 306 ft. x 66 ft., both of which will be referred to in detail later.

By a quirk of fate, the industrial expansion of Wolverhampton overtook the residential area on the other side of Dunstall Hill, and by the time the 'A' shop was authorized, the GWR was able to acquire more land at a reasonable price; too late, however, to reverse any decisions concerning future development at Swindon.

The eventual retirement of Dean brought about a considerable reshuffling of officers at Swindon, and, for the first time, the promotions were given to Swindon men rather than those from Wolverhampton as had tended to happen previously. The battle for supremacy, or, at least, equality, maintained by George Armstrong, had finished with his retirement, and in any case, the long reign of Dean at Swindon had upset the former pattern of quick promotion favouring young men from the north, and had been eventually halted by the untimely death of 'Young Joe' Armstrong, described earlier. The organization of the GWR had been slowly changing during the previous years too, and the position of General Manager was beginning to emerge as carrying higher authority, although not until after the retirement of Churchward, at the end of 1921, was the General Manager to emerge as the recognized senior executive officer of the Company. G. J. Churchward, of course, succeeded immediately to the post of Superintendent on 1st June 1902, and very quickly made his new dispositions. As far as he was concerned, his starting salary, following GWR practice, was below the ceiling for the post for the first 12 months, but on the attainment of this, the figure was still set below that received by Dean. During the rest of his career he only received one more advance in salary, of 16.6 per cent, in 1919! Of course, he received many other emoluments, including the use of Newburn House, pupil's fees, patent fees, etc. Small though the salary may appear today, (1982), taking into account the changes in taxation and inflation, his gross salary would now equate to over £100,000 per annum. Certain staff had been moved into key posts prior to 1902 however, and it is interesting to examine the previous careers of some of these as we find they are similar. Experience was the key; however, the comparative youth of them all is noteworthy. On his appointment as chief assistant to Dean, in 1897, Churchward retained the post of Locomotive Works Manager, only relinquishing it on 11th February 1901, when F. C. Wright was appointed in his place. Wright had been assistant manager since 13th April 1896, that is during the same period that Churchward was Manager. Prior to this, he had held the post of chief draughtsman for a period, but the day after Churchward's appointment as Superintendent, Wright was made Works Assistant, and became chief assistant on 27th July 1903. Churchward was 45 years of age in 1902 and Wright 40 years of age. Following F. C. Wright was H. C. King, first as chief

Plate 96: The interior of the 'A' erecting shop shown in May 1904 shortly after completion.

British Rail

Plate 97: A busy view of the newly built first section of the 'A' shop seen on 30th April 1908. No. 1642, a saddle tank, in the foreground is particularly resplendent after its repair. The day of the pannier tank was only just dawning. Newburn House can be seen in the top left corner of the picture.

British Rail

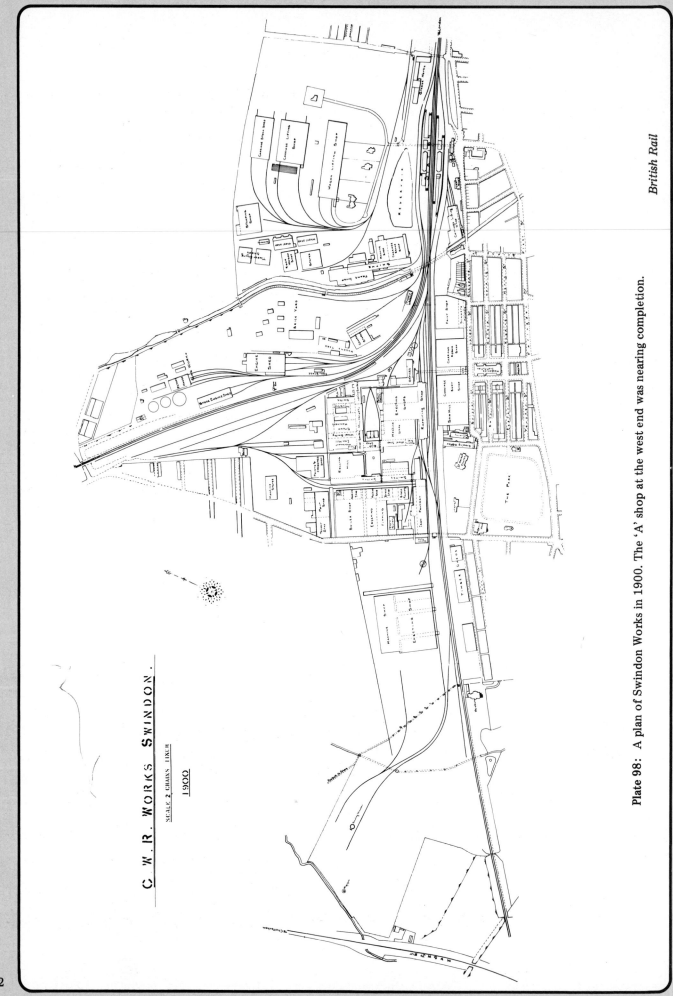

G.W.R. WORKS SWINDON.

SCALE 2 CHAINS 1INCH

1900

British Rail

Plate 98: A plan of Swindon Works in 1900. The 'A' shop at the west end was nearing completion.

draughtsman from 13th April 1896, then Assistant Locomotive Works Manager from 11th February 1901, and Works Manager on 2nd June 1902, being 42 years of age at this latter appointment. Similarly, F. W. Snell, who had become assistant chief draughtsman in July 1900, followed King as the chief there on 11th February 1901, although he was later to move to the Divisions, being about 40 years of age in 1902. On 25th February 1901, Churchward appointed a young man from the drawing office, C. B. Collett, as Assistant Locomotive Works Manager, also two supernumary assistants nominally under Collett, but reporting direct to Churchward. These were G. H. Pearson, son of W. Pearson former Superintendent of the B & E R, and J. W. Cross, both from the drawing office. All three were in their early thirties, and the latter pair were to supervise Churchward's many new ideas and his testing. The only 'old hand', and incidentally a Wolverhampton one, was W. H. Waister. Aged 55 years in 1902, and hailing from Newcastle, he was trained at Wolverhampton, but had been chief draughtsman at Swindon from 1885 to 1887, and after other short appointments, had succeeded George Armstrong in charge of the Northern Division. He moved back to Swindon as outdoor assistant to the Superintendent, a position roughly equated to future motive power superintendents, a few months later. However, this was the one senior post that called for long experience and steady judgement, and Waister certainly possessed both.

Such was the engineering management team which surrounded Churchward. He had, by this time, a strong young element in the drawing office, laboratory and test house, and as materials inspectors, who were being carefully guided in their careers by judicious junior appointments, and encouraged to take active interest in discussions at the Junior Engineering Society. Holding the post of honorary secretary of this society, was in itself a signal mark of a man's future potential. Such names as G. Burrows, Oswald Barker, Frank Crossley, F. C. Coventry, Conrad Dumas, E. T. J. Evans, T. O. Hogarth, E. G. Ireland, F. W. Marillier, Surrey Warner, F. W. Hawksworth, W. A. Stanier, T. Simpson and Victor Bailey, to mention but a few, were to become household names either on the GWR, or with other railways or industries not many years later. Another drawing office man to become well known was H. F. S. Morgan, who left to form the motor company of that name.

We will now return to the subject of locomotive and carriage development before examining the social situation in these early years of the century. The stage had been reached where three considerably developed prototypes were in revenue earning service and showing the advances which Churchward had

Plate 99: Du Bousquet-De Glehn compound locomotive No. 102 *La France* seen carrying the livery in which it undertook trials starting in October 1903. There was one earlier temporary livery.

British Rail

advocated. In particular, enough progress had been made with the two standard boilers and steam circuits in general, to be able to start on the second stage of development. American practice had figured largely in the new designs, and in particular, it was the robust simplicity of these items which attracted Churchward. Indeed, he was on friendly terms with some of his counterparts on railways across the Atlantic. For some years now there had been continuing controversy on the advantages of compound versus simple expansion engines. F. W. Webb on the LNWR had already introduced compound locomotives and theoretically there was much to be said for their adoption. Churchward was not so convinced, however, and felt that equally good results could be obtained with simple expansion, if properly applied in practice, and in his view the only way of finding out was by trial. Perhaps the greatest strides had been made in France with the development of the du Bousquet-de Glehn method of compounding and many examples were now running there, particularly on the Nord, Paris—Orleans and Midi Railways. Authority was therefore obtained to purchase an example similar to the latest pattern on the Nord, from the Société Alsacienne factory at Belfort. This locomotive, to be numbered 102 (and later named *La France*), arrived at Poplar Dock on 19th October 1903 in parts. After re-erection at Swindon it entered service on 2nd February 1902. It was of the 4-4-2 (Atlantic) wheel arrangement, the two outside high pressure cylinders driving the rear pair of wheels, and the inside low pressure cylinders the leading pair. Boiler pressure was at the English equivalent of 227 p.s.i. The coupled wheels were the standard GWR 6ft. 8½in. Separate sets of Walschaert's gear operated the high pressure and low pressure cylinders.

Whilst the French engine was on order, Churchward prepared to build, in 1903, a two cylinder simple expansion locomotive, so that the proper comparisons and tests could be made. This was to be No. 171 (later 2971 *Albion*). It was very similar to No. 98, but the pressure in the developed standard No. 1 boiler was raised to a comparative 225 p.s.i. As a 4-6-0 it would not have been comparable with the French engine, by virtue of having nearly 50 per cent more adhesive weight available. Therefore, the frames were prepared for the normal wheel arrangement, but extra plates were fitted to accommodate alternatively a pair of carrying wheels at the rear to make it a 4-4-2. There now commenced two years of observed performance of the two locomotives working in the same link. Little difference was found between coal consumption, although that of oil was higher on the more mechanically complicated French engine. It was clear, however, that the smooth running of the compound, because of its divided drive, would result in much longer periods between major maintenance. Individual bearing surfaces also carried much lower

friction forces for the same reason. Churchward was still not fully satisfied, and obtained authority to purchase two more similar locomotives. These were to be slightly larger than No. 102 and were similar to those then running on the Paris—Orleans Railway. The main differences were increases in high pressure and low pressure cylinder diameters and a corresponding increase in boiler size to match. They were registered into stock in June 1905 and numbered No. 103 *President* and No. 104 *Alliance*, the names being added two years later.

By this time, nineteen more of the 171 class were either completed or in process of erection. Of these, thirteen came out as Atlantics with the modified rear frame, and the remaining six as 4-6-0. One of the former, No. 184, had a new bogie based on that supplied under No. 102. This highlights the interest in this particular unit, and Swindon was to adopt the main principles, although in different form, for its future locomotive bogies, and this fundamental design was to be used later by both the London Midland & Scottish and the Southern railways. By 1906, that is about 2½ years after the arrival of No. 102, the situation was becoming clear in the mind of Churchward, and the main points can be summed up as follows. The Swindon 2 cylinder arrangement, with long travel valves, operated from Stephenson motion, was equally as economic as the 4 cylinder compound du Bousquet-de Glehn locomotives with four sets of Walschaert's gear. The complicated driving techniques of the compounds necessary to obtain the best, and equal, performance was a disadvantage. Conversely they were much smoother running, due to the divided drive, and corresponding balanced reciprocating masses of the four cylinder arrangement which deserved consideration in order to reduce wear and tear. The bogie design was excellent and assisted in the smooth running of the locomotive, particularly on the twisting tracks in south Devon. Finally the advantage gained by the 4-6-0 versions of the 171 class from increased adhesion, particularly noticeable on the south Devon banks, could not be overlooked, although this point was not relevant to the trials, but needed bearing in mind for the future.

Churchward, therefore, decided that to clinch the matter he should build an experimental 4 cylinder simple machine. Design was put in hand in 1905, and it appeared in service in June 1906 as No. 40. There were many problems to be solved in this new venture so that it could use as many of the new 'standard' parts as possible. The cylinder dispositions were similar to that on the French locomotive, and a plate frame was used throughout. Churchward required only two sets of valve gear to work the four cylinders as he would never countenance outside gear in his designs, and there was not room for four sets of gear within the frames. A type of valve gear was devised by W. H. Pearce in the drawing office to meet these

Plate 100: No. 171 *Albion*, built by Churchward for comparative trials against compound No. 102. This was the first GWR engine to have 225 p.s.i. boiler pressure.

British Rail

Plate 101: Churchward's experimental split-drive four cylinder simple locomotive, No. 40, also built for comparison with the French compounds in 1906. Later named *North Star*, it was rebuilt as a 4-6-0 in 1909 and renumbered 4000 in 1912.

British Rail

Plate 102: No. 4002 *Evening Star*, the second in the series which was Churchward's masterpiece of design. It was built in March 1907.

British Rail

requirements, derived from methods used previously by Prof. Stévart on river boats, and later used by Belpaire on locomotives. Known at Swindon as the 'scissors' gear from its arrangement, it used many standard parts and incorporated ingenious rocking levers to actuate the outside cylinders. Being 'simple expansion' this locomotive could work very freely at short cut-offs, a thing which no compound could do. It was this feature that balanced out the theoretical advantages of compounding regarding cylinder heat losses etc. The four cylinders were 14¼ in. diameter by 24 in. stroke, and a standard No. 1 short-coned boiler was carried at first. Apart from the inevitable teething troubles arising from a prototype, which were soon corrected, the locomotive, to be named *North Star* proved to have an amalgam of all the best qualities of the French compounds, and of the new Swindon practice of the preceding nine years. It fully justified the continuous researching and testing over this period, so ably led by Churchward and carried out by a dedicated band of engineers.

Although No. 40 went into service in June 1906, building commenced, in August, of the 4 cylinder 4-6-0 4001 class, the 'Stars', a group of ten built to Lot 168 and entering service between February and May 1907. Apart from the wheel arrangement, the only basic differences were a fully coned standard No. 1 boiler, and the replacement of the 'scissors' gear by two sets of inside Walschaert's motion. The former had the disadvantage of deriving motion on one side of the engine from gear on the opposite side.

Therefore, in the event of breakdown on one side, the locomotive became helpless. However, there was not room to fit Stephenson's valve gear in the limited space available, so Walschaert's was used. The author is well aware, from personal experience, of the difficulties of accessibility between the frames even with this arrangement, but the elegance with which the undoubted problems of space and clearance was solved must be admired. Its enclosure so close to the longitudinal centre lines reduced the couple generated by outside motion gear, thereby aiding steady running. It was recognized that the fitting of Walschaert's gear would make acceleration away from stations a little more sluggish than if fitted with Stephenson gear. This was acceptable, however, as the four cylinder locomotives with their slightly higher power rating would be used generally on longer distance trains with only a minimum number of stops. It is usually stated that No. 40 was Churchward's 'masterpiece' and as a step in development this is true, but the author would tend to the view that Nos. 40 (later 4000) and 4001 were joint masterpieces. The theories were presented in No. 40, but in No. 4001 we see the fruition of all the previous work, to which has been applied the designer's practical engineering panache, providing a locomotive which would stand the tests of time in heavy service. The GWR Museum at Swindon is indeed fortunate to own one of the first batch, No. 4003 *Lode Star* in its collection, and without doubt, this is the one exhibit that should never be removed from Swindon or exchanged for any other GWR locomotive, however famous it may appear to others. Indeed, the country is fortunate that one of this Lot was preserved at all, representing as it does the culmination of a remarkable period of steam locomotive development. Variations and re-creation of the concept were to appear for many years after, brilliant in themselves, no doubt, but all of them resting on the cornerstone of this great achievement. Churchward's basic aims had been to produce express passenger locomotives with a drawbar pull of at least 2 tons at 70 m.p.h. Only a few years later, when fitted with proven superheating, these locomotives were capable of producing over 3 tons continuously at the drawbar for long periods at 70 m.p.h. thereby justifying the design.

The rolling stock under maintenance in 1904, compared with that at the time of Dean's accession in 1877, shows the great change in the workload at all the GWR works, but especially at Swindon:-

Year	1877	1904
Locomotives	1,471	2,198
Passenger Category Stock	4,177	6,932
Freight Category Stock	32,303	61,367

Apart from the problems of attracting the requisite tradesmen and other supporting staff, the training of increasing numbers of engineers for design and management was becoming a problem for such a large workload. The formal training of engineers until 1900 was still very rudimentary, being on the principal of 'throwing in at the deep end' in regard to practical training, (and there is not too much wrong in that), but the attainment of necessary academic knowledge was much more problematical. Technical schools, as those at Swindon, were now beginning to be effective, but with only minimal support from industry. Churchward, with the support of the Board, took some very far reaching steps to adjust this state of affairs in October 1903. It was announced that, as from the beginning of the next academic session, the Company was to award a number of 'day studentships'. These were to be open to Swindon apprentices between the ages of 17 and 18 (apprenticeships still often lasted 7 years), and who had already spent at least one year in the Factory, and were attending evening classes. The studentships were to be competitive, and based on annual examinations. They were to be as follows:-

1st year . . . . 15 students
2nd year . . . . 9 students
3rd year . . . . 6 students

Because of the reducing number, the competition was fierce indeed to complete the full 3 years and only the best students survived, but these were allowed to spend a part of their last year within the hallowed walls of the drawing office and laboratory. The subjects covered were practical mathematics and mechanics, geometry, machine drawing, heat, electricity and chemistry. Tuition at the North Wilts Technical School was during the afternoons, for which they were paid as if at work. The 1st year met on Mondays and Thursdays, the 2nd and 3rd years on Tuesdays and Fridays. When the 2nd and 3rd years' tuition continued until 9.00 p.m. in the evenings, they were allowed to miss the 6.30—8.15 a.m. Works shift the next morning. The whole arrangement was under the personal direction of Churchward, and was very effective in producing excellent rolling stock engineers and managers. The system was to continue in similar form until the end of the GWR, and in modified form until fairly recently, when it was superseded by other state systems. Later, 12 studentships were offered in each of three years, but still competitive annually, with 'fee paying' students. Success in these courses could lead to membership of professional engineering institutions, and later were part of the Ordinary and Higher National Certificate training courses. In this way, Swindon was able to meet the need for engineers to fill all the senior posts in drawing office, Works and outstation Divisions. Indeed, it was arranged that there was always a surplus, and many Swindon trained engineers were recommended, by Churchward and his successor, to posts on other railways both in this country and abroad. Examples of this were Surrey Warner to the L&SWR as Carriage Superintendent; G. H. Pearson to the SE&CR as Works Manager, Ashford, and Assistant CME; Lionel Lynes was recommended to Ashford as leading carriage draughtsman; Harry Holcroft also to Ashford, but 'under his own steam'; E. A. Watson was recommended, by Churchward, for Works Manager, Inchicore of the GS&WR of Ireland. Many others were to 'spread the Swindon gospel' in many parts of the world at this and later periods. Victor Bayley, who left Churchward's experimental section to spend a lifetime in India building railways, later related his Swindon experiences delightfully in a volume of mémoirs entitled *'Nine-Fifteen from Victoria'*, now sadly out of print. Engineers at Swindon were occasionally given the opportunity to venture abroad examining the opposition and picking up ideas. H. C. King was sent to France to observe the trials of locomotive No. 102 and later paid a visit to North America. Due to his intimate knowledge of American practice, gained from working both with the American Locomotive Company and the Pennsylvania Railroad, E. A. Watson was offered, by Churchward, the post of inspector at Swindon, on his return to this country. It is also evident from the proceedings of the Junior Engineering Society, that close watch was kept on the work of Goldsdorf on compounding in Austria, and it is quite possible that he and Churchward met. The author is happy to recount reminiscences to him by the late W. N. Pellow, under whom he had the pleasure of working for a period in the 1950s. 'Bill' Pellow was the last outdoor assistant to the CME & running superintendent of the GWR, and continued as the first motive power superintendent of the newly formed Western Region of British Railways after the retirement of F. W. Hawksworth, when major managerial changes were made. A Cornishman, apprenticed at St. Blazey, he came to Swindon in 1908 to complete his training, entering the drawing office in 1912 under the redoubtable George Burrows. He, too, recounted how men were sent abroad both to gain experience and to gather information on development taking place. In particular, he told how W. A. Stanier, sent to America by Churchward, came back with the idea of using outside steam pipes from boiler to cylinders. The French locomotives had these, and the provision of them in the early 'Stars' in an inside position for all four cylinders, was not considered the best solution in practice. On Stanier's return, Pellow was given the job of developing the idea, which meant, among other things, redesign of the smokebox. It was the habit of Churchward to spend a lot of time in the drawing office, as he did also in the shops. As with other work in hand, he regularly visited Pellow's board to discuss the ways in which the schemes were being 'worked up'. The progress and difficult points involved were discussed freely with the draughtsman no matter how young and lowly, and the problems thus drawn out and possibilities for solution considered. Churchward would then take the necessary decisions to allow work to advance until the next visit. This 'tutorial' method of approach, especially to his younger staff, could not be surpassed for encouraging them to produce and develop their own engineering philosophies. Equally, in the shops, he had an eagle eye for malpractice, and was quick to point out the error of his way to any culprit, at the same time ensuring that the foreman was acutely aware of his own portion of guilt for allowing such things to happen in his shop.

It was still the custom for all grades of assistant in Works and drawing office to be continually encouraged to suggest experiments or modifications which could be tried. In such circumstances the man involved, whilst still carrying out his normal duties, had direct access to Churchward for such special work. During these years a 'single' driver locomotive was allocated to the Works for the sole purpose of mounting and trying in practice such modifications, and if necessary to be run in service. Such an example was the first use of armoured hoses for engine/tender connections.

The staff allocated to rolling stock work in the drawing office prior to World War I was:-

Locomotive Sections (2). . . . . 6 men each
Boiler Section. . . . . 6 men
Carriage & Wagon & Special Vehicle Section. . 6—8 men
Experimental Section. . . . . 6—8 men

Pellow also said that union membership in the Works at this time, in his assessment, was about 30 per cent of the staff. The main organizers in the town were Reuben George (not a railwayman) and Sam Walters, both to become Mayor of the Borough. They were social reformers by inclination and persuasion, and Sam Walters, was, from 1917 until 1940, secretary of the Medical Fund Society.

Locomotive development was only one side of the business at Swindon, and the spotlight must now move to the Carriage Works.

We have already read of the success of the 'Birkenhead' and 'Cornishman' carriage stock, but this development should be seen against the type of vehicle now appearing on other lines, particularly the Midland Railway. Thomas Clayton, who had left Swindon in 1873, was still Carriage Superintendent, not retiring until December 1901. Although not amongst the forerunners of corridor carriage builders, the comfort and finish of his main line stock was of the highest order, and with which other railways were now being compared. This railway had pioneered third class accommodation of a superior standard, and had set levels which the public were beginning to expect from other organizations. The GWR stock benefitting most from this trend, was that for the major main line long distance services, although new sets of improved vehicles for use on specific branches were built at this time. Introduction of dining cars had inevitably been delayed until after the BG conversion and the final extinction of the ten minute refreshment stop at Swindon. Even so, the first three did not appear from Swindon shops until 1896, entering service in May. It is stating the obvious to report that they were 'first class only'. Further individual cars appeared in 1897 and 1900, but the first composite (1st, 2nd and 3rd class) dining car did not appear until January 1903. The 1897 batch of sleeping cars was an improvement on their predecessors and were well equipped and comfortable for their time. The clerestory style was retained, in a modified form, for the beautiful Royal Train provided to celebrate, in 1897, the Diamond Jubilee of Her Majesty Queen Victoria. The Queen, however, insisted on retaining her older standard gauge saloon, of 1874, including its oil lighting! L. R. Thomas was responsible for the main design work. The Queen's carriage naturally retained the domed roof, although other

Plate 103: Rail Motor Car No. 61 (1905) and Auto Trailer No. 34 (1906). The introduction of similar vehicles from 1903 onwards set the style of GWR branch line working for the rest of its existence. Note the monogram of the period.

British Rail

engineering items were discreetly changed. The rest of the train was lit electrically and this amenity was to be gradually introduced into main line stock from the turn of the century, taking nearly sixty years to replace all the gas lit carriages! The interior craftsmanship of this train was, however, superb, and showed what the men at Swindon were capable of achieving given the opportunity. The whole train cost about £40,000, a noble gesture, indeed, by the directors.

Churchward, once firmly established in the chair, was to start just as great a revolution with his carriages as with his locomotives. The first big change was the introduction, in October 1903, of the first GWR steam rail motors, for the branch line service between Chalford and Stonehouse in the Stroud Valley. These single vehicles had a small steam powered bogie, built in at one end, supplied from a vertical boiler. The body was slab sided, with a high elliptical roof, and could be driven from both ends. Further examples were built at Swindon, the first for the Plymouth and Saltash area, and others for branches nearer to Paddington. In 1904 trailer cars appeared, for attaching to the motor vehicles, and developed what was to become the standard branch line stock for the GWR for the rest of its existence. Later on, small steam locomotives replaced the original integral power units.

Carriages, prior to 1904, had always been less than 60 ft. overall, and whatever their shortcomings as far as the public was concerned, their compact clerestory outline, as developed by Dean, was visually very neat indeed. But in 1904 appeared successively a 70 ft. long rail motor trailer car, four composite dining cars and some passenger carriages, all built with a massive 'clipper' outline, with elliptical roofs and varying in

Plate 104: *Dreadnought*, 3rd class carriage No. 3277, built in October 1905. Body dimensions were 69 ft. long and 9 ft. 6 in. wide at the waist.

length between 68 ft. and 70 ft., and except for the trailer car, no less than 9 ft. 6 in. wide at the waist. This latter dimension made belated use of the clearances available as a result of the broad gauge, although limiting route availability to original broad gauge lines. Inevitably there was opposition from various quarters. The public were not ready for vehicles with only three doors per side, and thought them dangerous because of limited accessibility. Their higher individual cost and that of modifying points locking bars, necessitated by their greater length between bogies, was shown to be outweighed by their operating economies gained from greater carrying capacity per vehicle, therefore less vehicles per train. Finally, there was the aesthetic consideration of looks, which may seem strange today, but like locomotive No. 100, they were considered ugly. Massive they certainly were but, while still carrying chocolate and cream livery, photographs made them look very handsome and businesslike. A few years later when Churchward moved to 'chocolate' only, and then to 'crimson lake' finish, their massiveness did become rather overpowering. This later move highlights the fact that Churchward was not so interested in the aesthetics of design which had become the custom in all branches of engineering in the Victorian age. Indeed, he is reported to have remarked that as far as he was concerned, carriages could be finished externally with tar as long as the interiors and quality of ride was to the customers' liking, a remark with which not all railway lovers, and others, could fully agree. Public reaction to the doors was noted, and later vehicles from Swindon were fitted with inset doors to each compartment and the inevitable sobriquet of 'Concertinas' was earned from their serrated body sides. These were also reduced in width to 9 ft. to give wider route availability, particularly the South Wales main line. Further ideas from America were to be found, from 1907 onwards, with

the introduction of a new 8 ft. equalized bolster bogie, possibly based on ideas brought over by A. E. Watson and adapted by Churchward for use under his new carriages. There was a later 9 ft. design for heavier duties, and these were produced until about 1914.

The provision of the new erecting and machine 'A' shop, already described, raised once again the problems of services; gas, power and water. The former was not difficult to overcome since adequate provision had been made at the new, 1876, gasworks for future development, and we have seen how extensions and improvements had been made in 1888 and 1896. With the large increase of roofed acreage and much extended production requirements for gas, further authorizations were made in 1900/01 for additional carbonizing plant. This was followed by extensions; the provision of regenerating apparatus, a new methane hydrogen plant, condensers, scrubbers and other specialized equipment appearing between 1902 and 1907, when an additional gas holder of 1 million cubic feet capacity was installed. At this time, it was noted that consumption had risen by 50 per cent over that of 1900. Total expenditure over this period amounted to about £28,000 and much of it was defrayed by increasing gas charges to individual shops, to be carried on their general overhead costs.

The reason for this great rise in gas consumption was the decision, taken in 1901/2, to provide electric power for new shops and to gradually extend this service to cover the whole Works. In 1902 this was, indeed, a brave decision, since there was no supply available locally. One cannot escape the supposition, however, that the proposals were connected with the newly incorporated borough. The first mention of proposals to light the streets of New Swindon can be traced back to 1882 when still a local board. Discussions staggered along through the urban district period, 1894—1900, and then became mixed with a parallel proposition to provide a tramway system, which had also been toyed with since 1883. There were the inevitable clashes of interest leading to delay, and it was not until after the Charter of Incorporation had been granted that firm moves were made to provide a tramway and an electricity generating station in Swindon. Matters proceeded slowly and the official inspection of the new tramway system connecting Rodbourne, Gorse Hill and the Old Town by three radiating lines from the northern end of the main shopping artery, Regent Street, took place on 20th September 1904, the public opening taking place two days later. The supply of electric power to private premises had commenced on 20th May the previous year. It must be remembered that, for a major portion of this long development time, Churchward had been a member, or chairman, of the UDC and was Charter Mayor in 1901. The first Electric Light and Tramway Committee was set up on 9th November 1900. It is against this background of public acceptance of electricity as a major power source that we must view the Works' decision on electrification. Was Churchward hoping that the town

scheme would come first and be available to him, or was the reverse the case, in that railway expertise was being used to help along the new undertaking? Events in the Works made earlier provision of electric power necessary in the new 'A' shop. It was financed by the 'umbrella' vote of £35,000 for equipping the new shop as distinct from production machine tools. The alternative power sources were either steam reciprocating engines or the use of the faster running gas engines, coupled to d.c. generators. The latter method was chosen and the first three units, manufactured by Westinghouse, were installed in 'A' shop. These were closely followed by three more units to serve the older erecting and machine shop block of the original Factory. This second installation was to be the nucleus of the 'M' power station, and in turn to become the principal of the five stations which were soon developed. These were the 'M' station, the 'A' shop station, shortly to be doubled in output, the C&W Works unit, situated north of the railway station, plus two smaller units, one in the gasworks and the other to appear a little later to feed the new timber sawmills developed at the extreme west of the

Plate 105: The machine (AM) shop on 21st January 1907. This illustrates the small space required to operate the 'walking cranes' used so much at Swindon.

British Rail

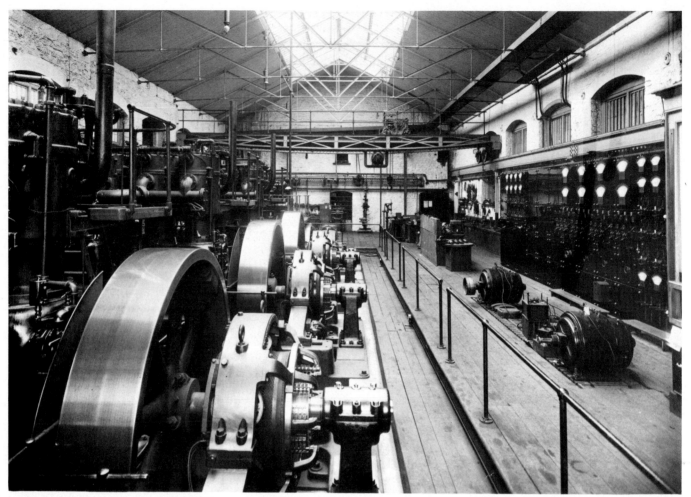

Plate 106: Gas engines driving electric d.c. generators in the 'M' power house shortly after installation. Note the early electric lamps in the roof. In 1980, the incoming power supply control board still occupied the site of the first control board seen on the right.

British Rail

Works, between 1904 and 1907. Some of the later gas engines (there were eventually 19 in all), were by Campbell of Halifax. Electric power was transferred to individual machine tools by utilizing the existing countershafting, originally driven by steam engines. This shafting was now isolated into smaller sections, each driven by a floor mounted motor, usually of about 40h.p. capacity. Within a few years of the Corporation generating station being established, we find, from correspondence, that its manager was constantly trying to interest the Works in taking further supplies from him. The rising demand in the town soon took up the spare capacity, and no further moves were made in this direction for some years. Incidentally, much of the preparatory work for the planning of the 3ft. 6in. gauge tramway system was carried out in the Works drawing offices, where reference copies of the large scale Ordnance Survey sheets have the route schemes added to them.

The much more troublesome water supply position had now to be faced. The new extensions, and those further ones which Churchward had in mind, demanded a complete review of the system. There was no chance of obtaining more water from the local water undertaking, as the town's expansion was such that it could barely meet its requirements, so it was decided to arrange to become completely self supporting in this matter. That the decision was correct is illustrated by the situation in 1980 whereby the greatly expanded supply system in the area is still not in a position to provision the Works. We have noted, in earlier chapters, the various attempts to find suitable local water supplies, ending in the use of existing, and later additional and deepened bores, at Kemble. The regular water trains, consisting of tank vehicles and modified old tenders, had been augmented, but with the new workshops, which were heated by steam, and other increased requirements, the system had reached its limit. The potential of the Kemble source, only about a mile from the source of the River Thames, was thought to be quite adequate, and it was decided, in 1902, to make this the future Works' supply, although a bore hole, near South Cerney, was also considered at the time. Whilst this may have been capable of a better yield, the higher costs involved in wayleaves for supply pipes over private land and under roads for several miles would be extremely costly. The space in the fork of the main Swindon to Gloucester line and the Tetbury branch from Kemble, and in which the existing wells were placed, was now used for a self-contained pumping station, the floor level of the new building being made 13 ft. 9 in. below rail level. This depressed level was selected to reduce the water lift from the head well, also to allow gravity fed coal bunkers to be provided, which could be replenished straight from coal wagons on the pump house siding with the minimum of labour.

The boiler house portion of the new building housed two hand fired Lancashire boilers working at 100 p.s.i. Steam was fed from these into the pumping hall which was built with its southern end over the head well of the bores. Two sets of pumping equipment, supplied by the Hydraulic Engineering Co. Ltd. of Chester, were installed. Each consisted of a two cylinder parallel compound steam engine of 24 in. stroke, the cylinder bores being 18 in. high pressure and 32 in. low pressure. Normal working speed was 12 r.p.m. A special motion linkage, of flitched steel and timber beams, transmitted reciprocating motion, first horizontally and then vertically, to a pump of the deep well bucket type having a diameter of 24 in. and stroke of 36 in. The head well, in which both the pump sets operated, was 48 ft. 9 in. in depth, but they were only able to draw down to 35 ft. of this depth. The water table, at this time, was well above this level and thought to be adequate. A water tank at the end of the station platform, and incidentally one of the few GWR water tanks still in use, was used as a receiver from these pumps. During the spring and summer of 1903 gangs of Swindon Works men, supported by a special supply train complete with steam crane, excavated trenches along the west side of the main line and laid a 15 in. diameter main. Of

Plate 107: Laying the 15 in. diameter water main near Minety, between Kemble and Swindon, in March 1903.

British Rail

Plate 108: One of the service trains for the Kemble water main pipe laying, headed by a 'Kruger' 2-6-0, in March 1903. Each bogie vehicle carried forty-five of the 12 ft. x 15 in. diameter cast iron pipes used for the main.

British Rail

cast iron socket and spigot pipes each 12 ft. in length, this main was laid at a rate of 1 mile per week for the 13 miles from Kemble to Swindon locomotive yard, and was completed on 28th July 1903. Occupation of the down main line was virtually continuous during this period, and, incidentally, this main, after nearly 80 years of use, is still in excellent condition. It was laid only about three feet below track formation level, whether along embankment or in cuttings, and so follows the gradients of the track. The rail level at Kemble station is 356 ft. above ordnance datum, and at Swindon yard 335 ft., so there is a nominal fall of 21 ft. to assist flow, but the main is actually bow shaped, falling to 299 ft. above ordnance datum about 8 miles from Kemble, rising sharply in the remaining distance to Swindon. Here it was fed into the high level coal stage water tank at the engine shed, and thence gravitated to the pattern stores tank in the Locomotive Works. The control of the pumping rate, to meet the varying demands at Swindon, was no mean undertaking, and ingenious methods were developed over the years to satisfy the requirements. The difficulty can be put into perspective when realizing that at the maximum pumping rate, the main held approximately 2,350 tons of incompressible water moving at a speed of about 10.5 m.p.h! Anyone inadvertently closing a 15 in. diameter valve against such forces would realize their mistake very quickly! Pressure drop alarms were fitted to the

system, and strict measures taken for safety in the GWR rule book. After an alarm, no train was allowed to pass between Swindon and Kemble, or vice versa, before a visual inspection had been made, usually from the footplate of a light engine moving at slow speed. However, a burst main on an embankment section, (the only burst of dangerous potential), has been very rare indeed. Even so, the care of the embankment sections of this line were the responsibility of Swindon Works from 1903 until about 1960, and special augers and other equipment kept, so that strengtheners of old rail could be piled into the embankment and tied together under the dual track. Many of these strengthening piles are still in position.

With this new supply in use there must still have been some misgivings, possibly because of the low levels reached by the water table at certain times of the year. Due to underground seepage rates this period of low ebb is always in November, gradually improving through January, nevertheless, at the period when demand was much higher due to the steam heating load in the Works, this situation, and the idea of further projected extensions at Swindon, led to the sinking of a new bore hole by the New England Boring Company in 1910. This was made from an existing dry head well just outside the pumphouse, the new 6 in. diameter bore extending down through both the upper or greater oolite and the inferior oolite below. These beds are separated by a

120ft. layer of Fullers Earth and other impervious rocks. Both oolitic layers provide good supplies, if fissures in the strata are struck. Cross connections were built between the two well heads later. After suitable lining, this bore made moderate yields, and a further 11½in. bore was made from the same well head by Messrs. Isler & Co. between March and October 1914. This latter bore was extended down to 325ft. but was unfortunate in not striking good fissures, and gave a yield inferior to the earlier 6in. bore, but was kept to make some contribution to the supply. These bores in total were to serve the Works adequately until 1967. With the completion of the new supply in 1903, the Works was fully equipped with new water mains and a greatly improved fire hydrant distribution, particularly in the timber yards.

The equipping of the new 'A' shop was significant in the provisioning, by Churchward, of an engine testing plant. The thinking behind this was not origi-nally for experimental or research purposes, although this was doubtless an additional consideration. The main purpose was for the 'running in' of locomotives when new, or after heavy repair. Such a process is essential for the satisfactory bedding down of the numerous high loaded plain bearings to ensure later dependability in service. The amount of track occupation required for such work was, by this time, very high, because of the huge output from the Works. Admittedly, some of this could be done for the smaller units on the 'Factory' line, but not for many years were the two main line tracks through Swindon to be increased. If the problem could thus be solved, the operating department would be very relieved. In the event, the idea was not too successful, as such a plant with the locomotive anchored and running on rollers, could not reproduce the external stresses on the wheels and frames transmitted from conditions and curvature of track, or by other parameters such

Plate 109: The earliest known photograph of the Locomotive Testing Plant in the new 'A' shop, taken in July 1904.
Author's Collection

Plate 110: Churchward's dynamometer car No. 790, photographed, when built, in June 1901. Note the flangeless recording wheel.

British Rail

Plate 111: An interior view of dynamometer car No. 790.

British Rail

as cross and head-winds and tail loading. The plant was never much used for this purpose after these shortcomings became apparent. However an interesting point which comes to light is that the original foundation drawings, completed in August 1900, for the shop, provided no less than four of these test beds! Each of these foundation plans are slightly different, presumably for varying wheel arrangements. In the event, only one plant was provided with adjustable power take-off rollers. Attached to these rollers was an air compressor, and when the plant was in use the other air compressors in the 'A' shop were shut off, and the power from the locomotive under test was not wasted, the compressor itself creating a 'load' against which to work. A dynamometer was also available for such experimental testing as was required. Research work at this time was to be assisted by the provision of a new dynamometer car completed in March 1901. Like other special service vehicles, this was built on Wagon Lot No. 293, possibly because the wagon building and repair budget could carry the expense!

In 1906 a new weighbridge house was provided just south of the new shop, capable of handling the larger locomotives, replacing the older one at the other end of the Works which was lifted and sent to Newton Abbot. In 1902 the large external traverser along the east wall of the 'A' shop was installed, and the 65 ft. balancing turntable which has served the Works ever since. Much of the machinery for the new machine shop was transferred from other parts of the Works, although, of course, some new equipment was purchased. This machine (AM) shop was equipped with single track 'walking cranes', supported above between runner channels attached to the Warren girders under the roof trusses. Four of these cranes, with their swinging jibs, two across both the length and breadth of the shop, effectively provided the necessary heavy lifting of items and assemblies such as crank axles and large steel billets for machining. Outside the north side of the shop a stock yard was provided which was served by a semi-goliath crane along its whole length. A rationalization of other machining and fitting activities took place in the rest of the Locomotive Works at this time resulting in much more economic production.

An acquisition which was to prove very contentious, was the purchase, in February 1902, of six Rochester time recorders, followed a year later by a further three. These were purported to be for better cost control. With the work card being punched with starting and finishing times, correct recording was shown of the time spent undertaking particular tasks. Arising from this introduction was perhaps the first major confrontation with the growing union strength, although their numbers were still in a minority. It also became an item of political argument between the local Liberals and Conservatives, but, for the time

being, not a lot more is reported about the system, although obviously imposed and used for some time.

In all, about £70,000 can be identified against building and equipping the new 'A' shop, although more may have been spent. But at this time, we find, from minutes of the LC&S committee of the Board, who considered all the submissions made by Churchward, that a certain 'wind of change' was blowing. The reasons are not clear, but it shows that, perhaps in the future, the LC&W Superintendent, senior officer of the Company though he was, could not expect the same freedom of action, particularly financial, enjoyed by his predecessors. This may have been no more than a small part of a demonstration to all departments that the Board intended to keep direction firmly in their hands. However it is more likely the first subtle move came from another direction. On 16th June 1903 the GWR General Manager, Sir Joseph Wilkinson, died in office, and shortly after James Charles Inglis, the Company's Chief Engineer, was selected to succeed him. Churchward had only recently been appointed, and there was shortly to be, due to retirement, a new Superintendent of the line, Joseph Morris. There had been suggestions previous to this time that the General Manager be accepted as the principal executive of the Company. The old tradition of departmental officers reporting direct to the Board, however, was well entrenched, and those already in such positions were unlikely to take kindly to this change, at least during their tenure of office. Inglis felt that the time had come to put the new concept into being, but his own Civil Engineering department was carefully taken care of by his co-appointment as consulting engineer of the Company, an 'engineer' being appointed under him for the day to day running of the department. A great engineer (he was President of the Institution of Civil Engineers for two successive years — a most unusual and significant point), he had, like Churchward, a very strong personality. Needless to say, Churchward showed great opposition and hostility to the new moves and, backed by other officers involved, managed to fight Inglis off. This situation, however, was not good for the Company in the long run, because it meant, amongst other things, that each department worked behind closed doors and there were huge gaps in communication, the very thing that Inglis was seeking to overcome. One particular result of this will be seen in a later chapter. This is the political climate in which Churchward found himself even a few months before Inglis's appointment. After reporting to the LC&S committee that, as well as the £35,000 required to equip the 'A' shop he was seeking a further £15,000 for machinery, he was 'instructed to obtain tenders in future, wherever practicable, for the supply of machinery and to submit the same to the committee'. This was a minuted instruction, and one can well imagine Churchward's reaction, being a man

Plate 112: A wide angle view of the L-shaped drawing office completed in 1904, seen here in unchanged condition in 1931. Note the steel framing referred to in the text. The Locomotive Carriage & Wagon sections are to the right and the general sections to the left.

both blunt and outspoken! But it is significant that only £2,033 can be found recorded as used against that particular £15,000 submission, and one is left to draw one's own conclusions.

An item now needing urgent attention was the office accommodation at Swindon, and in particular that of the drawing office staff. By 1902 there were no less than six drawing offices scattered around the premises, and these were as follows:-

a) The main locomotive drawing office situated on the floor above the Locomotive Works Manager's personal office.
b) The buildings drawing office also on the same floor as (a).
c) The general (i.e. Outdoor Machinery, in modern parlance) drawing office on the upper (i.e. first) floor of the main office block facing on to the London—Bristol main line.

d) The carriage drawing office also facing the main line, but from the south side and in the Carriage Body Shop (C & W No. 3 Shop).
e) The wagon drawing office in the Carriage Works Manager's office attached to the Brake Shop (C & W No. 15) adjacent to the station, and later to be the Assistant C & W Works Manager's personal office.
f) A general overflow office near the high level tank in Bristol Street in the building which is now the Works Fire Station and Hose and Fire Equipment Shop. This was used mainly for Locomotive and Carriage work.

This fragmentation must have been extremely inefficient for organizational and technical reasons, and would militate against the introduction of common design policies on standardization now being strongly followed. So it was that, on 11th November 1903, the sum of £7,000 was voted to add a further

storey to the L-shaped main office block, the whole new floor to be used as a combined drawing office. The resulting airy and light office remained the Swindon drawing office well into the days of nationalization, a portion of it being used for other purposes for a few years recently, but now gradually reverting again to the purpose for which it was designed. The structure of it is very interesting, the roof being supported by semicircular arches of Swindon rolled rail section to which are gussetted principals of the same section. These trusses run down the walls below the beautiful teak floor, alas now covered by mundane brown linoleum, and are tied together beneath this floor by transverse beams laid across the width of the building. The whole drawing office is thus mounted in a steel 'cage' resting on the original building below it. A similar method of construction, but on a larger scale, is to be found in the magnificent train shed at St. Pancras station. It was within these walls that generations of railway engineers were to gain wide experience and develop those special talents which were to carry many to high office on the GWR and other railways far and wide, or to success in other spheres. Further funds

were allocated for a new printing house built over the adjacent older erecting shop and reached by a bridge, arc lighting in the drawing office, and better toilet accommodation in the offices generally.

It was during this addition that the two stone bas-relief panels of a BG engine (one left hand and one right hand, of the same model) were built into the wall of the principal entrance to the offices, the one used more or less exclusively by the senior staff at that time. These were referred to in Chapter Two as being originally mounted on plinths, one at each end of Gooch's original running shed. As there were moves around 1885—90 to demolish this building (an event finally taking place in 1930), they were removed into safe keeping. It is presumed that they needed some restoration when remounted, having had only one further treatment since in about 1955. Many have enquired which locomotive is represented on these carvings, and it has been assumed to be one of Gooch's 'Firefly' class. Detail, although believed to be twice restored, is still excellent, and a study of all available diagrams leaves little doubt of its source. It is the distinctive boiler mountings, only apparently carried by one (or two) engines, which makes identi-

Plate 113: The general offices after the addition of the drawing office floor. Note the tie-plates clamping the steel framing to the cross-beams. Also of interest are the stone bas-reliefs of a broad gauge engine, which were moved from their original home on the engine shed, in their new position.

British Rail

fication clear. In G. A. Sekon's celebrated *History of the Great Western Railway* (1895) it was illustrated clearly and without doubt on page 67 over the name *Premier*. If correctly named, it is wrongly attributed there to Messrs. Sharp Roberts. (This *Premier* must not be confused with the later Gooch freight engine). Later researchers have shown *Premier* to be not a Sharp Roberts machine but from Mather Dixon & Co. Identity is further confused in that *Premier* had a sister locomotive *Ariel*. It is clear from the carvings that the driving wheels are certainly no more than 7 ft. in diameter by proportion. The plaques must also have been finished and in position some time in 1841, and one must assume that they were modelled either by direct observation by the sculptor, or taken from an existing set of drawings. *Premier* and *Ariel* were two of Brunel's unfortunate purchases, and both were withdrawn by the end of 1840, so presumably available for the sculptor to 'work from life'. It does seem strange that an unsuccessful machine was used for such important representation. The other arguments for presuming the carvings are of *Premier* are that G. F. Bird in his 1901—3 series of articles, quotes this name to the diagram involved, and his informa-

tion came from the sketches and drawings made by E. T. Lane at Swindon in 1848/9. E. L. Ahron's series in *The Locomotive*, 1915/16, also gives the same information, although this may have been a straight copy from Bird. That Sekon got the manufacturer's name wrong is surprising. Conversely P. J. T. Reed when compiling part two of *Locomotives of the GWR (Broad Gauge)* for the Railway Correspondence & Travel Society, did not use this excellent illustration at all, and suggests that both *Premier* and *Ariel* might have only had inside frames. It would be interesting to know the background of this statement. There has appeared another attribution, that of the Fenton Murray & Jackson engine, *Ixion* of the 'Firefly' class, the locomotive later selected for the Gauge Commission trials. A diagram of its immediate sister, *Gorgon*, shows none of the obvious boiler mountings however, and the proportion of the driving wheels to the top of the boiler is not correct. Furthermore, it was not delivered until October 1841, when building of the running shed would already have started, and the provision of these stone plaques are shown on the original drawing made perhaps in mid-1841. On balance the author supports the view that

Plate 114: The well-known bas-reliefs over the main office entrance at Swindon. They were originally mounted at each end of the 1840 engine shed.

British Rail

Plate 115: A close-up view of the bas-reliefs after restoration in the 1950s.

British Rail

the locomotive depicted is *Premier* from comparison of the detail work, the only artistic licence being taken, understandably, with the number of wheel spokes shown. Putting aside all these technical arguments, one must accept that as decorations, these two reliefs are very fine indeed, and much admired by those visiting the Works, and passengers glancing across from passing HST IC125 services. They do depict a typical broad gauge locomotive, and as such are exactly right for their situation.

Opportunity was taken, when adding this extra floor to the main office block, to extend the tunnel entrance subway northward under the offices, and thence under the Gloucester branch to the general stores building. Further direct access to the Carriage Works was provided by a new bridge over the North Wilts Canal in 1903. Main access to both sides of the Carriage & Wagon Works was improved, in 1904/5, by another tunnel entrance, latterly known as 'Webb's' entrance, which ran northwards from Station Road West giving access to the shops inside the boundary walls to the south of the line and emerging north of the main line outside the C & W Manager's offices. Access to all these tunnels in the Works was by 1 in 7 slopes.

The introduction of the tramway system in 1904 meant the lowering of the road under the Rodbourne Road bridge built in 1889. In so doing, this interfered with another Works pedestrian subway under this road between the east and west parts of the Factory. It was decided to abandon this and build a new one between what had then become the boiler (V) shop, and the yard adjacent to the 'A' shop. Opportunity was taken to provide two 30 ton hydraulic lifts, one each side of the road in this new subway, in order to convey boilers direct from one side to the other, thus eliminating considerable shunting mileages for these items. On the west side a few years later, in 1911, the boiler mounting and test (P1) shop was built, covering the westward lift.

A rather unknown piece of engineering below ground, however, had been slowly carried out, commencing in December 1900. The Factory was by then nearly 60 years old, and many of the different supply mains were becoming old and damaged by constant traffic. Leaks were hard to locate and often unseen until a gradual seepage of water or pervading smell of gas made it apparent. The problem for principal distribution was overcome by the provision, right across the Works from the running shed yard east of the Gloucester line to just inside the 'A' shop, of a 7 ft. internal diameter brick service subway. It took 3 years to complete, those sections deeper than 16 ft. to invert being tunnelled. A general slope from both ends to the centre of 1 in 200 for drainage meant that both end sections were shallower and could be built on the 'cut and cover' method. Two right angle turns were made in the centre of the

Works to attain the necessary service alignments, and a branch off this diversion section led south to the iron foundry. In all, the length of this subway was 2,229 ft. of which 1,092 ft. was tunnelled. The latter work was carried out by a gang of 5 men, three in the tunnel excavating and running spoil, and two surface men lifting spoil. They were able to proceed about 5 ft. each nine hour shift, the material being stiff blue clay inlaid with boulders. Final shaping and the insertion of timbering proceeded at the rate of 2 ft. 6 in. per day with five men. Finally a gang of three bricklayers and two labourers were able to line the subway at about 4 ft. per day. Lining was with Cattybrook Brindle bricks set in composition composed of 3 parts ground brick dust to one part of Portland cement. On completion of the three-ring brick lining and footway over the drainage channel, steel supports built into both sides of the culvert were to carry the 24 in. Factory Kemble water main, compressed air, electric cables, hydraulic power at both 1,500 p.s.i. and 750 p.s.i., one power gas and two lighting gas mains. Originally the subway was lit throughout electrically, but the damp atmosphere led to its abandonment, and for the same reasons electric cables were later withdrawn over most of its length. This excellent service subway is still in use today, although used only by the maintenance staff and almost unknown to others.

The arrival of Kemble water finally removed the need to draw water from the North Wilts Canal, although by this time its ability to supply was very limited. The two reservoirs north of the station were back filled in the early years of the century and when a large extension to the carriage brake shop was made in 1910, the south-east corner brick foundations had to be set 29 ft. deep to bed below the puddling of the pond. This shop was now gradually developed into a machine and fitting shop (No. 15) for C & W activities. A large extension to the wagon (No. 21) shop was also made in 1907, and the replacement houses built in Armstrong's time for senior staff were almost surrounded by the expanding Works. In 1907 the engine shed was almost doubled in size by the addition of a roundhouse extension, and this effectively ended brickmaking activity at the Works. Much of the stockpiled brick clay was used to fill in the reservoir just mentioned. The only other large extension in this period was the provision of a timber shed in 1906, followed by a logging sawmill at the far west of the Works, adjacent to the M & S W J R line. This enabled the existing sawmill next to the body shop to concentrate on secondary forming, thicknessing and planing, and the final machining of timber stock items. These latter provisions were partly the outcome of a major change of policy by the Board on 3rd July 1901 when the stores superintendent, who had been operating as a departmental officer for some period and not under control of the

Plate 116: Part of the large timber stock at the west end of Swindon Works. This December 1928 view shows the 'A' shop with Newburn House in the background. Old Swindon Hill is to the right.

British Rail

LC&W Superintendent, took over control of all timber supplies. This removed the timber manager's post in the C&W organization. Bearing in mind the money value then, it is interesting to know that the book value of timber transferred was £497,018! There remained the other materials scattered over the Works in some 30 different stores, valued at £160,000, and together with the appropriate storehouses these were transferred to the new department. This was another whittling away of the LC&W Superintendent's authority. Before looking at the concurrent social changes, we note, that in the LC&S committee minutes of 7th October 1903, Churchward 'reported that it was recently thought desirable, with the object of reducing the number of visitors to the Works, to make a nominal charge of 3d (about 1p) for each person and that the result was satisfactory. It was agreed that, for the present, the fees should be applied to the benefit of the New Swindon Park'. How long regular visiting parties of this kind had been allowed around the Works is not certain, but the local guide book of 1870 clearly states that the visitors are taken around the Works on Wednesday afternoons. So the tradition is at least 110 years old at the time of writing.

One great loss to the history of engineering occurred in 1905. For many years the old BG locomotives *North Star* and *Lord of the Isles* had been preserved in the Works, and indeed, from time to time, had been used for exhibition purposes. Space was becoming very difficult by 1903 for locomotive repair, and both were offered to the Science Museum. After long consideration the offer was declined, a surprising decision, and in 1905 the order was given to cut them up. A bald statement appeared in the GWR Magazine of March 1906 mentioning the 'passing' of these historic machines, and that the name *Lord of the Isles* had been transferred to Locomotive No. 3046. This action, which was soon regretted by the Board who had apparently acquiesced to the action, perhaps showed another side of Churchward's nature, as being uninterested in things of the past, but more enthusiastic about plans for the future.

The death, on 22nd January 1901, of Queen Victoria, ended an era in Great Britain, and similarly marked one in Swindon. The Boer War was still taking its course, not ending until 31st May 1902. Expansion at Swindon had been constant since 1841. As far as housing was concerned, there was still a problem in the mid-1890s, although not as pressing as in previous years, but much remained to be done by the urban district councils. The shape of the combined towns was like a dumbell, Old Town and the New Town, plus the Works, being connected by a narrow row of connecting streets down the steep hill from Old Town. To this should be added the Rodbourne area directly north-west of the Works and Gorse Hill, still a separate village some way east and north of the station. Gorse Hill was connected to the Old Town by a carriage road, tree lined for most of its way and known as 'The Drove', named after the cattle traffic using it for access to the market. This name, or Drove Road, applied at that time right from the railway bridge, east of the station, to Christ Church, the new parish church for the Old Town which had replaced the older manorial Holy Rood in 1851. We have read of the difficulties in the acquisition of land from the Rolleston Estate, the principal landowner in the New Swindon area. The policy of the owner changed towards the end of the 19th century. By the mid-1890s the thin part of the dumbell area had been developed and, using the new Commercial Road as its artery, streets of new houses were developed on either side. The real breakthrough came in 1897, however, when, under the control of local agents Bishop & Pritchard, but working under the direction of the Manchester firm of Maxwell & Tuke, a large tract of land of nearly 54 acres (21.75 hectares) was leased for housing. This was in one complete parcel almost square in shape and bounded roughly by the GWR main line to the north, the Wilts & Berks Canal to the south and the Drove Road to the east. This was laid out in grid iron pattern with two main east/west thoroughfares each 42ft. in width between housing plots, Manchester Road and Broad Street, the rest consisting of mainly north/south 36ft. wide roads, although a few did run east/west to retain a proper balance of house blocks. In all, no less than 1,208 houses were planned for this area. The plan is dated 1st February 1897 and a copy appeared at once in the GWR drawing office register for reference purposes. Housing plots varied from 14ft. to 20ft. frontage according to position, and averaged 80ft. in depth with back lanes 10ft. wide provided in all cases. All built as terraced houses, they provided, for the period, good and substantial homes for the railwaymen and others still coming to the town. Most were either two or three bedroomed, but larger ones were built along a portion of The Drove, which was renamed County Road a few years later. These houses, nearly all owner occupied, still form a major housing area of the town and are in excellent condition. With a total density of about 22 houses per acre, this development enabled Swindon to catch up at last with its housing problem of 60 years, and although much development was still to take place in the immediate future and continue to the present

day, it was generally at a pace which balanced the current demand. The rapid expansion in these two areas, coupled with other developments at Rodbourne and Gorse Hill, gave the impetus for further amenities. Among new churches opened were St. John's in Aylesbury Street near the station (1883), and a daughter church of St. Mark's. The foundation stone was laid on 27th June 1883 by the deputy chairman of the GWR, Sir Alexander Wood. About one fifth of the total cost came from an investment held in trust for the St. Mark's parish by the GWR Company, from the fund originally opened in 1843, and which had helped finance St. Mark's. A further appeal had been made at a half-yearly meeting of the proprietors in 1859. At a similar meeting held on 28th February 1873, another appeal was made by the directors (Minute No. 8), and a special form issued to accompany subscriptions. It was pointed out that, by then, the population at New Swindon was 12,000, but church seating only amounted to 1,200. It was hoped that £10,000 could be contributed, but at the next meeting on 10th September 1873, minute No. 17 sorrowfully reports that only £1,500 had been received and further appeals were made. Contributors were able to allocate their gifts to the Anglican or Nonconformist churches as they wished. Amounts were possibly contributed from this fund to some of the new Methodist, Congregational and other churches opened after 1873. The £650 granted for St. John's apparently closed the fund, as no further grants were ever made. Other St. Mark's extensions were St. Saviour's in the highest part of the parish. This church was built up by voluntary labour, mostly GWR men in their spare time, many giving up their 'trip' holiday for the task. Land was given by Mr Sheppard, and local firms gave much of the materials. The work was inaugurated by William Dean's daughter in 1889 and the church was ready for use on 11th January 1890, many men working their Christmas holidays to ensure completion on time. Later, in 1903, came St. Luke's in Broad Street. Other churches were St. Barnabas' Gorse Hill (1885), and St. Augustine's, Rodbourne (1908). The large Baptist Tabernacle, recently demolished, opened at the top of Regent Street in 1886, and the new Congregational church in Sanford Street replaced an earlier 'iron church' in 1894. The Roman Catholic church, which had stood on a site in Regent Circus, moved to a new building, Holy Rood in Groundwell Road in 1905.

In 1897 the Queens Theatre was built, seating, when opened, about 1,000 people. Renamed the Empire Theatre in 1905, it was to be enlarged in the 1920s to seat 1,350. For many years it was on the main circuit for all types of theatrical entertainment, with the most famous in the profession appearing there during

Plate 117: The Children's Fete. Nostalgic memories to those who were children in Swindon in the early decades of the century. The free roundabout ticket still carries the greasy stains from being packed with the half pound of cake. Also seen are entrance tickets for 1932.

Author's Collection

its life. The town's water supply was further strengthened by additional sources at Ogbourne in 1902. Some employment problems were arising, due, in particular, to the need for female employment, in an area which could not absorb the numbers in the usual outlets of shop or domestic work. Already a uniform clothing works had been extended by Messrs. Compton in Sheppard Street in 1901, and this was assisted further by the opening in Rodbourne of the Cellular Clothing Company's factory in 1902. It is not quite clear how much of a blessing this was. Starting with 75 employees manufacturing ladies' underwear, the staff had risen, by 1904, to about 300, but the hours expected of the girls and young women, 8 a.m. until 7 p.m., were so excessive that a Miss Reeves brought them out on strike in desperation. It is reported that girls were fainting from fatigue. However, the management kindly reduced their hours to 8 a.m. until 6.30 p.m! Another newspaper, the weekly Borough Press, was introduced in 1904. It came out on Saturdays and was mainly a sporting sheet. Because of its colour it became known as the 'Green un'. Records also show that in 1904 there were 131 hotels and inns in the town, together with 51 off-licence shops, and assuming they were all making a living, it infers a reasonable prosperity in the town. On the debit side in the same year, 1,106 were in receipt of outdoor relief, although only 136 of these were able bodied. Although not comparable to present day labour statistics, this does represent the recognized unemployed out of a population of over 40,000. The total sum paid out to these people in the year was, however, only about £125, representing only 2 shillings and sixpence (12½p) each -- not much for a year! Added to this were the 263 registered destitute at the Stratton Workhouse. More schools were being successively opened to meet the rising demand for places: Jennings Street, and the higher grade school in Euclid Street, both opening in 1904.

One big social occasion which has already been referred to as commencing in 1868 should now be reviewed, as it had become a regular happening on the Swindon scene. The Children's Fete, organized by the committee of the Mechanics Institution was to continue annually until the outbreak of World War II, only missing one or two in World War I, but developing into a big social event in the town. Usually held on the second Saturday in August, it attracted large crowds from its inception, which were to become an embarrassment in later years. It was always held in the GWR Park, and a large group of helpers was pressed into service, organizing such things as catering, admissions, ticket offices, dances etc. By about 1890 the pattern had been firmly established, and being an afternoon and evening event, the many touring showmen would arrive the previous evening, setting up their paraphernalia on the Saturday morning. Gates usually opened at 1.30 p.m. with the entrance fee at this time being 3d for adults and 2d for children, (about 1½p and 1p). From at least 1880 each child received, on entry, a packet containing a ½lb slab of fruit cake, together with a free ticket for a roundabout ride, and this became traditional. By 1890 the attendance had reached 20,000 and a fire-

work display provided by Wilders now became a feature as dusk set in. That year the set piece, which always ended the display was 'The Forth Bridge with a Train', a topical, as well as popular, choice, with that structure having only recently been completed. We have a very full description of the event in 1891, which is particularly interesting because of the cake distribution. Baked for the past 10 years in 5lb slabs by Mr Monk of High Street, the problem of cutting them into 10 half pound pieces and wrapping them had become a very time consuming affair involving a large number of lady and gentlemen helpers. In 1891 the trimming shop foreman Mr Harvie, mentioned earlier when entertaining his lady employees, devised a cake cutting machine with four cross blades and one longitudinal blade in a press mechanism actuated by a lever. The machine was equipped with canvas feed belts which conveyed wooden trays, each containing a 5lb cake, to the cutter, then the cut cake was fed away to tables where the ladies quickly dealt with the packaging. That year there were 2 tons 16 cwt. of cake supplied, (2,85 tonnes), and the machine reduced packing time to 4 hours, with about 6 cakes being bagged per minute, although they did manage 10 per minute for short periods, and even-

Plate 118: Cake cutting and packing, prior to the Fete. The patent cutting machine is seen in the centre.

Swindon Museum

Plate 119: 'Trippers' waiting to entrain in Swindon Carriage Works. These trains, headed by No. 3817 *County of Monmouth* and No. 3834 *County of Somerset* would be for Weymouth or Weston-super-Mare.

D. Bird

tually the normal bagging time became 12 per minute. Cakes were not the only problem however, 680 gallons (3,090 litres) of tea was brewed in the mess rooms and conveyed, in huge urns, to the marquees. As always, the Aylesbury Dairy donated 30 gallons of milk (136 litres). 40lb (18 kg) of tea was required, together with 4 cwt. (203 kg) of sugar. Large tanks, (usually modified from engine tenders) were available with drinking water supplied from Kemble. Oatmeal water was also obtainable free to children. Prior to the fete a 1d subscription was raised from each employee in the Works and was used to provide entertainment for all children in the Stratton and Purton Workhouses. These were looked after by 'aunts' and 'uncles' and a grand tea awaited them in the drill hall adjoining the park, each child being given 6d (2½p) to spend; quite a large sum for a youngster then. Any monies remaining after this, and there was always plenty, provided a treat for adult inmates of these institutions. In 1891 the fete included three of the largest steam roundabouts with their magnificent horses and steam organs, one of the

three proving less popular with the crowd because the horses were not of the galloping kind, i.e. there was no up and down movement. Other roundabouts were provided especially for boys, girls and infants. Apart from the usual fair machines, swings, etc., there were the side shows and prize fighting galleries, and even an exhibition of the 'New Stereoscopic Views' in the specially prepared cricket pavilion. The Swindon Town Military Band was in more or less constant attendance, but strong drink was not allowed in the park! A stage presentation, accompanied by a string band, gave several shows during the afternoon and evening, after which everyone waited about for the spectacular firework show, and these were often watched by crowds of people in Okus Road, a westward branch of Swindon Hill overlooking the park. The gate entrances were decorated with 'V.R.' displays, tastefully illuminated at night by gas jets! After the workhouse childrens' tea, the drill hall needed to be cleared in preparation for the evening dance, where music was supplied by Mr J. Carter's Quadrille Band, and there was a special refreshment marquee for this event. So ended an eventful day, but more fun was to be had on Sunday morning, when early risers watched the departure of the show-men with their gleaming steam engines and smart horse teams and caravans. An event to be savoured for long afterwards!

Of course, sometimes, there was the disaster of a wet day, and in 1892 when this happened, only 10,000 adults and 7,000 children paid for admittance. Usually the cake distribution only lasted from 1.30 p.m. until 4.30 p.m., when all was disposed of, but on this occasion, although distribution was maintained until early evening, of the 1,268 cakes supplied, seven bushel baskets of cut cake were left and 100 cakes left uncut. It is not recorded how this was disposed of. The firework set piece that year was 'The Mechanics Institution'. However, generally the event expanded, and by 1904 the attendance was no less than 38,000 requiring about 4 tonnes of cake! By this time the baking was being shared with the Co-operative Bakery in order to cope with the quantity. Quality was never allowed to decline, however, and the author, as a boy in the 1920s and 1930s well recalls the special flavour of them.

By the turn of the century the trip holiday had also gained in popularity to the extent that, in 1905, there was an exodus of 24,500 people within a few hours — about half the total population! In this particular year there were 22 special trains, for which locomotives and approximately 300 carriages needed to be available and ready for use. They were positioned both at the station and in many of the Works' sidings, loaded with families and luggage, and despatched with split minute timing. The whole operation was completed in just over two hours! The numbers travelling to the most popular districts were:-

Weymouth		5,420
West of England		5,332
Weston-super-Mare		3,807
London		3,782
South Wales		2,730
North of England		2,370
Unclassified	approximately	1,000

One unpopular side to this annual trek was removed in 1913. Prior to this the unpaid holiday had always covered a full working week, with the result that on the following pay-day, what was termed the 'grand march' past the pay tables took place, as there was no pay to draw. In 1913 the holiday was altered to mid-week dates, so there was at least half a week's pay to draw either side of the holiday. Even 70 years on, the 'grand march past' is still wryly recalled by older inhabitants.

A glance at the Mechanics Institution activities shows its continual growth. At the Annual General Meeting in February 1907 it was reported that

membership had risen to 10,176, almost the total number employed. The library now housed 30,143 volumes. They were still organizing impressive entertainments. On 14th January 1902, the large baths, (covered over for the winter), was the venue of a visit during their tour of Britain by J. Sousa and his military band from America. Again at the same venue we find, on 18th February 1907, the very first films shown in the town. The first cinema to open in the town came on 11th February 1910, on a site in Regent Street where Woolworth's store now stands. It was named County Electric Pavilion Cinema. It was followed two years later by the Arcadia Cinema, just a hundred yards down the road. The institute was now no longer the only centre of entertainment in the New Town area and was to amend its policy accordingly. The amateur theatrical, choral, orchestral and band organizations however continued to thrive, although three more cinemas opened in 1913. The inaugural meeting of the Swindon branch of the Workers' Educational Association took place at the town hall on Saturday, 7th May 1908, under the auspices of the Mechanics Institution, Swindon Education Committee and the University Extension Group. One of those present was Reuben George, the local social reformer. Also of interest is the speaker from Oxford University, a certain W. Temple, later to become Archbishop of Canterbury.

By 1900 the number employed was about 11,500 and the annual bill for the wages staff at Swindon was £600,000, which averaged out at £52 per man per year. In fact the range was still about 30 shillings (£1.50) for the higher skills to well under £1 for labourers, and it was even worse in other industries. In the report issued by the Board of Trade in 1908 entitled *Cost of Living of the Working Classes*, much information about Swindon can be gleaned. Wages in 1905 had reached from 33s to 31s 6d. for the skilled trades in engineering (£1.65p to £1.57½p), and were by now tending to be lower than other southern towns, but slightly higher than Crewe. Rents were about three shillings (15p) per week for the smaller terraced houses, about 60 per cent of that charged in London, but higher than at Crewe. Rents were lower than they had been in 1895, however, because the overcrowding problem had been mainly overcome, reducing demand. The proportion of employed women in the town in 1908 was 7.2 per cent.

Locomotive and carriage building was still moving apace. We have followed the development of the 4-6-0 passenger class locomotives. Whilst this was proceeding, Churchward had continued producing 4-4-0 double framed locomotives to meet traffic needs, and the best known of these was the 'City' class. These locomotives were basically of the 'Atbara' class with the larger standard No. 4 boiler. It was the 1903 batch of these, named after cities on the GWR, that quickly established a name for speed.

They were used extensively on the Cornwall expresses until ousted by the new 4-6-0s appearing later. The exploits of No. 3717 *City of Truro* on a Plymouth to Bristol mail special in May 1904 and recorded by Rous-Marten, made history when a speed of 102.3 m.p.h. was claimed on the fall from Whiteball Tunnel. Although not publicized, because of the possibility of adverse public reaction, the point to point running of this class on frequent runs such as this showed their capacity for sustained high speed with extremely smooth running. Railway pundits were therefore surprised at the emergence of the 'County' class 4-4-0 in 1904, the first to Lot 149. The 4-6-0s had already appeared, and in many respects they were a 'short version' of these with a standard No. 4 boiler. Their power was over 15 per cent higher than the 'Cities' but supplied by outside cylinders and with only single frames they were pretty rough riders, particularly at short cut-off, although they did good work on secondary main lines. Two further Lots were to appear in 1906 and 1911, making 40 in all, but no more were built after this.

In February 1908, after quite a number of the 4 cylinder 4-6-0s were in service, Churchward produced in Swindon his Lot 171, a single locomotive, No. 111 *The Great Bear*. The first Pacific (4-6-2 wheel arrangement) to appear in this country, it was a massive machine indeed, combined engine and tender weighing 142 tons 15 cwt. (145 tonnes). The engine portion was almost identical to the 'Stars', the main difference being 15in. diameter cylinders against the 'Star' 14¼in., producing a small increase in tractive effort. There has been, and continues to be, much discussion over the 'reasons' for the single example of this type, but it is not the author's intention to enter further into these arguments. Whatever the events leading to its appearance, however, the opportunity was clearly taken by Churchward to extend his know-ledge of large boiler design and try to break new ground for future use. It was fitted from the start with a superheater, originally of the Field-tube Swindon No. 1 type, later replaced by a two-row pattern. The firebox, however, was of the wide variety allowed by the wheel arrangement, and in some ways a normal advance from that fitted to No. 36, but incorporating many of the later developments in taper barrel construction. As an advertisement there was nothing to touch it, and whatever may be thought of its performance, in the following years, it brought much kudos to the GWR, and Swindon men were certainly proud of having built it.

If any vindication of Churchward's designs are wanted, they were certainly given in the exchange trials with locomotives of the LNWR in 1910. This event is purported to have arisen from complaints by certain members of the Board that the LNWR could build three express passenger locomotives for the same price as two of Churchward's 'Stars'. No. 4005 *Polar Star* worked between Euston and Crewe in tandem with LNW No. 1455 *Herefordshire* of their 'Experiment' class, and these workings were balanced between Paddington and Plymouth by No. 4003 *Lode Star*, now in the Swindon GWR Museum, and LNW No. 1471 *Worcestershire*. There was no doubt about the results of these comparative trials, but even after these it was plain that locomotive engineers had still to realize the great advances in design that were to be found in the 'Stars'. The other class of note was the 43XX mixed traffic 2-6-0 (Mogul) engines of 1911. This was additional to the six types contemplated in 1901. They were so successful that the remaining 'standard' 4-6-0 with 5ft. 8in. wheels was not to appear until long after Churchward had retired. They became one of the most numerous class on the GWR.

All this later locomotive development continued

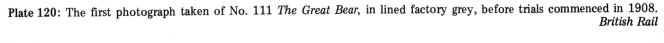

Plate 120: The first photograph taken of No. 111 *The Great Bear*, in lined factory grey, before trials commenced in 1908.
British Rail

Plate 121: The iron foundry, looking west, on 18th April 1907.

D. Bird

under darkening clouds however. Costs of living were gradually rising, with no change in wages, and labour was still not organized sufficiently to make much impact. The railways still did not officially recognize unions, although were prepared to hear grievances from, and discuss matters with, 'conciliation committees'. Most of such moves came from the operating grades of the railways, and they had a great asset in a locomotive driver from Wales, now resident in Swindon. He was 'Jimmy' (later the Rt. Hon. James) Thomas, a member, and later president, of the Amalgamated Society of Railway Servants. This organization became one of the main constituents of the 1913 National Union of Railwaymen, and 'Jimmy' became general secretary of the NUR before entering politics and Parliament, and finally becoming a Minister of the Crown. Living first at 32 Broad Street and later 17 Faringdon Road, he did much to organize the running staff at Swindon, and defeated W. H. Stanier in local elections in 1901 when only 26 years old. There was much consternation over this! No clerks were in a union in 1901 and it is estimated that less than 30 per cent of the Works

staff belonged, although this can only be supposition. Jimmy Thomas moved from Swindon in 1907 when ominous shadows were again darkening the Works' horizon. There were two basic reasons for this. One was the recession in trade, partly due to the industrial unrest generally. Organized labour in some industries was becoming able to show more solidarity and gaining concessions in wages and conditions. No railways, were, at this period, prepared to go along with this. The second reason, as far as the Works was concerned, was the great economic success of Churchward's policy of locomotive design and standardization combined. Locomotives were capable of running for longer periods between repairs, particularly to the boilers, usually the deciding factor for withdrawal. The rapid introduction of interchangeable parts meant that store holdings could be drastically reduced, not having to maintain separate spares for each class of locomotive or carriage. Short time working again reappeared, and then a considerable list of discharges. The issue of notices, was, to say the least, unfortunately timed, appearing a few days before the annual 'trip' holiday, spreading much bitterness amongst the staff. They thought it a poor reward for producing such engineering wonders as the 'Stars' and *The Great Bear*. Mass meetings were held on 7th July 1908 outside the town hall and a petition sent to the Board, but to no avail, and much hardship became apparent. It was now that the unions confirmed commitment moved to the Labour party. Churchward, being an autocrat, although extremely well liked by his men, is reported to have replied to a union man on one of the conciliation boards that, 'if you and those you represent are not satisfied with conditions in my department, I shall be pleased to receive your notices'. (P. S. Bagwell — *The Railwaymen: History of the NUR*).

Many men left their families in Swindon and sought work elsewhere, some remaining away for three or four years. An Unemployment Relief Fund was inaugurated in the town, and by August of 1909, £1,472 had been paid out to 572 individuals and some were employed in extending the Old Swindon town gardens, which was being gradually transformed from the original Goddard quarries of earlier centuries. Matters were not helped when, on 1st February 1911, a serious fire severely damaged the carriage paint shop, with the loss of much rolling stock. A serious accident on the line added to the financial pressures on the Board resulting in more lay offs. Whether as an indirect result of poverty or not, there was a bad epidemic of diphtheria in the town in 1912, adding to the troubles. After much argument on both sides of the industry, the unions threw down the gauntlet and called the first National Railway Strike on 18th August 1911, which lasted several days, until the intervention of Lloyd George. There had been partial stoppages at some places earlier in the year, which had caused an easing off of traffic. Even though the Railway Works were unaffected by this strike, it lessened even more the repair work load. It was after this strike that the combination of constituent unions into the single NUR took place, as it was then evident what solidarity could achieve. Other trades and organizations also took due note for the future. Even when work was becoming more plentiful, there was considerable drainage of staff, with many emigrating, particularly to Canada, where the transcontinental railways were in great need of staff for expansion. There was also an exodus of groups to other parts of the United Kingdom. An example was a party of 60 or 70 boilermakers leaving from Swindon Town station on Saturday, 7th August 1911, to work at John Brown's shipyard on Clydebank. Here they would practically double their pay immediately, with rivetters being paid 10 shillings (50p) a day, a very high rate indeed. Only giving their notices late on the previous day, (they were hourly paid staff), they caused considerable embarrassment to the Works management. They were sent off with cheers by officers and mem-

bers of the Boilermakers' Association, in addition to their families. The work situation was not helped by the National Coal Strike commencing 1st March 1912, bringing a steep reduction in railway freight business, and reductions in services to conserve fuel stocks, which in turn brought further short time working to Swindon. More trouble was created by the installation in the Works of electric clocks in every shop, working on the 'Magneta' master and slave clock system. Apart from the simple requirement of having standard time available in the shops, they were to be used by staff to note the starting and finishing times on job cards — a general extension of the previous Rochester system reviewed earlier. There was an immediate allegation by the men that times would be compared between individuals, and all would eventually be expected to work at the speed of the fastest. Of course, the national press quickly reported the details of the matter. It was expected that the 'measured time' system was to replace the well entrenched 'piece work' method. The trade unionists seized upon this in a bid to strengthen their membership, following as it did upon the periods of short time and laying off of staff at short notice. However it was explained that the times were only needed in order to meet the requirements of the new Railway Accounts Bill (1911), necessitating more detailed departmental accounting, and many extra clerks were to be employed as a consequence. Sir William Plender (of whom more later), and government auditors were proposing new methods of machine costing. It was also hoped that proving by such means the lower costs at large factories such as Swindon, they would attract more work, and a delegation from the unions accepted this explanation. The Amalgamated Society of Engineers' delegates had to satisfy a huge meeting of 1,500 of their members — a sign of the allegiance now emerging as the normal pattern for unions in the Works. Incidentally, these electric clocks were only withdrawn from service in about 1970, and two beautifully craft made master clocks now stand in a place of honour in the entrance hall of the main office block, although few who now admire their workmanship are aware of the trouble their introduction caused early in 1913. Much of the uncertainty arising from the incident was fanned into flame by the Liberal Member of Parliament, R. C. Lambert, who was shortly to face an election in what was very much a floating vote situation, the Liberals being, at the time, the radical party. Failing to keep this dispute going, a much larger red herring was raised over the latest dismissals in 1912/13, making a case in the national press that men had been selected for dismissal because of their party allegiance. This matter raged for some three months, although nobody ever questioned how the Company could know the private views of their workers. In any case, many 'working class' families

Plate 122: The tool room, then above the original machine shop, on 30th May 1907. Later used as a store, this floor has now been removed but the timber trussed roof was the only one so remaining in 1980.

British Rail

Plate 123: The steam hammer shop on 29th June 1907. The machine, seen indistinctly in the far left of the picture, has a rivetted frame and thus, probably, is one of the earliest installed in the Works by Nasmyth in the 1840s.

D. Bird

Plate 124: A view, northwards, over the Locomotive Works from the Bristol Street water tank. The higher building in the middle distance, housed the tool room on its upper floor. The west end of the 1841 engine shed, also in the middle distance, shows the blind stone arch which carried one of the stone bas-reliefs (Plate 115).

British Rail

Plate 125: The east portion of the 'B' shop re-organized as a tender shop as seen on 30th May 1907. Of interest is the small steam traverser, but through the aperture at the top left of this can be seen one of the wheels of the original erecting shop crane, illustrated earlier. This old erecting shop was still in use at this date.

British Rail

Plate 128 (above): The energy losses from complicated countershaft drives can be well imagined from this 1907 view of the brass (T) turning and fitting shop. Steam locomotives were, of course, very heavy on the use of brass and copper fittings. Prominent here are injectors, brake valves and ejectors.

British Rail

Plate 126 (top left): The springsmiths shop (then T2 shop) on 22nd June 1907. Note the original hearths and timber roof. Only one hanging gas lighting fitting can be observed, but there are some four-branch jet fittings at face level in places.

British Rail

Plate 127 (bottom left): The cylinder shop (then P2) on 21st January 1907. This was later called W shop. Note the very early boring machines, 'walking' crane, overhead countershafting and floor steam heating ducts.

British Rail

of that time were Nonconformist in their social alignment, and, because of this, generally supported the Liberal policies of the day. So the chances were that if many were dismissed, the majority might be Liberal voters. After much vituperative journalese, a statement was issued on 1st April 1913, and signed by Churchward, completely and firmly refuting the allegations. Effectively killed, the arguments again moved to pay and conditions, and a long battle ensued which was not resolved before World War I broke out.

As stated earlier, many were leaving for Canada and a local shipping agent reported that, in April 1913, he had arranged for 70 people from the area to emigrate to Canada where skilled workmen of good character and no explicit age limit were badly needed by the Grand Trunk & Canadian Pacific Railways. They could earn up to £4 per week, and at least 100 men from the GWR had left in the past 12 months. (*Daily Mail*, 1st May 1913). The agent rightly pinpointed the main reason for the situation — 'the invention which doubled the life of a locomotive boiler was no doubt admirable, but its result is that a good many of the men of Swindon find themselves left with no work to do'. Finally, the Daily Chronicle of 27th May 1913 noted that:-

'whilst the Labour Exchange bulletin at Swindon was seeking fitters at 28 shillings (£1.40) per week, in the same street a Canadian Pacific Railway official was offering contracts at £3 14s 4d (£3.72) per week, and sea passage paid. He hoped to take 100 picked men over on 28th June'.

A few days later the number was purported to be 300, but this may have included drivers and firemen who were being offered £30 and £16 per month respectively.

Our premise that it was not the effects of depression which was the main cause of the decline of work at Swindon, is supported by many pointers of heavy financial commitment on the GWR. At Swindon the century had started with large additions to the Factory, accompanied by heavy expenditure on new locomotives and carriages. Parallel with this was the successive completion of several large railway projects. The first was the commencement of the huge Fishguard Harbour project with a view to capturing a large portion of the transatlantic shipping traffic. The next was the opening of the South Wales direct line from Wootton Bassett to the Severn Tunnel, and in reality completing the great work of tunnelling under the estuary. This was in 1903, and the following year a new express was inaugurated between Paddington and Plymouth non-stop, covering the 246 miles via Bristol in 4 hours and 25 minutes, to be supported in 1906 by the new route to the West via Westbury and Castle Cary, cutting the distance by 20¼ miles. During most of the period covered by these schemes there was gradual development of the Paddington to Birmingham direct line via High Wycombe and Ashendon Junction, and in much the same period the South Wales to Birmingham direct line via Cheltenham and Stratford-upon-Avon. There was no shortage of capital for all these major and many other minor projects such as improvements to the main line throughout the length of Cornwall. However, care still needed to be taken that the financial scales did not fall in the wrong direction. These new lines attracted enough increase in traffic to balance the outlay. So that we find, in 1908, the LSWR receipts were up by only £400 over the previous year, but the GWR figure was £36,000. Not riches, perhaps, but satisfactory enough in the circumstances.

This brings us to one of the last projects to be attempted before war brought such expansion to a sudden halt. On completion of his large locomotive and carriage development programme, Churchward received authorization from the Board for large orders of the new rolling stock to these standard designs. He was immediately faced with a problem,

manufactured by himself. Whilst the 'A' shop had been necessitated by the increase in locomotive size in the late 1890s, and cranage of 50 ton capacity had been installed, the new locomotives in their dead state were already over this weight, and much longer also. Manufacture of small numbers had been no special problem, but the batches of 4-6-0 types now on order would use uneconomic building methods due to lack of capacity. The drawing office now prepared schemes for a major extension to the 'A' shop. Exactly when the work started is not clear, but some sketches and shot estimates must have been prepared in 1910/11. The earliest scheme still existing was completed in January 1912 and shows a *Great Bear* outline under 70ft. span overhead crane. This extension only shows what was to become the main erecting shop. There is no provision for the large wheel shop which was also built at its west face. But, as was intimated earlier, the days were passing when the chief executive at Swindon just said the word and the Board complied. Admittedly between 1903 and 1913, some £90,000 was granted for general improvements in the Works, but these were all small individual projects. The Board was now faced with the new Railway Accounts Bill coming into force in 1911, which, in effect, called for closer scrutiny and control of the finances of these huge public corporations. In 1911 therefore, faced with the recommendation for large Swindon extensions, the Board decided to call in Mr (later Sir William) Plender to make:-

'an independent investigation as to whether Swindon Works should be extended to deal with the increasing arrangements of the Company and to submit information as to the system of accounts, records and arrangements generally in operation at Swindon to enable the Board to come to a decision as to future policy in regard to the Works'.

Three separate reports were eventually presented, one each for locomotives, carriages and wagons between August 1912 and June 1915. By the latter time, war had completely altered the situation, and it is indeed fortunate that the first report to be presented was for locomotives. The other two will be dealt with chronologically in the next chapter. Because of their importance to the future policy of expansion and development at Swindon, the Board minutes appertaining to each report are quoted verbatim. Received in August 1912, the report was carefully considered by the LC&S committee whose meetings Churchward attended, (they were often held in the Swindon boardroom in any case), and the GWR Board, and on 1st November 1912 No. 3 minute reads:-

'The general effect of the report is that Sir William Plender is satisfied that some re-arrangement and extensions of the

Plate 129: The Carriage & Wagon trimming shop (No. 9) seen in 1907. This is a 'set piece' to show the range of activities from axle-box pads (foreground), to carriage seats and office chairs. The ornate settees and individual chairs (centre) are obviously from one of the Royal waiting rooms. Again note the low level gas jets, (fire risk!).

British Rail

Plate 130: The Carriage & Wagon Works management office block to the north-east of the station, backed by the No. 15 machine & fitting shop, photographed on 30th April 1908.

British Rail

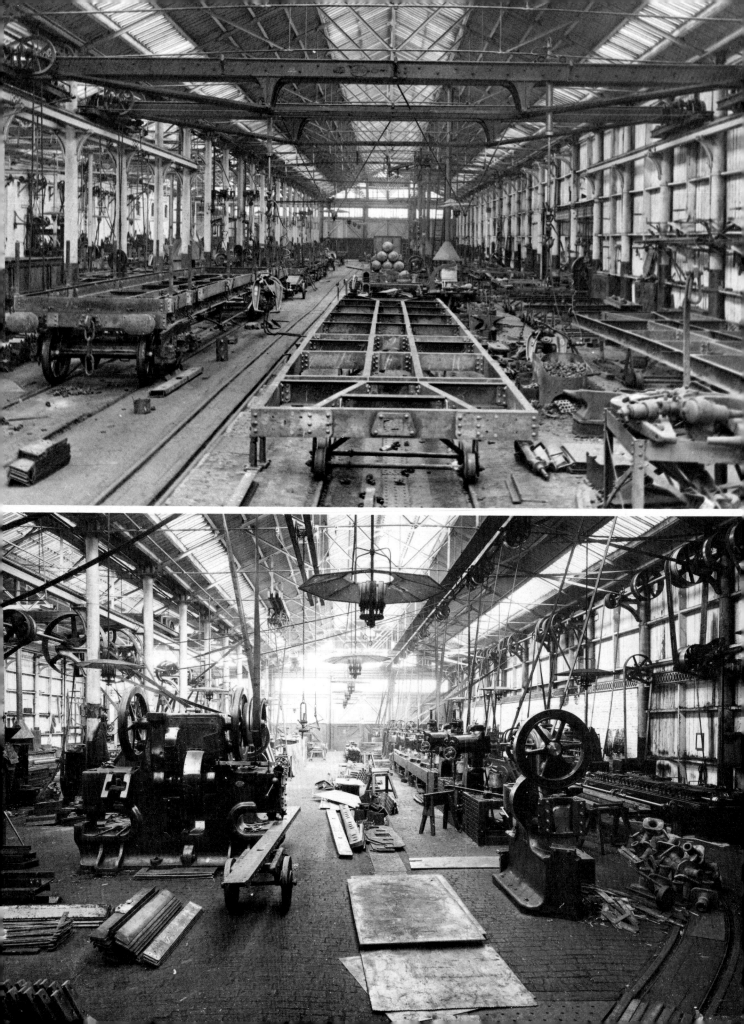

Plate 133 (below): A June 1907 view of the west bay of the Carriage & Wagon (No. 16) wheel shop, showing tyre and wheel turning lathes. The slender spoked wheel centres were from the small goods trucks of the day.

British Rail

Plate 131 (left above): Wagon frame (No. 13) shop on 1st August 1907. The overhead cranes are really positioners for the power rivetter which each crane carried. Positioned by means of hand ropes, the rivetter and its lifts were hydraulically operated, power to the vertical lift cylinder being ingeniously carried up inside the ram to the carriage housing above.

British Rail

Plate 132 (left below): Another part of the wagon frame (No. 13) shop with heavy shearing and punching machines in the foreground. Behind, the multiple drilling bench for longitudinal frame members can be seen.

British Rail

Plate 134: Part of the east bay of the Carriage & Wagon (No. 16) shop, showing the way in which the timber-centred Mansell wheels were built up for use on the carriages. These were used partly to absorb rail noise and it was generally accepted that a 'softer' ride resulted. Worn blocks were re-used for factory flooring and many floors were, in 1980, still using these blocks.

British Rail

Plate 135: A distinctive period piece. The road motor (later road wagon No. 17) shop, on 25th July 1907. Early motor bus bodies are seen in the foreground. An extension to this shop had been opened during the previous year.

British Rail

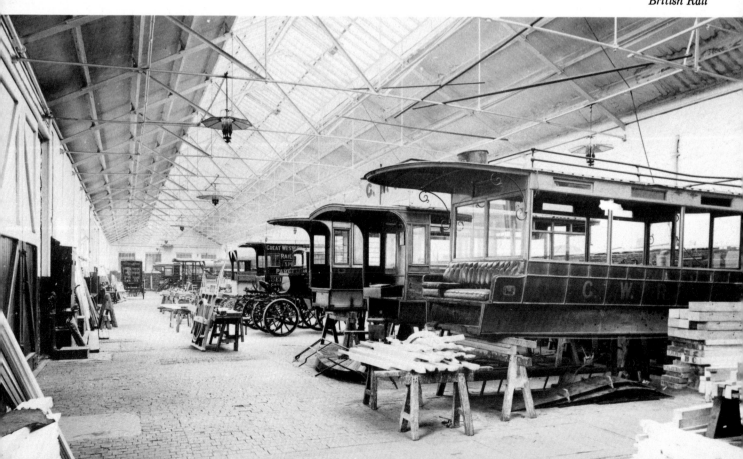

existing Works are necessary to relieve present congestions and to meet the current and growing need of Engine accommodation efficiently and economically, but is of opinion that no extension should be made beyond what is necessitated by the requirements in the normal maintenance of the stock. In indicating briefly some of the reasons which have led him to this conclusion he states that although the existing methods of costing at Swindon are not sufficiently scientific to supply exact statistics to enable a comparison between the costs in constructing locomotives there and the costs of outside Firms for similar work he has in certain instances been able to contrast the Company's stated costs of building with those of other Companies and Firms and these comparisons appear to justify the view that the cost of building at Swindon is lower than that shown by such Companies and Firms. Important questions other than relative cost have to be considered, however, such as labour unrest, difficulties and cost of providing Capital and the need for heavy expenditure in other directions.

'Sir William suggests therefore that the Directors would be well advised to sanction an extension of the Works necessary for meeting the needs of the efficient upkeep of the present locomotive stock, it being understood that any slackness in repair operations should be taken advantage of to carry through constructional work, but that no extensions should be authorised which are based primarily upon the proposition to build additional stock.

'He states that his enquiry has not extended to the Coaching and Wagon Department. He, however, considers that any contemplated extension of Shops for new Stock in this Department should be deferred if not altogether abandoned and that any present deficiency in wagons should be remedied without the Company itself embarking on Capital outlays for extending the Works for the purpose.

'On the other hand adequate shop accommodation for vehicle repairs and renewals is obviously a necessity and should be duly provided.

'The Board after fully considering the matter determined that the policy to be adopted in regard to the Works at Swindon should be based generally on the lines recommended by Sir William Plender and requested Mr Churchward to prepare and submit the plans and proposals for a comprehensive scheme such as he considers it would be necessary to adopt to meet the requirements during the next 10 years for repairs and renewals of Locomotive, Carriage and Wagon stock as distinct from the construction of additional stock and indicating the portion of such scheme which he deems it necessary to carry out forthwith. In preparing the scheme regard should be had to the necessity sooner or later of providing two additional down and up lines through Swindon'.

If there was a sting emanating from the report, it is to be found in the second paragraph of this minute,

Plate 136: The 1913 version of the 70 ft. carriage. Corridor third, bars 2, 'Toplight' No. 2566, of lot 1214, with American type equalized bolster bogies. It is finished in the standard 'lake' of the period.

British Rail

where it was recommended that only the needs for locomotive maintenance should be covered, new building to be covered by fluctuations in the repair programme. With this serious proviso from Churchward's viewpoint, we see from the last paragraph that in general the main recommendations were adopted. The principles contained therein became the genesis of a comprehensive scheme for the next decade, despite, or perhaps because of, World War I. Churchward needed no second bidding to start preparing final schemes for the huge 'A' shop extensions now agreed in principle. This put the Swindon engineers on their mettle, and on 11th December 1912 a full scheme for a very comprehensive extension was completed and costed. Structural drawings were also being prepared by this time in readiness. One can but think that Churchward's tongue was suitably positioned in his cheek!

The additional building planned fell into three main sections. Moving westwards from the original (old 'A' shop) came boiler manufacturing, and repair bays running north to south at 420ft. x 170ft. A 35 ton overhead crane of just under 75ft. span was to traverse the length of this bay, whilst a cross overhead crane above this (known as the 'attic' crane), was to service a huge 28ft. gap rivetter, sunk into the floor beneath. The top of its foundation block was to be about 35ft. below floor level. West of this were the erecting bays in an area 480ft. x 240ft. There were to be two bays of 20 pits each, and served in between by an 80 ton shallow pit traverser 42ft. wide. The repair pits 95ft. long were to be served with two 100 ton overhead traversing cranes to each bay, four in all, with rail centres at 75ft. Being double crabbed, these would lift the heaviest locomotive, and would be able to carry it clear up or down the shop. The forty pits could accommodate 80 locomotives at a time if pressed. West again was to be the lower roofed wheel (AW) shop where locomotive wheel and axle fitting, retyring, turning and balancing

could be achieved. This area was to be served by 'walking' cranes similar to those already in the AM (machine) shop. With this section 420ft. x 198ft., it made a total extension of 257,520 sq. ft. Adding to this the old 'A' shop area of 226,386 sq. ft., it was to make the whole structure a staggering 483,906 sq. ft. (44,955 sq. metres) or 11.11 acres (4.495 hectares) in area. Additional outbuildings made the total approximately 11¼ acres.

These were the proposals and the question of equipping the new shops would have to be discussed later as detailed planning developed. The building itself was estimated at £165,000 and a sum of £20,000 was added for overhead cranes, though which is not specified, and these amounts were authorized by the Board on 11th December 1913 and 9th July 1914 respectively. With war breaking out on 4th August, it was clear that a major revision of plans would be necessary, and on 6th October the main vote was reduced by £150,000 and the £20,000 vote withdrawn for the time being. The remaining £15,000 allowed building to commence however, and foundation work was quickly in hand. The work was to be carried out as before, mainly by the Factory's own mason's and steelwork shops, although it is suspected that many of the compound columns and girders required, came from the steel mills already fabricated. Considerable drainage work for the area had been completed at appropriate depth when the old 'A' shop had been built, so only additional connections were required. Also some of this new extension was to be on land already built up for sidings to house the redundant BG stock in 1892. As the land fell gently westwards, the furthest extent of the new AW shop was some 20ft. above original level, although only about 8ft. at the AV (boiler) shop end. Architecturally, the style of the old 'A' was continued with the use of the top bowed window frames, smooth faced Cattybrook red brick and with

Plate 137 *(left top):* Horse box No. 8, built in 1889, shows typical frame and suspension details of the short wheelbase vehicles of the Dean period. It was photographed at Swindon in September 1898.
British Rail

Plate 138 *(left bottom):* Horse box No. 359, built about a quarter of a century later than the previous vehicle illustrated, shows the development of body styles in vehicle building and that of running gear.
British Rail

blue brick sills and arches, giving a very pleasing appearance to such a large building. The frontage on to the main line of the other two main blocks of the Works, the iron foundry and the original erecting shop and engine shed building, had not been laid down in a straight line, but as the track curves gradually southwards from Swindon station, each of the blocks in turn had been set out with their centre placed tangentially to the track at that particular point. The same thing was done when the 'A' shop foundations were set out. This fact is not appreciated by most people in the Works, but is aesthetically very satisfying where large blocks of buildings are concerned, in that looking from either end one can actually see all three of these long building faces over nearly ¾ mile length. This gives a much more compact and foreshortened sense of perspective to these large buildings, which would not be the case if laid out along parallel lines.

The year 1913 saw considerable changes in the management structure. W. H. Waister who had been the chief outdoor running assistant to Dean and Churchward since the autumn of 1897 was now reaching the age of 65, and during the last 15 years his long experience had been of great support to his younger chief and colleagues. He was succeeded by his assistant W. H. Williams, originally from the Monmouthshire Railway. A Whitworth scholar, he had served a term as chief draughtsman at Swindon before becoming Swindon Divisional Superintendent. In the Works itself, H. C. King, also a Whitworth scholar, had masterminded the great production problems arising from the radical changes in locomotive policy in the ten preceeding years. In particular, the continuous building of classes of engines with dimensions and weight higher than the Factory was equipped to handle, had shown his capabilities. At the end of 1912 he was appointed as an assistant to Churchward, possibly because of the politcal situation, and knowledge of the probable requirements of Swindon in the event of war. He was replaced as Works Manager by C. B. Collett, and W. A. Stanier who was only a little younger than Collett became his assistant. The heavy building programme in the Carriage Works had been in the charge of F. W. Marillier, since his appointment there from a similar post at the Saltney Works. He was to remain C&W Works Manager until the end of 1920. For four years of this period (1907–11), E. A. Watson had been an assistant under Marillier, before leaving to become, as we have heard previously, Works Manager at Ashford (SE&CR). He was followed by E. T. J.

Evans, who was to have a long and distinguished career in the C&W Works, and who eventually took G. H. Pearson's post as Assistant C&W Works Manager in February 1914, when the latter also moved to Ashford as Assistant Locomotive Carriage & Wagon Superintendent of the SE&CR under Marsh.

The Works had now experienced about 15 years during which Churchward had been in nominal or full control. During that time two monarchs had died, and Swindon had become an incorporated borough. Many other changes which were to have a lasting effect had come into being. It was a period when organized labour had started to be more effective and to become at the end of the period a force to be reckoned with. Socially, life for the common man had greatly improved, particularly in the areas of medicine, education and travel. Unemployment or short time working was still a problem with the inevitable poverty following in its wake, but even in this sphere the introduction of small allowances to pensioners was the first step towards the development of social services. Although economic depression was close for some of the time, Britain was still the most prosperous country in the world, with the United States beginning to catch up. Against this background the Works had nurtured the greatest growth in railway, especially in steam locomotive, technology, which that particular science was ever to see. Coupled with this was the efficient application of new principles as applied to production and standardization. This was the corner-stone on which the Company was able to continue to flourish until after World War II, despite the great transport changes which were to take place to the detriment of railway profitability. It can be said that Churchward's life work was completed by 1911, after only nine years in office. Other work was to come from him, but only building on the firm foundations laid previously. The final fruition for the Works was the great 'A' extension now being commenced, but under the darkening clouds of war. The conflict to come was to be met by Swindon Works from a position of strength which was to stand the country in good stead, but which was achieved with great cost to itself.

On that fateful day of 4th August 1914, ten long blasts on the Works hooter signalled to Swindon that hostilities had commenced, and a pre-arranged signal for reservists in the area to prepare for muster, many from the railway Works, which had always encouraged volunteer corps. They left next morning

Plate 139 (right): Two views of a Merryweather fire-engine used by the Works Fire Brigade at the turn of the century.

British Rail

Plate 140: The Dennis motor fire-engine, purchased in 1912, and used for many years at Swindon Works. It is now part of the Bristol Museum collection.

British Rail

by train for Plymouth and embarked thence for India. Within 10 days, 17,000 troops had gathered in the Swindon area, and 45 trains were needed to convey them on the first stage of their journey to their eventual destinations. War had begun in earnest, and with it the end of an era when railways had provided the principal transport services for the country.

Chapter Seven

1914~1922 The First World War and its Aftermath

It has been rightly said that Britain was better prepared for the commencement of hostilities in 1914 than for any conflict before or after. Discussion had taken place over a considerable number of years as to the part the railways should play in such circumstances, and how they would best be controlled. This had led, ultimately, to the formation, in 1912, of the Railway Executive Committee (REC). This body was made up of the general managers of the nine largest companies under the official chairmanship of the President of the Board of Trade. This latter post was to be nominal, since it was through this government department that policy decisions were to be channelled. The General Managers were to elect, from amongst themselves, an acting chairman who would be the de facto chairman of the REC. The railways were to be run exactly as before, but national needs were to receive priority, and co-ordination on the various lines would be controlled by the REC. On 4th August 1914, an Order in Council was made by which the government assumed powers to control 130 of the 176 railways in the country. Of the 130, the REC had direct relations with 80. REC control was concerned mainly with railway operations, so the effect on main works such as Swindon was the provision of rolling stock requirements for the train services required. Swindon's main contribution to the war effort was through the Royal Ordnance Department, under the general heading of 'munitions'. The word hardly does justice to the wide range of items dealt with ranging from complete locomotives down to leather straps for soldiers' personal equipment. One item which did come under the aegis of the REC, however, was the provision of ambulance trains. Plans were already in being for the conversion of existing carriages for home service ambulances, and the Swindon Advertiser reported that the first such converted train left the Works on 26th August, only 22 days after the declaration of war.

A heavy carriage building programme was in being at the outbreak of war, particularly of 'toplight' vehicles, the design which had superseded the earlier 'Dreadnought' and 'Concertina' styles. These were generally of 56/57ft. length and ideally suited for ambulance train use. All the production runs of this period were purchased by the government, those already nearing completion being modified, and new vehicles emerging directly as ambulance vehicles. The C&W Works Manager, F. W. Marillier, was much involved with this work, and personally designed many of the specialized interior fittings. The extent

of this project will be discussed later when making a full assessment of the total war effort. The very first order on the C&W Works was for the immediate conversion of a number of open wagons to a high sided arrangement suitable for the conveyance of horses, still the main form of motive power for the army. 410 of these conversions were carried out in all, most of them in the earlier part of the war. A corollary to this, not affecting the Works itself but the GWR generally, was that 221 heavy draught horses used in parcels and goods distribution were immediately purchased in August 1914, and 52 light draught animals also, a total of 273. These could not be replaced by new orders on workshops.

Orders to the Works from the Royal Ordnance Department (ROD) were quickly placed, the first ones being fabricated parts for 4.5in. howitzers and 60 pounder guns. Items for the former were mainly heavy plate pressings, together with machined actuating gear for the mountings, and were despatched for assembly elsewhere. The two main parts for the 60 pounder guns, however, were to show the capabilities of the Works, being highly complicated one piece upset forgings, and finally machined overall. From now on orders for the widest possible range of war material was placed, with the inevitable development of large portions of the Factory for their exclusive production.

It will be recalled that the outbreak of war left outstanding wage demands unsatisfied, and this was to be remedied before the end of 1914 by an ubiquitous war bonus on wages, which was to colour wage structure in the Railways Works for many years to follow. There was an immediate labour problem, as the Swindon reservists had already left, and many, or most of these were from the Factory. There was also a quick response to the call for volunteers, there being 2,634 of these in Swindon within the first two months. The number of railwaymen within this total is unknown, but it must have been a high percentage. Ardour must have been dampened, however, when it became clear that it would not 'all be over by Christmas' which was optimistically claimed at the beginning of the hostilities. This is clear from a recruiting rally held on 5th October 1915 when, although a reputed 7,000 people attended meetings in different parts of the town, including one outside the tunnel entrance of the Works, there were only 6 volunteers!

It is in World War I that we find for the first time the effects of security policies, and as the months progressed the lack of information becomes increasingly apparent. This makes it difficult for the historian to deal in detail with the individual items of interest taking place in Swindon, owing to the lack of source material. Bulk statistics were made available in publications around 1922, particularly those by Edwin A. Pratt. The records of rolling stock built for government service were not covered by Lot numbers, these only being allocated when vehicles were repurchased for railway service, and not necessarily all the vehicles returned. The locomotive situation is a little clearer, and will be dealt with as a complete review. Of great help, however, is a collection of photographs of many of the processes, parts and complete items of military equipment, compiled for internal use in the Works. One or two folios of these have survived, but lack explanatory texts, just giving group headings such as '6pdr Hotchkiss Guns' or '6in HE Shell Forgings (2 Operation Process)', and have to be studied carefully to ascertain the import of any particular photograph. Of great help is a detailed knowledge of the buildings within the Works, enabling a particular wall or corner in a picture to be identified, thus helping to discover which shops were specially set aside for such work and how they were organized. We will now examine the main groups of wartime work for the duration of the war.

LOCOMOTIVES

Only two classes of GWR locomotives were to be specifically used for war service. These were the 'Dean Goods' 2301 class, and earlier 'Armstrong Goods' types, obviously selected for their power, simplicity and rugged design. Even with locomotives there is discrepancy as to the number involved. Pratt in his *War Record of the GWR* makes a bald statement that 95 locomotives were furnished for overseas and 105 tenders. Figures published in 1956 by the Railway Correspondence & Travel Society (RCTS) and obtained from Swindon records, now dispersed to other known and unknown places, are more explicit, but the totals do not quite match. The first to leave Swindon were six Armstrong '388' class in November 1915, but these were returned in March 1916. Three of these were then repurchased by the ROD and sent to Serbia in August 1916, two only returning in 1921. A further eight of this class left for Salonika in May 1917, but their ship was sunk by enemy action in the English Channel. The same month a large batch consisting of 62 of the Dean 2301 class was handed over to the ROD for France. To replace those previously sunk, a further eight of the 388 class left for Salonika in September 1917 arriving safely, four only being returned in 1921. The final batch to leave was sixteen 2301 class, also sent to Salonika in January 1917, of which seven never returned to England. During the whole period there were also loans to the LNWR and MSWJR of small

numbers. All the locomotives sent to France were reported returned in mid-1919. Some of those not returned from the Middle East worked for some time in the stock of the Ottoman Railway. The modifications to the engines varied according to the conditions in which they were to work, the main alterations being to braking systems, elongated cab roofs for solar protection and, in some cases, the addition of pannier tanks to augment the tender water supply in hot countries. All were of black finish, with large identification ROD numbers in white on the tenders.

CARRIAGES

There is general agreement that 238 carriages for ambulance trains were either modified from vehicles already under construction in 1914, or built from scratch. MacDermott and most other authorities equate this number of carriages to 16 separate trains, but the number included special vehicles other than standard ambulance carriages, such as infectious case wards, staff carriages, kitchen/offices and kitchen/mess vehicles, and those fitted out for pharmacy, stores and personnel. The size of made-up trains varied from nine to sixteen vehicles. One train was supplied at six weeks notice in 1915 to meet a special fund raised by the United Kingdom Flour Millers. Many of the complete trains were sent to the Continent. Some sets were later prepared for use by the American forces in France, and accordingly had the addition of Westinghouse brakes, and other standard items of American practice. Four trains were kept for home use from the Channel ports. Many of these vehicles were equipped under the control of a special sub-committee of the REC, of which F. W. Marillier was a prominent representative. Most of these carriages were purchased back into the GWR at the end of hostilities. Whilst some reverted to their original design, others became 'nondescript' carriages or saloons for specific services. In some cases only the frames were reused, therefore tracing all the vehicles concerned is very difficult.

As well as the 238 ambulance train vehicles just described, a further 638 passenger coaches had to be provided, mainly to meet the requirements of augmented and new services run for the huge number of workers employed at munition factories. Many of these were spread over the GWR system and generally away from large towns.

WAGONS

The largest number of vehicles provided for war service falls into this category, although the range of types precludes detailed description. There was an immediate call, in August 1914, for adapted vehicles for special purposes, and within a very short space of time, as well as the 410 high sided open horse wagons already alluded to, 101 unfinished open wagons, (i.e. without sides), 171 paired sets of timber trucks and 213 bogie 45ft. rail and timber vehicles were supplied. These were for the transport of guns, limbers, carts etc., which had to be entrained from end-loading rail docks, similar to present day motorail trains. The GWR continued providing vehicles at a high rate throughout the war to the total number of 216,350. Many of these were of the 45ft. bogie type already mentioned, but how many were new it is not clear; according to the types involved, it must have been a large proportion. There was also the daily provision of uncounted numbers of ordinary goods wagons required for the conveyance of government traffic of all types. It should be remembered that the level of normal freight traffic did not reduce in quantity, although much was due to war requirements. Also coastal shipping, was not generally available now, so this traffic needed to be transferred to rail.

Under this heading, since it was a Wagon Works activity, must be recorded the building of 1,100 road wagons for the Army Service Corps and general military use, together with 50 horse drawn water carts. Posts for picketting horses numbered 3,850 together with 38,000 picketting pegs. Also some 2,950 ambulance stretchers were produced from these shops. Many of these assemblies called for a huge number of forged, fabricated and machined parts in themselves. as can be seen from accompanying illustrations (*Plates 141 and 142*).

Plate 141: One of the 1,100 Army service vehicles built. Exhibited in the foreground are all the metal parts required in its manufacture. The Carriage & Wagon Works offices are in the background.

British Rail

Plate 142: A similar view to the previous picture showing one of the fifty water carts manufactured.

MUNITIONS (General)

Railway workshops in time of war, particularly the large ones, never fail to surprise those who should know better, by the wide range of their capabilities. Admittedly, writing in 1980, the picture would not be the same as in 1914 or 1939, since the rationalization of many primary activities to perhaps only one factory or completely to private industry, has reduced total capability in some measure. Nevertheless, by the nature of their normal work, it is necessary to retain many processes 'in being' even though not regularly used. Again the scope of the work has always been wide, for the same reasons, from delicate tool room work right through to heavy engineering and fabrication on a par with the ship-building industry. These capabilities are not to be found just in the equipment, but in the retained craft skills which are necessary to keep alive a large transport organization. Railways are still, as Gooch

was always ready to point out, an engineering organization first, and by application of such equipment and skills, able to provide a transport service. This little matter is often overlooked even in these so called enlightened days.

The facilities available at Swindon were soon in great demand by the War Office, Ministry of Munitions, Woolwich Arsenal, the Admiralty, and, as sub-contractors, to many private firms involved with similar work. Just to quote a catalogue even of the major items can be boring, but it is desirable that such information is discussed in order to sense the heavy workload now taken on in addition to the normal railway work. To assist the Factory in 1915 a special arrangement was agreed with the War Office concerning munitions work. Under the agreement a considerable amount of machine tools and equipment was purchased by Swindon and charged to the government account. Rearrangements were made in some shops in order to set aside specific areas for the new commitments, but in others, rows of machines were installed wherever there was room, around the edges of the shops, or in storage areas usually used for part machined items. A particular example of this was the points and crossings ('X') shop. Here the normal activity was squeezed into the minimum space, and a complete installation made for the manufacture of 6 in. high explosive shells. No less than 265,652 tons of steel, in billet form, was fed through this plant in about 2½ years, and output stood at 2,500 shells per week. Manufacture was very complicated, requiring many heavy duty turning and boring lathes, vertical borers, treatment ovens, hydraulic presses etc. In addition, storage and loading facilities, under cover, were necessary. Another most interesting item was the development of existing 1,500 p.s.i. hydraulic presses in the smiths' shop for the deep drawing of circular heavy duty steel sheet into hemispheres for the manufacture of mines. Apart from the deep drawing process, other presses were used for the further forming of flanges and the separate production of the register rings by which the two hemispherical pressings were joined. The same presses and adjoining furnaces were used for the billet preparation and drawing for the 6 in. HE shells already described. The particular forging presses used for these special processes were of 250 ton capacity. As experience of this latter work was gained, the preparation and centre hole drawing of these 6 in. shell billets was developed from a two operation process to a single one, thereby saving much labour, power and heat, and obtaining better metallurgical properties in the billet.

Although aircraft bombs in this war were small, a considerable number was made, weighing about 50—70 lb when ready for use, and were pear shaped with four-finned tails and nose detonating fuses. There is also a photograph in the collection of what may be a primitive incendiary bomb body. A specialist job for the navy was the manufacture of rotary davits, including roller race rings about 3 ft. 6 in. diameter. The davits were tubular steel fabrications, about 14 ft. high, and with varying cross-sections. Special load testing devices were prepared for this activity. Shell manufacture also necessitated the rolling of 9.2 in. steel billets down to 3 in. diameter for the manufacture of 18 pdr field gun shells. A total of 1,863,000 copper driving bands were also made for these shells, and 5,329,000 cartridge cases were reformed from returned cases of which 43,328 needed to be brazed before re-use. A large tool room type of order was for 103,127 graze fuses and a further 240,000 supplied complete with adaptors. Manufacture of other fuses and gaines reached 484,566, whilst the provision of major parts for other types numbered 384,651. A major inspection and supply activity was that of

unloading, sorting, checking and re-loading a huge number of miscellaneous steel billets from America. Some of these were re-rolled at Swindon before despatch.

Perhaps the most interesting work was with guns themselves. A complete manufacturing line was installed in the boiler (V) shop for 6 pdr Nordenfelt anti-aircraft guns, and the 6 pdr Hotchkiss and Woolwich pattern guns. Of particular interest here were the machines and equipment, either adapted from existing, or supplied new, for the deep boring and rifling of the barrels and machining of the breeches, these being made from a single solid forging. This activity was carried out in the machine (R) shop. Some of these guns were complete with mounting platforms and protective skirting. The total number produced was 327 of the Hotchkiss type and 682 of the other types, the latter being rifled at Swindon but bored elsewhere. A very special project was the manufacture of large field carriages for the mounting of 40 large 6 in. calibre naval guns sent in for this purpose. The fabrication of the carriages for these was done from heavy rivetted plate in the boiler shop. Cradles, trunnions and all the actuating gear, worm driven elevating quadrants and other parts requiring a very high standard of machining, including gear and tooth cutting, were made in the 'A' machine (AM) and tool (0) shops. The final erecting was laid out at the north end of what was then the most westerly bay of the 'A' erecting shop, and adjacent to the 'temporary' west wall. This wall was dividing the original part of the shop from the new extension now being slowly erected *(Plate 143)*. The other illustration *(Plate 144)* shows some of these huge guns, complete with their limbers, which were included in the order, proudly photographed outside the main offices. Of roughly the same size were similar carriages and limbers supplied for massive 8 in. howitzers, although only 12 of these were made. The carriage assembly sets for the 4.5 in. howitzers and 60 pdr guns mentioned as one of the first orders of the war ran to much larger numbers as follows:-

338 gun carriages . . . . (27,662 parts)
1,078 ammunition wagons . . . . (126,004 parts)
1,078 limbers . . . . (53,854 parts)
338 carriage limbers . . . . (17,249 parts)

These foregoing are only the main items of material dealt with. There were continuous orders for large numbers of small items, and in particular the many small leather items for pack saddlery, cases, carrying bags, which the trimming (No. 9) shop was able to supply together with much stitched webbing equipment.

All this activity, which represented a considerable workload, was undertaken in addition to the normal

work programme. We have noted the extent of carriage and wagon building, but locomotive building continued at a considerable pace considering the conditions, and about 175 new locomotives were constructed in the four war years. The total maintenance programme, however, increased as the years progressed. It had been anticipated that ordinary passenger traffic would decrease, but pleasure and business travel continued, in fact, passenger traffic in 1916 exceeded that of 1913. Further, during the war period, the GWR operated 37,283 extra passenger trains for naval and military use. Additionally, some 550 special leave trains were run. Unaccounted in this, and extra to the normal business and pleasure travel already mentioned, there were millions of special tickets issued for use on normal trains for civilians and military travelling on government business. The ambulance trains made about 6,000 loaded journeys, and there would have been a corresponding balance of return light loadings. Locomotive activity at docks was also greatly increased. From these figures the rising amount of maintenance work to locomotives and rolling stock becomes clear, and a large proportion of this was done at Swindon, working with a reduced staff due to war service. The huge pressure on the railway services could not continue indefinitely, and from 1917 onwards, some express trains were taken off and restaurant and sleeping car services discontinued, although there was little fall off in the number of passengers travelling.

We have already heard how the town calmly adjusted itself to the war situation, with the largest number of people leaving for the services in the early weeks. This was followed by a longer period of resettlement of occupations until conscription was introduced in 1916. Certain interesting changes were taking place in Swindon. On 23rd October 1913, the Swindon Corporation had applied for Parliamentary sanction to take over those parts of the Wilts & Berks and North Wilts Canals lying within the boundaries of the borough as they then stood. By this time the canals, being no longer used, were becoming a series of stagnant pools due to the falling banks and unauthorized tipping of rubbish. The length involved was about 3¾ miles, and agreement being obtained in 1914 gradual infill commenced, although this was not to be fully completed and the canal land reused until over 50 years later. The acquisition of these lengths of waterway included Coate Reservoir, a lake of some 70 acres to the south of the town. Originally a valley dammed and flooded as a high level feeder to the canal system, this was now available to be developed over the succeeding years as a fine amenity

for the town. The whole transfer was made for £10,000. While speaking of pleasure grounds, an interesting item appeared in the *GWR Magazine* describing the Royal Agricultural Show held at Shrewsbury in June/July 1914. For the first time the railway used a new advertising kiosk. This was a sectional building capable of easy erection and carried in a normal railway wagon, being used for many years at similar functions. Years later, after laying unused in the General Stores at Swindon, it was purchased and erected permanently in the Town Gardens in Old Swindon where it is still in occasional use as a refreshment kiosk, although few Swindonians know of its previous history. One other aspect of the old history of Swindon was to disappear in 1916. This was the final closure of the spring at the top end of Wroughton (now Croft) Road. This is the one that had served much of Old and New Swindon by courtesy of water carriers in the early part of the GWR days in the town. It was now completely built over to form a terrace on which a row of houses, known as The Knoll, were later built.

The labour situation was a little slow in changing, but by 1915 there was a move to place women in some jobs previously undertaken by men. Employment of railway lady clerks increased in 1915 and by 1916 the number was large enough for group photographs to be taken. In these early days they were expected to conform to dress conventions almost akin to a uniform, with high necked white blouses, and a dark or black neck bow or tie strings, long dark grey or black skirts, black stockings with tie up or strapped shoes to match. This invasion of clerical offices was one which was to stay for good. In particular, they were employed on the new mechanized accounting systems, introduced after the 1st January 1913 implementation of the Railway Accounts Bill (1911). In addition, there were the huge accounting procedures introduced for assessing locomotive and train mileage for government special trains, and also for the Factory accounting for the big programme of work for the ROD and Ministry of Munitions. Much of this work was done on new office machinery being introduced by the Hollerith and Powers-Samas companies. Indeed, a photograph of one of the large machine offices at Swindon, complete with female staff, appeared on the covers of the latter firm's sales and instruction literature for some years. In many ways, therefore, the young ladies now taken on were doing extra work rather than taking over work previously done by men, the latter being a much slower process. It was suggested in 1917 that female workers should appear in the Factory but

Plate 143 (left top): Some of the 6 in. naval guns, with mountings and limbers provided at Swindon. Normal business is being carried on close by.

British Rail

Plate 144 (left bottom): Display photograph of the same 6 in. naval guns, mountings and limbers, outside the general offices on 25th October 1916. Note the magnificent gas bracket. Macaw 'B' wagons, Nos. 84215 and 84262 are nearest the camera.

British Rail

Plate 146 (above): The same kiosk, as it stands 68 years later. Acquired by the borough council some years previously, it now serves as a refreshment stall in the local Town Gardens, unrecongized by most as a particularly fine railway relic!

D. Bird

Plate 145 (left): The ornate advertising and enquiry kiosk built in the Works in 1914. It is seen here on 30th April 1915, after its overhaul, ready for the season's work at agricultural and other shows. The war did not appear to be affecting these shows or the standard of workmanship at Swindon.

British Rail

Plate 147: Ladies from Mr Stamper's accounts group on 1st June 1916, when several such group photographs were taken. All their maiden names are given below. Miss E. Calladine (end right, second row), is believed to have been the first such lady employed in 1912:

A. Tolchard, J. Powell, C. Griffen, B. Mockeridge, M. Carpenter, E. Field, K. Bury, H. Craddock, M. Brown
P. Peters, O. Gabb, N. Tomkinson, E. Swatten, G. Godsell, N. Ford, O. Fido, E. Davies
M. Wright, G. Solven, Miss Molden, H. Dowding, F. Denning, L. Kirby, E. Calladine
C. Dawson, Miss Thomas, G. Noble (i/c), M. Trebilcock, M. Davies, G. Buckland

British Rail

Collett managed to fend off this proposal.

In other parts of Swindon things were somewhat different. In 1915 the Wills Tobacco Company opened a factory, advertising for girls not over 15 years of age to commence work at 5 shillings (25p) per week, and to receive unstipulated half-yearly advances thereafter. The factory opened in October of that year, and is still an employer of, mainly, female labour. This was followed in the next year by a new munitions factory, known locally as the 'Powder Factory'. Here again mainly women were employed, and at much higher rates for the dangerous job of shell filling with explosives of all types. It was also a very messy and dirty job. An outbreak of scarlet fever, in Swindon, in November 1915, effectively put the town out of bounds to the many thousands of troops then in camps in the surrounding areas. It also apparently extended the leave of the lucky few in the town at the time!

One GWR man in particular entered the limelight in 1915. This was Alfred Williams, who lived in South Marston, a village to the north-east of the town. Born into very poor circumstances in February 1877, he received a scant education in the small village school. As a lad he was attracted, like many others, to work in the ever expanding Railway Works, because of the high rates of pay compared with the incredibly low farm workers' wages in the area. He was, by nature, a country lover, and the work which he obtained in the new C&W stamping (No. 18) shop must have come as a great change to him. He was, nevertheless, an excellent workman. After entering as a rivet hotter at the age of 15, he was subsequently moved to the stamping shop, and 3 years later was chargeman over three steam hammers and six men, and for the following 20 years was a head drop stamper. He was, however, a born poet, but this realization did not come until the turn of the century when he entered as a correspondence student to Ruskin College, Oxford. From then on he engaged in a life of strenuous study, working late into the night after the 4 mile walk home from work after 5.30 p.m. He needed to leave home at 5 a.m. in order to arrive at work on time. His diligence affected his health and

Plate 148:   The Carriage & Wagon stamping (No. 18) shop on 3rd June 1907. Alfred Williams was employed at these hearths and hammers at this time.

British Rail

eyesight, to some extent, but he became a proficient and accomplished scholar in Latin, French, Greek and English Literature, and later he had a working knowledge of Sanskrit. Sometime during this period he started writing very good poetry indeed and published several small volumes, the first being *Songs in Wiltshire* in 1909. Most of his work in these years was of the country, and a few of his lyrics were set to music. In 1914 he resigned from GWR service due to ill health and tried to make his way in the literary world, but this was almost impossible with the onset of war. He also wrote patriotic poems, mostly in the style of the period, but in 1915 he published his famous work *Life in a Railway Factory*. In it, one can sense all the feelings and frustrations of a man with an acute artistic temperament and with eternal longings for the beauty of the countryside. It is inevitable that his views are sometimes whiter than white, and at other times the complete antithesis. Putting it bluntly, at the Works he was a 'square peg in a round hole', but without doubt a man of great talent and integrity, and a good workman at the tasks he undertook to earn his living. As one would expect from such a temperament he had strong feelings concerning social justice and spoke out against working hours and conditions which, in his case, were generally superior to similar work elsewhere in the country. Inevitably there was a strong re-action to the book when it appeared, and a rather bitter review of some length, appeared in the *GWR Magazine* in particular. The following month he was justly given considerable space for a letter in reply, pointing out that the criticisms made were limited to some of the views contained in the book, and not of the work as a whole. With the benefit of hindsight, this volume earns a place on the shelves of social historians of the Edwardian period, and should be valued by those who appreciate English Literature. If one has been intimately concerned with the fabric and internal organization of the Swindon Works over many years, as has the author, the volume can become a mine of information, as much by inference as statement. In November 1916 Williams volunteered for the Royal Field Artillery and served in India for a period where he became interested in Indian culture. After the war he returned home to his native village, building a small cottage there, and dying, in some poverty, in April 1930, never quite achieving the publicity his work deserved.

Labour relations generally in industry changed during the war period, and the unions were able to demand, and achieve, improvements in pay and conditions. Because of the war effort, long hours continued to be worked but within the Works, as in other places, union representation began to make itself felt. Political support was also moving from the Liberal Party to the younger and more radical Labour Party, and the Swindon branch of this organization was formed on 28th August 1916. In that year also,

the pressures of war became much more evident with the cessation of professional football, a sport in which Swindon Town had been very prominent in the pre-war Southern League with international players in the side, such as Harold Fleming and Jock Walker. Also, in 1916, the 'trip' holiday was abandoned for the duration. Air raids by German Zeppelin airships had become common particularly on the more vulnerable south-eastern part of the country, but these raids were becoming more daring and penetrating much further into the country. Although never affected, Swindon was prepared by the adoption of the Works hooter as an air raid warning, when six long blasts would be given. This hooter was to serve the same purpose in World War II.

During the early years of the war, work on the new 'A' shop proceeded, although only slowly as the labour force had to meet the changed conditions after the large number of reservists had left for service. There did not appear to be appreciable materials shortage, however, and by 1915 the walls were in process of erection. As soon as most of the main roofing was in situ, the area was used at least for storage of war material, and some work may well have been carried out in the section nearest the older shop. As we read in the previous chapter, further reports from Sir William Plender were not forthcoming before hostilities broke out, and this may well have modified the views produced in the reports for the carriage & wagon departments which were submitted on 19th March and 11th June 1915 respectively. As before, they were considered carefully by the Board and a portion of the minute No. 6 of 19th March 1915, after suitable introduction reads:-

'The general conclusion at which Sir William has arrived is that while the Company's carriage stock has been increasing the average age has also increased, which points distinctly to the necessity for the adoption of some scientific basis for renewals and that after carefully considering the various factors he is of the opinion that the provision for carriage renewals should be based on an estimated life of 33 years for the steam drawn coaching stock and 15 years for the electric coaching stock. On this basis 3% and 6.6% respectively of the actual cost value of the stock should be set aside annually, which would mean for 1915, £170,000, and it is recommended that this basis be agreed to.

'Speaking generally Sir William's report confirms the view as to the desirability of definitely adopting the policy of a programme of renewals to be submitted to the Directors each year and it will be necessary for the Officers to agree not only the character and types of rolling stock to be provided on Renewals Account but also the extent to which such renewals will meet the expanding requirements of the undertaking and the amount of additional provision to be made on Capital Account'.

Sir William also recommended that smaller vehicle repairs be separated into group or type costing, while

Plate 149: Work in progress on the new vertical retort bench at the railway gasworks on 23rd May 1922. Note the crane tank engine No. 18 *Steropes* and the wooden oil barrels.

British Rail

heavy repairs be subject to individual costings. However, due to war conditions, it was felt that this system should be deferred. Again he was convinced that, as for locomotives, the construction costs of vehicles was considerably lower than that charged by outside manufacturers. The minute considering the wagon report was on similar lines and with corresponding recommendations.

Following the full scheme submitted for the large 'A' shop extension, the full annual programme was drawn up and sent to the Board on 7th May 1913. It included the authorized amount for the 'A' shop, and apart from the £165,000 for this latter scheme, referred to in the previous chapter, £16,200 was also set aside for the new 'A' power house together with

£2,100 to start improvements to the sawmill and £6,500 for other power stations and sawdust gas producer plants around the Works. The only other shop extension commenced was to the older 'B' erecting section at £16,800.

Further schemes, amounting in all to £176,000, did not obtain sanction due to war time limitations. Major schemes which sank, some not to surface again, included a new masons' shop, extensions to the engine shed, carriage stock washing and lifting sheds, a large wagon shop extension and a new laundry. Some of these major schemes were eventually to be completed piecemeal fashion in the 20 years between the wars.

One major problem to be exacerbated by wartime

restrictions was the urgent need for extensions to the gasworks, and £30,000 was voted for this in April 1914, but it was not possible to undertake the work until 1920. Instead, small additions and improvements were made to increase output as and when equipment was available, some work being done in each year. Following this to its conclusion, it was recommended, in January 1920, that a modern vertical retort house on the Dempster-Toogood system be built to replace the old horizontal retorts. Coke washing and briquetting was also to be introduced, the total cost being £275,000, the largest single sum to date ever to be requested for the Works. It was inevitable that the Board examined this major scheme in great detail, and Churchward had to produce very convincing arguments for the scheme in general, and the reasons for selecting the particular equipment. The sum was eventually sanctioned on 30th July 1920 and work commenced in October, and was completed in July 1922. Even this was not the end of the saga, however, for it became clear that the four existing gas holders, with a total capacity of 1,690,000 cubic feet, were not adequate. Also one of the small holders was now beyond economic repair after 45 years use, and a further holder of 3,000,000 cubic feet capacity was suggested at a cost of £60,000. The repercussions of this request were widespread and although authorized in December 1922, was amended, three months later, to a holder of 2,500,000 cubic feet capacity at a cost of £49,000. This large expenditure on gas manufacture was to have effects on the whole power policy of the Works for years to come.

Financing of the 'A' shop extension was done by grants to match the speed of progress, the main building being covered by sums of £52,000 both in December 1915 and February 1917, and a further £46,000 in February 1919. Regular sums were also made available for the provision of new sidings and for equipping the new shop with cranes, traversers, and installation of machinery. In all, between 11th December 1913 and 8th November 1923 when the final certificate was issued, a net sum of £433,853 was allocated to this huge extension to the Factory. It has been published, from time to time, that the cost of the shop was £438,262, but the former figure is the total specifically voted by the Board. As said earlier, portions of the shop, when finished, were taken over for munitions purposes, and railway work also overflowed into the new area from time to time. The first area to be opened for the purpose for which it was intended was the westernmost locomotive wheel (AW) shop in March 1920, followed by the central erecting (AE) section, and finally the boiler (AV) shop in August 1923. The new shop therefore took about ten years to complete and the whole 'A' block evolved over a period of about 24 years.

Virtually all the other authorizations made during the war years were for plant and equipment of the widest variety. Only one item of plant required extra building and this was the extension of the heat treatment house necessary for extra furnaces for gun work. One removal made early in 1918 was that of machinery from the upper floor of the original machine shop of 1843. This had, in later years, become the tool room of the Works, and in spite of an increasing load of vibrating machine tools, the floor had always been supported on heavy trusses made entirely of yellow pine. This floor, with its supporting trusses, was retained in use for storage purposes until about 1955, by which time it was showing notable signs of stress!

By April 1918 most munition work had ceased, except for the ROD on locomotives and ambulance trains. Consequently, for the ridiculously low price of £7,586 the Board purchased, for its own use, the machinery and plant which had been bought by the Ministry of Munitions and installed at Swindon. Of interest in this connection is the sale to the government of certain unspecified machine tools in April 1917, to which the Works fitted individual electric motors before being despatched to railway workshops in France.

Changes in Works personnel were inevitable under wartime conditions, but these were not as widespread as might have been expected, no doubt due to their being of greater use producing munitions than elsewhere. W. H. Stanier, who had already moved to Paddington in 1915, retired in 1916 after a long and honourable career at Swindon and in public life. Churchward's post was redesignated Chief Mechanical Engineer (CME) in 1916, in line with the same moves on other railways, and his chief clerk since 1902, Joseph Lockyer, retired in February 1918. He was replaced by A. J. L. White, son of a former chief clerk, R. L. White, of the previous century. A. J. L. White had done much to put Swindon 'on the map' through his informative articles prepared for the *GWR Magazine*. Apart from regular reports on output and special projects, he pioneered the issue of locomotive 'names and numbers' lists for the already large numbers of railway enthusiasts. Commencing in 1910, a long series of articles on different shops, their equipment and operations, appeared in the *GWR Magazine* and, although sparse during the war years, the series eventually covered every aspect of all departments.

In the Birthday Honours List in 1918 appeared the following awards for their services to munition production:-

G. J. Churchward (CME) . . . . CBE
C. B. Collett (Locomotive Works Manager). . . . . . OBE
F. W. Marillier (C&W Works Manager). . . . . OBE
J. M. Llewellyn (Chief Inspector C&W Dept)
(For Ministry of Munitions). . . . . OBE

Plate 152: A view from the south-east of the 'A' shop, shortly after final completion. The de-tubing house (The Barn) is seen on the right. The nearest locomotive is No. 3317 *Somerset* and the locomotive weighbridge is in the distance to the right of the signal box.

Plate 150: A view of the same project on 25th July 1921, chosen for the early Swindon Works version of a mortar/cement 'Premix' vehicle (right).

British Rail

Plate 151: The foundation tank for the new 2.5 million cubic foot gas holder pictured on 27th July 1925. The view is interesting for the building activity on the new Ferndale Road. All the land visible is now built upon.

British Rail

One loss to the C&W Works was the death, from wounds, of Major C. S. Wilson on 21st October 1918. He had previously been an assistant manager from 1907 until war service. The town itself had about 5,380 men serving in the forces, many from railway families. Of these around 1,000 were killed or died on active service. Taking the total railway staff of the CME's department which included drivers, firemen and other running shed staff, 9,252 enlisted out of a total of nearly 30,000 (in 1914), and of these 825 died in the war. Of particular poignancy to the town was the effect of the German offensive in Flanders in early 1918 when on 21st March, the 2nd and 6th Battalions of the Wiltshire Regiment were virtually wiped out, and a large proportion of these men had Swindon connections. Eventually, at 11 a.m. on 11th November 1918, the Great War came to its weary close, and Works and town alike, together with the rest of the country needed to remake its life, but one which would never again be the same. Great social changes had already come into being, and more were to follow. The Works had borne its burden well, but the equipment was becoming run down as well as the railway as a whole. Changes such as the nationalization of the railways were being spoken of, and the pattern of both passenger and freight transport was to have to face the rapid development of road competition.

One more major design was to appear from Churchward. For some time there had been the need for a locomotive capable of handling heavy vacuum braked freight traffic at higher speeds. To meet this need, a diagram was developed which below the frames was, in effect, an extended version of the mixed traffic 4300 2-6-0 class. The new engine was to be to the 2-8-0 wheel arrangement with the same 5 ft. 6 in. diameter driving wheels and with most of the motion gear interchangeable. The cylinders were to be increased by ½in. to 19 in. diameter. To supply this large machine, a new boiler was to be designed, and work commenced on this project. The first engine was built to Lot 214, the order for which was issued on 31st January 1919, but design work had been progressing for some time. The design of the new boiler presented a weight problem, as the maximum allowable axle load was still 19.5 tons. In this boiler Churchward was possibly looking forward to the needs of the next generation of passenger locomotives and took great care with the design. As a result, the new standard No. 7 boiler was not ready for the first locomotive and a standard No. 1 boiler was fitted so that its basic capabilities as a locomotive could be proven. No. 4700 was completed on 15th July 1919, and was a great success but for the limitations of the boiler fitted. The author has been told by those who worked on the standard No. 7 that much of the experience from the *Great Bear* boiler was used in its development. Keeping much the same barrel

length as the standard No. 1, the cone diameters were increased by about 6 in. allowing for a 17.7 per cent increase in total heating surface. The order for the remaining batch of 8 locomotives was placed on 14th May 1922 and they were completed on 19th October 1923. The boiler order was for 9 so that 4700 could be fitted similarly, and this was done in May 1921. The boilers themselves cost £2,387 each as against £1,178 for the standard No. 1. They were therefore over twice as expensive, although, of course, this cost would have to encompass the provision of the new large flanging blocks. In final form the engines without tender cost £7,544 each. Although the class was never increased they were, in the minds of many, one of the finest of Churchward's creations.

The relief of the country at the signing of the armistice and the subsequent celebrations were soon followed by the inevitable reactions. Labour relations in the country generally had not been too happy in the latter months of the war, and the upheaval arising from the cessation of lucrative war work, together with the returning war heroes expecting to resume their former employment, was soon to result in near chaos in industry. The country was virtually bankrupt and the railways, like many other firms, were in a completely run down condition. The master/servant relationship of pre-1914 days, already souring then was never to return. The unions, understandably, became extremely militant with strike action being their main weapon. On 1st January 1919 the 47 hour week was introduced at Swindon Works, the first change in official working hours for 47 years. At last the early (breakfast) shift was dropped, and the new hours were to be:-

Monday to Friday
8.00 a.m. until 12.30 p.m. and 1.30 p.m. until 5.30 p.m.
Saturday
7.30 a.m. until 12 noon

One repercussion of this new arrangement was the disappearance of the coffee taverns situated and well established near all the main entrances. Although used also at midday, their main business had been the provision of beverages with hot and cold meals at moderate prices, particularly for the short (45 minute) breakfast break when there was not really sufficient time for men to go home, unless living nearby.

The great years of the railway were passing, together with the whole edifice on which had been built the country's industrial supremacy. Prosperity could only be restored to the railways by a long period of heavy and lucrative freight and passenger traffic. The reverse was the case in these conditions, and the rapid rise in motor freight traffic, due partly to the cheap sale of unwanted military transport vehicles, sealed their fate. The rates which the companies could charge

Plate 153: Churchward's stately 2-8-0 mixed traffic locomotive, No. 4704 with the standard No. 7 boiler as running in 1937 with the more proportionate Collett 4,000 gallon tender.

British Rail

had been pegged during the war, by control, and it was not politically possible to alter this situation. Inevitably, the control of the railways through the REC was not lifted and there was a call for nationalization, or some other large reorganization of the railway structure. Railway employees wanted retention of government control to continue the betterment of pay and conditions which had been readily met during the conflict. War bonuses had been one of these benefits, and the threat to withdraw them resulted in a national rail strike in September 1919 which lasted nine days. Although the General Election held on Saturday 14th December 1918 voted in another coalition government, the change in representation brought new views to bear, and dropping the idea of nationalization, introduced, instead, the Railways Act in 1921. It is not appropriate to discuss here all the details leading to the drafting of this Bill. Suffice it to say that the proposals finally adopted, divided nearly 180 separate organizations into four main groups, the LNER, LMSR, GWR and SR. Of all these, only the GWR group retained the name and management structure of a former undertaking. This was due, in part, to some quick thinking by the Chairman and General Manager of the Company during the final drafting of the Bill. Details of this are

given in Sir Felix Pole's memoirs *Felix Pole — His Book*. This was possible because of the size of the GWR compared with the smaller constituent companies, mainly those in Wales, making up the rest of the new 'Western' Group. The Act came into force on 1st January 1923, but the take-over (for that is what it amounted to) of the other railways was carried out systematically, but piecemeal, over nearly two years, being almost completed by then.

The importance to Swindon of this arrangement is obvious. It was to become the unchallenged senior Works of the new railway and was to escape, at least for a few more decades, the rivalry now to spring up between places such as Derby (MR), Crewe (L&NWR) and Horwich (L&YR) for instance on the new LMSR; or Eastleigh (LSWR), Brighton (LB&SCR) and Ashford (SE&CR) on the new Southern Railway.

During these immediate post-war years, Churchward was approaching his retirement age, he would be 65 on 3rd March 1922. His style of management was no longer applicable in this new age and he could not stomach the confrontation of the more militant and less respectful representatives of the unions which he now had to face, and remarked inevitably that 'it is time the old man retired'. This he did at the end of 1921. When this intention was announced there was a great surge of affection shown in the demands from all levels of his huge staff, possibly the largest of its kind in Europe, for a suitable presentation to be made. This took place at a great gathering in the main hall of the Mechanics Institute. Despite his bluff and apparently stiff demeanour, he was overcome at this demonstration of respect and congratulation. Receiving the cheque he said he could not possibly accept all the money personally, but that after the purchase of a first class salmon and trout rod and tackle, he wished the large balance to be put into a trust fund. The Churchward Memorial Fund (later renamed The Churchward Trust) provided yearly prizes for students at the local technical school.

There may have been a further reason for Churchward's decision to leave when he did. In June 1921, Felix Pole had been appointed General Manager of the Company, and was to put his particular stamp on the undertaking. Having to lead it through the difficulties of the grouping, he saw it as inevitable that he be master in his own house. The moves made previously by Sir James Inglis as General Manager to gain supremacy over the chief officers had been allowed to remain in abeyance after a few tentative trials of strength. The war had made it inopportune to go further, but the time was now ripe for the change. The change was implemented by the institution of the monthly chief officers' conference, when the General Manager laid down the targets to be met appropriate to the department, and more importantly, decided financial priorities. Although perhaps resulting in over centralisation, this very fact had advantages for Swindon, although not so much for the future standing of any CME or other chief officer.

H. C. King, who had been Churchward's principal assistant since the beginning of 1913, retired on 14th March 1920, but just previous to this, C. B. Collett, whilst still holding the position of Locomotive Works Manager, was also designated deputy CME on 9th May 1919, relinquishing the former post on 1st January 1920. W. A. Stanier replaced him on the same date in charge of the Locomotive Works. It is a pity, perhaps, that there was only about five years difference in the ages of these two engineers. Collett's background had originally been civil engineering, and he had not joined the GWR until 1893, whereas Stanier had entered a year earlier in 1892. In the usual way of things at that period, however, Collett's seniority in age ensured that he remained one step ahead of Stanier all the time. Surprise, and indeed astonishment, has been expressed in some quarters in the past, that Collett was selected to follow Churchward. There are indeed grounds for this amazement, particularly on aspects of the personalities of the two men in question. There is little doubt that the GWR lost the chance of lifelong service from Stanier at this

Plate 154: Charles Benjamin Collett, OBE, Chief Mechanical Engineer 1922–1941.

British Rail

appointment, and from a social point of view this was unfortunate for Swindon, and meant the eventual loss of a great locomotive designer. Conversely, the Board needed a 'strong man' to head the department which was to see so much reorganization, and Collett certainly fitted this description. He was a brilliant production engineer also, but was content to leave design problems to the extremely talented staff which he inherited from Churchward.

F. W. Marillier, who had served as manager of the Carriage & Wagon Works since 1902, retired on 20th November 1920, and was replaced by his assistant since 1914, C. C. Champeney. This gentleman was not to hold this office long, however, accepting a post with the Midland Railway Carriage & Wagon Company at Birmingham in July 1922. For a few months he was replaced by R. A. G. Hannington from the Locomotive Works, but the appointment of W. A. Stanier as Works Assistant to Collett in September 1922 brought Hannington back to take charge of the locomotive side. E. T. J. (Teddy) Evans took charge of the C&W Works, a reign which was to last even longer than Marillier's — 24 years. It is reported that Collett did not altogether approve of Stanier's appointment, but not having any interest in more social matters, he made full use of him, leaving all such activities to Stanier. As a result Stanier became the 'Swindon' representative at most functions, both inside and outside of railway life, and gained much affection and respect in the process.

The C & W Works found itself in some trouble. There was an inevitable fall off in wagon work, and short time working was introduced in 1920. In the carriage department too, the main work was the conversion of the ambulance train vehicles repurchased from the government for normal passenger services, although a small amount of new building took place. No orders for new locomotives were placed for nearly three years, as a batch of ROD 2-8-0s were purchased from Woolwich Arsenal. These were the Robinson Great Central type locomotives adopted as the wartime utility model. Twenty were acquired in 1919 and a further 84 were hired. Those hired were returned to store in 1921/2. Consequent disposal of them was slow and the GWR finally purchased another 80 in 1925 at the bargain price of £1,500 each (including tender), although all needed extensive workshop attention before entering service. This added an extra £1,000 each to the total book cost, averaged over the whole 80 engines. This was the one class to run on the GWR never to be 'westernized' as they remained virtually as purchased throughout their long service, some lasting until 1958.

Thus in a very troubled situation in the Works, (and in the Locomotive Divisions) Collett took up his new post. His first important task was to present his proposals for the new departmental organization. Most of the constituent railways now being amalgamated had their own officers and workshop facilities. With one exception, the Works facilities were in different parts of Wales, in particular Oswestry (Cambrian Railway), Caerphilly (Rhymney Railway), Cardiff Cathays (Taff Vale Railway) and Barry (Barry Railway). There were also smaller establishments at various places on other smaller undertakings. The one works outside of Wales was at Cirencester on the M & S W J R. It was inevitable that all the railway undertakings had devised their own pay structures over the years, and the grouping made it necessary for this to be examined before the inevitable rationalization of staff took place. The matter was taken to the Industrial Court, resulting in the well known Judgement No. 728 dated 8th July 1922. This laid out in great detail the specific basic rates for railway shopmen, whether in Works or at depots for the whole of England and Wales. Allowance was made for rates in special areas such as London, and skill differentials were clearly made. The adoption of this agreement went a long way to assist the movement of labour which was inevitably to come. Arising from the Plender report, it was accepted that, with the completion of the 'A' shop, no further large exten-

sions should be made at Swindon, and that the best of the smaller works now being taken over should be retained for specific repair work. Traffic patterns were also changing so that a complete review could be made of the Divisional organization. This had systematically developed on the GWR and had been very flexible in the early days. Originally divided into the Southern and Northern Divisions, areas or districts responsible for local control had evolved. The depot from which these had been individually controlled changed quite frequently, possibly because the responsibility was placed on the senior shed foreman at any particular time, that foreman continuing in charge of his own shed. However, posts sometimes referred to as 'Area Foreman' or 'District Superintendent' gradually evolved, and as more railways were amalgamated such as the B & ER or SWR, these became Districts or Divisions in their own right. Amalgamations of Districts had also taken place, and occasionally splitting as traffic developed. By World War I, the GWR was operating eight Divisions under Churchward which were controlled by his outdoor running assistant at Swindon. However, under wartime conditions, a reorganization had quietly taken place during 1914/15 when the Swindon Division had been divided between the surrounding Divisions. There were thus seven GWR Divisions at the time of the grouping. The Swindon Division had played a great part in the development of the GWR and comprized, apart from a section of the main line roughly from Didcot to Chippenham, those lines known as the 'Wilts & Dorset' and some of the 'Wilts & East Somerset' group. It stretched southward to Weymouth, and in its Divisional Office had been trained many of the picked young engineers of the future. Working very much under the eye of Armstrong, Dean or Churchward, they were able to show their mettle. Two new Divisions were to be formed; Cardiff Valleys, comprising basically of the TVR, RR and BR, and the Central Wales, based on the old Cambrian system. Newport and Neath Divisions also had additions, and boundaries generally were tidied up. The one big change, however, was the acquisition of considerable port facilities on the South Wales coast, notably at Newport, Cardiff, Penarth, Barry, Port Talbot and Swansea. Prior to this the GWR had operated facilities at Plymouth, Fowey, Weymouth and Fishguard, but apart from Fowey, these had been as much passenger ports as freight. The new acquisitions were entirely different, having been born through the coal and steel trade, and technically different near the Severn estuary by virtue of the complicated locking facilities necessary for the massive tide variations experienced. It was now arranged that the maintenance of the wide range of facilities be assisted in a major way from the millwrights and other specialist shops at Swindon. This was done through Divisional Offices which

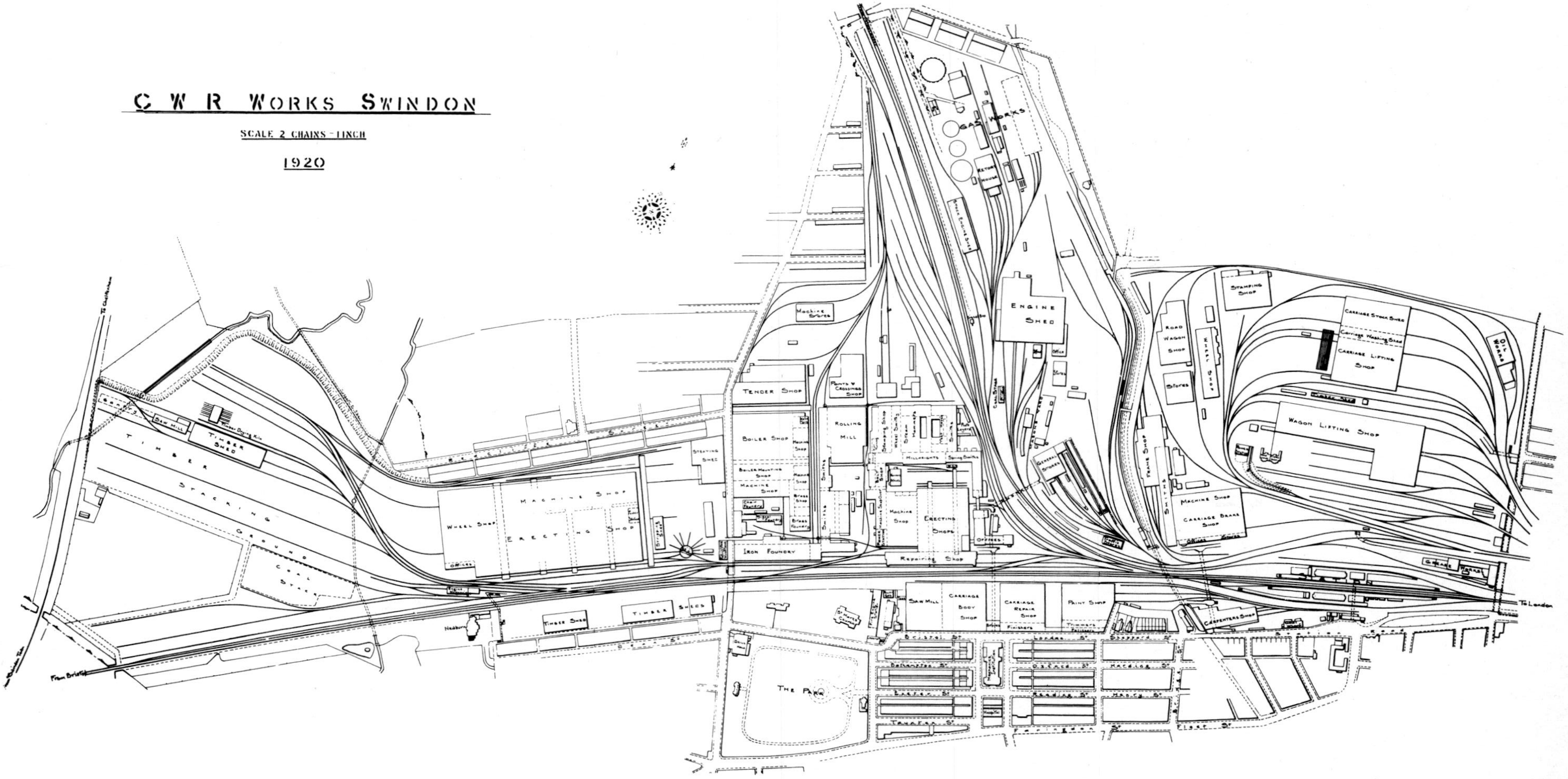

G W R WORKS SWINDON

SCALE 2 CHAINS = 1INCH

1920

Plate 155: A plan of Swindon Works in 1920.

Author's Collection

194

retained specialist dock engineers on their local staffs.

The other problem was the provision of suitable posts for the officers and technical staff of the companies now joining the GWR. Some, naturally, decided to retire, but others were appointed as Superintendents or assistants in their old area, and some moved to Swindon. In particular, John Auld who had been CME of the Barry Railway came to Swindon in September 1922 as docks assistant to Collett and was able to advise him on this new aspect of work. Other men, later to be well known on the GWR found their way to Swindon and into the drawing office or junior assistant posts in the next year or so. Considering the complexities of this rationalization, things went comparatively smoothly and the new people fitted in well. It is notable, however, that only a small number entered the ranks of locomotive or carriage designers at this time, although they may have had the chance later.

Whilst the retention of female labour in factories ended abruptly with the war, the inroads made into clerical work were here to stay. This was aided by the suitability of girls and young women particularly to the work of the accounting and mileage offices now becoming increasingly equipped with what was really the first generation of fully mechanized accounting methods. These new facilities were to revolutionize office methods on the railway in the next few years, and places such as Swindon were amongst the first to fully adopt the new methods. At this time (1920) new rates were introduced for 'girl clerks', commencing at 17 shillings and sixpence (87½p) per week at 16 years of age, and 21 shillings and sixpence (£1.07½p) a year later. Two higher grades of lady clerk was also open to them in certain designated posts. For the lower Class 2 these ranged from 18 shillings (90p) at 18 years to 60 shillings (£3) at 30 years. Class 1 (and there were very few of these) commenced at 65 shillings (£3.25) per week, rising to 70 shillings (£3.50) after 4 years. There was, of course, no age range for these senior appointments. At this time a fitter's base rate under the 728 Agreement was 46 shillings (£2.30), to which bonus and piecework enhancements could be added, and a range of about 60—70 shillings (£3—£3·50) was general at Swindon.

The population of Swindon in 1911 was around 51,000 and by 1921, in spite of the war, had reached 55,000. Railway employment at Swindon now reached its maximum, and including the large number of staff at the engine shed, station and goods depot, numbered about 14,000. The Locomotive and C&W Works on their own probably accounted for 10,000 of these, the CME's HQ staff and the stores department accounting for approximately another 1,500. The social life engendered by the Mechanics Institution was also changing. For many years there had existed the GWR Temperance Society, but this had taken under its wing much social activity in its later years. Parallel with this was the reduction in the need for temperance movements, and a new organization to be known as the GWR Social & Educational Union evolved. Although keeping its separate identity for many years, the Mechanics Institution and S&EU were to work closely together for the welfare of the Swindon railway families.

Finally, in the Works, the new 'A' shop extension was systematically becoming completely equipped and with the transfer of the old 'W' shop machinery, final completion took place in the early weeks of 1923. Improvements to the brass foundry were also put in hand in 1922, and a production landmark reached in the iron foundry, when a new anvil block replacement had to be made for one of the largest drop hammers in the Works. This iron casting successfully cast in 1921, weighed no less than 65 tons, and remained a record for this foundry until the end of its long life. It was machined on the Detrick & Harvey open sided planer. Such was the capacity of the Works for 'doing the impossible at once, and working miracles on Fridays by arrangement with the Management' as certain notices in offices jokingly, but also, proudly, displayed.

Thus the Works entered a new era, equipped for taking any opportunities that may be offered, but under a cloud of economic gloom and rising discontent and unemployment from the country's labour force. Furthermore, the railways were beginning to lose their monopoly, although the full effects of this was still decades, rather than years, away. The question was, whether Swindon could withstand the lowering economic conditions as it had forty years previously. From an equipment and manpower point of view this should be possible, but the major controlling factor, finance, was now in the hands of different people. It was going to be a struggle indeed.

Plate 156: The oxygen manufacturing plant installed in 1924. The fractionating column is in the centre of the picture which was taken on 24th April 1928.

British Rail

Chapter Eight

1923~1939 Between the Wars

By the beginning of 1923 much of the reorganization of the GWR brought about by the Grouping Act was either in hand or already accomplished. The locomotive department, however, was to continue feeling the change for many years to come, as 925 'foreign' locomotives were added to the stock books. Although the majority of these (720) came from only six major constituent companies, the influx of this large number of locomotives of almost infinite variety had, in the short term, a catastrophic effect on the system of standards so carefully developed since 1900. There was almost immediate scrapping of some engines arriving at Swindon, usually because of their poor state of repair, compared with Swindon standards, although they were not necessarily old. The volume of traffic in South Wales was such, however, that it soon became clear that a motive power shortage would result from this policy. Such replacement by existing or new designs was not immediately practicable so the alternative of equipping 'foreign' locomotives with standard GWR parts, where possible, was followed. In particular this was applied to boilers, and in time nearly all the locomotives retained were fitted with suitable GWR boilers, and these invariably of larger steaming capacity than hitherto. To aid this process, existing GWR boilers of the 2301, 'standard No. 2' and 'Metro' types were specially modified for this purpose and became GW standard Nos. 9, 10 and 11 in the process. Some ideas from the South Wales railways were also taken up and fitted to applicable GWR engines. As a result of these modifications, most of which were necessarily done at Swindon, many locomotives from the constituent railways had long lives on the GWR, some staying in service almost to the final withdrawal of steam in Great Britain.

One post in the Swindon hierarchy which changed in 1922 in the early days of Collett was that of the former Outdoor Assistant, always based at Swindon. This officer had been the de facto head of the Locomotive Divisional Superintendents. The changes were made for two reasons. The first, and most important, was the arrangement, peculiar to the GWR, whereby the CME was in complete control of the drivers and firemen as well as the locomotives. Co-operation with the operating officers of the system had always been necessary, but with the final withdrawal of the one driver/one engine concept, the rostering of footplate staff in line with guards and other train staff became very important. It should be mentioned here, in parenthesis, that in earlier days, when a repaired locomotive was returned from the Works after overhaul, it was always addressed with labels on the cab handrails to 'Driver Smith, Old Oak Common', or similar. From the time of Charles Crump's appointment at the end of 1922, the title became Locomotive Running Superintendent & Outdoor Assistant to the CME. In the former of these two roles, Crump was responsible to the Superintendent of the Line as a principal assistant for all matters appertaining to the running of trains. The latter half of the post, responsible to the CME, was for the day to day maintenance of the rolling stock and constant review of the shopping for heavy repairs. The second reason for the redesignation of the post was that under the Judgement No. 728, already referred to, all grades in it worked a standard 47 hour week. Staff employed in all aspects of train operation, however, came under a different agreement as 'conciliation staff' and worked a basic 48 hour week. The new post took charge, on behalf of the CME, for this 48 hour staff with a separate clerical support group. In like manner, the new Assistant (Works) to the CME was responsible for all 47 hour staff, that is all craft and support trades both in main Works and in running sheds. This may sound a complicated arrangement on paper, but in practice it worked extremely well. The chief foreman at all depots was always drawn from the conciliation grades. The mechanical foreman at a depot was nominally under his control for the provision of serviceable locomotives, but worked through the Divisional mechanical inspectors for technical control. The holder of this revised post under the CME occupied offices on the ground floor of the main administrative block at Swindon, formerly occupied by the, now defunct, Swindon Division.

Early in 1923 the final extension to the iron foundry (J shop) was completed, forming a shop 660 ft. long by 80 ft. wide. During the next 40 years this was to supply difficult and complex castings of high quality, not only for locomotives, but for all types of plant and equipment for the railway and docks. During the period now under review, there was to be only one large extension to the Factory, the Board no doubt bearing in mind the Plender reports, but advances were made in new equipment and tooling. In particular, the use of oxy-acetylene methods of welding and cutting were greatly increased. This particular process commenced in 1910 when one welder only was available, but by 1925 the number had risen to over 100. This rise meant heavy supplies of the basic materials and, to this end, a complete oxygen making plant was installed towards the end of 1924. The method used was the fractionation of liquid air, compressed for the

197

Plate 157: A view of the now fully working final extension of the erecting (AE) shop on 18th March 1925. This is particularly interesting because of the stripped locomotive frame on the left, one of the French compound Atlantics. The variation in diameter of the high and low pressure cylinders can be clearly seen. It is either No. 103 or No. 104 as No. 102 was withdrawn a year after this photograph was taken.

British Rail

purpose to 55 atmospheres. Air was drawn in through caustic soda columns for purifying and, after compression, was dried by passing over caustic potash en route to the fractionating column. Here pressure was gradually allowed to fall from the input pressure down to 0.3 atmospheres, the various constituent gases of air boiling out at their particular temperature (Nitrogen — 194 degrees centigrade; Oxygen — 182 degrees centigrade). The oxygen, thus separated, was fed into a miniature gas holder and drawn out as required via a three stage compressor filling air bottles at a standard 1,850 p.s.i., or into a series of reservoirs feeding mains at 500 p.s.i. The oxygen was 98/99 per cent pure. At the same time four new acetylene manufacturing houses were erected in various parts of the Works and, after production by the normal calcium carbide and water process, was similarly bottled, or piped to the necessary shops.

New additions to the main office block were made, mainly in 1924, by a new three storey section bridging a roadway between the two separate buildings forming the eastern boundary of the original Works. For many years a steam raising plant had existed in the centre of the Locomotive Works where a collection of locomotive type boilers had been installed. Votes had been made in 1920 to the extent of £35,000 for the extension of the smiths' (Q) shop including a modernized boiler station on the old site. However, as a result of the expense involved in the gasworks extensions, a full investigation was required by the Board on the whole question of power supplies in the Works. These extensions, together with a new masons' yard and additions to the C & W stamping (18) shop and other smaller items amount-

ing in all to £174,700, were the only authorizations out of a list amounting to £1,075,200 made by Churchward just prior to his retirement. His submission for this large programme was to provide space for more men due to the shortening of hours from 54 to 47 per week. Churchward argued that a full double shift was impracticable, but the stern economics of the period ensured that financial demands from a CME were no longer 'given the nod'. This was the situation which Collett faced when he took over.

Reverting to the power situation, Mr J. A. Robinson, Consulting Engineer to the Metropolitan Vickers Electrical Company was asked to advise on this matter in July 1923. In his report, submitted the following March, he recommended immediate construction of a central steam driven electric power station to replace the numerous gas powered stations in use, but the report was too late. The gasworks had just been expensively extended and Collett had already started refurbishing the central boiler station in June 1923, indeed the first Stirling 3-drum boiler, with underfeed stoker, had been commissioned for use and evaluation in September 1922. Collett was strongly against the proposals costing £105,000, arguing that there would be no savings over the present arrangement, and that a further 3 gas engine generating sets were the only addition now necessary. He was strong enough to get this accepted.

The acquisition of the M & SWJ line in the grouping meant that passenger services between Swindon Junction and Swindon Town station were reintroduced on 22nd October 1923 after a period of 38½ years, lasting until the line expired with the Beeching cuts. Connections were never great, townsfolk going directly to the Town station if they wished to use the north/south services offered, so very little transfer of passengers from the main GWR line ever took place. The M&SWJ Cirencester Works, opened in 1895, was run down and the work and some men were transferred to Swindon.

There was an urgent requirement to replace much of the freight locomotive stock and the principal type was to be 42XX 2-8-0 side tank engines of 1910 design. These were ordered in regular batches from 1921, 110 being completed between then and 1930. They carried the standard No. 4 boiler. Also ordered in quantity, starting in 1924, were further 2-6-2 passenger tank locomotives of the 45XX class, a type built first under Lot N3 in 1906 at Wolverhampton. These had the smaller standard No. 5 boiler and were capable of a good turn of speed when necessary.

The need for an addition to the main line express passenger fleet of engines had been forseen for some time. It is interesting to speculate what Churchward's solution to the problem would have been, possibly a Pacific, or, even more likely a 6ft. 8in. wheeled version of the 47XX class. Although Churchward and Collett were not, personally, particularly close, Collett had a high regard for the principals of locomotive design laid down in the preceeding 20 years. It is not surprising, then, that the proven 4-6-0 4 cylinder arrangement was favoured, and obviously use of the new standard No. 7 boiler was desirable. This diagram, when checked out, however, would have made weight increases above the 19½/20 ton axle limit still apparently demanded by the civil engineers. The boiler was, therefore, reduced in diameter by about 3in. over its continuously coned length to become a new standard No. 8. Cylinder diameter was increased, from the 14¼in. of the 'Stars', to 16in., and many other minor, but important, changes made in detail design to assist in both running efficiency and improved production in the shops. The result was the 'Castle' class, the first, *Caerphilly Castle*, being shown at Paddington on 23rd August 1923. With a tractive effort at 85 per cent boiler pressure of 31,625lb it was rated some 26 per cent above the 'Stars' and nearly 14 per cent above the *Great Bear*. Although this method of quoting the real power of a locomotive can be misleading, the figures were seized upon by a lively publicity department under the businesslike eye of Felix Pole, and extolled as 'the most powerful locomotive in the country'. That the locomotive was to prove itself one of the most successful designs ever, there is no doubt, but that was to be vindicated later. As far as Swindon was concerned, another engine in the long tradition was to be a world beater, and they were able to turn it out in the full lined-out livery and with polished copper and brass, a practice discontinued in the war. Just prior to its appearance, a new train to become known as the 'Cheltenham Flyer' had been introduced on 9th July 1923. Worked by 'Stars' initially, it was timed to cover the 77¼ miles from Swindon to London in 75 minutes, but even these engines were regularly cutting this time to 72 minutes and less. The 'World's Fastest Train' was to reach greater heights when the run-in 'Castles' were put on this service. Arrangements were made that *Caerphilly Castle* be exhibited alongside Gresley's new Pacific at the British Empire Exhibition in 1924, against which it appeared quite small, although claiming to be more powerful.

Appearing at about the same time as No. 4073 were Nos. 7 and 8 for the 1ft. 11½in. gauge Vale of Rheidol Light Railway. These two engines were similar to No. 9 built, in 1902, by Davis & Metcalfe of Manchester for the line when opened. These three steam locomotives are still in service at the time of writing, having been recently fully overhauled at Swindon, and they are the only steam locomotives remaining on British Rail's books. In 1924, No. 2925,

Plate 158: Collett's No. 4073 *Caerphilly Castle* of 1923. Note the original cab roof with rain strips already removed in this picture taken on 15th January 1925.

British Rail

Plate 159 (left top): A well posed view of the carriage finishers (No. 7) shop taken on the day after the Royal visit in 1924. No doubt the shop had been specially tidied as it was on the official route.

British Rail

Plate 160 (left bottom): The Royal visit of 28th April 1924. A lady, in her best overall, is making luggage rack netting and is being watched by Her Majesty Queen Mary.

Author's Collection

Plate 161: Their Majesties watching the casting of a welcome message in the iron foundry (J1) shop. Their message still adorns the west wall of the (now No. 9) shop.

Author's Collection

St. Martin was modified by fitting it with 6 ft. diameter wheels in place of the 6 ft. 8½ in. diameter of the 'Saint' class. Thus it became close in detail to the only one of Churchward's original six diagrams not built, because of the success of the 43XX class 2-6-0 machines. With greater boiler capacity than the 'Moguls', and the better riding characteristics of a longer frame, it proved, in tests over four years, to be an excellent design, and we shall follow the development chronologically later. It is of note though that this was the only time when Collett tested a single locomotive over a long period before producing a class series.

An event of great note to both Swindon and the Works took place on 28th April 1924. This was the visit by King George V and Queen Mary, the first official Royal visit to the town. The whole visit was planned to take less than three hours, indeed, the official illustrated programme, on sale beforehand, allowed only 2¼ hours. Their Majesties departed in the GWR Royal Train from Windsor at 12.55 p.m. taking luncheon en route. Arriving at Swindon Junction at 2.10 p.m., they were received by the Lord Lieutenant of the County, the Mayor of Swindon, Alderman T. C. Newman (not a railway

mayor that year), and the local Member of Parliament, Mr Mitchell Banks. The Works' representative was Mr C. B. Collett. A fleet of cars carrying, amongst others, the Chairman and General Manager of the Company, then accompanied their Majesties via the main shopping streets to the cenotaph, where the customary wreath was laid. After bouquet presentations and the signing of the visitors' book at the nearby Town Hall, the procession made its way to the Victoria Hospital in the Old Town for an inspection of recently opened wards. Departing at 3.10 p.m. the remainder of the visit was in the hands of the GWR. After presentation of officers of the Medical Fund Society, their Majesties drove past a company of 200 retired railway servants. Arriving at the Sheppard Street entrance of the Carriage Works, they were received by Messrs. Collett, Stanier, and E. T. J. Evans (Manager C&W), and they inspected the shops engaged in carriage trimming, finishing, polishing and body making. In this section a number of female employees were seen engaged in trimming and polishing work. A visit to the saw mill completed this part of the visit. They then crossed the main line into the Locomotive Works and were met by the Manager, R. A. G. Hannington. The iron foundry was visited first where a special floor casting of 'Welcome' was made as they watched. This is still exhibited on the west wall of the shop, now the No. 9 diesel engine repair shop. A large locomotive was observed being turned by one man on the 65 ft. turntable, and various types of locomotive were displayed for inspection. Naturally, a 4300 class locomotive was found to be running at full speed on the test plant, (although little used at this time). The procession made its way, via the 'A' machine shop, to the main (AE) erecting shop where a locomotive was being lifted by one of the four 100 ton overhead cranes. The tour finished with visits to the wheel turning and balancing section of the AW shop and the adjacent locomotive weighbridge where 76 men, all with 50 or more years service on the GWR, were paraded. The longest serving amongst them, G. Bayliss, was arrayed in a set of spotless white overalls and was introduced to the King.

It was here that the much publicized 'change of programme' took place, although it had been carefully arranged by the publicity conscious Sir Felix Pole. The locomotive 4082 *Windsor Castle* was waiting at the head of the Royal Train and the King and Queen were ushered up special steps to the footplate where much photography took place before the King 'drove' the train as far as the station, the train finally leaving at 5.00 p.m. A memorable day for Swindon, and quite a tiring programme for the participants. An item of interest from the correspondence concerning the visit is that Driver E. Rowe and Fireman A. Cook, who were in charge of *Windsor Castle* received a letter of thanks, a copy of the souvenir programme and £2 and £1 respectively. The GWR Chairman, Viscount Churchill, had an aide-mémoire of facts prepared for him, and the following 'round' figures for Swindon are quoted:-

No. of employees CME Dept.,	45,000
at Swindon	14,000
No. of women at Swindon	400

Capacity of Works (p.a.)	New	Repairs
Locomotives	100	1,000
Carriages	200	4,000
Wagons	4,000	10,000

Swindon Works 1½ miles in length ½ mile in breadth
310 acres

Wages Bill (p.a.)	
CME Dept.	£8,500,000
at Swindon	£2,500,000

Costs	£
Express Passenger Locomotive	6,700
70 ft. Dining Car	4,600
70 ft. 1st class Carriage	3,500
70 ft. 3rd class Carriage	3,000
20 ton Mineral Wagon	240
12 ton Goods Wagon	165

Another important visit to the Works was on 30th May 1924, consisting of a large party from the

Institute of Transport, Doubtless the place was still spick and span from the Royal visit a month earlier. During this visit they were shown a new class of engine which was being built. The Welsh railways had numerous tank engines of the 0-6-2 arrangement, and many of these had been sent to Swindon for repair or scrapping. There was a need, however, to produce replacements for many of these. In general the 2-6-2 wheel arrangement was preferred on the GWR because of the better riding around curves facilitated by the 'pony' wheels. However, the 0-6-2 arrangement had worked well in Wales and as the faster running was made down the valleys, and the engines invariably worked smokebox leading up the valley gradients, the cheaper arrangement was acceptable. On 8th June 1923 the Locomotive Committee authorized the building of 50 such locomotives to Lot 228 and these went into traffic in the latter half of 1924. They were the 56XX class and 150 were to be built at Swindon by the end of 1928. A further 50 were built by Messrs. Armstrong Whitworth the same year. Carrying the standard No. 2 boiler, 8 in. diameter piston valves, 18 in. by 26 in. cylinders and 4 ft. 7 in. diameter wheels, these powerful locomotives were ideal for the heavy South Wales coal traffic.

During these years numerous handsome war memorials, honouring those who had served, were wounded, or died, on active service, appeared in the various shops. Always unveiled with a religious service, gatherings took place around them annually on Armistice Day and they were always kept in first class order with Flanders poppy wreaths and regularly adorned with vases of fresh cut flowers. A level of prosperity had again come to the Works, although this was to be shattered again shortly. This prosperity is indicated by the 'trip' figures for 1924 when no less than 29,000 railwaymen and their dependants, accompanied by a further 2,000 non-railway folk, left Swindon in 31 special trains for their annual holiday. This year the arrangements at the Mechanics Institution had not been made by Harry Southwell who had retired the previous holiday. He had served the organization unstintingly as secretary for 31 years since 1892, and had been a council member for seven years previous to that, a record of service to the GWR community difficult to surpass.

The workload in 1924 is indicated by the production figures for new rolling stock in the annual report. This was a year when much constituent stock was passing through Swindon, and therefore, the rate of new building of locomotives was somewhat reduced. The figures were:-

	New	Repaired
Locomotives	59	912 + 720 boilers and 545 tenders
Carriage Stock	210	4,000
Wagons	2,760	12,600

Plate 162: The north (cupola) bay of the iron foundry (J1) shop. Here the large floor mouldings for cylinders etc., were made.

British Rail

Plate 163: The south bay of the iron foundry where, generally, the smaller box mouldings were prepared.

British Rail

Plate 164: An 0-6-2T locomotive, No. 5600, the first of its class, photographed in factory grey immediately on completion on 19th November 1924.

British Rail

The year 1925 was entered full of hope, but already clouds were looming with unrest in the coal industry. The Works saw the provision of a new pattern shop to meet the demands of the enlarged iron foundry. The increasing dock work also necessitated extension of the millwright facilities, and further Stirling boilers were installed at the central boiler station. Working at 130 p.s.i., eight of these boilers were eventually installed, each capable of producing 14,000 lb steam/hour. Their chimneys became a landmark in Swindon, each being formed from six 2301 class boiler shells, 10 ft. long and 4 ft. 5 in. in diameter bolted end to end. Including the height of the boilers themselves, the chimneys reached to over 80 ft. from ground level. Each separate chimney weight approximately 12 tons. Electric transport trucks were also introduced at this time.

Great excitement was caused by the locomotive exchange trials between the LNER Gresley Pacifics and GWR 'Castles', but the publicity got out of hand in newspapers and other publications, and what was intended to be a serious interchange of ideas between engineers, became completely side tracked and soured

relations between the two railways. The centenary of the Stockton & Darlington Railway was to be celebrated in September 1925 and in anticipation it was decided to build a replica of the BG *North Star* in its original form. It will be recalled that the original locomotive had been cut up early in the century. As soon as the decision was made public, it was surprising what was 'found' lying about in Swindon Works. Major items were the driving wheels and crankshaft, the nameplates and parts of the motion. How these had been hidden away successfully is not clear, but the Works was a big place! The headlight was at Paddington, and some of the horsehair stuffed leather buffers were being used as stools in Bath. The replica, incorporating these original parts, was ready to play its part in the celebrations together with modern GWR locomotives and rolling stock.

In order to make the movement of coal more economic the GWR introduced, in September 1925, 20 ton all steel mineral wagons, hoping, in due course, to replace the old timber 10 ton vehicles which had been standard for so long. The adoption of these by the colliery owners was to take a long time, but many were now built, particularly by outside contractors.

It was at the Stockton & Darlington celebrations that Sir Felix Pole met Daniel Willard, President of the American Baltimore & Ohio Railroad whose centenary was to be celebrated two years later in 1927. Willard, and an associate Edward Hungerford, travelled to England to get ideas for their forthcoming event and the possibility was mooted of having one or more British exhibits, although little more than generalizations were discussed.

Seventy-three new locomotives were built during 1925 and 1,060 heavy repairs passed through the shops, 753 boiler repairs and 653 tenders, showing a slow, but significant, rise in the level of work. The repair of carriage stock was particularly high at over 4,500, and it was expected that, in 1926, an average of 91.3 vehicles per week would be dealt with (on a 50 week basis). In addition, 2,350 new wagons were built and 15,650 repaired. The staff level was not increasing and productivity had reached great heights for a basic 47 hours per week. However, disaster was close with the tragedy of the General Strike, although this affected the railways for only about 10 days from Monday, 3rd May 1926. It was the prolonged struggle in the coalfields that had such a devastating effect on the GWR in particular. Most of the constituent railways taken over in the grouping needed coal traffic and export through their docks as their 'life blood'. This business quickly disappeared and was never again to reach the proportions which had been the norm for so many years. The GWR therefore was hit more than the other railways, not only now but in the long term. It was the Welsh steam coal which was exported in the main, and not that from the more northern coalfields, and the GWR was never able to recover from this setback. The effect on Swindon was to be expected and considerable reductions in workload were effected in the latter half of 1926 and in 1927. Reverting to the railway strike, it became clear for the first time that the country could fall back on to road transport if necessary and a railway system was not entirely essential for distribution of needful commodities.

On 30th June 1925 a significant land deal had been completed between the GWR and the Borough of Swindon. The GWR Park had, over the years, gradually changed its activities. There had been so many demands for its use for functions, that Saturday cricket had to be transferred elsewhere, and the use of the ground, was, in any case, spoiling the turf for the game. Things came to a head in about 1906 when it was clear that if sport was to continue there, the whole area would have to be returfed. As funds were not available, this was not done, and the matter was settled, a little later, by building a bandstand in the centre of the Park. In ensuing years the borough had raised the question several times of enforcing their own by-laws there in common with other public recreation areas in the town, but this had been resisted by Churchward. The Park committee, (still the senior officers), met at least annually during the war years, but only one meeting was held under Collett on 6th February 1922 and from then on no further meetings were recorded, the minutes of that meeting not even being signed. Interest in the park had obviously waned, and it is therefore not surprising to find on the date mentioned above that an exchange of land took place. The corporation was to take over the park completely and the GWR was to receive a parcel of land, roughly the same area in extent, which lay to the north of the C & W Works. It was part of the Ferndale Road Recreation Ground, and was required for the extension of facilities for painting vehicles and (the old story again), the storage of carriages required for summer season traffic only. Although work on the buildings was not to commence for a few years, filling of the land at the east end of the site on which the approach sidings would be laid began almost immediately.

Despite the troubles emanating from the coal traffic situation, the passenger business was still healthy, but there were some particular areas of concern. Although, with hindsight, we know what excellent locomotives the 'Castles' were to be, in their early days, although completely outshining engines on the LNER and LMS, they were not quite so satisfactory as could have been wished in their timekeeping, particularly on the heavy West of England expresses. The need to use imported coal in 1926 also showed that their narrow firebox design could not so readily accept fuel other than the Welsh steam coal, with which the GWR had always been supplied. Furthermore, the operating difficulties over the South Devon banks between Newton Abbot and Plymouth, with a ruling gradient of 1 in 37, indicated a need for at least a small number of even more powerful locomotives. It is fortunate that the Locomotive Committee of the Board was now headed by Sir Aubrey Brocklebank of the shipowning family, who took great interest in, and was extremely well informed on locomotive matters. Collett made the point that as long as the 20 ton axle load limit remained, although a larger locomotive may be desirable, little could be done, and instanced the trouble with the standard No. 7 boiler considered for the 'Castle'. Recently the SR had introduced their 'Lord Nelson' class which, using the tractive effort notation, was now the most powerful locomotive in the country but the axle loading was 20¾ tons. It will be remembered that when James Inglis, as General Manager, had taken steps to exercise executive power over other senior officers, Churchward had led the rebellion and one of the consequences was a lack of interchange between departments which had never been a strong point of the GWR management structure in any case. The present

Chief Engineer, J. C. Lloyd, now questioned by Brocklebank and Pole, calmly stated that bridges had been built or brought up to at least 22 ton standard for many years and only four, between Paddington and Plymouth, remained not so treated! The outcome was an immediate decision to authorize Collett to work up to 22½ tons, and for Lloyd to strengthen the remaining bridges at once. There is also the implication that the 'Castles' could have had the standard No. 7 boiler after all in 1923, if the departments had been communicating with each other!

Design work was put in hand early in 1926, and a mock-up photograph appeared in the 1926 CME's Annual Report (which would have been completed in the early days of January 1927) of a 'new heavy powerful engine, tractive effort 39,000lb'. It further stated that the building of 20 'Castles' had been deferred because of the difficulties arising from the coal strike, and after cover up explanations concerning the Bridge Stress Committee, that it was proposed to build these 20 engines to a heavier and more powerful design. The drawing office was now able to design into a large engine all the best practices of previous classes. The new boiler provided, standard No. 12, took care to preserve the ratio of dimensions which had been proven over the years. Preserving almost the same diameters as the standard No. 7, it was only 1ft. 2in. longer and therefore the diameter/length ratio on the standard No. 8 was similar to that on the standard No. 12. A very much larger firebox was required, however, and the length was increased from 10ft. on standard Nos. 7 and 8 to an unprecedented 11ft. 6in., about the maximum distance a fireman could expect to place coal accurately from a moving footplate!

Sir Felix Pole now had his 'Super-Castle', but was still not satisfied that the nominal tractive effort was 39,000lb. To do the job properly it had to top the 40,000 mark! Already the stroke, at 28in., was 2in. more than the 'Castles' and the boiler pressure raised by 25lb to 250p.s.i., but to attain the magic figure, a cylinder diameter of 16¼in. was required and a slight reduction in the driving wheel diameter. Although completely against standard practice, the wheels were reduced from 6ft. 8½in. to 6ft. 6in. diameter, and this gave Sir Felix a figure of 40,300lb for his publicity! Class names were already in mind. Amongst the flood of publicity emanting from Paddington had been two beautiful volumes on the historic and architectural details of the Abbeys and Castles served by the GWR, and from which locomotives had been named. Now a third volume was produced, on Cathedrals, and it was obvious to all that these names were in mind for the new locomotives. Preparations for the Baltimore & Ohio Centenary Exhibition were now taking shape, and Sir Felix took all the necessary steps to see that the new GWR engine should be the British exhibit. In this he was successful, but it was felt that the name should, perhaps, be more representative of the occasion. So, as had happened for the 1851 Great Exhibition, when *Lord of the Isles* had been substituted for *Charles Russell* permission was now obtained to name the first locomotive *King George V*, others of the class to bear the name of previous Kings, moving backwards in time.

The Baltimore & Ohio Exhibition gave the Works great problems in timing, since, as well as the very short design and building period available, there was little or no time left in which to rectify teething troubles. Everything needed to be right first time. *King George V* was ready for exhibiting at Paddington on 1st July, and had its maiden trip on the down 'Cornish Riviera Express' (CRE) on 20th July. It was already fitted with its Westinghouse pump and other American requirements. On 3rd August it was loaded aboard the *SS Chicago City* at Roath Dock, Cardiff.

The public impact of the new class was enormous at Swindon. There had always been a large number of people visiting the Works, but for a considerable period, and especially whilst the rest of Lot 243 was being built, visitors came in their trainloads to see the work in progress. Indeed, on 3rd November the first of many excursions was run from Paddington to Swindon. About 700 people availed themselves of this half-day inclusive outing, and it was arranged that the train would be hauled both ways by one of the new 'Kings', and booked timings, similar to the now famous 'Cheltenham Flyer' were made. These continued for some time, and journeys were also arranged from other centres.

In America, *King George V* was in the care of William Stanier, supported by chargeman erector F. W. Williams and fitter (later chargeman) Dando. These latter men were from the 'new work' gang in the 'AE' shop and knew every bolt and bearing. The engineman was Mr Young of Old Oak Common, one of the top drivers of the Company. Also to be photographed frequently with the engine, was 'Britannia' in the person of Miss Bruhl, Sir Felix Pole's granddaughter. A week after the departure by sea on 10th August, Swindon was alerted by the news that No. 6003 hauling the down 'Cornish Riviera Express' had derailed at Midgham whilst travelling at 60m.p.h. Luckily for the GWR, it was on straight track, and because of this the cause of the trouble was clear, as only the bogie had derailed. One can imagine the consternation in the drawing office! A detailed enquiry was immediately held and Stanier was cabled that *King George V* was not to be allowed any main line running in America until authorized. A fault was identified in the springing arrangement of the bogie, which was of radical design. A young designer hailing from the Taff Vale Railway, and becoming

Plate 165: Perhaps the best known and finest photograph of No. 6000 *King George V*, one of the first photographs taken on 16th June 1927 whilst the locomotive was still in factory grey.

British Rail

Plate 166: *King George V* in America. Also Britannia (Miss Bruhl) with 'Bill' (later Sir William) Stanier. To his right are Swindon chargeman Williams and fitter Dando of the 'A' shop.

British Rail

Plate 167: The temporary hospital extension shown three weeks after its official opening. The lower glass fronted case (extreme left) carried daily bulletins of all patients. Note the ornate tramway column and 'Cars Stop by Request' notice. The Wesleyan Church, now the GWR Museum, is in the background.

British Rail

well known at Swindon in later years, A. W. J. Dymond, quickly modified spring calculations and design details were sent, by cable, to Stanier, who had new springs made and fitted. No further trouble was experienced in this matter.

It is sufficient to say here that the locomotive was a huge success in America and brought great kudos to the GWR and to Swindon in particular, making the whole town proud of their part in railway history. A strange sequel should be related. The reader will recall how much of Churchward's original 4-6-0 types were based on American practice. After the visit of *King George V*, a locomotive completely in the Churchward tradition, the Baltimore & Ohio Railroad and others began to build new, or to modify engines to conform to Swindon practice, and many of these efforts appeared in photographs of the *GWR Magazine* in ensuing years. Some of these changes were concerned with the removal of all the typical outside clutter of American locomotives and it was from these changes that the ideas were developed for streamlining American locomotives a few years later.

Pressures on the Medical Fund had been increasing, and in particular the capacity of the accident hospital was causing great concern. Although the Victoria Hospital was well established, the advances in medical knowledge in World War I had turned surgery into a regular method of treatment, where previously it was often resorted to as a last hope. The functions of the

small hospital had radically changed therefore and the Council of the Society issued a special report in 1925, and at a subsequent meeting it was agreed to ballot members, now numbering 15,000 and equating to 45,000 possible patients, on the advisability of extending facilities. Although increases in weekly subscriptions were necessary, there was an overwhelming number in favour of such extensions. Matters were urgent enough to consider the building of a temporary wing to obtain benefit as early as possible, and consideration given to the possibilities of a completely new hospital.

It was agreed with the trustees, that the garden space in front of the existing hospital be utilized for the new wing, and a general meeting held in February 1926 authorized the project. A loan of £4,000 at low interest was negotiated with the GWR and the design work placed with the local architects Messrs. Beswick & Son. Mr Palmer, a Swindon contractor, erected the new building, which was to be utilitarian in appearance because of its 'temporary' nature. Site work commenced on 6th September 1926 and the new wing was ready for its opening, by Sir Felix Pole, on 26th February 1927. This gave to the Medical Fund an increase in beds from 12 to 42, but pressure was still on for further facilities as soon as they could be arranged. Further discussion now took place so that all possible alternatives could be assessed. Again the likelihood of amalgamation with the Victoria

Hospital was examined, but it was found almost impossible to come to any satisfactory arrangement between the Friendly Society basis and Voluntary Hospital basis of the two organizations. The only alternative, therefore, was to build a completely new hospital, and the committee was unanimous in their decision to propose this to the members.

In November 1930, a small booklet, prepared by the same architects, was issued to members outlining the proposals for a four floor building utilizing the whole block on which the present hospital stood, and including the row of cottages then standing at the back of the site. The new hospital was to have a total of 80 beds arranged on the 1st and 2nd floors, with consulting rooms, casualty ward and X-ray room on the ground floor. Living quarters for the nursing staff were to be located on the 3rd floor. The estimated cost was £44,000 and running costs of about £21,600 per annum would be double that of the recently enlarged hospital. Although it would mean a further increase in weekly charges, the voting amongst members was heavily in favour. The reader will, however, have noted the date of issue of the explanatory booklet. Already the effects of the Wall Street financial collapse in America was influencing the Worlds' economy, and within a few months the situation at Swindon made it impossible to go ahead with the project. The 'temporary' hospital was going to have to serve for about forty years.

Demand for increasing amounts of electrical power was being felt in the town, and plans were prepared by the Borough Corporation for extensions of generating capacity. The site of the original power station, in the middle of the town, was incapable of any large scale extension, and in any case would be detrimental to the surrounding residential area. If a new station was to be built, it was essential that the planned capacity be large enough to meet estimated future demands, and greater efficiency could be expected from a larger plant. An offer, therefore, was made to the GWR to provide capacity for both them and the town at the same time. Collett was pleased to accept this, as it relieved him of the pressure to provide his own steam operated plant, which had been recommended in the Robinson report, in the Works. Agreement was reached and the building of a new power station at Moredon, to the north of the town, was commenced. Alternating current was to be produced, replacing the direct current generated by both the corporation and the Works' gas-engined plant. Because of the lead-time problems, preparations had to be made in the Factory for the purchase and installation of a.c/d.c. conversion plant ready for the acceptance of power from the new station. On 27th November 1924, a sum of £10,000 was allocated for this purpose and went ahead in the 'M' sub-station so that a.c. power could be accepted as soon as Moredon was ready and the gas engines

Plate 168: The proposed new hospital of 1930.

Author's Collection

Plate 169: A typical motor bus body fitted to its chassis, pictured outside the road wagon (No. 17) Carriage & Wagon shop, where it was built.

British Rail

Plate 170: The huge stock of cast iron brake blocks maintained to the east of the Carriage & Wagon (No. 15) shop. This 1928 picture includes an interesting rake of 6 wheel carriages in the 'water sidings' next to the station.

British Rail

successively removed. Although small by modern standards, the new power station, rated at 11,250 kW output, was sufficient. The GWR took about half of the load, having its own feeder cables into the Works, a facility which still exists from the National Grid switching station. By 1926 a gradual transfer to the new supply was taking place and the final completion of Moredon and withdrawal of generation equipment in the Works was attained by 1930. The rising demand for gas in production processes in the Works was now possible to satisfy with the loss of electricity generation requirements, so that no further extensions were required. Finally, electric current was now much cheaper than heretofore, and much conversion from other power sources took place progressively over the years.

The trials of modified locomotive No. 2925, over nearly four years being successful, an order for 80 locomotives of a similar type was placed on 23rd December 1927. Main differences from the modified 'Saint' were the pitch of the boiler, frame layout in line with current practice, and detail changes to the valve gear. This order was completed on 13th May 1930, but was to be followed by further orders, almost yearly, up to 1950, amounting to 330 in total. The 'Hall' class, as they were known, became the universal workhorse of the GWR, being economical to build (£4,375 each at the outset), and also to run and maintain. This continuity of building throughout so long a period helped to stabilize an otherwise variable work load, particularly through the depression years.

The year 1927 saw almost the end of the large programme of conversions of constituent railways' stock, when 29 were reconstructed, together with 98 new GWR types coming out of the shops. In the same year 130 locomotives were condemned and it can be seen that Collett was able to keep within the earlier Plender recommendations namely keeping new building levels equal to replacement requirements. New carriage vehicles numbering 295 and 2,200 wagons were also built. By the middle of 1928 the rebuilt locomotive shops at Caerphilly were completed, and from then on much of the locally based 'valley' locomotives were able to have heavy repairs carried out there, thereby relieving Swindon of much of the extra work not foreseen when the final 'A' shop extensions were planned. Similar work was in hand at Wolverhampton and, increasingly, repair work, especially to the smaller tank and tender locomotives, was concentrated at these two modernized centres.

There was another kind of Royal visit to Swindon on 21st March 1928, when King Amanullah of Afghanistan paid a visit. Somewhat notorious in his lifestyle, and to be deposed not long after, the visit was followed with great interest and the usual courtesy by Swindonians. On the lighter side, a Railway Employees' Carnival was held at Belle Vue, Manchester, in September, at which one of the main

contributions was an amusing musical play *A Visit to Juja* or *The GWR Goes East*. Written in the pantomime tradition by Hugh Mytton of the Estate Surveyors Department at Paddington, and with music by Walter Collins, the show was cast with people well-known in Swindon amateur stage circles. The 'dramatis personae' listed here will give an idea of the type of entertainment, and also call to mind well-known Swindon railway folk:-

Tutt	Sultan of Juja	F. Westlake
Hushcash	Grand Vizier	R. H. Wood
Jee Whizz	Chief Slave &	
	Executioner	S. Ellison
Pulsem	Court Physician	S. Griffiths
Jim Driver	GWR Engine	
	Driver	F. Yates
John Order	GWR Station	
	Master	A. E. Ford
Jack Whistler	GWR Guard	E. Mooney
Joe Snipps	GWR Ticket	
	Collector	W. F. Church
Jeff Dumpem	GWR Porter	W. Richardson
Pi-Jaw	Ex-Sultana	D. Adams
Aha		D. Perrot
Oho	Dancing Slaves	M. Perrot

After its Manchester performance it travelled to other GWR centres, and the author clearly remembers the production at the Mechanics Institute at Swindon when a huge full-size flat canvas of *King George V* moved across back stage in the final scene! One would like to know what became of the words and score of this romp. It may be worth one of the larger railway preservation societies staging it again in aid of funds!

In 1928, an interesting development in the Carriage Works was the introduction, together with the LMS and LNE Railways, of 3rd class sleeping cars which immediately proved popular. Although 92 new locomotives were built at Swindon in that year, orders were also placed for 50 of the 56XX class 0-6-2 tank locomotives, for South Wales, from Messrs. Armstrong Whitworth & Co., Newcastle, and the same number of the 57XX 0-6-0 pannier tank type from the North British Locomotive Company. These orders helped to alleviate unemployment now increasing in the northern parts of the country. Whilst passenger vehicle production remained high at 280, wagon production fell heavily to 1,761. There was, however, a large amount of dock work carried out at Swindon at this time. In 1929 steps were taken in the boiler shop to improve production methods and wasteful handling of these heavy items by the introduction of special 'Wageor' drilling, reaming and tapping structures with variable work platforms and counterbalanced air driven power tools. Rivetting and caulking methods were also greatly improved.

A great social event was the GWR Musical Festival

Plate 171: The first 'Hall' Class locomotive, No. 4901 leaving the Works on 11th December 1928.

Plate 172: A particularly fine view of one of the 'AE' shop 100 ton cranes in action. It is moving No. 4288 out of the shop after repair. Since it was necessary to house two repairs per pit, the locomotive away from the engine traverser had to be lifted out if completed first..

Plate 173: Construction of Carriage & Wagon(No. 24) shop, as seen on 23rd March 1929. Note the building up of the ground and also the remains of the lock and keeper's cottage of the derelict North Wilts Canal, in the foreground.

British Rail

held at the Mechanics Institute and in other buildings. Sir Walford Davies was the honorary music adviser to the Social & Educational Union (S&EU), and brought with him a formidable array of adjudicators including Armstrong Gibbs and Dr Adrian Boult. A large party of French railway officials visited the country in May 1929, and whilst on GWR territory looked around the Works, but it is noticeable that C. B. Collett did not appear, and they were escorted by W. A. Stanier. A great loss was sustained by the GWR on 6th June 1929 when Sir Felix Pole announced his resignation as General Manager. Although he had a worthy successor in James (later Sir James) Milne, the latter did not have the flair for publicity which had always kept the GWR in the news for the previous nine years to the advantage of its finances. One other interesting item in 1929 was the recurring list of locomotive name plates for sale at Swindon, which seemed very hard to sell! In particular, those off many of the 4-4-0 type locomotives now being withdrawn were on offer.

Although the year of many record runs of the 'Cheltenham Flyer' it was also the year of a govern-

ment Relief Bill which enabled the financing of projects by advantageous government loans in order to provide work. Many projects were started on the GWR in general, but one at Swindon brought the end, after 88 years, of its earliest building — the original running shed. This was demolished in November to make way for southerly extensions to the 'B' repair shop. This was to be the last major extension to this shop. The construction of the large new No. 24 carriage shop was going on apace on land exchanged earlier for the GWR Park, being finally completed by February 1930. This was supposed to be used primarily as a paint shop, and included a fully equipped paint-mill for manufacture of the basic paints. It also had its own self-contained boiler house with two Lancashire boilers. With the main portion of the shop 600ft. by 400ft., it had a total area of 6 acres (2.43 hectares), and was to be the last large rolling stock repair shop built at Swindon.

Two deaths of note occurred towards the end of 1929, one being that of the CME's chief clerk A. J. L. White on 24th October. His father had occupied the same post in the previous century, but A. J. L's claim to fame was the pioneering of engine name and number lists, described earlier. His extremely informative articles on the Works are now almost the only records of the machinery and equipment used in the first 20 years of the 20th century. The other death was that of Dr G. R. (Roddy) Swinhoe, late Chief Medical Officer of the GWR Medical Fund, who died on 10th October. Succeeding his father Dr G. M. Swinhoe in 1907, he served in the post until 1917, and successively they occupied this senior post for some 58 years.

The highest annual locomotive mileage recorded to date was attained in 1929 with a reduced number of engines. These over the year had diminished from 3,940 to 3,858, but the train miles worked rose from 95,060,251 in 1928 to 97,130,000 in 1929. It was going to be a watershed of fortunes, and in 1930 the effects of the slump began to bite. Already, in 1928, the whole staff, from directors down, accepted a 2½ per cent reduction in wages, and it was to be some years before this was finally restored. A prudent Board, however, was effecting very wide economies in the hope of weathering the difficult period which they foresaw and, to a large extent, they were successful. Gradual losses of traffic were countered with vigorous new policies in the affected areas, but the flood could not be adequately stemmed. By the end of August 1930, Swindon Works was going on to short time in many departments and this was eventually to spread to the whole Works. But, as in the previous century, the work that was available was being funnelled into the larger efficient organizations at Swindon, assisted in the C & W Works with the new No. 24 shop now completed. New trains were built for the 'Cornish Riviera' and 'Torbay' expresses, as the motor car had not yet begun to effectively invade this area of business. There was pressure to support industry in ways other than civil engineering and building work, and the GWR took advantage of this by placing orders for 100 locomotives of the 57XX 0-6-0 pannier tank class, 25 each to the companies of Armstrong Whitworth, Bagnall, Beyer Peacock and North British Locomotive. This order amounted, in all, to about £250,000. These contracts allowed Swindon to concentrate on building the final ten 'Kings' and another batch of 'Halls'. From the Wagon Works came a special vehicle, a 4 x six-wheeled bogie well beam wagon capable of transporting a 120 ton load. Special beams were also available to carry large electric transformers. This vehicle was 89 ft. 6 in. long overall and was soon in great demand for the special loads it could carry. The carriage side also commenced building the 'super saloons' for the lucrative transatlantic traffic between Plymouth and London. Many ocean liners made calls at Plymouth, and passengers and mail were loaded on to GWR tenders meeting them in Plymouth Sound. A day in transit could thus be saved and, not having

had much success with Pullman trains, it was decided to build similar luxury stock which could also be available for private service at other times. These beautiful vehicles, 9 ft. 7 in. wide at the waist, were preceeded by some very handsome 'nondescript' saloons for private hire. These left the Works during 1929-1931. Some of these latter types became, in BR days, 'semi-royal' vehicles, used when the full Wolverton Royal Train was not justified.

In the Works further contracts based on the Development (Loan Guarantees & Grants) Act of 1929 were carried out. The main undertaking was the provision of the new 'concentration yard' (C shop), where all scrapping could be concentrated for economic cutting up, and the resultant scrap materials sorted and despatched. As well as a main covered shop with overhead crane and crackerball attachment, a large outdoor area was served by large goliath cranes equipped with electro-magnets and grabs. Sorted scrap material could then be stored until the market prices were advantageous. The new 24 shop was only about half utilized due to lack of repair work, but the new 'deinfestation plant' attached to it commenced work. This consisted of a large steel tube 16 ft. 6 in. diameter by 85 ft. long into which a complete coach or a number of grain wagons could be run. With the end circular door moved into position and hermetically sealed, a pump evacuated the chamber to 28 in. of mercury while internal steam pipes raised the temperature to 120 degrees Fahrenheit (49 degrees Centigrade). After 6 hours, no vermin of any sort could remain alive, but if the vehicle was suspected of having been in contact with infectious diseases, a measured dose of formalin would be injected to become formaldehyde as the vacuum was slowly destroyed, thereby completing the treatment. At this time, a start was made on converting shop lighting from gas to electricity. Starting in some carriage shops where a four-line a.c. circuit was installed to cover power as well as lighting, this programme was not to be completed until after the start of World War II. Also, large capacity air compressors, with motors working at 3,300 volts, were now installed at strategic points in both Works.

At the beginning of 1930, W. A. Stanier announced that a new sports ground, for railway staff, would be available within a few months. The site was a large field of about 13 acres south of Shrivenham Road on the east side of Swindon. The land was purchased from the Goddard estate on 17th August 1928. As a young boy, the author remembers holding one end of the plan showing the proposed layout, the other end being held by his father, A. W. J. Peck the S & EU Secretary, whilst a couple of directors and local senior officers discussed the project. The magnificent ground, to be further developed over a period of years, was a great boon to the large number of employees at the Works, and a separate

Plate 174: The de-infestation plant adjacent to No. 24 shop. The sealing door is swung aside to admit brake third multibar 'Toplight' carriage, No. 3801, of 1924 (later No. 3401).

British Rail

Plate 175: Machining the airtight door ring for the de-infestation plant. The late Alec Clissold is here seen utilizing his exceptional millwrighting skills in maintaining the perfect eccentricity required on this steel ring on the old, but indispensable, large-swing facing lathe in the millwrights (G) shop in December 1930. The setting up of the ring on the special extensions to the face plate, without deformation, must have been a nightmare in itself!

British Rail

Plate 176: Only the fashions have changed for the holiday-makers boarding one of the west country 'Trip' trains in the 1930s. The train is standing adjacent to the original Clayton carriage shop on the 'down' side of the main line to Bristol.
British Rail

organization, the GWR (Swindon) Athletic Association was formed to run it. One social occasion which should not be overlooked was the first 'Open Day' at the Works. It was held on 12th April 1930, in aid of the Railway Benevolent Institution and approximately 6,000 people attended. It is believed to have been the first time that employees had been able to show families and friends around their place of work, although, of course, regular guided tours had taken place for over 70 years. Over £142 was raised that day. Amongst the attractions were fire fighting demonstrations arranged by C. T. Cuss, one of the assistant managers, who had a penchant for fire training, and other odd activities as well, such as blowing up old tree trunks. Visitors were allowed to direct fire hoses at targets, and to blow engine whistles, all at one penny a time! The first GWR Arts & Crafts Exhibition to be held in Swindon took place on 1st November 1930 at the large baths, and was to be held many more times in Swindon.

The Mechanics Institute was unfortunate, when late at night the theatre stage portion of the large upper hall was destroyed by fire on Christmas Eve, and much damage to other parts of the building was sustained due to the effects of smoke and water. Under the energetic leadership of W. A. Stanier however, steps were quickly taken to make good this loss. Also improvements on former facilities were made. On 3rd September 1932 the new 'Playhouse' as it was now named was opened by the Mayor, all other rooms having been systematically cleaned and repaired, and a new ground floor dance hall installed. The new theatre was leased for a period by the Wilson-Claridge Repertory Company, and they opened with a play well known at the time entitled 'White Cargo'. A little later there was to be another serious fire, this time in the Works, when the C&W carpenters' shop was gutted. This building, on the south side of the line, had expanded from the old lifting shop of 1868. It was now entirely rebuilt to

Plate 177: A Collett 2251 Class 0-6-0 when new in 1930. Note the automatic train control contact shoe at the front end.

British Rail

a modern layout and reopened in 1935.

The short time working and dismissals now taking place had a detrimental effect on the number of people taking the annual 'trip' holiday, with a noticeable reduction in those travelling. This trend continued in 1932 when only 26,000 people travelled, even so, 430 carriages had to be found. Although some left on the Thursday evening, 7th July, between 9p.m. and 12.15a.m., between 4.50a.m. and 8.05a.m. the next morning, no less than 26 trains were loaded and despatched. Staff had fallen to about 11,000 at Swindon, so 40 per cent of the town's population were away for the holiday. The main fall back was in repair work, particularly in the wagon department, although it was also very keenly felt in the Locomotive Works. New building proceeded with little change and in 1930 came the first new 0-6-0 tender locomotives (2251 class), since the 'Dean Goods' almost forty years previously. Indeed, these new engines were wanted specifically for the lower axle-load lines mainly in Wales. Later in the year the special saloons referred to earlier were put into service. Built at Swindon, their interior fittings were carried out by Trollope & Sons, coach-builders of London. By 1931, 3,119 out of 6,828 carriages were electrically lit, and conversion was proceeding at a steady pace. Experiments with ball bearing races for carriage bogies had not proved successful, but now roller bearings were being tried for the first time. On 20th March, the locomotive *City of Truro*, completely overhauled and painted in original colours, left Swindon, hauled 'dead', en route

for York Railway Museum where it was to remain for many years before being worked again in the last years of steam operation. The year saw the intro-duction of the 'Whitewash Coach', or Track Testing Car, to be more precise. Originally a 'toplight' carriage of 1911, it was now converted for rear inspection and housed the 'Hallade' recorder which had been tried in ordinary train compartments since 1929. Damaged areas of track were indicated by auto-matic drops of white or colour wash from the coach to denote the specific areas to track maintenance teams. This vehicle, now DW139, is still in similar use today, but with its bogies modified enabling it to run regularly at 100m.p.h. In about 1976, side sheeting was removed for examination and only very minor repairs were needed to its timber body framework after 65 years of continuous use!

Consternation was felt in Swindon at the end of 1931, when it was announced that W. A. Stanier had accepted the post of Chief Mechanical Engineer to the LMSR. Well known and respected by the railway community, and Swindonians in particular, it was he who had been the visible representative of the GWR at Swindon, certainly since Churchward's retirement and, for many years previously, had undertaken many of the social duties so necessary in keeping a large organization cohesive. Always active in local and church affairs, his imminent departure would provide a vacuum which could not be adequately filled by those remaining. From Stanier's point of view it was the chance to extend his locomotive and rolling stock ideas from the sound Churchward principles, in which

Plate 178: One of the magnificent 'super' saloons for the Plymouth boat trains and other special services.

British Rail

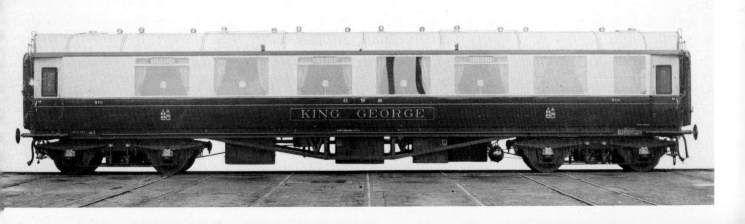

he had absolute faith, in ways which he would have wished Swindon practice to go after 1922. Being always in close touch with his previous chief, these ideas were possibly parallel to those which Churchward himself would have chosen. Due to the closeness of ages between Collett and Stanier, it was plain that the latter might never succeed to the top, and even if he did it would not be long enough, in an engineering sense, to be effective. With him went the best wishes of his Swindon friends, but also, in a short time, some of the design staff from the drawing office. These people possessed much valuable design experience of locomotives and boilers on which could be based the huge programme of locomotive building now facing Stanier in his new sphere. In his place John Auld, late of the Barry Railway, was appointed as principal assistant, who tried as well as he could to take over the public and social activities relinquished by Stanier and in which Collett steadfastly took little or no interest.

A not so well known, but equally colourful figure in his way also retired at the end of July 1931, James Kibblewhite, of a numerous Purton family. He had been a chargeman for 40 of his 50 years of service, but became famous in the years 1886—94, when he held, at various times, virtually all the open running championships in the country from ½ to 10 miles. In 1889, 1890 and 1891 he was the one mile champion of all England. He won the four mile championship twice, and the ten mile once. His main training was a daily jog and run between work and Purton, his home village situated a few miles distant. Amongst the lucky few with interesting changes in their normal occupation in 1931, were a select group of carriage finishers and trimmers, who visited the Gainsborough Film Studios to assist with setting up carriage compartment and corridor 'sets' for some shots of the film 'The Ghost Train' in the famous Jack Hulbert production. All railway location shots were carried out on the GWR on the Basingstoke and Camerton branches, and at the Barmouth Swing Bridge. It was also the year of years for No. 15 C&W shop, which seemed to contain all the talent of the Factory within its walls, with awards either individually or in groups for boxing, running, swimming, cricket, football, cycling, fishing, best essays, the conductor of two prizewinning orchestras, brass playing and even highest subscriptions to hospitals and other charities, and finishing with the highest award at the GWR Arts & Crafts Exhibition.

The Annual Report of the CME for 1931, which appeared early the following year, showed a drop in locomotive building to 93 at Swindon, although carriage vehicle production was still at 295. However, wagons at 1,835 were only 45 per cent of capacity. During these difficult years, Wolverhampton Works was being remodelled after the style of Caerphilly, and starting in 1929 was completed in 1932, 74 years

after its adoption as a locomotive building establishment. The Board was now obliged, because of their investment policy, to see that all the three main factories had a fair share of the work load, and this was enforced by political considerations also. Locomotive book stock had fallen since the peak of 1928, of just over 4,000, which was never again to be reached. By 1935, it was just below 3,700 although there was a rise just prior to and during the coming war years. In 1932 Swindon was beginning to feel the pinch and 192 engines were scrapped. During this same year the workshop staff of the CME over the whole system had been reduced by 2,700, over half of these at Swindon, and by 1933 all works were continuing with much depleted staff and short time, just 3 days per week being worked in many instances. This state of affairs improved during the year, and some normality was restored. There was a long term effect on the town, however, and the population fell steadily from 63,000 in 1934 to about 60,000 in 1938, whilst the total number employed at Swindon stabilized around the 10,000 mark, which was to be the norm for the next 20 years. One outcome arising from the labour dislocations of this period was the agreement reached on new machinery of negotiation for railway staff, introducing the Railway Staff National Council and Railway Staff National Tribunal early in 1935, and these are still in being at the time of writing.

In 1911 the GWR had purchased, for trials, a small petrol rail car, but development of this form of traction had not progressed enough for its adoption. Between the wars, however, the use of the heavy oil engine was being introduced in different parts of the world with a measure of success. The Locomotive Committee of the Board, ever watchful of developments of this sort, felt the matter should be investigated, and early in 1929 had asked the CME to submit a short paper on the use of diesel-electric power units, either independent or in the form of multiple unit traction for passenger trains. The resulting memorandum, dated 20th March 1929, gave the findings vis-a-vis GWR requirements. The idea of electro-diesel sets for use both on the Hammersmith and City lines and on normal suburban routes, was considered unsatisfactory because of the lack of adequate acceleration. A Beardmore proposal offering two 500h.p. diesel-electric sets, one in each end vehicle of a 6 coach train, and able to be used as two 3 coach sets, was compared with similar steam hauled local trains. The estimated cost of the 2 x 3 car train would be £34,000 as against £17,700 for two 517 class 0-4-2 auto-fitted locomotives and six suburban carriages. In addition, the former would have seating for only 336, as against 384 in the latter. In the heavier sphere of operations it was suggested that to improve upon steam performance and acceleration, separate diesel-electric locomotives would be needed, and the cost differential of complete trains would become £60,000 to £22,000, using the cost of a large suburban tank locomotive. Finally, for branch working, a 500h.p. locomotive from Beardmore was quoted at between £11,800 and £14,300 as against a steam one of higher power at £3,000. It is plain that there was not much enthusiasm for the idea, but noteworthy that little or no account was taken of the savings possible in intermittent workings both for fuel and labour, which should have closed the financial gap considerably.

In 1933, Swindon Works was supplied, by Fowler, with a small 70b.h.p. diesel mechanical shunter which proved very useful. Perhaps more surprisingly, on 4th December 1933 in the Reading area, streamlined rail car No. 1 started running, a product of the AEC Works at Southall with bodywork by Park Royal Coachworks Ltd., although to general Swindon specifications. The first car, at 121h.p., was not as powerful as could be wished, although capable of 60m.p.h., but was followed in the next year by cars for an express service between Birmingham and Cardiff, with two engines fitted per car. The earlier car cost £3,000 and the next series £3,500 each, so prices, although not purely comparable, had changed drastically since 1929! Later cars were more expensive at about £4,885 from No. 5 onwards as they became more complicated mechanically. Bodies were later supplied by the Gloucester Carriage & Wagon Co. In

all, 18 of these vehicles, to several design arrangements, were purchased, but little of the maintenance was allocated to Swindon, as they were maintained by the manufacturer on a cost per mile basis until the beginning of the war. In 1936 a much larger diesel-electric shunter of 350b.h.p. was purchased for use and evaluation at Acton Yard (No. 2 later No. 15100), and this was not dissimilar to the well tried design in use today on BR. It was built by Messsrs. Hawthorn Leslie, with electrical gear from the English Electric Company.

So much for the dawning of the diesel age on the GWR. An era of the steam age came to an end on the misty Tuesday morning of 19th December 1933 when, at about 10.20a.m. the locomotive No. 4085, hauling the Paddington to Fishguard express, struck down and killed instantly the great engineer of the GWR, G. J. Churchward. Always retaining interest in the railway, he is thought to have been unwisely examining a loose rail joint on the track near his house. The body was noticed, a few minutes later, by the driver of a train travelling in the opposite direction. F. A. Drinkwater, a prominent first aider at the Works, was immediately at the scene, but there was nothing he could do. The Works was stunned at the news, as the 'old man' had been held in affection almost amounting to reverence by the staff long after he had left in 1922. He was buried as he wished, the

Plate 179: Southall diesel car No. 1 on 24th November 1933, a few days before entering service.

British Rail

Plate 180: The Zeiss optical lining up equipment:-
(a) Telescope set in the cylinders of No. 2804. Collimator set in No. 3 axle gap.

British Rail

Plate 181: (b) Collimator at No. 3 axle with transverse equipment for checking right angles across the frame. Also the micrometer 'clock' gauge at the end of the set length piece from the horn face of No. 2 axle.

British Rail

first Honorary Freeman of the Borough of Swindon in the churchyard of the Old Town parish church, Christ Church, and there was a very large attendance at this last office for a famous man.

Strangely, at the moment Churchward was run down, K. J. Cook, then assistant manager to R. A. G. Hannington, was in the erecting shop working with the new Zeiss optical aligning equipment which had recently been purchased. This specialized equipment, which made possible much more accurate aligning and squaring of all the main moving parts of a locomotive, was to have great and beneficial effects on the running life between heavy repairs, by enabling most mis-alignment stresses to frames and knocking of moving parts to be eliminated. It was used in conjunction with a purpose made horn-grinding machine laid down over the erection pits on machine grooved floor plates. This, in effect, allowed the locomotive frames to be set out as if on a large machine bed and the hornblocks could be ground square to the cylinder and crank pin line to within accuracies of 1/1,000in. in situ. The acquisition of this equipment led to the reorganization of the repair activities in the shop, where previously one gang of men had seen a complete repair through except for some specialist assistance. Now the circuit was split into four groups of activity and the staff reallocated to these four discrete sections. They were:-

a) Stripping, cleaning and distribution of parts to particular machine, fitting, and other shops for repair.

b) Frame examination, repair, Zeiss aligning, with necessary attention to cylinder bores, hornblocks, etc.

c) Replacing of boiler, refitting of motion bars and axle-boxes, and other main frame items, and finally rewheeling onto the repaired driving wheels.

d) Completion of erection including all motion gear and other fitting and boilermaking work, followed by valve setting on the new plant now installed for this work, and finally lowering onto bogie or pony trucks.

Painting and other similar activities were conveniently worked into the programme at suitable stages, so that only final connections now had to be made, including coupling to the tender, if not a tank engine. Lighting up and trial runs then followed. It was practice at Swindon for Factory repaired engines to proceed to the Swindon running shed, where, for a period of about two weeks, they were allocated to various agreed 'running-in' turns. Therefore it was quite normal to find the two or three coach 7.35 a.m. stopping train to Bristol via Badminton hauled by a gleaming 'King' or 'Castle'. During this period the locomotives were under the care of the 'works gang' of fitters at the shed, who made any adjustments necessary after service turns before the engine was finally released to normal traffic and worked to its

home depot. Boiler repairs had been equally improved by the adoption of the 'Wageor' drilling rigs already mentioned, resulting in high productivity together with accuracy and efficiency. This was a specialist equipment patented by Constructions Electriques Wageor of Paris and St. Etienne. Using all these new methods, the average mileage between Factory repair gradually increased, reaching about 155,000 miles by the beginning of World War II.

One effect of the depression was the changing pattern of freight and mineral traffic. This made many of the 2-8-0 tank 42XX class locomotives redundant. A major modification design was made which considerably increased their coal and water capacity, by elongating the bunker and adding a pair of carrying wheels under the extended frame to become 2-8-2T. With an extra 2 tons of coal they had about the same range as a tender engine and were able economically to replace many of the old 'Aberdare' 26XX class locomotives. These conversions were done in three batches between 1934 and 1939, being withdrawn from the 52XX and 42XX series, and renumbered the 72XX class. In all, 54 locomotives were dealt with in this way, making them much more useful because of their wider range of operations.

After laying, more or less, unused for very many years, the decision was taken to turn the old Churchward test plant into a modern piece of research and testing equipment. This was done with the usual amount of Swindon reticence. The old air compressor which had previously been driven by the locomotive on 'test' as its workload was removed, and new dynamometers took their place for the accurate measurement of drawbar horsepower and other power factors, together with full instrumentation. This was the time when the LNER and LMS were suggesting that a national plant should be set up. Attempting to gain the support of the GWR, they were brought to Swindon to see No. 2931 developing maximum power, and full tests in progress. Even now this plant was not used to its maximum capacity, but much experience was gained by some of the younger engineers at Swindon, which was to be put to great use some fifteen years later.

The centenary of the GWR occurred in 1935, and coincidentally the Silver Jubilee of King George V and Queen Mary. Among all the railways in Britain, the GWR had been alone in retaining its identity over such a long period and naturally much was made of the occasion. Most of the celebrations were held, of course, at places other than Swindon, but there were two contributions which did emanate from there. The major one was the building of the two new complete trains for the 'Cornish Riviera Express'. Each consisting of 10 passenger vehicles plus a three-car kitchen and dining set, they were built to the same 9 ft. 7 in. waist as the super saloons and offered a very high class of accommodation suitable for the prin-

Plate 182: 'Centenary' stock brake composite No. 6652, with inset doors, on this 9 ft. 7 in. wide stock.

British Rail

Plate 183: The new pavilion at the GWR Swindon sports ground, opened in 1935.

British Rail

cipal train of the GWR. It was indeed a fine 'present' to the travelling public who supported the line. The inaugural run of this stock took place on 8th July. The other contribution was the assistance given in producing the centenary film, 'Romance of a Railway'. For this *North Star* was removed from its usual home in the 'A' shop, and brightened up to become the star of some of the sequences made of the railways' early history. Many of the participants in the scenes were members of the dramatic societies connected with the GWR.

The 'Bristolian', a new fast service between Paddington and Bristol in each direction was also inaugurated on 9th September. The 'up' train of this service was due to pass the Factory at about 5.10 p.m. not long before cessation of the working day at 5.30 p.m., and it was usual for many to creep out of the shops to hide between the 'dead' engines awaiting repair, to see this great advertisement of their handiwork pounding through at full cry. A stirring sight indeed, especially to apprentices, of which the author was a member. There was also a radio programme lasting an hour on what was then the 'National' programme on the eve of the centenary, 30th August, in which the Mayor of Swindon, Alderman W. H. Bickham, appropriately an employee in the 'A' shop, made a contribution concerning the developments at Swindon.

This was also the year in which the new sports ground was finally completed with the provision of a fine new pavilion opened formally by one of the directors, the Rt. Hon. Lord Dulverton, on 26th April. Designed under the direction of the GWR Chief Architect, A. E. Culverhouse, it was constructed by Messrs. J. Harrison & Co. of Camberwell, London. The S&EU, very shortly to be named the GWR Staff Association, also opened new premises on 26th September 1936 in Bridge Street, Swindon, thereby still preserving their identity from the Mechanics Institution. These club premises included on the first floor a well equipped Little Theatre which was regularly used by the dramatic section of the large theatrical society which had run for many years in the town. This active organization, which had its roots in the early days of the establishment at Swindon had, for many years previous to those now under discussion, produced at least annual major musical plays, comic operas, and Gilbert & Sullivan operas, in the Mechanics Institute Theatre, but later at The Empire Theatre in the town. Their productions were always in friendly rivalry with another such group, the Swindon Amateur Musical & Dramatic Society dating from 1923. During the 1930s, these two societies reached a very high level of competence indeed, and regularly played to near capacity houses for their annual productions, a major number of their members being employed on the GWR.

The last major classes of engine to appear before World War II were the 'Granges' 68XX, built between 1936 and 1939 and the 'Manors' 78XX in 1938/39, although a few more of the latter were to appear in 1950. The 'Granges' were more exactly the locomotives foreseen by Churchward in his 1901 diagrams than the 'Halls' of 1928, as they had 5 ft. 8 in. driving wheels. Sets of motion and wheels for them were retrieved from the scrapping of many 43XX 2-6-0 class withdrawn shortly before. Both classes met a need for secondary mixed freight traffic services, and the 'Manors' were a specially light design with a new boiler, the standard No. 14, but they were again a typical 'developed' Churchward design, carrying on all of his precepts.

It may be noted here how the Works had recovered from the depression years, by quoting the new building figures for the years mentioned:-

Year	1933	1934	1935	1936	1937	1938
Locomotives	103	106	122	149	150	122
Carriage Stock	172	249	324	393	478	282
Wagons	1,392	2,470	3,180	4,260	5,340	2,807

It can be seen that 1937 was the peak year for output, and it should be remembered that over and above this was the main annual 'bread and butter' work of about 1,000 heavy and 1,000 light repairs to locomotives, over 4,000 heavy repairs to carriages, and 11,000 to wagons. All this with a total staff of around 10,000, of whom, of course, only about 8,000 would be workshop staff, and these carried a large 'outstation' workload for the railway and docks! Much credit must go to the management teams in the two Works for the organization of labour and work methods necessary to obtain these output figures. The wide use of short time working, distasteful though it was to all, greatly lessened the number who would have received notices to leave. As a result only a comparatively small number left not to return, and the basic large skilled staff was kept intact for the inevitable rise in workload. In the Locomotive Works, this function had been skilfully carried out by the Manager, R. A. G. Hannington, but he met a sudden and tragic death by an accident on 26th June 1937 at the early age of 53. Entering the service as a pupil under Churchward in 1903 he venerated his old chief and applied his principles assiduously throughout his career. He was succeeded by K. J. Cook who was at the time his assistant in the Locomotive Works, and H. Randle was now appointed in Cook's place.

The large rise in workload again put great strain on the various services in the Works, but the provisions made since 1920 were such that they were able to accept the extra output. Of great assistance was the addition at the central boiler station of a large Ruth's steam accumulator. Peak calls for steam at certain parts of the day were met by the storage capacity

Plate 184: No. 7800 *Torquay Manor* on leaving the Works, in unlined green, on 13th January 1938. The boiler was the new lighter standard No. 14 type.

British Rail

Plate 185: The first 'buffet' or 'quick lunch' car, No. 9631 of July 1934. This vehicle is still beautifully preserved by enthusiasts.

British Rail

of this equipment of 30,000lb of steam at line pressure. The steam mains layout was such that there was a constant supply into the unit and when the demand was low, boilers could be completely shut down for periods, rather than work at low efficiency. Steam would then be drawn from the accumulator. This huge steel reservoir was 80 ft. 3 in. long and 15 ft. 6 in. in diameter, resembling an airship resting on expansion supports. At Kemble the steam pumps, which had been in use since 1903, were augmented in the same well by two electrically driven turbine pumps, each capable of moving 75,000 gallons per hour against a head of 229 ft. The steam engines and pumps remained in position as a standby, but the boilers were made redundant. For emergencies, arrangements were made for a small locomotive to stand on the pump house siding and supply steam via flexible and fixed piping to the steam pumps. This arrangement released a large number of stokers which were difficult to recruit. At the same time yet another bore of 24 in. diameter was made in the well outside the pump house, and at a depth of only 72 ft. 5 in. struck a large fissure in the oolite, considerably increasing the yield. The maximum daily demand had now reached 2 million gallons, the yearly requirement being 650 million gallons. A new laundry was opened in the C&W Works in 1938 on the eastern boundary, replacing the original basement laundry, dating from 1893, in Sheppard Street. It was fully equipped with modern laundry machinery and dealt with a large amount of the GWR requirements for refreshment rooms and hotels as well as the stores and LC&W departments. A measure of the C&W workload may be gained from the statistics of the paint mill. In 1937 this mill produced 1.5 million lb of wagon paint, 900,000lb of carriage paint, 30,000lb of timber filling and 20,000lb of stopping.

In the carriage body shop, where the main work was still in timber, although sheathed in steel sheet, a special machine was installed for preparing the longitudinal frame members on which the body was built. This was supplied by T. Robinson & Son of Rochdale. The machine bed itself was 48 ft. long, but with the roller approaches placed at each end and on which further machining was done, the whole unit was 190 ft. long. Although its official name was a 'Trenching Boring & Reaming Machine', there was only one name to which it answered in the Works — the 'Loch Ness Monster'!

Although the effects of the recession on the town of Swindon were small compared with the suffering of such communities as Jarrow and others in the north of England, the Corporation could see that it was not in the common interest to remain a one industry town. In the middle of the decade the first steps were taken to alter previous policy and try to attract more industry to the area. A large council housing estate had been developed at Pinehurst to the north of the

town, and further expansion was now within their control since the borough boundaries had been considerably extended on 1st October 1928. This had increased its area from 4,264 to 6,020 acres (1,723 to 2,432 hectares), most of the increase being undeveloped land. Little effect could be expected in the short term and it was the coming war which was to bring about the transfer of firms to the area. Although outside the borough area, the firm of Vickers moved to an extensive site complete with airfield, in 1937/8, and this acquisition can be seen as the first real move in the future industrial expansion of the district.

The increase of responsibilities due to the boundary changes had meant that the old Town Hall was becoming too small for its purpose, and the building of new civic offices on a site nearby in Euclid Street was approved and put in hand. These new buildings were opened by the Duke of Gloucester on 5th July 1938, and after the ceremony he made visits to the main industries in the town, including a short visit to the Locomotive Works. A rather more colourful Royal visit had been made about a year previously, at the time of the Coronation of King George VI. This was by the Alake of Abeokuta, the Paramount Chief of Nigeria. This gentleman, 6 ft. 4 in. in height, clothed in splendid gold and white robes covered with decorations of all colours, was accompanied around the Works by an equally be-decked entourage, including a huge gold state umbrella, which was held above him even when on the footplate of a locomotive.

The Munich crisis of 1938, with its relief of war averted, nevertheless marked a change in outlook and increased rather than decreased steps being taken to put Britain on a firmer war footing. Particularly on the railways, air raid precaution (ARP) methods and drills were stepped up amongst staff, and steps to improve the defence of the huge Works were put in hand, including the provision of air raid shelters. Pre-fabricated material for such purposes was prepared in the Factory and sent to other depots and there was a concentration on rolling stock repairs, to make ready for use every locomotive and vehicle that was available. There had always been Territorial Reserve units based at the drill hall situated in the GWR Park, usually connected with units such as the Royal Wilts Yeomanry. There was need for a unit of another type, and H. Randle, then Assistant Locomotive Works Manager, formed the 5th Anti-Aircraft Divisional Workshop Company, RAOC (later REME). This was to become very much a 'Swindon Works' unit, although many volunteers came from other parts of the town. Most of the officers were recruited from those of the drawing office or Works who were already graduate engineers. A good selection of veterans of the previous war, older tradesmen, storemen and clerks, formed the warrant officer and NCO sections, and the rank and file came largely from apprentices and young journeymen. There was of course the added attraction of a yearly bounty and two weeks paid extra leave for the annual camp. At the outbreak of war this was the only unit of its kind up to strength.

Things were still progressing in the hope that war could be averted. Nationally, the political moves for 'Equal Treatment with the Road Industry at the Hands of Parliament' became very active, and a deputation of the Chairmen and General Managers of the four groups met with the Minister of Transport to discuss the matter. The last of the schemes under the Guaranteed Loan Act at Swindon was commenced. This was yet another carriage stock shed, but this time the place chosen utilized the site of Newburn House, empty since Churchward's death and not required by C. B. Collett, and a strip of land westwards to Wootton Bassett Road, which, although owned by the GWR since 1900, had been used as a part of the Westcott Recreation Ground. This land was now filled up to rail level, and a building, 1,800 ft. long and 122 ft. wide, with six tracks inside capable of stabling 265 carriages under cover, was erected. It took 35,000 wagon loads of spoil from other parts of the system to build the land up, and it was about three years before the final structure was erected and was completed in 1939, after which there was little stock to be stored! This additional 5 acres of roofed buildings brought the total in the Works

to 79 (32 hectares), but this figure excluded small outbuildings. The Works now extended over an area of 326 acres (132 hectares), the maximum it was ever to cover, and by far the largest engineering complex in Europe, if not the World.

Events in Europe in August 1939 made it clear to many that war was becoming unavoidable, and suitable arrangements were put in hand. As in 1914–18, the Railway Executive Committee came into being and before hostilities commenced on 3rd September 1939, eighteen selected LMS carriages were already in Swindon Works for conversion to ambulance vehicles, 12 for overseas use and 6 for home use. The 5th AA Divisional Workshop Company went to their annual camp in Cornwall in August and were not to return to work, sub units taking up their war stations spread over the south and West Country. Being up to strength they also manned 1st Division depots in the London area at Hemel Hempstead and Kidbrook. In their own area they stretched from Swindon to Southampton and the Isle of Wight and west to Plymouth and even Fowey. Within the Works the well organized war arrangements came into operation, and for a second time in 25 years Swindon Works was ready to serve the country with its specialist skills and services. But this time its resources were to be stretched to the limits of endurance, and it was to emerge into a completely different world.

Chapter Nine

1939~1950 World War Two and the End of the GWR

Whilst it is true to say that people were expecting hostilities with Germany to commence sooner or later, the country was not as prepared for war as in 1914. Disarmament policies in the previous ten years had reduced an already depleted defence strength on land, sea and air. Only in 1937/8 did the government noticeably react to the situation in Europe. A major problem was the supply of the necessary equipment for the forces. As a result, in addition to the factories normally producing such items, new 'shadow factories' started to appear in different areas of the country, but not until 1939 was there any appreciable move to assess the capacity of the large railway factories. Although some heavy work was undertaken early on at certain factories such as Horwich, where Matilda tanks were put in hand, action at Swindon was limited to exploring possibilities and giving quotations. In fact there was a distinct reluctance on the part of some, and C. B. Collett in particular, to get embroiled in munition work. This was possibly due to experience during World War I, when there is evidence of difficult situations arising with armament work tending at times to affect equally important normal railway work, with resultant wrangles between different government departments, the Works being 'piggy in the middle'.

As mentioned at the end of the previous chapter, carriage conversions to ambulance trains were on hand as soon as war was declared, and the GWR had had the foresight to ensure that all rolling stock was in first class condition. It was, therefore, inevitable that no extra overtime was necessary at Swindon for normal throughput and this matter did not pass unnoticed by the staff, particularly when most other factories were working as much overtime as possible. But it showed that a much needed manufacturing capacity was available, and this state of affairs could not be overlooked.

By the outbreak of war, some of the Dean standard goods locomotives had, of course, already been withdrawn and cut up. However nine, which had recently been withdrawn from service pending disposal, were reinstated and, as in the previous conflict, a large number were 'called up' for military service. At first 100 were called for but eight more were added later. During 1939/40, the main batch was overhauled and fitted with the Westinghouse brake, and automatic train control equipment was removed. Some were fitted with additional pannier tanks and condensing gear. Fifteen of these locomotives were dealt with at Eastleigh, and seventy nine were already in France when the German invasion of that country succeeded. They were then formally sold to the government and written off. Many of these 'lost' engines continued to work in France under the occupation, but, of course, some had been destroyed. Amongst these locomotives were some which had served abroad in World War I. It is interesting to know that at the cessation of hostilities, many of those left in France were sent to China under the UNRAA arrangements, two went beyond the Iron Curtain, a few went to Tunisia and then Italy, and some were returned to Britain for cutting up. During hostilities these locomotives were replaced on the GWR by loans of 0-6-0 types from the LNER and LMSR and GWR reinstatements of withdrawn stock.

Arrangements to combat air raids, in common with other places, had been made before the war started. The Works 'hooter' was the main air raid warning system of the town, although the ubiquitous sirens were also installed. Shelters were provided in strategic places throughout the Factory. Due to the type of buildings there, it was possible for some of these to be above ground, and good use was made of the built up nature of parts of the land where it was easy to excavate and install suitable bunkers, often formed from old boiler plate. The disused portion of the underground foot subway, originally running from 'Newburn' towards the hamlet of Shaw, became the main shelter for the 'A' shop, with an entrance inside the shop. One great problem was the blackout. Most of the Works buildings relied on roof lights because of the large area they covered, and all of these and the side windows had to be painted over at once. In a few cases it was possible to leave a small portion of the lower side windows clear, but these were provided with night screens, particularly in the hot shops. This meant that nearly all work had to continue in artificial light and this was still mostly gas, a great difficulty for some of the exacting work carried out. It did bring the benefit of speeding the introduction of electric lighting generally however. In the first instance, all machine tools were equipped with individual electric lights as soon as the equipment was available. Light anti-aircraft posts, armed with machine guns, were established on the roofs of some of the shops. Some 400 staff volunteered for ARP duties and were suitably trained. Later, when fire-watching against incendiary attack came, nearly

Plate 186: The first Swindon version of the diesel railcar. No. 19 was completed in March 1941.

British Rail

600 people were on the roster. These duties, although essential, interfered with output, but when, in later years the Factory was working seven days a week, no doubt the change of activity was beneficial.

In this war, security became of paramount importance and, as a result, less definitive information is available concerning the special work undertaken, as compared with World War I. However, many of the more important undertakings were photographed for future reference, and this collection is useful in supplementing the comparatively small amount of information published. It is perhaps best to deal now with this war work as a whole. The majority of the munitions work was done during the years 1941 to 1943. Much of 1940 was spent in fulfilling small orders erratically placed, and preparing staff and equipment for new production lines, whilst, by 1943, the American continent had become the armament supplier for the total war effort. The pressure on British factories could then be eased in line with material shortages.

One of the earliest large jobs undertaken at Swindon was the provision, from the wheel shop, of 12,500 armoured car turret swivel bearings, and in other general shops for thousands of parts for the many types of tank then in production and, in particular, the provision of 251 complete Rackham clutches and 320 sets of final drives for tanks. Both these items called for a considerable amount of fine machining and fitting for which the superior craftsmanship of the staff was especially suited. This concentration of skill, however, could not be allowed under war conditions. Whilst railway work in general was a reserved occupation, the existing skills of the country had to be reallocated to man all the new factories or production units being set up. It was not long before the powers of direction of labour were operating, and many of the skilled Swindon craftsmen were being sent to such places, to be replaced generally by new staff, often female, who had to be trained to undertake such work as could be assimilated in a short time. A great reshuffle of work had to be made, therefore, so that the best use could be made of the staff available. Special amenities also had to be provided for the influx of female staff. As in World War I, areas were allocated for setting up the new activities in the most suitable shops. All these requirements were an added burden to the management.

The Battle of Britain, fought in the skies, soon brought demands for many replacement parts for damaged aircraft and 171,000 components for Hurricane aircraft were machined in the Works. The carriage finishers shop also produced some replacement assemblies for this machine, built, as it was, of mainly timber airframes. Towards the end of 1940 came demands for both 3 in. mortar bombs and aircraft bombs. Some 6,000 of the former were produced, but the latter was to be a major under-

taking, starting with bombs of the 250 lb variety. At this time, Swindon undertook the design, assisted by the Ministry of Aircraft Production (MAP), of new heavy 2,000 lb and then 4,000 lb bombs. The first dozen were completed and ready for testing only a few days after a visit from ministry officials! After this 88 were quickly ready for live filling and operational use on a raid to Essen. Over 2,000 of these large 4,000 lb bombs were supplied from a grand total of 60,000 of all sizes. As in the previous war, bullet proof mountings and shields were built for Hotchkiss guns, 600 for the twin type gun and 3,000 for the single barrel type. Remaining with guns, special rail vehicles were adapted for mounting 6 in. naval type guns, and 14 in. and 16 in. naval gun barrels were received and stored, being loaded on to other specially prepared vehicles for distribution to the naval bases as required. Parts by the thousand for Bofors, 3.7 in. A A, and 25 pounder guns were manufactured, together with 400 non-recoil mountings for 6 pounder guns for merchant ships. Perhaps the two most interesting jobs were the manufacture of a number of multiple pom-pom guns for the Admiralty. Only the barrels and breeches were supplied, all the complicated swivel and elevating gear being made at Swindon and assembled for Admiralty inspection. Eastleigh Works of the Southern Railway also assisted in some of the machined parts for this venture. The other large undertaking was the redesigning, in the drawing office, and subsequent manufacture of the huge mountings for a 13.5 in. hyper-velocity gun to be mounted on the Kent coast for cross channel firing. This manufactured equipment was installed in Kent by specialist armament personnel. One piece of gun work of a different type was the preparation, in the carriage works, of a full size timber replica of a combined 95 mm and a medium Besa machine gun for use by the Ministry of Tank Design in the development of the tank turret into which these two weapons were later to be mounted. This was a fine example of the carriage finishers' craftsmanship.

The same shop undertook the manufacture of a full size model of a midget submarine, and subsequently built 50 superstructures for these craft. The superstructures were of mahogany with canvas side sheets which protected the diver pilot and his assistant from the water flow when submerged. Remaining with the Navy, No. 13 C & W shop undertook the manufacture, first of jigs, then of many complete landing craft for sea borne invasion. Only the diesel engines and propellers and shafts were supplied, and one such craft was turned out every eight days. Shell manufacture also became important again, and for this the Ministry of Supply took over a section of the 1930-built No. 24 shop and installed two production lines for 25 pounder shells, and 63,000 were made. The 'B' production line was lifted and shipped to America, but it is possible that this

Plate 187: Manufacture of the first 2,000lb and 4,000lb bombs, 'somewhere in Britain' — actually in the locomotive plate (L2) shop.

British Rail

Plate 188: Mountings for the 'hyper-velocity' 13.5 in. calibre cross-channel guns:-
a) The planing of mounting segments.

British Rail

Plate 189: b) A complete mounting set out in locomotive boiler (V) shop. Note the depressing effect of blacking out the roofing glass. One of the 'Wageor' boiler working frames can be seen in the background.

British Rail

231

Plate 190: Craftmanship at its best. A full size timber mock-up of combined 95mm and Besa machine guns for the Ministry of Tank Design. It was executed in the Carriage & Wagon carriage finishers (No. 7) shop.

British Rail

Plate 191: One of the fifty sets of midget submarine superstructures for the Admiralty, fitted to the dummy propellant body. Note the surrounding screens for this 'hush-hush' work.

British Rail

Plate 192: Building some of the landing craft in a bay of the wagon frame (No. 13) shop. As all roof glass was blacked out, worked had to proceed at all times, in artificial light.

British Rail

Plate 193: One of the many landing craft made in the Carriage & Wagon Works. Too wide for rail traffic, they were despatched by road.

British Rail

now lies at the bottom of the sea off Northern Ireland, as the ship on which it was loaded was believed torpedoed. Nearly half a million copper driving bands were made for many shell calibres.

One effect of the fall of France was that ports on the east coast of Britain became dangerous to use, with the result that an east-west move took place, with those ports facing Ireland and the Atlantic receiving all the imports and handling troop movements. Although well equipped already, their capacity had to be increased rapidly, and being impracticable to move much equipment from the closed ports, new had to be supplied. Swindon's contribution to this was the supply and erection of thirty four 3 ton dockside movable cranes for ship loading and unloading. Naturally the Swindon ones went to the GWR's own South Wales ports.

Other contributions to war work were the manufacture of 125 searchlight projectors of the 90 cm size, 1½ million various drop forgings, 21,865 sets of quick release gear for barrage balloons, 27,157 timber components for Bailey bridges, 125,000 parts for AA predictors, generator sets for the newly introduced radar sets, and the provision of bodies for many types of road vehicles, (wireless vans, mobile canteens, armoured cars). Another section of the C&W No. 24 shop was handed over to Messrs. Short Bros. for Spitfire production and the newly completed 'Newburn' stock shed became a stores depot. One huge asset to the Works in all this change in output was its ability to produce its own cutting tools for both machine and hand use, together with jigs and gauges. Indeed these facilities were in great demand from all quarters. Recorded amongst the output of the tool room was 62,936 ground thread taps, 10,000 milling cutters, 1,000 sets of screwing dies and 1,300 thread milling hobs, much of this going to aircraft factories.

The impression must not be given that the Works took all this in its stride! The reverse was the case due, rather naturally, to all the different ministries working without co-ordination to get their contracts completed, and these authorities were not much concerned with the real reason for which the Works existed. As stated earlier, the GWR stock was in first class condition in 1939, but the effects of war conditions rapidly took its toll. In particular, locomotive boilers began to suffer from indifferent washing out and maintenance at sheds under black-out conditions, stopgap staff, and almost continuous use. Although there was a locomotive building programme in being for which materials were still hopefully available, the main work was maintenance and with the shortage of steel, and particularly copper, now in evidence, the government departments belatedly discerned the folly of loading railway works with munitions to the detriment of .assuring their proper operation. The inevitable reaction was the clearance of as many con-

tracts as possible from this department and a complete upset of the labour position which these changes had made away from locomotive skills. Added to this there were orders to be placed for additional freight locomotives, thirty three of them to the GWR 28XX design, and ninety to the not dissimilar LMS Stanier '8F' class of the same wheel arrangement. These latter WD engines were required both for use in this country and for places such as the Iran—Russia supply route. This large order for WD freight locomotives, coming as it did just as the big orders for other munitions were in full flow, created the conditions feared by Collett at the beginning of the war, necessitating rapid changes in priorities in the Locomotive Works. The WD locomotives were ordered under four Lots: No. 348 (10 locomotives), 349 (20), 351 (10) and 353 (50), all orders being placed between 20th February and 14th August 1942. Building rate was controlled partly by the availability of materials. In the event, the last order was reduced by 10 on 2nd January 1945, so that in all only 80 were built, (Nos. 8400 to 8479). Some 1,600 wagons were required also for WD service. All assembled between September 1941 and January 1942 at the Ashford Works of the Southern Railway, most of the components came from other centres, Swindon being amongst them.

At last, Collett was persuaded to retire. Already 70 years of age, his effectiveness had declined in later years. His assistant, John Auld, was, in fact, a few months older than Collett and although wanting to retire much earlier, had been encouraged by him to stay on. Auld, however, felt that he had 'done his stint' and his resignation forced Collett to do the same, both leaving in July 1941, thereby ending a reign of 19 years. During that time there had emerged the 'Castles', 'Kings' and 'Halls', and other notable locomotives for various duties. All these had kept the GWR in the forefront of efficient railway operation. It was not until after nationalization that the real capabilities of the 'King' class were to be realized, and one must question the lack of impetus from Collett in not discovering this sooner. However, his withdrawn relationship with his staff did not encourage the same spirit of co-operation in such matters, as would have been the situation under Churchward. W. N. Pellow, in conversation, made the point that from Collett's appointment, until the time he (Pellow) left for a divisional post, the new CME never once entered the drawing office. Yet Churchward had done so almost as a daily ritual. Nevertheless the years between the wars saw the railway equipped almost completely with modern locomotives of most efficient and economic design, together with very acceptable carriages. Perhaps the greatest achievement was the introduction and maintaining of high degrees of dimensional tolerance, and excellent standards of boiler maintenance. This led to increasing periods

Plate 194: Frederick William Hawksworth, Chief Mechanical Engineer 1941—1949.

Author's Collection

between major overhaul. A few years later it was to be noted by some railway engineers that the engines being brought into Swindon for repair carried limits of wear equivalent to those with which engines were being outshopped from other factories after repair!

Collett was succeeded by F. W. Hawksworth, a Swindonian by birth, his father having held positions in the drawing office. His grandfather had been a foreman at Coleham, Shrewsbury. Attending first Sanford Street Boys' School and transferring to the new North Wilts Technical Schools when opened, to obtain secondary education, he spent his holidays at Shrewsbury where his grandfather used to take him into Coleham shops and interest him in things mechanical. This old gentleman also owned a steam launch which young Fred was able to potter with at weekends. He commenced an apprenticeship in Swindon Works in August 1898. He attended evening classes, (this was before the day studentship period), and his other interest was in the St. Mark's Church choir, of which he was a lifelong member. His father often undertook small design and drawing commissions for outside parties and passed some of these on to Fred as he gained experience. One of these jobs was an electric lighting scheme for the fairly new market building in the New Town. Entering the drawing office, he soon attracted the attention of Churchward, and one of his early major jobs there was the frame design work of *The Great Bear*, and the main frame drawings of this locomotive carry his signature. Attaining the rank of assistant chief draughtsman in August 1923 under O. E. F. Deverell, he succeeded to the senior post on the untimely demise, at the early age of 50, of Deverell on 4th April 1925. He was appointed assistant to Collett when Stanier left at the beginning of 1932. He was, therefore, reared in the overall engineering tradition

of Churchward. Being appointed in wartime, however, he was under the restraints of the time and rarely in a position to have a free hand, the Mechanical Engineering Committee controlling any new building for the major part of the time. The Board appointed F. C. Hall, the outdoor assistant, as principal assistant, which gave a distinctive change to the top team, but under the conditions of the period this was doubtless an astute move.

The centenary of the Works passed virtually unnoticed in January 1943, and another 25 years passed before suitable celebrations took place. In the town there was much change. A large number of Swindonians of both sexes were away in the forces or had been directed to work elsewhere. To balance this there were many 'billetted' in the town, either to avoid centres affected by heavy air raids, or, more particularly, manning the new industries and activities brought to the town. Although not more deeply inland than many centres which had received the unwelcome attention of the Luftwaffe, why this great engineering and transport centre received such scant attention from air raiders remains an enigma. Very little damage was sustained in the town, and virtually none in the Works or other war factories. There are the remains of an incendiary bomb which fell close to the gas holders in the Works Museum. Vicker's factory at South Marston, established just before the war, was engaged in aircraft production in a big way, and the equipment firm of Plessey had transferred a large portion of their capacity to the town, occupying first the old 'Powder Factory' of the previous war. Other factories were in the area such as the euphemistically named 'Marine Mountings' to the south of the town. All these moves meant a great change to the make-up of the population, which was never to revert to its pre-war form. What it did succeed in doing was to bring about the wish of the borough to have diversification of industry, and it was hoped that the end of the war would find the new firms wanting to stay, and this is what came about.

Local defence was in the hands of the Home Guard. The GWR were early in the field in forming units at all railway centres with the specific purpose of guarding railway property. Swindon Works had its own unit, the 13th Wilts Battalion (GWR) with Lt. Col. Dyer as Commanding Officer, and office facilities and staffing were provided by the Works on a full or part-time basis as required. All these units did great service and were not stood down until November 1944 when the allied landings in Europe had considerably progressed. The Swindon Battalion had its own band, and this was 'released' to other railway units, not so well blessed, when required for ceremonial.

The 'trip' holiday was suspended as an event as soon as hostilities commenced, as there were limits placed on travelling in any case, and many of the south and south-west haunts of Swindon people became restricted areas for either strategic or troop training reasons. Many did not take holidays at all, and those who did spent them at home or in the local countryside, which, when all is considered, is one of the most beautiful in England. Help was always welcomed on farms, and a few days working in the fresh air was as good as riding donkeys on the sands at Weston or Weymouth. Six such holidays were missed in the years 1940–1945 inclusive, but the 'trip' was re-instituted in July 1946. Although, naturally, not on the same scale as previously, many people took this chance to get away. Because of the difficult conditions still encountered, such special trains as could be spared left on the Saturday afternoon at the beginning of the holiday. There was, however, another reason for this change from the pre-war Thursday night and Friday commencement. This was because, at last, the holiday was now of two weeks duration, and had to conform to normal weekend bookings at resorts, and, in addition, it was now two weeks with pay. Gone were the days of the 'grand march past'.

Entertainment during the war years was indeed difficult, but much was organized locally by amateur organizations of all types. Theatricals and concert parties were activities in which railway people had always excelled, and many people worked hard to keep engagements for local workers and troops. One such group was the Swindon Male Voice Choir, formed in 1919, under the baton of W. J. Evans. This choir had gone from strength to strength, and from 1928 and on through the war period, was under the direction of George Morse of the C&W Works. It was formed mainly of railwaymen, and has, at the time of writing, just celebrated its Golden Jubilee. A civic undertaking of note got under way in 1943 with the opening of the first public library financed by the rates. The Mechanics Institution library, formed a century earlier, was, by now, very large indeed, and had in addition a considerable membership by special subscription, providing for non-railway employees. This had lessened the priority of providing civic facilities of a similar nature, but wartime conditions had made it clear that this could be left no longer. It first opened in part of the large

Plate 195: The GWR Male Voice Choir, on 1st July 1930, after winning at the Lydney Music Festival. Conductor George Morse is 8th from left in the front row.

British Rail

store of William McIlroy in Regent Street, which was of course very understocked just then, and the library remained there until a few years after the war.

One item more beneficial to railway people than usual in wartime, and not mentioned previously, was the coal and timber issues. For many decades it had been possible for railway staff to obtain coal supplies, at concessionary rates, bought at bulk prices by the Company. Over the years two coal wharfs had been set up in the Works, one near the station and the other in Rodbourne Road at the north end of the Works. Coal was sold in units of 2 and 4 cwt. and ordered from staff and shop offices on a fortnightly basis. Suitable 'coal tickets' were issued for the amount ordered and the cost deducted from pay packets. Delivery was made by coalmen with their shire horses and flat carts built in No. 17 C & W shop. With all the wartime difficulties of distribution, although the private coal merchant may not have obtained regular supplies, the railway coal supply rarely failed. Buying steadily over summer and winter also enabled the amount available to be eked out and delivered more realistically. House coal and anthracite were the two grades available, but, of course, during the war it was a case of what could be obtained, and briquettes were well in evidence, and later on the well named 'nutty slack'. An extra privilege was the timber sales which came in the form of 'refuse' and 'old timber', and before the war, sales had amounted to 1,500 tons a year. The 'refuse' could be either the outsides of logs from the primary sawmills or offcuts from the ends of planks or butts. Old timber was from broken down wagons or carriages. This was not delivered by the railway, but could be collected from timber sales yards set up for the purpose, although 'wood tickets' were issued as for coal. All types of transport could be seen, in the town, bringing home the spoils from these sales, and there were a few entrenpreneurs who could collect timber in bulk from the yards and deliver it to the houses for a small commission. As is the way of things, such men often had the pick of what was available. Most of these services lasted well into nationalization years, finally disappearing some 10 to 15 years before this volume was written. During the war years, timber was not so readily available, but from time to time wood, which was too poor for 'chipping' processes was sold to eager purchasers.

Another activity carried on over the years at Swindon, but particularly busy during wartime, was the special loads yard, situated on sidings to the north of the station and part of the Carriage Works. Many of the special vehicles built over the years for the transport of specific items such as transformers, together with a selection of the vehicles code named 'crocodile', 'macaw', etc., were kept here ready for the particular duties which they could perform. Large stocks of timber packing, wedges, securing chains and 'bagging' were always available. Often the awkward loads were pieces of specialist equipment made in the Factory for docks or other depots, machine tools on transfer, etc. Here they were carefully loaded and packed ready for transit. Staff, known as special load inspectors, visited places where such items were awaiting despatch and returned to prepare vehicles for the item concerned, having special timber cradles made if necessary. These men often travelled with the special load in transit, if necessary, and always if it was 'out of gauge', and ran under strict control when normal traffic would not interfere with its movement.

An organization which has been particularly well supported at Swindon Works is the St. John Ambulance movement. A Works group of the movement was formed around 1883—1885, and, after a shaky start, grew rapidly into a very efficient body, being supported whole-heartedly by the Company in general, and the local management and medical officers in particular. Starting with only a handful of recruits, the strength of trained ambulance men grew steadily, reaching its highest figure in 1937, when some 500 were serving a staff of just over 10,500 through 103 dressing stations. With a reduced total staff in 1980, upwards of 13.5 per cent of them are available to render invaluable service to their fellow men and women. Long service awards upwards of 25 years are quite common, and it is a measure of the dedication of these people that over the years 47 members have been promoted to the rank of 'serving brother' (or sister) and 6 to the rank of 'officer'. During both the war periods their service was especially appreciated in the Factory, but continued devotion to this service for nearly a century has been of inestimable value to the workforce generally. Incidentally, the training of first aiders, over numerous years, has been ably assisted by 'Phyllis', indeed, she is older now than any of the members in the Works, having been a member of the staff since 1923. A long service perhaps? However, as she is a well looked after skeleton, housed in a suitably tall box, there is a good chance of many more decades of service yet!

Other locomotive building proceeded during the war to meet shortages, but naturally not at the rate which had been the norm a few years previously. Not only were materials difficult to obtain, but the repair programme was becoming very heavy indeed due to the inevitable conditions of operation. Other than the 28XX freight locomotives already mentioned, the output was limited to 0-6-0 pannier tanks, 20 more of the Collett 2251 0-6-0 tender engines, and further additions to the 'Hall' mixed traffic class. In the drawing office Hawksworth was carrying out some preparatory design work on new weight and main dimensional diagrams. The collection of locomotive diagrams dating from this period bears this out. Hawksworth was obviously keen to produce engines to his own design, but war conditions limited his ambition. However, a redesign of the frame arrangement, including new cylinders and a longer wheelbase for the bogie, resulted in the 'Modified Hall' or '6959' class. From now on most of this class carried 3-row superheaters, and individual engines carried various experimental items for evaluation in service. The first of these, No. 6959, appeared in March 1944 and thereafter all the class were built to the new pattern. Hawksworth's wish, however, was to produce a new passenger engine, and his thoughts inevitably turned to the Pacific arrangement. In Hawksworth's 90th year, the author had a conversation with him, and he spoke at some length on this matter, and it is to be regretted that this was not tape recorded, although it is doubtful if Hawksworth would have encouraged such an exercise! He was frustrated in his project of building even a prototype, as it would have been a passenger engine, and not suitable for mixed traffic. As such, it could not be allowed by the Railway Executive Committee responsible, although the SR Pacifics were allowed as they came into the mixed traffic category. He found a compromise in the 1000 'County' class. This class emerged from the shops in August 1945 and was, in many ways, a final expression of Churchward's 'Saints'. Most of the new features of the '6959' class were included in the new locomotive, but a non-standard departure to 6 ft. 3 in. diameter driving wheels was made, a dimension which had been considered for the Pacific. The boiler, (standard No. 15), was completely new and pressed to an unprecedented 280 p.s.i., but using the same flanging blocks as the LMS '8F' WD engines, which were, of course, still available, and in use at Swindon. The first of the class also carried a double chimney, a glimpse of things to come, but only after extensive experimental work. The tractive effort, at 32,580 lb, was slightly higher than the 'Castles' and therefore high for a two cylinder arrangement. They did particularly good work between Plymouth and Penzance on that heavily graded and curved section, and were much liked for their 'punch' by the drivers in that area.

More 'Castles' were also built; 10 in 1946, with more to follow in 1950. The point that has to be made is, however, that a new Pacific would not necessarily have been a 'super-King'. It was not the policy of the GWR to run increasingly longer and heavier trains, as was being done on the LMS and LNE Railways. The argument was that a more frequent service was the best way of solving loading problems, and that longer trains, (the maximum was usually 13 vehicles), would necessitate extensive alterations to stations serving the main lines and, in many cases, extension of platforms was virtually impossible. Any time gained in running would, therefore, be negated by the need for time-consuming 'moving forward' to release passengers from coaches left standing off the platforms.

The end of the war brought long awaited relief to the pressures at Swindon and was celebrated with the same fervour as elsewhere. The railways of the country were, by this time, in a state approaching collapse due to the huge backlog of maintenance in all departments. It was evident that a long struggle was ahead if the railways were to regain the level of efficiency they had enjoyed in 1939. Acute shortages of materials and, in particular, fuel, were to continue for a long time and the General Election of 1945 brought a government into power intent on nationalization of major undertakings such as railways and the coal industry. Within the shops the blackout paint had been removed at the earliest opportunity and the special staff brought in to assist with war work returned to their homes. With them went most, and eventually all, of the female labour who had proved their worth so much during the dark days of war. Although the political and supply position engendered a standstill situation generally, certain moves at Swindon showed that there were still plans for the future. Whilst the General Manager, Sir James Milne, was in Switzerland in 1946 with F. W. Hawksworth, for the International Railway Congress, an order was placed with Messrs. Brown Boveri for a gas turbine locomotive. A second was ordered shortly afterwards from Messrs. Metropolitan-Vickers. The first of these, No. 18000, was only the third in the world, but the type was seen as a likely alternative to the diesel-electric locomotive now entering service in large numbers, particularly in North America. It was also hoped that the type could eventually be developed to use an indigenous fuel in the shape of pulverized coal, although at this time the problems of turbine blade erosion had not been fully realized. The extra problems which fly ash would have given in this context is not difficult to envisage!

With virtually prototype machines, there were many problems, both mechanical and electrical, arising. Although some of these were dealt with under the direction of engineers from the two respective suppliers, the shop staff at Swindon adapted themselves to the new problems, in the same easy way as they had during the recent war. The locomotives, although ordered in 1946, were not delivered until 1950 and 1951 respectively, when the effects of nationalization were already being felt. This readiness and ability to switch to new methods and processes was, indeed, an augury for the not too distant future when steam began to be superseded by a new form of prime mover.

One other major design, apart from a large batch of modified 0-6-0 pannier tanks of the 84XX and 94XX classes, which came from Hawksworth, was the 15XX outside cylinder 0-6-0 tank with Walschaert's valve gear. Built for easy maintenance and for long spells of continuous duty particularly in the Paddington area, these were a completely new and successful departure and received favourable comment from the running department.

With the low level of raw material and other shortages already alluded to, the repair programme, completed in 1946, was remarkable. As well as 80 new locomotives built, including the last 17 of the 2-8-0 WD type, heavy repairs were carried out on 733 engines, 2,520 carriages and 10,000 wagons, and 1,455 new wagons were built. Also of note were the 17 diesel mechanical shunters on order from private manufacturers and this illustrates the thinking evolving in the use of oil fuel, which was apparently then more easily obtainable than coal! Furthermore, a decision was taken to convert some steam locomotives to oil firing. In 1946 the GWR got away to a fine start with the adoption of a very good oil burner. Tried first on some 28XX freight locomotives, of which 20 were finally converted and renumbered in the 48XX range, the modification was extended to eleven in the 'Hall' class and five of the 'Castle' class engines. Design work was put in hand in the drawing office to install oil fuelling depots at strategic points on the system. These locomotives were found to steam easily and performed well, resulting in econo-

mies at running sheds where ash cleaning and handling was eliminated on those converted. But the government then found that it could not accept the balance of payments problems which large scale oil conversions would make, and so the scheme was brought to an end, and all locomotives were reconverted to coal by 1950. The GWR had been very pleased with the scheme, and unfortunately expended much more capital than the other railways. Considering the very few years which were to elapse before dieselization began to develop, it is to be regretted that the fuelling depots already built were not retained. More importantly, perhaps, the life of steam locomotives using oil fuel could have been extended considerably, allowing for a much more rational change-over to diesel traction than in fact occurred.

Changes of senior personnel at Swindon took place with the retirement of E. T. J. Evans from the Carriage & Wagon Works on 27th April 1946, after almost 23 eventful years as manager. He was, for about a year, succeeded by Hugh Randle, with C. T. Roberts taking up the post in 1947 when Randle returned to the Locomotive Works. This quick change was due to the appointment of K. J. Cook, (who had been awarded the OBE in recognition of his wartime

Plate 196: No. 5083 *Bath Abbey* (rebuilt on the frames of No. 4063 in 1937), as converted to oil burning in December 1946. A Swindon type portable fire extinguisher is fixed to the running plate near the cab.

British Rail

services in the Factory), to the post of Works assistant to the CME. Appointed a year later, in 1948, to principal assistant, Randle followed him as Works assistant, and C. T. Roberts and H. G. Johnson became managers of the Locomotive Works and C&W Works respectively in 1948.

The year 1947 saw the re-commencement of carriage building, when 100 were completed, together with 77 locomotives and 1,707 wagons. Heavy repairs were carried out on 777 locomotives, 2,722 carriages and 12,585 wagons, so that the Factory was slowly beginning to return to a more normal situation. Machine tool replacements were still hard to acquire, with often a 2 year waiting period; however, a few vital machines were obtained. A new Swindon Works brochure was issued, no doubt to be current before nationalization could place any limitations on its production. One employee becoming well known, in a different sphere at this time was Hubert Cook. An accomplished artist, his studies in the Works, particularly of spectacular processes such as welding, and executed in various media, brought wide acclaim and led to his acceptance in the professional artistic world.

Much attention had been given, in the years immediately prior to World War II, to development of testing proceedures, both on the test plant and with the dynamometer car. This work was pioneered by a group of young engineers of whom C. T. Roberts was one. They cast serious doubts on the theory of constant speed tests, which were particularly applicable to stationary testing. Churchward's work early in the century had shown the flaws in this type of approach if definitive results were to be expected. From these deliberations and discussions arose the basis of testing locomotives under conditions of constant evaporation rates, later to become the framework of 'controlled road testing'. This concept was brilliantly developed by S. O. Ell and another young team of men in the immediate post war years, and this system was to be adopted as standard by British Railways. Over a period of time, enough information was gathered, from different types of locomotive, to enable the experimental section to forecast realistic timings for specific train loads over any given section of line without leaving the office. Furthermore, the performance figures recommended would be for the most economical use of the locomotive concerned. S. O. Ell's breakthrough on this matter was based on his elegantly simple method of measuring the evaporation rate. This was done by an appliance constantly recording the pressures at both the base and the nozzle of the locomotive blast pipe, the differential so registered giving the necessary information. The footplate staff, by reading straight from the manometer could adjust cut-off accordingly for rising or falling gradients, using brakes if necessary to reduce speed, but keeping steam consumption steady. It was found that by this method, road testing and plant testing could give precisely the same evaluations technically, and thus the scope of testing was appreciably widened.

The inevitability of nationalization crept nearer when the Act of Parliament invoking the formation of the British Transport Commission (BTC), which was to take over all forms of public inland transport, received Royal Assent on 6th August 1947, with vesting date to be 1st January 1948. It had been the tradition at Swindon, and at other railway depots, to 'blow in' the New Year from all available engines in steam at the stroke of midnight, together with the firing of rows of detonators. The 'blow' on that fateful night heralded not only the new organization but to many in Swindon, with great sadness, the end of the 113 years of existence of the GWR. The population of Swindon had changed considerably during the war years, but it was still a railway town, engendered almost in its entirety by the GWR. The removal of the Board of Directors from the scene, who had corporately over that long period been the support and, often, mainstay of development, created a vacuum that was not readily discerned by many at that time of political change. But it was final and irrevocable. Although immediate effects were not apparent, it was gradually to be realized that the year by year fortunes of the great Works organization was to become a pawn in the wider field of railway and national politics. Although it may be argued that the removal of such control as the GWR imposed on the community was overdue, the corollary had to be accepted that with it went the self interest of the old company in always making the maximum use of what was one of its largest single assets. In future, work and development was not to fall into Swindon's lap as of right but had to be negotiated and worked for by every means at the disposal of the management and staff. If any part of this structure failed it could spell disaster, a lesson which took many years to learn and digest.

The onset of nationalization did not, and could not, bring much immediate change to personnel and work, but the new officers of the Railway Executive, working under the BTC, but not appointed by it, began to formulate their policy for a unified railway system. All the senior officers, and most of the middle management, now at Swindon, had been trained there, a state of affairs almost unique in the annals of its history, strange as that may seem. Equally, none of these officers were to be included in the higher echelons of the Railway Executive engineering management group now being formed. By and large, for reasons that were deemed right at the time, most were to come from the LMS fold. This was to have the same effect on Swindon in the ensuing years that the grouping had placed upon the internal machinations of the new LMS, LNE and

Plate 197: The new look carriage outline from Hawksworth. No. 787 of lot 1629 of June 1948, is seen with a low level destination board. This stock saw the re-introduction of the GWR coat of arms, replacing the 'roundel' of the 'thirties'.

British Rail

Plate 198: The locomotive testing plant was heavily utilized in the 'forties and 'fifties. This picture was taken during improved draughting experiments on No. 6001, resulting in alterations to the single chimney liner and the blast pipe.

British Rail

Southern Railways in 1923. This effect, however, was to be more vital and long lasting at Swindon than the dissensions of 1923/4.

The slowness of change was such that the building of locomotives to GWR design continued at a cautious rate. However, a long and detailed series of trials of a wide range of selected locomotive types was put in hand on specific routes all over the country. These 'Locomotive Exchange Trials' in 1948 aroused great interest, and the Swindon drawing office was much involved through S. O. Ell's experimental and research section. A large amount of the work fell on this department who, as has already been noted, were the acknowledged experts in such matters. A huge amount of technical information was amassed which could be used for the design of the new standard steam locomotives now envisaged. It was also a chance for the new senior engineering officers to 'pick the brains' of all the design centres now under their control. Many secrets were now laid bare, and some unpleasant discoveries were made!

F. W. Hawksworth retired on 31st December 1949 after serving the nationalized Western Region for two years, remaining, for that time, as CME. His full tenure of this post was the shortest of all the GWR locomotive 'chiefs', and lasted just 8½ years. His departure heralded the reorganization of the old department on the lines laid down by the new authority. It was to be split three ways. The close-knit structure of manufacture, repair, maintenance and running of all rolling stock which had served the GWR so well since the appointment of Joseph Armstrong in 1864, was now to give way to separate Mechanical & Electrical, Carriage & Wagon and Motive Power departments.

Thus K. J. Cook as Mechanical & Electrical Engineer succeeded to the locomotive factories and outstations work such as Severn Tunnel pumping station. Hugh Randle became the new Carriage & Wagon engineer, and W. N. Pellow, who had been Hawksworth's outdoor running assistant, became Motive Power Superintendent, taking charge of all engine sheds, (or motive power depots as they now became), and the entire locomotive divisional organization. These changes resulted in a lot of split loyalties for quite a time, and were to mean the removal of many members of the Swindon staff to other centres in due course. Docks and Waterways were to be hived off as completely separate nationalized bodies, and the loss of dock work, in particular, had a great impact on the work of the maintenance and machine shops at Swindon. But, again, the transfer of work was gradual and it took some time for the loss of work to be noticed.

The last express engine to be built by the GWR at Swindon was 'Castle' class No. 7007, and although carrying the name *Ogmore Castle* for a while, was appropriately named *Great Western* in January 1948, commemorating the old Company, and the first loco-

motive built at Swindon in 1846. It was actually being built in the Works just over 100 years after the original *Great Western*. A month later, in February 1948, No. 7001 was renamed *Sir James Milne* after the last General Manager who had retired at the demise of the Company. The remaining 'Castles', Nos. 7008 to 7037 inclusive, appeared between May 1948 and August 1950. The very last of the series was nameless until a visit to the Works on 15th November 1950 of H.R.H. Princess Elizabeth. The tour was almost a repeat of that carried out by her grandfather 26 years previously. Before taking her leave on the special train waiting for her near the engine weighbridge, she carried out the naming ceremony on No. 7037. When unveiled the name was seen to be *Swindon* and with the Borough Coat of Arms on the splasher below. This was, indeed, a fitting recognition of over a hundred years of steam locomotive development there.

It was not only the GWR itself which was being bowed out. We have, in this volume, followed the fortunes of that great organization the Medical Fund Society. It had reached its flowering by the turn of the century, and had continued to supply a full medical service of extraordinarily high standard to some 45,000 people in Swindon and district. Discussions of a National Health undertaking, together with other major changes in social services, had been taking place, particularly under the leadership of Lord Beveridge. One of the places in which study in depth had been made was at this great institution at Swindon, and the old members of the society are aware how much of the main ideas for the new Health Service were taken from it. There have been claims to have been the sole basis for the new scheme from other places, but they are under a great misapprehension. Fortunately, the committee of the society saw fit to issue, in 1947, an excellent history of its life entitled *A Century of Medical Service*. Prepared by Bernard Darwin, this small volume sets out very lucidly the story of its formation, early vicissitudes and later triumphs. It is no longer available, although copies may occasionally be found in reference libraries. The 'Medical Fund' as the whole organization was always called in Swindon, ended its service on 31st March 1949 when the new National Health Service commenced operations, and on that date a bronze memorial tablet was affixed to the wall of the 1892 block of consulting rooms and dispensary, — known to all Swindonians as 'the surgery'. It stated:-

'This tablet was erected to place on record the existence of the Great Western Railway Medical Fund Society, which, from 1847, provided a Medical Service for the employees of the railway and their dependants. The Society ceased to function upon the introduction of the National Health Service Act on 5th July 1948 and was dissolved on 31st March 1949.'

Plate 199: 'Castle' Class, No. 7037 *Swindon*, the last of the long series and built under nationalization, photographed a few days after the naming ceremony by H.R.H. Princess Elizabeth during her visit to the Works on 15th November 1950. The town's coat of arms is carried on the splasher. The engine was fitted with the final type of 4,000 gallon tender.

British Rail

The society remained in being for a while after the transfer of the medical staff and buildings, since the swimming, turkish and washing baths housed in the same building were not subject to the new service. These were eventually transferred to Swindon Corporation. At the close, there was a balance of £37,084 to distribute amongst the membership. Legal steps needed to be taken to remove the organization from the Register of Friendly Societies, and this was stated to have been the largest dissolution on record. When completed, the final meeting formally ending its life was held at 5.30 p.m. on 1st May 1950, 103 years after its formation. It is of note that 'the surgery' is still the main Health Centre in the town as this volume is written in 1980.

St. Mark's Parochial Church Council also, in 1945, issued a centenary volume describing the growth of the original church and the daughter churches which arose under its guidance. This volume is a fine record of the work and witness of the Anglican Church in the railway community and town.

The Mechanics Institution also reached a turning point in its long history. As with similar organizations, social changes were taking place. We have already heard how two weeks holiday, with pay, was now granted, and also, incidentally, a 44 hour week was introduced on 30th June 1947. For the shop staff, at least, the latter eliminated Saturday morning working, although the change came more slowly for technical and clerical staff in the offices. They had first, one Saturday off in three, then alternate ones, until abolished completely. The turning point of the Mechanics Institution, however, was the assumption by the railway itself, of the annual 'trip' holiday arrangements. These had always been made by the Institution and the travelling 'pass' for the holiday was dependent upon membership. Claimed to be an 'unfair' limitation by the unions, the arrangements for the holiday were taken over by the staff section in the Swindon general offices. Since the opening at last of a public library in Swindon during the war, the Institution's own service was paralleled, and although their library was to carry on for a few years more, it was eventually to close its doors, leaving an organization which was now only a social club, but still able to offer a wide range of excellent facilities for its members.

So within the period of a few months, the whole edifice, which had been carefully built up for over a century, slipped away. It was a period of great social change throughout the country, and in the main, people were not concerned with what was passing, they were concerned only with what they believed to be 'a brave new world'. Perhaps only the older people in Swindon realized what they were losing. Already 10 years had passed since World War II had commenced in 1939, and this represented the span of a fresh generation who had grown into adulthood in a completely different world of shortages, direction and controls. The large and important chapter in the life of Swindon had closed, and never more was it to be the 'Great Western at Swindon'.

Chapter Ten

1950~1980 Great Western No Longer

It is over 30 years since the life span of the GWR ceased, bringing to an official end the connection of that great company with the town of Swindon, but it is not desirable or, indeed, proper, that the story should suddenly come to an end there. The reasons are not hard to seek. The narrative could not finish abruptly at 23.59hrs. on 31st December 1947, since no noticeable change came over Swindon at that fateful hour, and it remained generally thus until about 1950, and even then the changes were gradual.

A new railway telephone exchange had been found very necessary during the war years, but it was not until 1948 that the authority to proceed could be obtained, and design work then commenced. With war conditions very much in mind, it was to be built on air raid shelter principals, with much of the equipment below ground level. The site selected was just outside the general offices, an area between the offices and the main Bristol line. The old telephone exchange had been in the south-west corner of this office block since the original installation in 1893. The new building required heavy excavation into the blue clay subsoil and, during this work, two matters caused certain excitement. The first was about half way down the excavation, when the top of what was discovered to be a four feet diameter brick culvert was uncovered, much to the consternation of the engineer who had prepared the drawings, (the author, one must be honest to state), and to the general amusement of the rest of the staff! It was averred that the navvies had inadvertently hit the Bakerloo line! But in more serious vein, the oldest plans knowingly available, and dating back to 1880, had been studied, and the area shown to be clear. However, a closer search was made after this discovery, and an old tin case with much earlier drawings now came to light from the drawing office loft. On a plan, dating from 1846, this outflow sewer, for such it was, was clearly shown. In fact, it was the original outgoing sewer from the Works, but had been superseded some years later as the Works enlarged, but some connections were, unknowingly, still fed into this older one. This underlined the importance of retaining, for ready reference, any drawings, however old, and this precept has been followed ever since. Also on this old drawing was the pipe which carried the original canal water supply to the stand pipes in the village, before the drinking supply, which also ran across the site now being excavated, came from the new Water Co. in 1867. Its position was scaled off and this 4in. cast iron pipe was discovered a few feet down in the exact position predicted!

The other matter of interest was the discovery, at almost the lowest depth of excavation, of three queer stone-like objects in otherwise stone-free clay. Fortunately, they were laid aside and later identified, by the Natural History Museum in South Kensington, as three fossilized vertebrae of the extinct marine reptile 'ichthyosaurus'. As we shall see later, there were to be even more interesting items to be unearthed in the Works, and it was also found that other 'discoveries' had been unearthed around the turn of the century, but with little interest being shown in them at that time. After these little excitements, the new automatic telephone exchange was finally commissioned during July 1952.

Arrangements were proceeding for the provision of new standard classes of steam locomotives for British Railways after the conclusion of the interchange trials. This work was under the control of R. A. Riddles at HQ. The reasons behind the decision to develop a new range of ten types of locomotive are clear. The new organization had inherited close on 20,000 locomotives of some 448 different types. Whilst some steps towards standardization of parts, introduced on the GWR by Churchward 50 years earlier, had taken place within the three other railway groups, this affected, in the main, only the more recent designs. It was now that the pull of old loyalties began to have its effect at Swindon, whereas such problems had been avoided in 1922. The new designs, as they evolved, had obviously close affiliations to LMS practice, which is not surprising with the preponderance of former LMS engineers now in the top posts. There was cold comfort for Swindon in knowing that many of the original ideas for LMS designs had been transferred to Derby, in the 1930s, by Stanier. Certainly boiler design was still closely allied to Swindon practice, but many things, both in general design principles and in such important matters as close limits and fits, which had been sacrosanct over decades, now had to be unlearned by the Swindon designers who held such things as a sine qua non.

The organizational changes made for both rolling stock design and building were quite rational in the situation where it was desirable to co-ordinate such activities into a single cohesive force. Still scattered around the country, usually at main works, the drawing offices were allocated specific work of detailed design such as boilers, boiler mountings, bogies, etc., and individual offices were designated as 'parent office of design' for the various new classes. The parent office, for a particular class, undertook the gathering together of all detail work for the particular class or classes allocated to it, and prepared

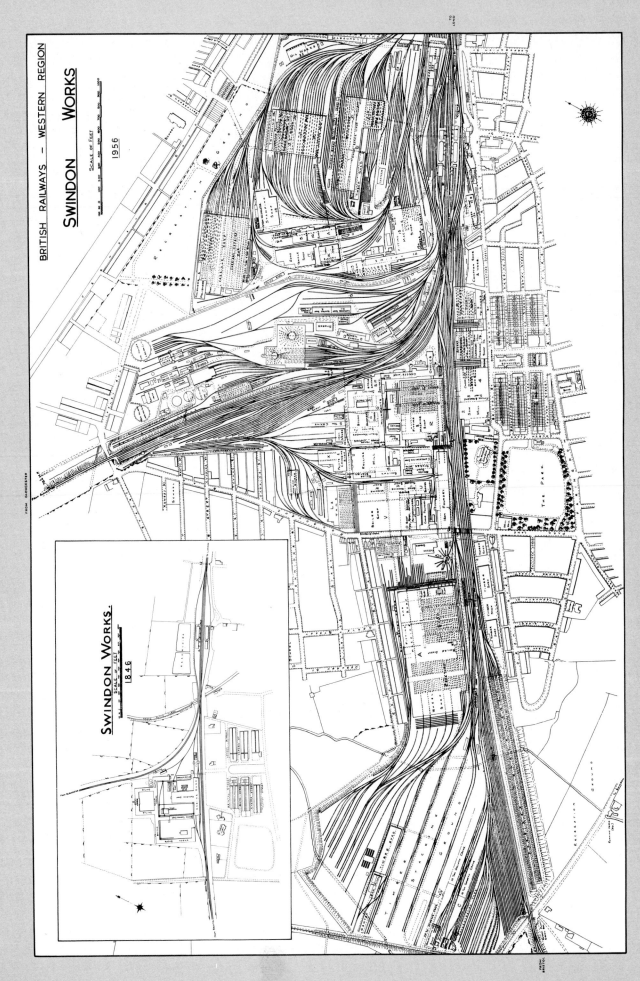

BRITISH RAILWAYS — WESTERN REGION

SWINDON WORKS

1956

SCALE OF FEET

SWINDON WORKS.

SCALE OF FEET

1846

Plate 200: A plan of Swindon Works, 1956.

Author's Collection

Plate 201: The erecting (AE) shop during the 'Standard' steam period. An R. A. Riddles design of Class 3 Mixed Traffic 2-6-0, No. 77000 is being outshopped on the 42 ft. traverser. No. 5020 *Trematon Castle* is lifted by one of the 100 ton cranes, for transfer to the valve setting plant.

British Rail

the final set of general arrangement and assembly drawings ready for manufacture. A similar state of affairs was constituted within the various factories, although, at this stage, it was not possible to introduce such a wide range of product rationalization as evolved 10—15 years later. Finally, the location of a 'parent office' did not necessarily mean that the locomotive was to be built in the adjoining works, although in many cases it was so.

As well as locomotives, standard designs were brought out for new carriages, and some types of wagons, similar methods being used. From all this preparation, a good supply of new work fell to Swindon for a period of a few years. The steam locomotives built were batches of the 75000, 77000, 82000 and 92000 classes, and a batch of the LMS 46500 design for light branch line work, with the building period stretching from 1951 until 1960. By the latter year the dieselization programme was already in full spate and the end of steam already close at hand.

The other area of rapid change was in the formation of the new motive power department already described. Whilst the principal Western Region Divisional Officers, (now known as District Motive Power Superintendents), and their assistants were to be drawn, for some time, from the engineers trained at Swindon, a start was made for the new department to institute its own management development scheme. At first a number of younger men were seconded from the drawing office to a lengthy training period both at depots and district offices. This training experience covered the mechanical, stores and accounting work of a depot, as well as that of daily locomotive servicing and rostering, and included a period on the footplate. Work at District Office was as a supernumery assistant working directly under the District Motive Power Superintendent. In due course, such men were to supersede the shed foremen, and these posts on the GWR had traditionally been filled by former footplate staff.

It was inevitable that such sweeping changes as those

quoted, together with many others in areas such as accountancy, storekeeping and staffing arrangements, led to much disorientation of the people concerned. Loyalty to their own evolved systems was strong on all railways, and that on the GWR, with its lifelong span of about 115 years was particularly, and understandably, so. Whilst it was patently necessary to attempt to transfer such loyalties to the new BR, any action destroying old loyalties appears to have been counter productive in the long run, and an obvious case of 'throwing the baby out with the bathwater'.

The election of 1951, with the inevitable change of policy towards nationalized industries, brought the Conservative Party into power once more. A second Transport Act, in 1953, brought considerable changes to the organization of BR, when the intermediary Railway Executive was abolished and a reshaped BTC was to control the respective regions directly, and these were given back some of their autonomy. The new Chairman was General Sir Brian Robertson, and he was able to move some of the difficulties that had been present in the three-tier control. With hindsight, the RE had been conservative in their outlook and should have been grabbing at chances much earlier to obtain dieselization or electrification where applicable. With the revised management structure came a new impetus to change over from steam to diesel. First moves came with shunting locomotives of tried and tested types, which had been running for many years. Swindon had its manufacturing share of both 204 and 350h.p. types over the next few years.

The implementation of the new control structure of the 1953 Act took until 1955 to complete, by which time the regions were under the charge of area Boards, consisting of senior officers of the particular region, together with eminent industrialists and other people conversant with both business and social requirements of the area served. In December 1954 the *British Railways Plan for Modernization and Re-Equipment* was published. This was to take place over a 15 year period, but was optimistic in more ways than one, and as governments only last for five year periods, the chances of final completion must always have been doubtful. However, we are only interested in the work, or lack of it, that would come to Swindon. In the short term, it was soon obvious that a full order book was assured, but even so, there were thoughts in the minds of some that the final outcome would not be so happy, and thus it turned out.

Although a large sum of money was involved in the new plan (a figure of £1,240 million was quoted at the outset, revised to £1,660 million two years later in 1957), there was an obvious call for ensuing economies, and it was hoped that this could be obtained by higher efficiency in all departments. All works, were, therefore, to be subjected to new ideas of what was

then entitled 'work study', and officers were now trained specially in this subject in order to introduce new methods, particularly on the factory floor. In the Swindon offices, the services of a large firm of industrial consultants were chartered, and studies of methods were made in depth, reports were published and some action taken. In particular, the drawing office was modernized and at last the huge drawings boards, some 6ft. in length, with their tee-squares disappeared, to be replaced by much more comfortable draughting machines. Incidentally, some of the largest tee-squares, in use on the locomotive and carriage sections, were cut from the table top on which Brunel used to work at his office in Parliament Street. This table was cut up in 1893 and these squares had been used in the drawing office since that date, although few people were aware of it. A few unused blades were never made up properly, and two of these are to be seen in the small Works Museum. Methods in the drawing office and other offices were revised with financial savings in view and were to some extent successful, but there was the inevitable reaction to change. Acceptance of new methods on the shop floor were not so easy, and taking the long view it is plain that much of the dissention with the trades unions which was to follow a few years later can be seen to stem from this period.

There were changes in the hierarchy at Swindon over this time of upset. Firstly, K. J. Cook, Mechanical & Electrical Engineer, moved to a similar post at Doncaster in July 1951. He was succeeded by R. A. Smeddle from the Eastern Region. At about the same time, H. Randle, the C&W Engineer moved to the Midland Region to be followed in the post by C. T. Roberts. The Locomotive Works Manager vacancy was filled by J. Finlayson who hailed from north of the border, and brought with him a type of 'knock-about' management which Swindon had never known and, which, quite frankly, did little to help in a situation which called for much more delicate handling, if good industrial relations were to be maintained. He was in the post four years until 1956, when the Works was glad to welcome back S. A. S. Smith as Manager, Swindon trained and a former assistant. It was under Smith's four year period of control that the whole type of work was to be changed, and it was fortunate that a man who knew the place and people so well was available to carry the changes through.

Morale in the Works rose and fell with rapidity in these difficult years of change. But all was not gloom, just under the surface there was always a touch of humour to be found. Always the time honoured myths of the place could be discussed, such as membership of the 'Calathumpians' and other abstruse 'goings-on' connected with ancient organizations which were reputed to exist if staff were gullible enough to believe it! It was good at that time to have a Works magazine called *Swindon Railway News* which was produced free by the Region, but was edited in the Works by Arthur Humphries, all the articles being internal contributions. In this magazine nothing was sacred, from the 'boss' to the Works committee, but everything was in good taste and gave much amusement and fun. To illustrate this, an article. 'A Visit to the Royal Festival Hall' by a certain character calling himself 'Timon Motion', will not come amiss. This appeared in the October 1961 issue, when work study was very much in people's minds:-

'1. For considerable periods the four oboe players had nothing to do. The numbers should be reduced and the work spread more evenly over the whole of the concert, thus eliminating peaks of activity.
2. All the violins, twelve in number, were playing identical tunes; this is unnecessary duplication. Staff should be drastically cut and if more volume is required it could be obtained by means of electronic apparatus.
3. Much effort was absorbed in the playing of demi-semi quavers, an unnecessary refinement. It is recommended that all notes should be rounded off to the nearest semiquaver. In this way it would be possible to employ trainees, or lower graded employees, more extensively.
4. There seems to be much repetition. No useful purpose is served by repeating on the horns a passage which has already been handled by the strings. It is estimated that if all the redundant passages were eliminated, the whole concert time of two hours could be reduced by 20 minutes, and there would be no need to waste time on an intermission.
5. On methods, there are several aspects where engineering principles could be successfully employed. It was noted that the pianist was carrying out his work as a two-handed job, and was also using both feet for pedal operations. However, some notes called for extensive reaching, and it is suggested that the keyboard could be re-designed to bring the notes within the normal working area. In many cases the operators were using one hand for holding their instruments. A suitable jig could be designed to render the idle hand available for other work. It was also noticed that excessive effort was being used at times by the players of wind instruments. Provision of a small blower fan would provide all the necessary air under more accurately controlled conditions.
6. Obsolescence of equipment is another matter requiring investigation. The leading violinist's instrument was already several hundred years old. This instrument should be written off and more modern equipment purchased'.

Nearly all the various ploys used in this new science are very humourously given an airing in this piece of nonsense.

We left the Borough of Swindon in 1950 still struggling back to normality after wartime, as other towns, but with problems almost diametrically opposite to many communities. These latter were often bereft of whole town centres, from the effects of air raids, with housing also destroyed or extensively damaged. In Swindon there had been virtually no damage to the town centre, and only a few houses were lost. Their pre-war determination to expand the range of industries was now even more important, as the politically minded could foresee that loss of the GWR patronage made the Railway Works even more dubious as a long term employment asset. The war had aided the position by the arrival, already recorded, of Vickers Armstrong and the Plessey companies into the area, together with Marine Mountings run by Lister's of Dursley. It was clear that these firms intended to stay. Together with Garrard's, the gramophone company and Wills', already established, there were still, in addition, the three clothing companies of Compton Sons & Webb, Cellular Clothing, and Nicholsons. With the railway, this was the major industrial line-up in 1953.

However, in 1952 the Town Development Act gave local authorities greater power to attract industries, and to provide appropriate housing to support incoming population. It was now up to the town itself to make the effort, and this was successfully accomplished by attracting an 'overspill' population from the London area, particularly Tottenham, and a large engineering firm in the Pressed Steel Fisher plant, part of the Nuffield group. This new large factory, built to design and manufacture press dies and finally car body steel pressings, commenced operations in 1955, attaining full production in 1957 and enlarged further in 1959. Amongst other engineering companies attracted to the town during this period were Deloro Stellite, Metal Box, and Square D (electrical switchgear). Thus in the span of a few years, a very much wider based engineering industry became the support of the town, although BR was still the largest employer. Needless to say there was some transfer of staff, both skilled and unskilled, from the railway to these industries, who, at the time, were able to offer better conditions of employment.

Co-lateral with this influx was the building of large council housing estates, to the north and east of the town, and the population began substantially to increase again, although the rate of expansion was not so high as in the previous century. Thus a subtle change took place in the railway position, in that the maintenance of an employment level of about 10,000 at the Works was no longer politically necessary, since there was a constant labour demand, particularly of the skilled variety, in the area. This point could not have been lost on the higher echelons of the BTC when considering long term policy where economies loomed large. There were to be several removals of staff to centres other than Swindon in the ensuing years.

Once the new top management structure of the re-formed BTC had settled down it became plain that a complete change of policy was to take place, and that steam locomotives were to be replaced at the earliest opportunity. Whilst there were some moves for the adoption of electrification, such planning was centred mainly on suburban schemes. The main change was to be to diesel traction. We are aware that already such traction had been accepted as standard for shunting and other similar duties, but also various main line prototypes had been running on the former LMS and LNE Railways from about 1947 onwards. These had been of the diesel-electric type and the electro-diesel on the Southern Region. Specifications and designs were now drawn up for a massive increase in the number of units in service, and orders placed for a wide number of types, both with railway work-shops and private locomotive contractors. Interest had been shown in the performance of the 'V200' class diesel-hydraulic units in use on the state rail-ways of West Germany. This type of locomotive offered very attractive power/weight ratio possi-bilities, and it was considered that this alternative type should be tried in strength. The Western Region was offered the chance to adopt the type for its main line use, but if it did so, design and development would have to be done internally, as there were at that time, insufficient manufacturers with the necessary expertise in the country. Need-less to say, not much encouragement was needed for the Western Region to plough its own furrow again, and the drawing office at Swindon was soon busy on the job of adapting the 'V200' into one of their own, which would be within the limits of the BR building gauge. Orders were also placed with the North British Locomotive Company of Glasgow for five locomotives of similar type. The Swindon design was the D800 'Warship' class of 2,250h.p. Power was derived from two high speed diesel engines, each working through separate hydraulic transmissions to both axles of two x 4-wheeled power bogies. The body was of monocoque construction, mounted on two parallel tubes and in general no plate work was thicker than five sixteenths of an inch. The drawing office thus presented a completely new challenge to the work force, particularly in the sheet metal, boiler-making and fitting trades. Previous to this, most welding had been done on plate, generally in the range seven eighths to one and a quarter inches thick, and techniques and equipment had to be drastically changed to accommodate working on thin sheet. Also the steel alloys now used to reduce weight posed simi-lar problems. Even though the carriage department was gradually moving over to steel body shells, these were not yet stressed structures and, therefore, a much simpler problem to the staff and the processes not comparable with the new locomotive methods.

The main units such as diesel engines, transmissions, final drives, etc., were, of course, 'bought out', but the accuracies required for fitting these units in position were not only very exacting, but also much more numerous than on steam locomotives. This latter was not, however, such a problem, as in the past decades very high accuracy had been called for in all steam motion and running gear. Later when repair work became due, great changes in shop working had to be faced, particularly on the transmission equip-ment. The first locomotive to this new design was released to traffic on 13th September 1958 and 38 were to be built between 1957 and 1961.

It was quickly being recognized in other quarters that a locomotive of the power output of the D800 class (about 2,000h.p. was available for traction), was not really sufficient for long heavy hauls. Design work was therefore put in hand for a larger 2,750h.p. type on two x 6 wheel bogies, all axles being driven, but with the same basic layout of two sets of power and transmission equipment to each locomotive. The advantage of this arrangement was that individual units were fairly light and small enough for exchanges to be made at running depots only moderately equipped with lifting gear. Such engine or trans-mission changes could be completed in a comparatively short time, thereby saving long periods out of traffic for attention at main works. The D1000 'Western' class appeared in 1960, and 30 had been built at Swindon by 1964.

In general, all diesel-hydraulic locomotives, built by outside manufacturers at Swindon and also at Crewe for the Western Region, had engines built to Maybach and MAN designs, and transmissions to Voith and Mekydro design, although license to manufacture was generally held by British firms. An experiment using the current equivalent design of Paxman engines was also tried. In the early days, problems not encountered before, needed to be solved. In particu-lar, trouble with hydraulic transmissions, which had not been experienced in Germany, raised doubts on the advisability of adopting the type at all. However, careful and painstaking work, carried out by the research and experimental section and in the motive power department, eventually made it possible for the transmissions to become highly reliable. An interesting fact coming to light during these investi-gations was that, although design rated to a certain continuous torque output, the 'V200' class had rarely been expected to work above 75—80 per cent of this in service on the German system. On Western Region main expresses, continuous output of near maximum design was necessary and, indeed, expected, from the specification under which they were purchased, and was one of the early contributory causes of failure.

The work on diesel-hydraulic locomotives was a product of the Railway Modernization Plan, and alongside it had developed a large building pro-gramme of diesel multiple units, (d.m.u.) for branch and suburban work. In addition, large orders were placed in outside railway industries, and many of these units made their way into operational service

Plate 202: Diesel-hydraulic locomotive No. D800 *Sir Brian Robertson*, the first of this type. Subsequent locomotives were named after British warships.

British Rail

Plate 203: The larger 2,700 h.p. diesel-hydraulic 'Western' Class. The first of the Class, No. D1000, is shown here painted in the desert sand livery, a colour which modellers have been trying to authenticate in recent years. However, official photographs were always in monochrome.

British Rail

Plate 204: One of the later designs of d.m.u. sets to come from Swindon. This six car set was supplied originally for the Hull—Liverpool cross-country service in 1960.

British Rail

via Swindon Works where modifications and running adjustments had to be made first. The plan dictated, inevitably, the modernization of both the Locomotive and Carriage & Wagon Works, in order that the change over to the new processes would be economically viable. Changes were not carried through as a single project however, but individual schemes were prepared in the general drawing office following the priority in which they arose.

In the first instance in 1957 and early 1958 this amounted to the acquisition of shop equipment necessary for the new processes. The development of schemes was allowed to take place naturally as soon as enough information and experience was available.

As the pace gained momentum, however, the scale of the necessary work became clearer, and by June 1960 the CM&EE was able to produce a ' General Plan for the Future of Swindon Works'. This encompassed individual schemes for 13 Locomotive Works areas, 11 C&W Works areas, 15 supplies and contracts department warehouses and offices, and three major separate schemes for the gasworks, central boiler station and new points and crossings 'X' shop, and were set out in some detail, with general arrangements and estimates. By this time, two small schemes had been completed, many were authorized and others at the estimating stage. The summary of costs

for the separate departments at June 1960 were as follows:-

	Estimated Cost £	Authorized to date £
Locomotive Works	949,000	369,600
Carriage & Wagon Works	948,745	447,745
Supplies & Contracts Dept.	367,250	217,090
3 separate major schemes	1,841,255	500,255
Totals	4,106,250	1,534,690

The reader may gasp at the figures being considered, but the changes needed were enormous. Whole shops, some of them with areas measured in acres, had to be virtually gutted of their contents, and relaid out for completely different work. Also steam traction was still almost at full strength, although orders already placed for the new standard designs were being cut short and four Lots were withdrawn entirely (Nos. 413—416 inclusive). The work could not be done as one combined operation, but each shop had to be dealt with separately, sometimes split into four separate stages.

It must be recalled that the modernization plan was to spread over 15 years, and the Works alterations were phased to supplement this. Before giving details of the shop changes, attention should be drawn to the '3 major schemes' which amounted to 45 per cent of the total estimate. One of these schemes was the closure of the Factory's gasworks, and acceptance of supplies from the Gas Board instead. There was to be some transfer of equipment and re-use or demolition of old plant and buildings. No estimate was given for this scheme as it was intended to deal with any work on a 'day to day' basis, as convenient. The huge sum of £1.84 millions therefore, was for two schemes only, one which came to fruition, the other to die before it could be started. The new points and crossings 'X' shop was to be built adjacent to the motive power depot and between the two Works. Authorized at £500,255 this new shop was to include a large stockyard for rails, and the whole shop serviced by overhead cranes. The shop measuring 360 ft. x 160 ft. was of modern barrel-vault construction and equipped with its own offices, stores and amenities. For the first time in the Works, heating was achieved by its own HPHW system. Opened in 1959, it took some little time to become fully operational, mainly because of delays in the delivery of large planing machines. When it finally reached its planned output, railway policy was already taking a complete volte-face, and it only lasted in use about four years. This one and a third acre building was the final addition to the Works, which had not stopped expanding for over 116 years. From now on the reverse process was to set in.

The largest scheme was for a new central boiler station to serve the whole Works and estimated to cost £1,341,000. In theory the 'single site' approach for the whole Works was correct, but in the author's opinion the whole scheme was, in finality, ill conceived, and probably the result of 'too many cooks'. The idea of a central station was not new and schemes had been under consideration by the Swindon drawing office for some time. By 1959, however, the maintenance of buildings including heating and ventilation had been taken over by the Chief Civil Engineer at Paddington. They in turn, faced with a scheme of such magnitude, called in consulting engineers to submit various proposals. The resulting recommendations, however, were not firm and gave alternatives. The Works used a considerable amount of steam for processes and had naturally adopted the same medium for heating over the years. The adoption of a modern HPHW system for heating now 'in vogue' was recommended, and there were commercial pressures to use this method. The sensible suggestion of using back pressure turbines in the generating station to produce electric current in normal hours for the Factory could not be discounted, although this would mean considerable discussions with the Electricity Board to re-negotiate what were very favourable existing terms. Some of the suggestions were incompatible, and it was even proposed that separate steam producing plants be built in strategic parts of the Works for production use, thereby destroying the economic concept of a single boiler station! Comparison of the various schemes to hand showed that the CM&EE, CCE and consulting engineers were using different parameters of reference, and at one stage there was disagreement on which buildings should be included. What was to happen in those excluded was not made clear! The scheme was not helped by the General Manager of the Western Region asking why the station and Mechanics Institute were excluded from the scheme. Inevitably the sorting out of all these matters took a considerable time, and this delay was effective in killing the scheme entirely as other events caught up. By February 1961 we find that Swindon drawing office were putting up three minor schemes; for HPHW boiler plant in No. 2 (C&W) shop, a larger unit in the centre of the Locomotive Works and a process steam plant for the C&W Works group of the laundry, oil works (No. 22) shop, and oxygen house. These three schemes were to total only £91,000 although there would have been extra costs for the heating pipework in the shops.

Although some of the other schemes produced for the plan floundered for varying reasons, the main one was that of expedience to unforeseen and rapidly changing national railway plans. The one major project which did proceed to completion, through necessity, was that of the diesel testing station, and work on this proceeded over seven years, commencing in 1958 with facilities for testing diesel-electric shunting locomotives. After this section had been installed at the south end of the boiler de-tubing house ('The Barn'), and just east of the 'A' shop block, authority was obtained to completely demolish the remainder of the building so that the rest of the equipment required could be properly installed. Next to be completed was the 'small engine' testing cell with three Heenan & Froude DPY5 dynamometer beds to provide facilities for d.m.u. and other similar engines up to 230 h.p.

The provision of a large complement of diesel-hydraulic locomotives on the Western Region presented a problem of testing peculiar to this form of equipment. The testing of a diesel-electric locomotive is relatively simple in that after it is completely assembled, the engine may be started, and by taking the current straight from the electric generator, it can be passed through suitable variable resistance banks, allowing the locomotive to be put through the whole of its range of duties whilst stationary. The only equipments not tested are the traction motors, but static testing of these is also a simple matter. Such an arrangement is not possible however with hydraulic transmission and the engine and transmission unit have to be tested separately against dynamometers before installation in the locomotive. In the transmission test cells, 'slave' engines had to be provided to operate the units being tested under all conditions of speed and power output required by the accep-

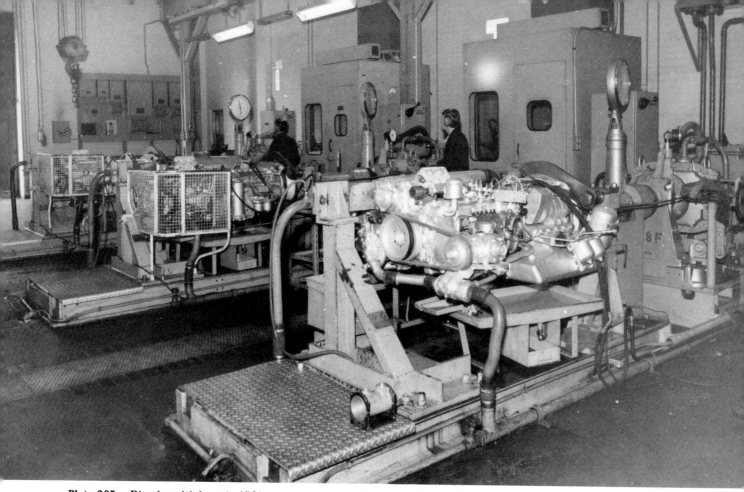

Plate 205: Diesel multiple unit 150 h.p. engines on the Heenan & Froude DPY 5 dynamometer test beds at the diesel testing station (No. 8) shop, in September 1966.

British Rail

tance specification. In an attempt to speed the through-put in the engine cells, the engine cell dynamometers were centrally placed and could be driven from engines mounted either end. This allowed for 'rigging' of one unit whilst the other was tested, although it was found later that this arrangement generated further problems. The dynamometers in all these cells were capable of absorbing from 650h.p. up to 1,920h.p. at the revolutions required. Heat produced in the circulating water in these test systems was dissipated in adjacent cooling units. A 20,000 gallon underground reservoir provided the necessary water circulation for the systems. Fully instrumented control panels and desks were provided behind protective glass windows for safety and reduction of noise levels. This station was a very complicated installation, but had the advantage of being designed and specified in step with the experience being gained in both the Factory and running service of a type of motive power new to the country. In all the plant cost around £500,000.

Other major schemes, which proceeded to at least two or three stages, included a new diesel engine repair layout in the 'B' shop, (the extended site of the original repair and erecting shop of 1843), and major alterations to layout of the 'A' erecting shop, but the proposals to modernize the 100 ton cranes at this time did not proceed, although equipment was purchased for the modifications. An X-ray testing house was provided adjacent to the 'A' block for the proper inspection of welded assemblies and sub-assemblies, particularly bogie frames. With a shielded chamber 27ft. x 24ft. and height clearance of 18ft. to the overhead crane provided, this facility has been of increasing value to the Works as the use of welded structures and equipment has greatly widened.

In the Carriage Works, two major schemes were completed more or less as planned. These were the modernization of the C&W (No. 16) wheel shop with modern wheel and axle turning lathes, overhead cranage and other up to date equipment; and the (No. 19) carriage lifting shop where a new three road extension was provided complete with electric lifting jacks for the diesel multiple units and the 'Blue Pullman' sets now being introduced on the Western Region. To the west of the shop a large 68ft. span carriage traverser was also installed. This was of adequate capacity to serve all 32 roads to the shop and eliminated a large amount of time consuming shunting over a complicated track layout which was expensive to use and maintain. Like the Locomotive Works, other minor jobs were carried out such as the diesel multiple unit power testing shed, and a separate shop for vacuum brake cylinder repairs.

Plate 206 *(left):* One of the two main engine test cells in the diesel testing station on 6th February 1967. Two engines could be rigged simultaneously on either side of the dynamometer.

British Rail

It is impossible to assess the actual total expended on Swindon modernization schemes of this period because of the complications and variations which arose, but in the author's estimation about £1.75 million was spent before events caught up, not only with Swindon Works, but with the railway system as a whole. As we read earlier, the motive power department had been formed after the retirement of Hawksworth. During the ensuing years it was natural for it to become more closely allied to the operating department at Paddington, and indeed W. N. Pellow had an office there as well as one at Swindon and there were frequent meetings between the staff of both departments and direct telephone lines were in constant use. Inevitably, a decision was made to move the whole department to Paddington, and this took place in March 1957. This was a new experience for Swindon staff, and the move did not pass without its predictable troubles, with families having to uproot their homes, where they had, supposedly, settled for life.

As a direct result of the success of the experimental and research section of the drawing office, a replacement dynamometer car was authorized. A vehicle of the Hawksworth type was used for this purpose, and it was fitted out with the most modern equipment available, with the specific purpose of diesel traction testing as well as steam, which still occupied a major part of the railway traction power. This vehicle was eventually transferred to Derby where it is still in use for particular purposes. On 21st November 1957 the BTC authorized the building of an Apprentice Training School, in order to bring the training of young people into line with the new ideas then being formulated. Planned in the Swindon drawing office, the final design was carried out at Paddington by the CCE staff, and opened fully on 17th September 1962. It was built to accommodate 120 apprentices for their first year of service, and equipped with machine tools and all necessities for the basic training now required as standard before entering the workshops service proper. Lecture rooms for theoretical subjects were provided (although this work was later transferred to the Swindon College), together with a gymnasium and assembly hall. It was the original concept to accept lads from both the Works and the Western Region, but in later years apprentices, including girls, from other major companies in the town were accepted. It is still considered one of the best of such schools in the south-west.

The final closure of the gasworks took place in January 1959. Gas of some sort had been manufactured in the Works since 1842, and on the site now closed, since 1874. Other closures affecting Swindon's work load, were those of the Barry and Newton Abbot Locomotive & Carriage Works, and the Locomotive Works at Oswestry. Some still remained as maintenance depots, but the repair work

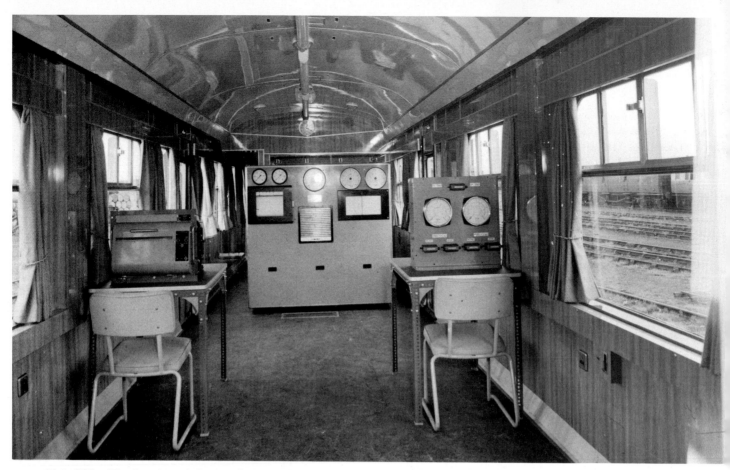

Plate 207: The interior of the last Swindon dynamometer car No. DW150192, rebuilt and equipped over a period of two years from Hawksworth carriage No. 796 and withdrawn in 1961 for this purpose.

British Rail

Plate 208: One of the first of the Swindon designed 'B4' bogies being assembled in Carriage & Wagon (No. 15) shop in 1962.

British Rail

formerly done came mainly to Swindon, in the midst of the modernization plan. Only the Works at Wolverhampton, Worcester and Caerphilly continued for a few more years to do locomotive repairs. In 1960, S. A. S. Smith became the Works assistant to R. A. Smeddle, and S. Ridgeway succeeded as Locomotive Works Manager.

There is record of the artificial limbs made in the Works still being maintained in 1960, although the National Health Service had been operating for 13 years. A few were actually made as replacements, but after this date the chargeman specialist carrying out this work was transferred to other work before retiring.

The introduction of the 'Blue Pullmans' on the Western Region brought new experience to the staff at Swindon. With their power cars at both ends, they were the forerunners of the later High Speed Trains (HSTs), so successfully launched on the Western Region some years later. As with all new designs there were fresh problems to be overcome, and one of these was with the riding and movement of the bogies. Arising from these difficulties and with other ideas forming in the minds of the carriage engineers, a completely new bogie was designed. This was the famous B4 bogie, which was the first of a large series to be put successively under British Railways' vehicles. Although requiring high accuracy in building, it was essentially a very economic unit, and when first in production its total cost was approximately equal to the basic steel casting alone of the Commonwealth type of bogie then in general use. After prototype building, a production line was installed in the C&W No. 15 shop. Later, the manufacture of this bogie was transferred to other works, particularly to Derby, and it was almost forgotten, or overlooked, that this was originally a Swindon product.

Equally interesting was the design of a new prototype coach. Work on this vehicle, actually the first Mk. II coach for BR, commenced in the drawing office in 1961, the vehicle going into service in 1963. The new, but now familiar, profile had bowed and curved roof ends. For the sake of convenience, the body sides of this prototype were produced on the diesel multiple unit jigs in use at the time. Slight adjustments to this form were the only ones made to the final profile drawings for the production runs of the Mk. II carriages. This important item in the history of British railway carriages was No. 13252, built as a 1st Class compartment vehicle. Many new methods of construction were used, including sprayed polyurethane foam for sound and heat insulation, replacing the standard blue asbestos (still to be used for some years, before its dangers were fully understood). There was also a wide use of aluminium, plastics and adhesives, and the vehicle ran on the newly developed B4 bogie. Full testing of the body

was carried out at the SNCF research establishment at Vitry in France. It is indeed unfortunate that papers have been written on the Mk. II coach overlooking the initial development done at Swindon and, indeed, the impression could be gained that the design was a Derby product. The transfer away from Swindon took place because carriage building was to cease there entirely.

Even by the end of 1959 doubts were being raised in government circles regarding the correctness of the heavy railway expenditure then beginning to gain momentum, and a decision was made to obtain a private view of the organization and efficiency of the BTC. This work was entrusted to a special advisory group, led by Sir Ivan Stedeford, who had already advised government ministries on similar subjects. It is perhaps not surprising that a Parliamentary Select Committee was also interested in the railways, considering the large amount of public finance being allocated to them by the government. The latter's findings were not too harsh, but that of the advisory group was much more critical, although as is usual, the findings were not published. It was felt that the BTC had completed its job of co-ordinating the four main railway groups and was now itself redundant in its present form. Furthermore it was thought that a more commercial outlook should take the place of what had become a service to the public to be maintained at all costs, a situation which had developed over the years from the original Acts of Incorporation of the companies and subsequent legislation upholding the railways as a 'common carrier'.

A change of direction in the railways was to come quickly. The BTC Chairman, Lord (formerly Sir Brian) Robertson retired at the end of May 1961, and he was succeeded by the then Technical Director of Imperial Chemical Industries, Dr. Richard Beeching. It is not surprising to find that the new Chairman had been a member of the Stedeford committee, and had been chosen presumably for his support of the findings in the report. Great activity was at once apparent, and resulted in the introduction of the Transport Act of 1962, the third since 1947. Even before the introduction of this act, Dr. Beeching had put into motion a large number of specialist studies on all aspects of the railway organization. Under the new act the BTC was to be abolished, as were the area Boards. At this latter level they were to be replaced by regional Boards, chaired by the General Managers of the regions, and these were to be answerable direct to the new British Railway Board (BRB), which was to come into being on 1st June 1963.

The policies of the years immediately prior to Dr. Beeching's arrival had put the main workshops into a position which could not auger well for their future without some drastic changes taking place. Workload

Plate 209: Prototype carriage No. 13252, the prototype Mk. II vehicle for British Railways, after design and building at Swindon early in 1963.

British Rail

during the 'standard steam' period, which had also included replacing most passenger stock and much of the old wagon stock with new vehicles, had kept all these works extremely busy. The quick change-over to diesel, particularly towards the end of the decade 1951–60, meant withdrawal of large numbers of steam locomotives and replacement by much smaller numbers of diesel powered vehicles, many of which had been supplied by private contractors. It was inevitable that this crash programme of re-equipment would mean a period of slackness, and obvious that many establishments would quickly become 'excess to requirements'. To meet this problem in 1962 the main workshops, 31 in all, were transferred away from the regional CM&EE's and grouped together as the Workshops Division of BR with a headquarters set up in the first instance at Castlefields House, Derby. The new organization formed its own small advisory HQ staff, which was greatly enlarged later, under a General Manager and operated as a separate 'region' of BR. Shortly afterwards, in September 1962, the 'Main Workshops Future Plan' was announced. This drastic scheme called for the closure of 15 of the 31 main works, and famous names such as Darlington, Gorton and Brighton, to mention only three, were to disappear from the railway works scene for ever. Those who were not aware of the likely out-

come of Dr. Beeching's investigations, now in hand and to be made public in the famous 'Re-Shaping of British Railways' of May 1963, were certain that the draconian measures for the Workshops Division were ill conceived and quite unnecessary. With hindsight, we can see that future capacity requirements were fairly accurately assessed, and the cuts only slightly on the 'heavy' side. It is, however, fair to state that if slightly more shop areas had been retained, they may have had to be 'mothballed' for a few years. However, considering the slowness with which redundant factory premises and land has been disposed of, there would have been little financial loss over the period, and great benefit derived by about 1977, when reasonable building and refurbishing programmes were again well under way.

The effect of the 'Reorganization Plan' as it was called to differentiate from the previous BTC modernization plan, was to be drastic at Swindon. Out of a total sum of £17.2 million for all the remaining works, the largest portion, £2.33 million, was allocated to Swindon. The C&W Works, developed and extended since 1868, was to be totally closed, and the retained activities to be housed in the remaining Locomotive Works buildings, suitably altered for them. Having reached this point in the story of the Works we must examine the changed situation there.

As stated earlier, up to and during the 'standard steam' period, workloads and therefore staffing had remained more or less static in the Factory, but the sudden policy changes brought this building programme to a halt. Also the repair load of steam locomotives fell sharply as their life span was shortened and new diesels introduced, these not requiring major maintenance for some time. Similarly on the carriage side, the provision of an almost new stock of vehicles and the new diesel multiple units for suburban branch line work, also meant reduced repair work. When it is remembered that heavy repairs generally accounts for 80 to 90 per cent of the activities, the seriousness can be realized, and, as we know, before the reorganization plan, 31 works were competing for work which was gradually becoming enough for only about half that number. It was here that political pressures, not encountered before at Swindon began to pinch.

It was indeed fortunate that by this time moves made by the borough in previous years, and particularly under Ministry approval on 25th June 1952, for the development of industrial estates and reception of 20,000 'overspill' population from the London area, began to show its advantages to local people.

With many engineering firms already arrived and expanding, and more to come, railway artisans were in great demand with a continual transfer from the Works to these new industries, and these losses generally kept in line with the reduction in work. Furthermore, it was clear to those who had sensed the probable change in the fortunes of the railway industry in Swindon, that it might be wise to move to the new companies in the area. A landmark was passed when, on 18th March 1960, the very last steam locomotive to be built for BR was outshopped from Swindon Works. This was No. 92220 *Evening Star*, very appropriately named, not only for the occasion but, also, for the re-use of the name of one of the very first engines to run on the GWR. This was finished with loving care by the staff in the full lining out of earlier years, copper chimney band and as much brightwork generally as possible. The nameplate was supplied in the 'Egyptian slab serif' lettering which had been used, with only a little deviation in the 1870s, through the life of the GWR. The ceremony, attended by almost all the Works personnel, was led by the Chairman of the Western Area Board, Reggie Hanks, once an apprentice at Swindon, and by that time deputy to Lord Nuffield at Morris Cowley. This event, sad indeed to Swindon, brought home

Plate 210: The last steam locomotive for British Railways, Class 9, 2-10-0 No. 92220 *Evening Star* outside the 'A' shop after the naming ceremony on 18th March 1960. It carries the full GWR lining, copper chimney band and Brunel Egyptian slab-serif lettering for the nameplate. This locomotive has since been preserved.

British Rail

Plate 211: The machine moulding bay of the reorganized non-ferrous foundry in September 1966, specially photographed to illustrate the improved lighting. Note the overhead telfer for feeding the moulding sand hoppers.

British Rail

forcefully the way in which things were going, and before the start of the reorganization in the Works, staff would drop, in round figures, from 10,000 to 8,000.

The new scheme called for major changes in the way that building and repair of railway rolling stock was to be organized. Firstly, some works were to be set aside primarily for new building, none of these to specialize in more than one type, i.e. locomotives, carriages or wagons. The others were to be repair works only. Secondly, repair works were to undertake the repair of certain types of vehicle, no matter where geographically located, thus reducing the store-holdings of spares in many centres. Lastly, many primary manufacturing functions were to be located at one or, at the most, two works. It was to be expected that the first and second ideas could not be meticulously adhered to, as manpower had to be kept evenly occupied over long periods and some workload adjustments had to be made. The last item, however, the rationalization of primary facilities, was governed by the plant installed and available. Thus iron founding was to be concentrated at Horwich, and the large

foundries at Swindon and other places, were to be run down and closed. Swindon was to become the centre for non-ferrous founding, and also for coil spring manufacture. In general terms Swindon together with Glasgow, (formerly St. Rollox), were the only two retained works to deal, in the future, with locomotives, carriages and wagons, the others covering only one, or two, of these activities.

R. A. Smeddle retired at the time of the formation of the Workshops Division, and was also the last CM&EE to occupy the chair at Swindon. His successor Tommy Matthewson-Dick, took up his post at Paddington. S. Ridgeway also left the Locomotive Works at about this time, and the appointment of a Chief Works Manager was made, to cover both Works during the time of reorganization and the gradual amalgamation of the activities which would finally take place. To this post, in 1962, J. S. (Jock) Scott, who had very wide managerial experience all over the railway network, was appointed. H. G. Johnson, who had been C&W Manager for 14 years, retired on 31st December 1962. H. W. Mear came from Derby to take over the Locomotive Works, and E. T. Butcher was promoted from assistant to manager of the C & W Works, both appointments effective from 1st January 1963.

These were the officers who were to either start, or see through the great changes now imminent. The primary planning was, however, carried through by three long serving Swindon staff, in the first place. These were, A. A. W. Loveday, Assistant Works Manager, the author, then plant engineer, and K. Jones, then chief estimator. Their first brief was to produce proposals and 'shot' estimates to meet the workload parameters laid down. This work was done mostly 'after hours' when there were no interruptions, and the original proposal sheets in the author's own handwriting and with Mr Jones' supporting estimates, are being referred to as these paragraphs are written.

The workloads on which the schemes were drawn up were as under:-

Repair of:-	Per Year
Main line locomotives	300
Diesel-electric shunters	100
Diesel engines (main line)	400
Hydraulic transmissions	400
Locomotive bogies	400
DMU engines and gearboxes	600/700
Train heating boilers	150
Wagons (heavy and light)	10,000
DMUs (including WR and LMR Pullman trains)	1,000/1,100 single vehicles
Containers	3,000
BRUTE Trucks (manufacture)	10,000
Non-ferrous castings and machining	2,000 tons
Points and crossing units	4,000

In addition, there were general services to regions lifting tackle, stores stock items, etc.

Some pride is felt that the first estimate was £2,533,250, and this figure was indeed close to that authorized and eventually spent. It was inevitable that the BRB would commission specialists to advise on this huge project, and in particular Sir Steuart Mitchell made a masterly survey of machine tools and equipment available in all the Works with recommendations for future purchasing policies. The first formal submission for authorization was made in November 1963 at the slightly higher figure of £2,868,000, but this was revised to £2,503,000, to be reduced further to £2,427,000 the following March. The civil engineering contractors, Messrs. C. J. B. Limited, were first allocated the Swindon project, but after certain investigations and abortive preparatory work, they withdrew when their own estimate of £2,778,000 was not accepted. This was on 1st July 1964. In the meantime certain revisions had been made to proposals, and a two stage version was finally undertaken by Messrs. Wilson Lovatt, who commenced work on 16th November 1964.

To relate the difficult times now met in the Works for the period of physical reorganization would need a book in itself. Production was expected to continue, and of course the diesel locomotive building programme, still in hand, had to be completed, although new locomotive building was not in the future remit. In addition to the D800 and D1000 locomotives, there was also an order for 56 diesel-hydraulic 650h.p. 0-6-0 plate-framed locomotives still in hand. These were nicknamed the 'Teddy Bears' for some abstruse reason, and were the last locomotives to be built at Swindon for BR, and No. D9555 left the Works in October 1965.

Orders for new carriages had now ceased, and the total Works staff figures of 8,022 in December 1962 had fallen, twelve months later, to 6,805, and were to drop to 5,104 by July 1967. This meant that about 3,000 were to become redundant, a formidable number indeed for the town. However, although there were the inevitable individual problems, the bulk of men not near retiring age found work comparatively quickly in the new industries in the town and district. But it was not surprising that much heartache was felt amongst those affected. The railway had been the traditional form of family employment, in many cases for a century. To have to move, perhaps fairly late in one's working life, to a completely new environment, was not at all easy.

As in the previous modernization scheme, many of the projects concerned were reorganizations of equipment to new places. The major item concerned the old iron foundry. This building, 660ft. long x 80ft. wide, was completely transformed into the diesel engine repair shop with all special facilities self-contained, including a fuel injection pump repair room, stores and machining bay. One other similar project was the conversion of the old 'B' shop, some walls of which dated from 1841, into the new diesel multiple unit lifting and repair shop. One completely new boiler station was built near the 'A' block, and it is interesting that now one of the main firms of heating engineers in the country was able to say that the existing methods of heating, mainly by below floor steam pipes at 100p.s.i., could not be bettered for the type of shops in question — so much for the HPHW ideas! A completely new carriage shop had originally been given serious consideration, running northwards partly over some of the oldest buildings in the Works (the original smiths' and steam hammer shops, which were coming down anyway), but this was shelved in favour of using existing stone built buildings which still had a long life expectancy. The old 'Welsh' rolling mills disappeared finally in 1964 after over 100 years working, and with it went its last 1860 Swindon built single cylinder 28in. mill engine fitted with a huge 20ft. diameter flywheel purchased from J. Perry which had driven some of the rolls stands. It originally cost £300 and the flywheel £155.

261

Plate 212: Building the D9500 Class diesel-hydraulic locomotives in the 'AE' shop, giving a good idea of the locomotive's internal layout. The 650 h.p. Paxman engine is in the foreground. These were the last locomotives built for British Railways at Swindon.

Author's Collection

Plate 213: The diesel engine repair (No. 9) shop on 4th November 1966 after conversion from the former iron foundry (J1). Compare this view with that of Plate 121 taken in the same shop in 1907. The improved working conditions are self evident.

British Rail

Plate 214: This 28in. mill engine, with a 20ft. diameter flywheel, installed in 1860, was removed from service and scrapped in 1964. The driver sat on a stool in the foreground with the control levers in front of him and received orders through the opening cut in the partition.

British Rail

Plate 215: A three stand, two high set of rolls driven by the other 28in. engine, seen on 31st October 1921. The rolls were, left to right, roughing, round bar and fire bars. The flywheel can first be seen in the right centre of the picture.

British Rail

Plate 216: The carriage repair (No. 19) shop after reorganization. This view is taken from almost the same spot as that of Bourne's print of the engine house shown in Plate 17.

British Rail

Plate 217: A general view, photographed on 19th September 1966, from one of the 100 ton overhead cranes of the main east repair bay of the 'AE' shop (No. 5), during the reorganization period.

British Rail

Much emphasis was put on the amenity standards to be reached. Existing conditions, with a few notable exceptions, were very poor indeed. Each shop was now equipped with new washing and locker facilities, and a new dining hall and medical centre was built near to the Rodbourne Road entrance. The provision of this excellent dining hall had a rather droll consequence. Throughout this volume we have read of the involvement of the GWR with the social life of the town. With nationalization this apparently came to an end for ever. It did not take local organizations long to discover that this new hall offered the best dancing floor in the district, and could accommodate 300—350 people comfortably. Furthermore, the secondary dining room and kitchen facilities completed the requirements for staff and society functions. Dance halls in the area had closed, and the remaining opposition was a civic undertaking in the rebuilt part of the town's shopping centre, called, incidentally, the 'Brunel Rooms'. This establishment within the Works has proved so popular that it usually has forward bookings of eighteen months for Friday and Saturday functions! So the tradition of service to the town still continues in a different way.

Eventually a specialist railway team was formed to see the reorganization through, which included professional civil and electrical engineers as well as the mechanical engineers and supporting staff. It was inevitable that labour relations would be difficult. Change is always resisted, but the drastic changes now faced meant much more; a large industry continuously expanding for over a century and providing steady employment, was now being broken up. Men's job security was uncertain, and this led to attitudes of non co-operation, or at least the use of maximum tactics to slow progress in the various schemes. Naturally the local management was the butt of such actions. The shop staff were, however, aware that the policy decisions were not of Swindon origin, and such local action was their only resort, except to complain through their national union organizations or local member of Parliament. Since a similar situation was in being at every other railway centre, the attitudes at these higher levels could not be seen in the same parochial light, but were more concerned that all centres had at least some cut of the cake. It would be wrong to hide the fact that output suffered during this period, indeed deliveries of repaired and new work fell behind. However, relationships between management and staff never deteriorated to personal levels, which might well have happened in these circumstances. The understanding built up over decades now showed its strength. Wide differences of opinion were inevitable, but the Works committee, comprising unions and management, always 'kept talking', as the imposed diminution of the Works continued. The project was eventually completed at about the time

planned. The operational area of the Works proper before starting was about 283 acres (114 hectares), and the roofed areas were 3.7 million square feet (344,000 square m). When completed with the loss of the old C&W Works, this was reduced to 104 acres (42 hectares), and about 1 million sq. ft. (96,000 sq. m). In fact, another 40 acres of land at the west end of the Works, (the old timber yard and saw mills area) was retained for some years, and has only recently been fenced off as non-operational. About 91 miles of track were reduced to 26 miles, and of course there were similar reductions in other services in the Works.

It is perhaps to be regretted that the proposed new carriage lifting shop was not proceeded with. Under the early scheme, the diesel engine repairs would have remained in the 'B' shop where considerable capital had already been expended to set it up, and the 660ft. long iron foundry would have become the wagon repair shop. Transmissions and bogie repairs would have been set up in the boiler 'V' shop. However the effects of the Beeching report were already taking their toll, and the wide closure of lines put into question even the lower level of activities and the shop capacities now being retained throughout the country. A confidential letter sent to Swindon as early as 17th June 1964 gave a hint of things to come. This intimated a reduction of the annual predicted load of locomotive repairs on which the reorganization was based, and worse was to follow in the next few years. It was, therefore, obvious to those who controlled the Swindon project that there would be under-utilization of buildings in some cases, even after the drastic surgery now in hand.

By the latter end of 1966 the project was coming to a close, but much was still to be achieved before it could be said that the work was finally completed. From the beginning of planning the job had taken over 3½ years, of which 1¾ was spent in actual rebuilding. Steps had been taken to set aside one of the carriage shops as a sale hall for redundant machinery and equipment, and moves were made to dispose of the land and buildings now superfluous to requirements. In the event, two of the three parcels of land were conveyed to the local corporation, the C&W Works area to the north of the station, and that lying between the old canal and the Gloucester line. This latter area included the motive power depot which was also now closing, the gasworks site, and the almost new points and crossings shop. This area was to become the 'Hawksworth Industrial Estate', whilst the former was eventually used for the North Star College section of the main college in the centre of the town, which had grown from the original technical school buildings of 1896. The other large municipal project here was the 'Oasis Leisure Centre'. The old Works laundry was leased to the local Hospital Authority, and is still in business at the time

Plate 218: The chaos of reorganization. This view, on 6th September 1966, shows the yard in front of the old Locomotive Works Manager's office block during installation of the carriage traverser transferred from No. 19 Carriage & Wagon shop.

British Rail

Plate 219: Possibly the very last broad gauge track to be removed. This turntable had served the Works since its inception, prior to lifting in 1965, the lengths of broad gauge rail never being removed. The turntable is now preserved as a relic in the Works near to its original site. A hydraulic power capstan is seen in the centre right of the picture.

British Rail

Plate 220: The Maybach bay of No. 9 diesel engine repair shop.

British Rail

Plate 221: Redundant plant and machinery laid out for sale in the 'showroom', the old No. 4 Carriage & Wagon shop, in 1966.

British Rail

Plate 222: An historic moment. The handing over of the keys of the Carriage & Wagon Works, which lay north of the main line, on the transfer of the property to Swindon Corporation for demolition and development on 30th June 1967. In the Works Manager's office are:-

J. B. Morrison, Borough Surveyors Department; A. S. Peck (Author), Works Plant Engineer; G. V. Markham, Estates Assistant, Town Clerks Department; F. H. Poolman, Works Chief Watchman, and H. W. Mear, Swindon Works Manager.

British Rail

of writing.

During this time of upheaval and stress within the Works, one particularly notable event had taken place outside. It will be recalled that the original 'barracks' building had been taken over and converted by the Wesleyan Methodists in 1869. This large church had faithfully served the railway employees and others in the district for many decades. By the mid-1950s, however, the population had gradually moved away from this part of the town and was being taken over almost entirely for business purposes. The Trustees, therefore, decided to transfer its activities to more suitable outlying areas, and the last religious service was held there at the end of September 1959, after 90 years of use. A year later the premises were conveyed to the Corporation of Swindon, who had decided to transform it into the Great Western Railway Museum. This was in recognition of the services which the GWR had made in first giving birth to the industrial town, and then building it up into the flourishing borough which it had become. There had long been many relics held in various places, but

now it was possible to bring most of them together. The main exhibits were to be five representative locomotives. In date order, they were *North Star* (1838 reconstructed 1925); 'Dean Goods' No. 2516 built 1897; and *City of Truro* famous for its record breaking exploit on the Wellington Bank on 9th May 1904. The fourth exhibit is a representative of the most notable batch of locomotives ever designed and built; No. 4003 *Lode Star*. This locomotive, the only one of its type preserved, represents that great revolution in steam locomotive design which put Britain and the GWR years ahead of the world. No finer or more important exhibit could surpass it. Finally, there is a representative of the ubiquitous pannier tank 0-6-0 class, No. 9400 of 1947 Hawksworth design, the type so redolent of GWR practice over the last 60 years of its life.

All these locomotives were moved by special road trailers on Sunday mornings, when roads could be closed to traffic, into the museum when building was in progress, so that it could be enclosed and completed later. The main hall is named after G. J.

Churchward, and there are also Brunel and Gooch galleries. Some of the models which once graced the CME's office in the Works are also on show here, together with beautiful examples from elsewhere, which, after a chequered history, are now available for all to see. One particularly interesting exhibit is a panel of working samples of every safety carriage door lock used regularly on the GWR during its life. The museum was opened on 22nd June 1962 by R. F. Hanks, and is now recognized as part of the National Railway Collection, including the York and South Kensington museums, although it is run locally.

Again, in 1966, the borough decided to purchase the major portion of the original railway village for preservation. These cottages are included in the statutory list of buildings of architectural and historic interest. Over the succeeding 14 years their exteriors have been fully restored, the interiors being adapted with modern facilities as houses or flats. Subsequently the project has won many national prizes. In the year of writing, 1980, one cottage, next to the museum, has been restored and equipped as it would have been in about 1900, when inhabited by a railway foreman of the time. It is now an annexe to the museum and also open daily.

In 1967 the second exodus of Swindon staff to other railway centres took place. This time it was the turn of the important design, research and development offices, transferred to the new Railway Technical Centre being formed at Derby. This removed much of the technical 'heart' of Swindon Works and, indeed, that of other places such as Doncaster, York, Eastleigh, etc., which suffered the same indignities. Whilst a good case can be made out for such centralization, there is also the loss of direct contact with workshop practice, which is always so important, particularly when developing new methods and designs. A small 'outlier' section was left, as indeed was the outdoor machinery drawing office of the regional CM&EE. But the supply of that particular brand of engineer, trained in the Works, experienced then in the drawing office and ready to return as an engineering manager to the Works, now disappeared. Time and experience will tell whether his replacement, by mainly graduate engineers, with only short apprenticeship periods in works with more limited facilities and often no railway design experience, will be to the ultimate advantage of the Railway Works.

Dr. Beeching ended his period as Chairman of the BRB on 1st June 1965 after only 2½ years service, which will be remembered for its effects long after the shortness of its term is forgotten. He was replaced by Stanley Raymond, late General Manager of the Western Region, for a further 2½ years until the end of 1967 when another railwayman, Henry Johnson took over until 11th September 1971. In

1967 Jock Scott retired, his job of reorganization being over, and H. W. Mear was appointed 'Works Manager Swindon', in line with other railway factories.

One major social loss arising from the closure of the Carriage Works was that of the rehabilitation workshop. This shop, which was at road level in London Street, was opened in 1953 to rehabilitate railwaymen in the area who had become partially disabled due to illness or accident. Their normal occupation was of no account, since the treatment consisted of imposing controlled physical movements calculated to correct such disability as they had. Such exercises were achieved by adapting simple machines such as presses, punches, drills etc., with ingenious attachments controlling their mechanisms and compelling the required movement of limb or muscle. Machines were set up for hand or foot operation, and in many cases could be adjusted to suit the type of regular movement required. The shop was under the professional control of the Works Medical Officer, who made daily visits to assess patients' progress. At the same time, the shop could produce small items for use in the Works.

It was explained earlier that the gasworks had been run down and closed and the supply for the Works was taken from the South Western Gas Board, A 24in. diameter main was installed, which gives some idea of the quantity required at the time of transfer. This was, of course, in the days before North Sea Gas when high pressure mains could be used. With the demolition of the gasworks, the four gas holders would normally have gone, but arrangements were made with the SWGB for the transfer to them of the 2½ million cu. ft. holder. Repairs carried out to this holder to cover deferred maintenance cost £105,000 compared with the £49,000 it had cost when built in 1923.

Once again the water supply to the Works was causing disquiet. This time it was due to the lowering of the water table level in the Kemble area where it was abstracted. This had been brought about both by the huge increase of boreholes in the surrounding district, and the large acreage of gravel extraction which had been developed, with the inevitable formation of large man-made lakes. By 1962 the amount of water required at Swindon still remained high, whilst a large amount was still being used by the steam locomotives at the depot, and the Works had not yet begun to contract. The introduction of diesel locomotives also required a considerable amount of process water for high pressure cleaning before repair. Consequently, in successive late months of the year, particularly November and December, the highest daily abstraction rate, due to heavy steam heating loads, was having difficulty in being met when the water table at Kemble was at its lowest annual level. Cases were occurring when the pumps in the 48ft.

Plate 223: The western part of the restored 'Railway Village' as completed in 1974. Note 'A' shop on the left in the distance and the former GWR Park to the left in the middle of the picture. St. Mark's Church and the fine water tower with original tanks (now replaced) can also be seen.

R. C. H. Nash

deep service well were actually sucking air. Storage at Swindon was only sufficient for about 6 hours at full load, and therefore could not cope fully, even if full pumping was continued to fill storage at night. Although steam locomotives were disappearing and condense return services being fitted to the heating installations, records of well levels showed that the situation would soon be out of hand. So, in 1967, authority was obtained to install new pumps at greater depth. The existing electric pumps were now, at 32 years, nearing the end of their useful life, but as supply had to be maintained, and with no other source being available, it was necessary to sink an entirely new bore. A site was selected about 150 ft. nearer to Kemble station in the hope that good fissures would be struck. The initial bore was made down to about 390 ft., but saline water was mixing in at this depth. Investigation showed that adequate supplies were being tapped higher and the bore was

plugged at 280 ft. and acidification carried out to clear and open up the fissures in the oolite which had been struck. Resistivity tests showed the best yields at 56 ft. and 105 ft. depths. The main bore of 33 in. diameter from the 60 ft. headwell down to the 170 ft. level was equipped with two submersible two-stage pumps, each capable of 44,500 g.p.h. against 220 ft. head supplied by Messrs. Harland Engineering Ltd. They were suspended one above the other at a mean depth of about 85 ft. As the water level below the cill is now rarely higher than 30 ft., the pumps are usually about 60 ft. below this level, allowing for ample variation in years to come. The old electric pumps and the steam engines and pumps of 1902 were now removed and the old wells plugged. The pumphouse was demolished and the site covered. All that is visible now, just to the north of Kemble station, is the new well head and the small control house. This latter houses the robot control gear which is operated

Plate 224: The eastern part of the 'Railway Village' still under restoration at the same time as the previous view. In the foreground is the GWR Museum with the old GWR Hospital to the lower left of the picture. The cottage to the right of the Museum has now been equipped as it would have appeared circa 1900, and is part of the Museum. The well known *Glue Pot* pub stands on the corner behind the Museum and further civic developments can be discerned, in the top centre of the picture, on the site of the old Carriage & Wagon Works.

R. C. H. Nash

from a small console in the Works fire station at Swindon. Latterly the abstraction rate, for which a licence is held, has been reduced to suit present needs, and the pumps downrated accordingly. However, it is some comfort to know that when the new borehole was test pumped, a rate of 80,000 g.p.h. was obtained, with a draw-down in the well of only 10 in. Swindon Works' water supply problems had, at last, been solved.

During the chairmanship of Henry Johnson, yet another Transport Act, that of 1968, was placed on the statute books, the last to date! The railway undertaking has been subject to much political 'tinkering' and the investment necessary just to maintain, not improve, the general service to the public was rarely forthcoming for a period long enough to be effective. Most railway planning of any con-

sequence required a 10—15 year gestation period, and with Parliamentary sessions lasting only 5 years at the most, such firm planning commitment is still a forlorn hope for most of the time. In the 1968 Act, however, there was one item which was to become, in a short time, a branch to which Swindon could cling like a drowning man. This was the lifting of a control which had always existed on the railways, precluding them from undertaking work for outside parties, or selling their own products elsewhere.

Shortly after H. W. Mear took over as Works Manager, a decision was made over which engineers have disagreed ever since. This was the gradual withdrawal of all diesel-hydraulic locomotives, and retention of only diesel-electric locomotive traction and electric locomotives. This is not the place to reopen the argument, but its effect on Swindon was

271

to be catastrophic, as the whole diesel-hydraulic fleet was maintained there, and the locomotives which would replace them had their repairs already centred on other works on BR. The re-action of the staff was to be expected, and a very difficult period ensued when it was hard to get locomotives completed and released after repair with any certainty. Added to this the huge fall-off in freight traffic also meant a large cut in wagon maintenance. At a throughput of only 350 repairs a week, a figure that was rarely, if ever, attained, both through non-availability of wagons and manning problems inside the Works, the outlook suddenly became bleak indeed, and the staff level gradually fell until a time was reached when the non-viability of the Works was patently obvious. Great efforts were now made, using the provisions in the new Act, to attract 'private party' work, and to some extent were successful for a period. Such work included the manufacture of large hatchcovers for ships, and the repair of nationalized undertakings' single and double deck buses. Almost any work that could be found was undertaken.

Inevitably the whole railway expenditure was now under review in these particularly difficult days, and it was soon apparent to senior staff at Swindon that its life may be drawing to an end. Headquarters accountants produced figures to prove that the place was a liability and should be wound up, but the small group of managers who had originally planned the reorganization, together with the Works accountant, L. Rendell, fought a rear guard battle lasting well over a year, so that at least schemes were reluctantly requested for yet another reduction in size. This was based broadly on keeping the piece of Works either to the east or to the west of Rodbourne Road. In all, the author produced no less than 18 different schemes to be supported by financial statements which were always just able to counter HQ proposals. The unions, of course, were not standing by in this situation, and were equally active both nationally and locally through the member of Parliament.

Whilst it was recognized at the time in question that there was not the work to go round, many were convinced that more investment in new rolling stock would have to come in the not too distant future. Once the use of the available capacity at Swindon was lost, it could never be replaced unless capital was forthcoming, measured in tens of millions, and that was never likely to be the case, even if suggested for some other works or new site. It was towards the end of this continuing fight that H. W. Mear reached retirement age, in July 1972. Whilst in the difficult position of not being able to give overt support to his principal assistants who were keeping the battle going, but carrying forward as required his distasteful running down of the Works, he was nevertheless always prepared to put his signature to yet another submission prepared in order to try and keep Swindon Works going.

On 1st January 1970, the Workshops Division had become British Rail Engineering Limited, a completely separate subsidiary of the BRB, and overnight was formed one of the largest engineering enterprises in the country. This new arrangement completed the freedom to enter into home and export business of whatever type it could find, but especially for railway export business. Even if Swindon could not expect too much of the share of work now to be won, it did mean that if such work went to another works, it would, of necessity, displace some BR work, and Swindon could well pick up some of this.

The arrival of H. R. Roberts to take up the appointment of Works Manager in July 1972 was looked upon with some apprehension — not of the man himself, one must hasten to say, but in what his remit was almost certain to be — to close Swindon Works. It would not be proper to discuss at this short distance of time, too much detail of these last eight years of history. Suffice it to say that after a reasonable time in which to pick up the threads of the situation, Mr Roberts was able to see that the case being made locally for Swindon being retained in its present form was desirable and necessary. However, it was not easy to convince quickly the higher echelons, and an energetic effort had to be continued and increased, to get every scrap of work, both railway and private, that could be obtained. The efforts paid off, but the whole period was a proverbial cliff hanger. At last, there were signs of an increase in railway work, with the policy of accepting anything paying off, as this type of railway order began to bear fruit. Other Works with a more stable workload tended to be selective in acceptance, but Swindon got into the habit of never saying no, however distasteful the job may have been in normal circumstances. The unions in the Works played their part in accepting changes in practices to meet the demands. Soon there were larger private party orders, and some of these demanded very high standards of workmanship. Deliveries were back on time. One particular item, although relatively small, was very important. New body side jigs were required for the manufacture of the proposed Advanced Passenger Train (APT) carriages. Complicated in construction, and naturally required to high accuracy over a length of about 70 ft. these were constructed (incidentally using the Zeiss optical lining up apparatus so useful in the past), inspected and delivered a few days earlier than the deadline requested. Under such circumstances the Works as a whole began to regain confidence. Finally in 1977 it was clear that the capacity at Swindon was very necessary for the well being of BREL in the long term. But the work might be different from that in the past, and finance was made available for another 'mini-reorganization' so that the Factory could accept it. It was accepted that some shops might have to be abandoned, and steps were taken to

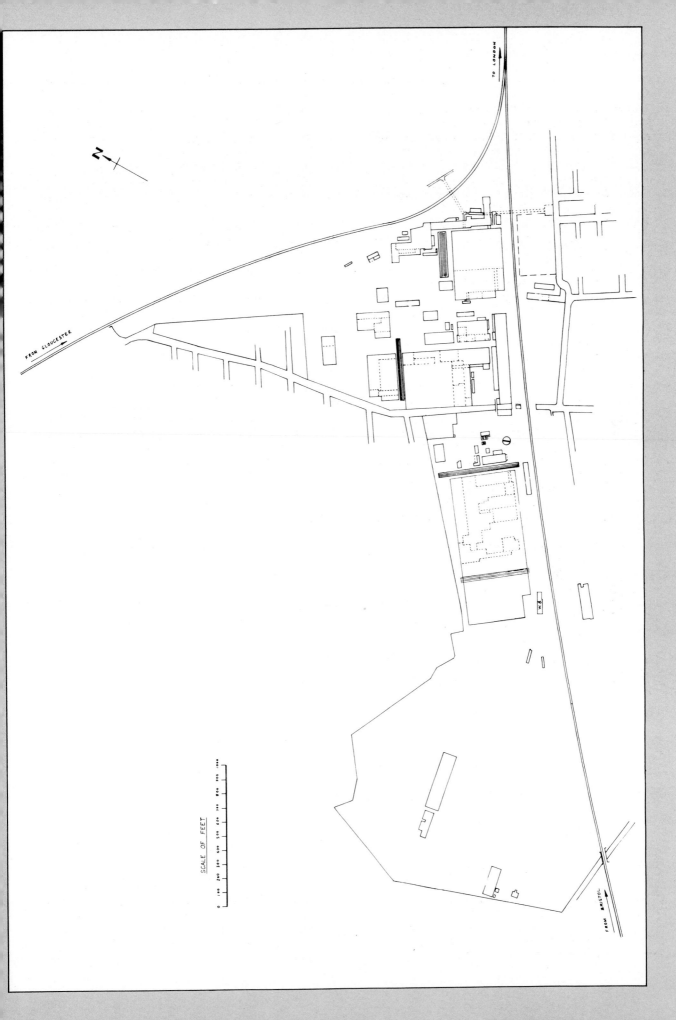

SCALE OF FEET

FROM GLOUCESTER

TO LONDON

FROM BRISTOL

Plate 225: A diagrammatic plan of Swindon Works, 1972.

Swindon Works Records

273

Plate 226: A phoenix rises from the ashes! The building of locomotives once again. One of the 625 h.p. metre gauge diesel-hydraulic locomotives of an order for twenty on Swindon Works is outshopped for export to Kenya in 1979. As in 1855, when No. 57 was built, track of a narrower gauge had to be provided in part of the Works for this Hunslet-designed locomotive.

R. C. H. Nash

turn them over to other railway use, but this policy had to be reversed.

As an interesting aside to these alterations, work to install a new piece of foundry equipment uncovered yet more prehistoric remains just below the surface. After much argument by learned people, it was identified as much of the skeleton of 'pliosaurus brachyspondylus' a rare reptilian creature which lived some 130–150 million years ago. Final identification was made jointly by Professors Appleby and Halstead of Cardiff and Reading Universities respectively. It was the most complete skeleton of the creature found in this country, only one other approaching it having been discovered, in 1880, near Cambridge. Now presented to the British Museum Natural History Department, it was featured on the BBC television programme for young people 'Blue Peter' on 22nd May 1975, and 5,000 people also visited a special display of the 'bones' at the Swindon Museum before the remains were sent to London.

The real breakthrough was to come in four particular orders, two railway and two private. The railway work was, firstly, the return to Swindon of diesel shunter repairs, initially in a small way, but now so that virtually all these were based on Swindon for major overhaul. The second was the order to refurbish completely certain whole classes of Southern Region electric multiple unit stock over about a 10 year period. This work, worth currently about £10 million a year, is now running to requirements. Of the two private orders, the first was for a large number of single and double-jib track relaying crane frames for an Austrian firm, spread over a four year period. The other work, and perhaps the most gratifying, although only lasting for about 1½ years, was an order for 20 diesel-hydraulic locomotives of metre gauge to a design by the Hunslet Engine Company of Leeds, and destined for Kenya. So after thirteen years locomotives were again built in Swindon.

In 1973 the total staff at Swindon had fallen to about 2,200, which put it at the lower end of the workshops staff league. What of today, (1980), only seven years later? The staff has risen to 3,800 and is still increasing as the right type of tradesmen required are found, making the Works third in the league after Crewe and Litchurch Lane, Derby. An amazing resurgence indeed, but once again Swindon is holding its head up high. One thing it must not do, however, is to forget the depths to which it was being plumbed only a decade ago. An institution so large and costly must always be aware of the economic and political pitfalls which are now, and perhaps have always been, a way of life. May we hope that the spirit that made Swindon such a great railway centre will encourage those now in possession, that continuance of this great heritage must be worked for, and never allowed to lapse, by default, in their own particular and individual effort.

Appendices

APPENDIX I

Daniel Gooch's letter of application for the post of Locomotive Superintendent, now preserved in the Great Western Railway Museum at Swindon:-

Manchester & Leeds Railway Office
Rochdale
July 18th 1837

I. K. Brunel, Esq.,

Dear Sir,

I have just been informed it is your intention to erect an Engine Manufactory at or near Bristol and that you wish to engage a person as manager. I take the earliest opportunity of offering my services for the situation.

I have until the last two months been constantly engaged on Engine Building and have worked at each branch of the business but principally at Locomotive Engine Work. The first 3 years of my time was with Mr Humphrey at the Tredegar Iron Works, Monmouthshire. I left him to go to Mr R. Stephenson and was at the Vulcan Foundry 12 months when I obtained leave from Mr Stephenson to go down to Mr Stirling of the Dundee Foundry Company, Dundee to get a knowledge of steam boat work. I remained with him 12 months and returned to Mr Stephenson's works at Newcastle where I remained until last October, when I left having had an offer from a party in Newcastle to take the management of a Locomotive Manufactory which they intended erecting, but which owing to some unavoidable circumstances they have now given up the idea of proceeding with, and we have countermanded the orders for the Machinery.

This has left me without a situation and I am anxious to engage Myself to some company where I will have the management of the building of Engines. At present I am with My brother on the Manchester & Leeds line where I have employment until I meet with something suitable.

I will be glad to refer you to any of the formentioned places for testimonial.

I trust you approve of my application. I shall be glad to hear from you stating the Salary and any other information you may think necessary.

I am, Sir,

Yours Obediently,

Danl. Gooch

(This letter is reproduced by courtesy of the Great Western Railway Museum)

APPENDIX II

THE FAWCETT LIST

List of names of all Officers, Managers, Sub-Managers, Foremen, Contractors etc. from the opening of the New Locomotive Works at Swindon on January 1st *(sic)* 1843 to December 31st 1865.

I. K. Brunel	Projector, Constructor and Engineer in Chief
Mr afterwards Sir Daniel Gooch	Chief Locomotive Engineer, Director and Chairman
Mr Archibald Sturrock	First Manager of the Works
Mr Minard C. Rea	Second Manager of the Works
Mr W. F. Gooch	Third Manager of the Works
Mr Samuel Carlton	Fourth Manager of the Works
Mr Joseph Armstrong	Succeeded Sir Daniel Gooch on his resignation as Chief Engineer of the Company
Mr Dougal Mack Mr Edward Snell	} Assistant Managers under Mr Sturrock
Mr John Budge Mr John Fraser Mr Wm Dakin Mr James Haydon	} Sub-Managers — Messrs. Snell, Fraser and Budge were all Chief Draughtsmen in succession before being appointed assistant managers
Mr John Johnson	First foreman in Smiths' Department
Mr Thomas Stewart	Second foreman in Smiths' Department
Mr George Ditchburn	First foreman in Boiler Shop
Mr Lancelot Young	Second foreman in Boiler Shop
Mr Joseph Fox	Third foreman in Boiler Shop
Mr William Nicholson	First foreman in Fitting & Turning Shop
Mr William Bickle	Second foreman in Fitting & Turning Shop
Mr James Haydon	Third foreman in Fitting & Turning Shop
Mr Robert Laxon	First foreman in Coppersmith Department
Mr Samuel Gray	First foreman in Patternmakers Department
Mr Thomas Rawlinson	First foreman in Paint Shop
Mr Robert Bishop	Second foreman in Paint Shop
Mr Thomas Jones	First foreman of Masons' Department
Mr William Falconer	First foreman of Wheel Turning Department
Mr Thomas Atkinson	First foreman of Erecting Shops
Mr Walter Mather	Second foreman of Erecting Shops
Mr Richard Pattison	Third foreman of Erecting Shops
Mr John Fawcett	First Contractor, having taken all Wheel and Tyre repairs under Mr Sturrock
Mr William Hamilton	First to take over Foundry Work by Contract
Mr Joseph Thorpe	Succeeded Mr William Hamilton

Mr William Laverick	First Contractor for Steam Hammer Work (Forgings etc.)
Mr Joseph Waterson	First Contractor for New Engine Wheels
Mr William Hogarth	Second Contractor for New Engine Wheels
Mr Richard Pattison	New Engine Erector, built the 1st engine *Premier*
Mr James Squires) Mr James Fairbairn) Mr John Taite) Mr Archibald Couts) Mr John Dudley) Mr George Youle) Mr Grey) Mr Hardy)	New Engine Erectors
Mr Robert Wardle) Mr Thomas Chilton)	First Boilermakers and Contractors
Mr Lee	First Storekeeper
Mr Dunn	Succeeded Mr Lee
Mr James Davis	First Chief Clerk and Accountant
Mr William Hall	Succeeded Mr James Davis
Mr John Brack) Mr Richard Tilley)	Came from Wigan and were the First Contractors for building Iron Trucks
Mr William Affleck) Mr John Miles) Mr Thomas Young) Mr Charles Hurt) Mr Peter Bremer) Mr Thomas Hammet)	Contractors for building Iron Trucks when Messrs. Brack and Tilley left
Mr George Hawkins) Mr Creacy)	Made all the Wooden Frames, doors etc., for the above Iron Trucks
Mr Thomas Ellis	Designed and Constructed and Managed the Rail Mills and also formed a Building Company amongst his workmen and erected all those cottages called Cambria Place for his Welsh workmen to live in
Rev. Joseph Mansfield	First Clergyman appointed to St. Mark's Church
Mr Alex'r Jas. Braid	First permanent Schoolmaster and Acting Secretary to the Mechanics Institution
Mr Henry Appleby	First Superintendent of the Running Department and the 'A' Shed, was removed from Haylane to Swindon before the New Works were completed

I myself contracted for and made the first 8 ft. wheels for the engines *Great Western* and *Lord of the Isles*. Mr J. Waterson and Mr William Hogarth made the remainder and all other driving wheels

Sgd. *John Fawcett*

Mr F. F. Foord,
Swindon Works,
October 10th 1904

Author's Collection

APPENDIX III

GWR   BR(W)   BREL

CHIEF OFFICERS AT SWINDON

1837-1864 Daniel Gooch	Locomotive Superintendent (not resident)
1864-1877 Joseph Armstrong	Locomotive, Carriage & Wagon Superintendent
1877-1902 William Dean	Locomotive, Carriage & Wagon Superintendent
1902-1921 George J. Churchward	Locomotive, Carriage & Wagon Superintendent
	Chief Mechanical Engineer 1916
1922-1941 Charles B. Collett	Chief Mechanical Engineer
1941-1949 Fredk. W. Hawksworth	Chief Mechanical Engineer

Mechnical & Electrical Engineer   **Carriage & Wagon Engineer**
1950-1951 K. J. Cook   1950-1951 H. Randle
1951-1956 R. A. Smeddle   1951-1956 C. A. Roberts

Chief Mechanical & Electrical Engineer
1956-1962 R. A. Smeddle

Works Managers
1841-1850 Archibald Sturrock
1850-1857 Minard C. Rea
1857-1864 William F. Gooch
1864   F. A. Bucknall
1864-1896 Samuel Carlton

Locomotive Works Managers   **Carriage & Wagon Works Managers**
1896-1901 G. J. Churchward   1868-1873 T. G. Clayton (Building Factory)
1901-1902 F. C. Wright   1873-1885 J. Holden
1902-1913 H. C. King   1885-1895 G. J. Churchward
1913-1920 C. B. Collett   1895-1901 L. R. Thomas
1920-1922 W. A. Stanier   1901-1902 T. O. Hogarth
1922-1937 R. G. Hannington   1902-1920 F. Marillier
1937-1947 K. J. Cook   1920-1922 C. C. Champeney
1947-1948 H. Randle   1922   R. G. Hannington
1948-1952 C. T. Roberts   1922-1946 E. T. J. Evans
1952-1956 J. Finlayson   1946-1947 H. Randle
1956-1960 S. A. S. Smith   1947-1948 C. T. Roberts
1960-1962 S. Ridgway   1948-1962 H. G. Johnson

1962-1967 J. S. Scott — **Chief Works Manager**

1962-1967 H. W. Mear   1962-1963 E. T. Butcher

Works Managers
1967-1972 H. W. Mear
1972-1981 H. R. Roberts
1981-   H. Taylor

Index

Illustrations are indicated by *italic* numerals